UNDEFEATED
ROCKY MARCIANO
The Fighter Who Refused to Lose

UNDEFEATED
ROCKY MARCIANO
The Fighter Who Refused to Lose

by
Everett M. Skehan

with family assistance
by **Peter, Louis, and Mary Anne Marciano**
photography by **Stanley Bauman**

Rounder Books

Cambridge, Massachusetts

Designed and typeset by Swordsmith Productions
Cover design by Jean-Pierre LeGuillou

Library of Congress Cataloging in Publication Data
Skehan, Everett M. Rocky Marciano.
1. Marciano, Rocky, 1923–1969. 2. Boxers (Sports)—United States—Biography.
I. Title.

200411 6699
796.8'3'0924 [B]
ISBN 1-57940-106-6

Printed in the United States of America

9 8 7 6 5 4 3 2 1

To Pierino and Pasqualena Marchegiano.
To the daughter Rocky loved so dearly,
Mary Anne, and to Rocky Kevin, the son
he knew and loved too briefly.
And to all Italians.
In memory of the son who gave them great love and honor.

Acknowledgments

THE AUTHOR WISHES TO THANK the many persons who gave their time and energy in lengthy interviews and shared valuable insights and knowledge of the life of Rocky Marciano. They helped tremendously in shaping the authenticity and originality of this book.

A special thanks to Ken Botty, my friend and managing editor at *The Evening Gazette* (Worcester), for his advice, encouragement, and for giving me the necessary leave of absence from my duties as a reporter to finish the book.

I am also very grateful to my editor at Houghton Mifflin, Grant Ujifusa, for taking a special interest in the project, working very closely with me, and in the process becoming a good friend as well as an adviser.

I would also like to thank my close friend and fellow reporter Nick Basbanes, who was a good listener and critic all the way.

The book could not have been written properly without the total cooperation, research assistance, and valuable sources provided by my friends and associates Louis and Peter Marciano.

Finally, my inspiration on the many nights spent at the typewriter is totally attributable to my beautiful daughters, Tracy, Laura, and Kelley, and I am especially aware and appreciative of the faith my father and mother, Louis and Helen Skehan, had in their son throughout the entire project.

For enhancing the insights into Rocky and his life and career in this expanded anniversary edition, the author appreciates greatly the contributions of Bill Nowlin, publisher and editor; Richard Johnson, agent and advisor, who campaigned strongly for the book; trainers Angelo Dundee, Lou Duva and Goody Petronelli; Rocky's brothers Lou and Peter Marciano; photographer Stanley Bauman; Brockton Mayor John T. Units, Jr.; Armond Colombo, Brockton High football coach and brother-in-law of Rocky; and Tommy Frizzell, baseball coach and professor at Massasoit Community College in Brockton. Thanks as well to Brad San Martin and Steve Netsky at Rounder Books for their work on this publication. Thanks also to Bob Gormley, former editor-in-chief of Northeastern University Press. He was a strong advocate for reissuing and expanding the Rocky book and continues to be interested in and supportive of the project.

Contents

New Text and Photographs

UNDEFEATED
ROCKY MARCIANO
The Fighter Who Refused to Lose

Introduction

FIFTY YEARS HAVE PASSED since Rocky Marciano's final fight, a ninth round knockout of Archie Moore in Yankee Stadium on September 21, 1955. It was Rocky's forty-ninth victory in a row. He had never lost a bout since turning professional in 1947. He retired in the spring of 1956 as the only undefeated heavyweight champion in history.

It seems that now is a fitting time to release this expanded edition of my 1977 book on Rocky's life and career, which was entitled *Rocky Marciano: Biography of a First Son.* This new edition includes the original story word-for-word, but has many more photographs and insights into the motivations that shaped Rocky's life and his obsession with winning at all costs. It documents his influence and rightful place among the giants of the sport, which has become clearer and stronger with the passage of time.

Many feel that Rocky was the greatest heavyweight champion of them all. Others give that distinction to such greats as Joe Louis, Muhammad Ali, Jack Dempsey, and Jack Johnson. The choice is often personal and biased and, in truth, it is impossible to accurately determine the real winner. For each of those great champions was by far the best of his era. They defeated all of the top contenders.

But Rocky Marciano was the only one who was never beaten. Of all of the champions only Rocky refused to lose. He never gave up no matter how bad things got.

For Rocky possessed the heart and courage of a lion that when badly wounded becomes more dangerous than ever. Bloody and battered and given little chance to survive, on several historic occasions the Rock defied ringside doctors, referees, trainers, and especially the fighters that threatened to end his reign as king of the boxing jungle. (The prime example was in 1954 when Ezzard Charles sliced Rocky's nostril in half. The blood was spurting out like a geyser, but, before the doctor or referee could stop the fight, Rocky stormed out and battered Charles unconscious.) Rocky found a way to knock them all out. He was the ultimate survivor.

All of Rocky's fights were thrilling and filled with drama and danger that rarely applies to modern contests, for Rocky never

1

clinched and rarely stopped punching. Had his fights occurred during recent times some of those bloody battles that brought forth the ultimate of Rocky's spirit and determination would have been stopped long before the final blows were thrown.

In 2005, as this book is being published, the heavyweight boxing scene is in such total disarray that few fans are interested in it. There is little exciting action but plenty of attempts at dancing and clinching by these masqueraders that should only be viewed as what Rocky would have called "cheese champs." For the once supreme title of *Heavyweight Champion of the World* no longer applies. There are watered-down divisions, such as the WBA, WBC, WBO, and IBF, each with its own so-called champion, none of which would have stood a chance against the greats of earlier eras.

The world-renowned heavyweight stars of the 20th Century such as Johnson, Louis, Charles, Walcott, Marciano, Ali, Joe Frazier, George Foreman, Larry Holmes, Mike Tyson, Lennox Lewis, and Evander Holyfield are gone. And they may never be replaced.

For there are much easier paths to fame and fortune these days to attract the most talented of America's athletes; they can make millions in baseball, football, basketball, and as the richest, most famous of them all, Tiger Woods, can attest, the non-violent sport of golf. It makes little sense for them to spill their blood and risk their brains and lives in the unforgiving arena of a square ring.

But back in Rocky's time there were far fewer choices for the sons of Italian immigrants and racially oppressed blacks; for many of them fighting or forever laboring in obscurity were the only options.

And so fight fans got to enjoy what many would view as the Golden Era of Boxing, the

1940s through 1980s. Those were the years when the truly great battles were staged by heavyweight champions such as Louis, Charles, Walcott, Marciano, Ali, Frazier, Foreman, and Holmes.

In addition to the superior heavyweights of the period, there have been no light heavyweights (other than Roy Jones Jr.) that come close to equaling such stars as Billy Conn, Gus Lesnevich, Joey Maxim, Archie Moore, Dick Tiger, and Bob Foster.

And the middleweights were also far superior; greats such as Sugar Ray Robinson, Tony Zale, Carmen Basilio, Dick Tiger, Carlos Monzon, Marvelous Marvin Hagler, Sugar Ray Leonard, and numerous others, along with superior welterweights, lightweights, and featherweights; Henry Armstrong, Willie Pep, Sandy Saddler, Robinson, Roberto Duran, Basilio, Leonard, and Alexis Arguello to mention just a few.

The only outstanding competitor in those weight classes these days, other than Hopkins, is the fast-handed smooth-moving Floyd Mayweather, Jr., who has won WBC titles as a super-featherweight, lightweight, and super-lightweight. At the time this book went to press, he was undefeated at 34-0 and also aspired to winning the welterweight championship. Many consider Mayweather to be the best performer pound-for-pound of any boxer on the scene. However, Mayweather is another product of those modern-day watered-down boxing organizations and weight-classes, and cannot come close to challenging the great Sugar Ray Robinson for the distinction of being the best fighter pound-for-pound in the history of the sport.

The modern heavyweights of the new millenium that call themselves champions but are really the creations of shrewd promoters, foremost of which is the shady manipulator Don

King, wear an assortment of belts that have been established more for the purpose of making money than developing talented fighters. They are an ungainly bunch of misfits with barely recognizable names such as Johnny Ruiz, Lamon Brewster, Danny Williams, Vitali Klitschko, Chris Byrd, and several other anonymous, inferior, and ponderous competitors. None of them would have stood a chance against the legends.

But Rocky Marciano was the genuine article. Considered to be too small, too old, too clumsy to ever become more than a journeyman club fighter, his was a greater story of sacrifice, determination, and beating the odds than even the popular fictional "Rocky" created by Sylvester Stallone for the movies.

When you read *Undefeated* you'll understand why and how Rocky defied them all and became one of the nonpareil champions in boxing history.

E. S.

Book One

Growing Up to Win

1.
Fighting Back

Brockton, Massachusetts (March 1925). On a cold, windy night, Luigi Picciuto stood forlornly at the corner of Brook Street waiting for the doctor to come, the one person who might save his grandson, gravely ill, the only child of his beloved daughter Pasqualena.

A powerful man, almost six feet tall and weighing 200 pounds, Picciuto had the broad chest and hard, muscular arms of a blacksmith, a trade at which he had labored for many years in the tiny village of San Bartolomeo, near Naples, Italy. There he had met his wife, Concetta, and began raising a family, saving money whenever he could and always planning for the future. Then in 1914, tired of the war, the politics, and the poverty, he came to America.

In Italy, Luigi Picciuto had been a proud man, a man who commanded respect. In America, he soon discovered things were different. Jobs were not easy to come by for immigrant Italians with little education. But Luigi was more fortunate than many of his paesanos, for he had a good trade and he was strong and forceful, able to survive in an atmosphere of prejudice.

In 1915, Picciuto returned to Italy to settle his affairs, and to bring his daughters Pasqualena and Carmella to America. They arrived in 1916, planning to work hard and to save every penny beyond what was needed for the barest essentials so that the rest of the family could join them as soon as possible.

Inside Picciuto's modest, white-shingled cottage, the neighborhood women were gathered around the crib, consoling Pasqualena Marchegiano (Mark-a-jahn-o). Her only child, Rocco, nineteen months old, lay critically ill with pneumonia, and very little hope remained for his recovery.

While the men sat in the kitchen with the boy's father, Pierino Marchegiano, the women held their rosaries, whispering prayers in southern-dialect Italian and broken English.

"Figlio mio. Figlio mio," Pasqualena Marchegiano kept repeating as she leaned over her pale and motionless baby. "Corra de ma ma." ("My son. My son. Heart of my life.")

A damp stogie jutted out from beneath Luigi Picciuto's thick black mustache. Rain had begun to fall, soaking his woolen cap and overcoat as he waited for the headlights of the doctor's car. Luigi was the patriarch of the family. It was his sad and solemn duty to greet the doctor and guide him to the side of his dying grandson.

"Whatsa matter, God don't want me to have kids?" Pasqualena Marchegiano kept asking. "And I love kids."

It was a question that her mother, Concetta, and sisters Carmella and Lena could not answer, burdened by the knowledge that Pasqualena had lost another son, who had died on the day he was born. And now it seemed that Rocco was also dying.

As Luigi Picciuto waited alone in the rain, he heard the wind rattling in the branches of the oak trees at the edge of James Edgar Playground and the voices of the men as they trudged by, going home wet and weary from work in the shoe factories. Luigi was a sensitive man, with dark, lonely eyes, who was deeply hurt when tragedy touched a member of his family. And in the cold March wind he fought back the tears as he concluded that perhaps his decision to come to America had been a mistake.

The injustice of "Palmer's Raiders" had enraged Picciuto. The United States attorney general, A. Mitchell Palmer, had personally directed a series of raids in the early 1920s that resulted in the deportation of many of Picciuto's countrymen. They were called "anarchists," guilty of unnamed political crimes.

Picciuto, and all of his friends in Ward 2, were enraged most of all by the Sacco-Vanzetti case. Two Italian immigrants, a fish peddler and a shoe factory worker, like the men in Ward 2, had been arrested on murder charges by Brockton police less than a mile from Picciuto's home in April 1920.

"Figlio di puttana" ("Son of a whore"), Picciuto had said to his friends. "There is no justice for these paesanos." Involved in the anarchist movement, Sacco and Vanzetti were held for a double murder in the payroll robbery of a factory in Braintree, Massachusetts. There was only circumstantial evidence against them, and many Americans, including every Italian in Ward 2, felt the men were innocent. But Sacco and Vanzetti were convicted and put to death.

"These bastards," Picciuto had said. "They make us suffer. They have no love."

But Luigi's problems in America had begun long before Sacco and Vanzetti. When the family first arrived in America, they settled in Bridgeport, Connecticut. Picciuto was hardworking and optimistic then, despite the hardships. But one day he was called home from work. His nine-year-old son Nicholas had been crushed to death beneath the wheels of a truck. The boy was riding a wagon his father had made for him for Christmas out of roller skates and two-by-fours.

After Nicholas's funeral, Picciuto gathered his family together and in Italian said tearfully, "My heart is broken. My life is over."

A short time later, he told his family it was impossible for him to stay in Connecticut, so close to the memories of his son. He was the patriarch, and they did not question anything he decided for the family. They moved to Brockton, Massachusetts, where a daughter, Carmella Cappiello, was already living.

Fiorena Foscaldi dipped her finger into a teaspoon filled with warm olive oil. She allowed several drops to fall into a shallow dish of water held in her wrinkled palm. Then she began to speak the privileged words to take away the "evil eye."

Pasqualena Marchegiano tried to remember who had seen her baby on the day he became ill, who had put the curse of the malocchio, the spell of the "evil eye," upon him.

Luigi Picciuto returned to the house with

Dr. Josephat Phaneuf, who immediately began administering to the ill baby.

"I've done everything possible," he said. "It will depend upon the boy's own spirit now, whether he has the will to fight this sickness. But, if he can overcome this, you'll have a strong son here, Mrs. Marchegiano."

But for more than a week after the doctor's visit the boy's condition worsened. He was pale and thin and he took no nourishment. The family lost almost all hope.

Dr. Phaneuf visited the child often, gave him medicine, and lanced his ears to stop an infection. But in 1925 there was really very little that a doctor could do for a baby with pneumonia. Many died from it.

Pasqualena Marchegiano removed her diamond engagement ring and placed it in a dish that held a candle for Saint Anthony. "God, I give you my ring," she cried, kneeling before the candle. "I give you my ring, God, so you save my son."

Pierino Marchegiano spent his days worrying about his son as he bent over the machine in the shoe factory. In the evenings he was unable to eat his supper and refused to allow himself any wine.

He was a frail man, under five feet eight inches tall and weighing less than 150 pounds. He had fought against the Germans at Chateau-Thierry in World War I, where he was seriously wounded, having been hit in the face with shrapnel and overcome by poisonous gas. Pierino was proud to have fought for America, though his health was permanently damaged. He coughed often and choked on the phlegm and constantly sucked hard, sweet candy to take away the foul taste of the gas, which seemed to linger inside him.

"Hey, Petey," his friend Mike Colombo said, as they sat in the kitchen. "You must rest, paesano. The baby, he'sa gonna be all right."

"My son, he'sa gonna die, Michelange," Pierino said. "My only son issa gonna die."

"Nay. Nay," Colombo said. "Your son, he's got a big heart. Don't you worry, eh, *compare?*" But Pierino seemed strangely detached from it all. He was an altogether different person from the tough, wiry youth who had grown up proud in Chieti, Italy, a small fishing village near the Adriatic Sea. The war, the shoe factory, and finally his son's illness wore heavily upon his spirit.

During this period of grave crisis, a bent and wrinkled old woman came to the house. Paolina Mangifesti, ninety years old, had not been expected to visit the deathbed of her nephew Pierino's son.

The neighborhood women were gathered around the baby as always, clutching their rosary beads. They still prayed, even though most of them had already given up hope.

"Why do you keep looking at him?" Paolina said in Italian. "Why don't you do something?"

"There's nothing to do," a woman answered, also in Italian. "He's too sick. Only God can save him."

"No," Mrs. Mangifesti said. "In Italy, I have seen the children with pneumonia. And if they are strong, they can live." Then she ordered one of the women to bring her a dish of warm water and a small spoon. She forced the baby's lips apart with the spoon and let the water trickle into his mouth. And to the amazement of the women, the child blinked his eyes and began to move his lips.

"You keep making him drink," the old lady said. "This poor baby is all dried up. Give him some chicken broth, and if he doesn't want it, push it down his throat."

That week the crisis passed. The fever subsided, and the baby Rocco was taking nourishment eagerly.

"You're going to have a healthy, strong boy on your hands, Mrs. Marchegiano," Dr. Phaneuf said.

Although it is quite possible that the pneumonia had taken its natural course, Pasqualena Marchegiano always credited the old lady with saving her son's life. And Mrs. Mangifesti died shortly after Rocco's recovery, never having really known the boy.

That spring, Pasqualena took her place among the proud young mothers of Ward 2. It was a happy season, and she had much for which to be thankful. There was no way of knowing the hard times that lay ahead in the Great Depression.

2.

King of the Hill

BY THE TIME the noon whistles echoed from the Brockton shoe factories, sending hundreds of young boys scurrying home from the ball parks for lunch, Rocky was already inside the Stacy Adams company building.

Every day Rocky carried his father's lunch to work. It did not matter if the boy was bruised or tired from his games of football or baseball or if he had someplace to go with his Ward 2 pals, there were no excuses for being late. Pierino Marchegiano expected his son to be inside the plant with the hot *spezzatto* (chicken soup), sandwiches, and coffee Pasqualena had made before the men put aside their labor.

Rocky loathed, hated, and feared the shoe factory. To him the factory was a prison, a place where good men were forced to sweat and toil and submit to injustices at the hands of the Irish foremen.

He was sickened by the sight of his father hunched over the number 5 bed laster machine, the nails protruding from his lips as he used both his hands and feet to keep up with the pace of the work. It was not a good job for a man so sickly as Pierino, but it was all that was available and he did not complain.

"Remember this place, Rocky, and when you grow up be somebody," Pierino told his son. "Don't ever work in a shoe factory."

"Don't worry. Pa," Rocky said. "Someday I'm going to make a lot of money, and then you'll never have to work here again."

In those days boys grew up tough in Brockton, even tougher than they do now. Twenty miles south of Boston toward Cape Cod, the city of some sixty thousand persons was, during Rocky's youth, a place where men spent their lives working in the shoe factories, a few textile mills, foundries, and other small industries. There was a large Irish population and smaller clusters of Italians, Lithuanians, Swedes, and Jews. The wealthy Yankee factory owners, businessmen, and professionals lived mostly on the West Side, but they were few by comparison to the middle- and low-income working class that dominated the city. It was not like some of the larger cities, which contained areas that would later be labeled ghettos, but it was a place where people worked hard for their money and dreamed of improving their lot.

From Rocky's earliest youth, Brockton was always a great sports city, which over the years has produced many high school football and basketball championships. And in the shadow of James Edgar Playground, Rocky dreamed of becoming a star, an athlete who could command respect and wealth and make his family proud.

Baseball was Rocky's first love. He idolized the power hitters like Babe Ruth, Joe DiMaggio, and Ted Williams. The sluggers were the biggest money earners and the most respected, and he longed for the day when he would join them. He never imagined that he would become a prizefighter.

As the young Rocky chased his dreams of baseball glory, the Marchegiano family lived upstairs in four small, unheated rooms in Luigi Picciuto's trim white cottage on Brook Street. When the family grew, the tiny apartment became very crowded, and Rocky slept in the parlor on an old fold-up cot beside his baby brother Sonny. It was the one thing he regretted about his grandfather's house, where he was to spend his entire boyhood.

"Gee, Ma," Rocky would say. "When will I ever have a room of my own?"

"Don't you worry. Rocky," Pasqualena told him. "Someday we'll have a nice big house with your own bedroom."

But the chances looked slim. In the twelve years following their marriage in the summer of 1921, the Marchegianos had five children: Rocky, September 1, 1923; Alice, October 10, 1925; Conge, November 16, 1927; Elizabeth, November 8, 1931; and Louis, September 29, 1933. Although Pierino worked hard in the factory, his pay remained low. It was the time of the Great Depression, when many families struggled to survive.

"We never had much in those days," Rocky's mother recalled. "But there was always a lot of love in our house, and we knew that someday it would be better."

Pasqualena managed her small budget shrewdly, getting the most out of every dollar. She cooked simple but nourishing meals of pasta, vegetables from the garden, and pasta e fagioli. She made fresh green salads, which Rocky loved, being particularly fond of the dandelion greens they gathered from the neighborhood lawns. And in the spring, after the rains, the family went into the nearby woods and fields and picked mushrooms.

"We used to get buckets full of them," Sonny Marciano said. "Ma would cook with them and use the mushrooms in sauces and salads. We'd dump them in a pan and throw a quarter in, If the coin didn't change color, we ate the mushrooms. We were really gambling with the mushrooms every day."

There was no talking allowed at the supper table, a policy which Pierino firmly enforced. "Enjoy your food," he would say. "There is plenty of time for talk afterward."

Rocky's appetite was insatiable. He often consumed several bowls of soup and two or three heaping plates of spaghetti before asking his mother for some fruit, usually dried figs.

He sat at the right side of his father in the place reserved for the first son. His father always gave him a glass of wine with his meal and instructed him to drink it slowly.

"Wine is good for you," Pierino said. "But only one glass. Don't ever let me see you drinking more than one glass."

FROM THE TIME they were old enough to swing a bat, Rocky and his friends spent every spare moment at James Edgar Playground.

They were determined to become major league baseball players, and some of them almost made it.

Rocky would stand at the plate for hours while his pals Eugene Sylvester, Izzy Gold, Nicky Sylvester, and others pitched to him.

Rocky was a catcher and one of the most powerful hitters for his age in the neighborhood, but he was a very slow and clumsy runner. He was determined that his slugging would make up for what he lacked in speed. He was of average height with dark, wavy, almost curly hair and a stocky build, wide, sloping shoulders, uncommonly thick legs, and powerful arms.

As long as the game involved only his close friends, Rocky could stay at the plate indefinitely. He loved this. But usually other boys showed up to play, some of them older, and eventually Rocky was forced to give up the bat. He never did so without a protest.

"Gee, Louie, I was just beginning to get some good whacks," Rocky would say. Or, "Cripe sakes, I haven't been up that long."

He hated to chase fly balls in the outfield, but he used the time to develop his legs by exercising and running in short bursts after every ball hit regardless of whether or not it was coming to him. But within minutes Rocky would be shouting, "Hey, how about it? My ups. I've got to get some hits."

From grammar school days, Rocky was a leader in sports. He was respected for his courage, determination, and ability. He was never a good basketball player, but in the sand lot baseball and football games, Rocky was usually a team captain. He played hard, and he always played to win.

"We were lousy losers," Izzy Gold said. "The only thing that mattered was to win. We didn't much care how . . . The Rock always liked to play against the best teams in Brockton. He never liked the easy games. But if we were losing he'd get all fired up, and he couldn't wait to get up to the plate. Lots of times he'd win the game for us, and that was beautiful. But if The Rock ever struck out or made an error or missed a tackle in football, forget it. You couldn't talk to him at all. He wouldn't be satisfied until we played the team again and beat them. We were all lousy losers, but, like in everything, Rocky was more determined than any of us. The Rock was never a good sport about losing. He'd never think of congratulating a guy for beating him. He'd always be too down on himself for that."

As aggressive as Rocky was on a baseball diamond or football field, he was an otherwise shy youth. He never really cared for school, and was a daydreamer who gazed out windows and imagined himself back at the ball park. His friends recalled him as more of a follower than a leader in things other than sports.

But Rocky was one of the most popular boys in Ward 2. Some chums like Nicky Sylvester and Vinnie Colombo would be life-long friends. Sylvester was the comedian of the group. He could always make Rocky laugh with his slapstick antics. He was close to Rocky throughout his boxing career, and in the championship years he provided a valuable service as the camp jester, the one person who could relieve the overwhelming tension of training for a fight.

In those grammar school days, Rocky's closest friends were Izzy Gold and Eugene Sylvester. They called themselves "The Terrific Three," and built a clubhouse in the dirt cellar of the old, wooden three-decker where Izzy lived. They spent part of every day together, and continued to do so until they had left school and World War II split them up.

"We used to sit down in my cellar, the clubhouse, and scheme," Izzy Gold recalled.

"The Terrific Three. We'd gotten the idea from a comic strip in the *Brockton Enterprise Times*. We were gonna steal from the rich and give to the poor."

"How're we gonna make a big score?" Rocky would say. "Chrissakes, we've gotta make some money here."

"Maybe we could rob a bank," Izzy would say. "I know. We'll hit the gamblers. Rock, we'll take them for a million."

"Naw," Eugene would say. "We're gonna make it, Rock. We're gonna be big-leaguers."

"Yeah, Euey," Rocky would say. "Yeah. But what's poor Izzy gonna do? Izzy won't be a big-leaguer."

"Don't worry, Rock," Izzy said. "I'll make it out of here. I'm gonna score big with the gamblers."

It was an obsession with them—baseball and money. Everything they did seemed to focus on those two things.

"We came from a respectable neighborhood, and our families really cared about what happened to us," Eugene said. "None of our gang was ever in any serious trouble, or in jail or anything like that. About the biggest thing we ever did was ring in a false alarm to the fire department once, and we really got our asses kicked for that . . . We had good, decent, hard-working fathers, who put in long hours every day sweating in the lousy shoe factories and still never made any decent money. Don't think we didn't notice that. We were always scared of being stuck in the shoe factories for cheap money the rest of our lives."

Eugene Sylvester was the unofficial leader of the Terrific Three, although Izzy Gold might dispute the claim. A thin, dark-haired boy, Eugene disguised his handsome, delicate features by a perpetual wise-guy smirk. He was the loudest talker, the biggest instigator,

and the one who got Rocky into the most scraps and fights.

Izzy Gold was a tough little Jewish kid who spent his first twelve years in the rough-and-tumble environment of Brockton's poorest neighborhood, the East Side. Long before his family moved to Ward 2, Izzy knew what it took to survive. He was an outspoken schemer who enjoyed taking risks and loved to gamble. This was the type of person that attracted Rocky throughout his life.

"Rocky never wanted to be a fighter when we were kids," Eugene Sylvester recalled. "If anything, you'd have to call the Rock shy, kind of quiet and easygoing. He never started things. Izzy and me pushed The Rock into just about every fight he ever had. Sometimes he'd even argue he didn't want to go after a guy. But we could always talk him into anything. I used to brag after The Rock became heavyweight champion that I got him into more fights than he ever had in the ring. And that was the truth."

"The Rock loved to wrestle and hit guys hard in football or do any kind of thing that would test his strength against another kid," Izzy Gold said. "He had this thing where he wanted to be the strongest kid in the world. But he wasn't a fighter. It took an awful lot to get him mad."

But Rocky was very gullible as a young boy, and Sylvester knew how to get him mad. Eugene considered Rocky his personal bodyguard.

"Hey, Rock, did you hear what that guy called us?" Eugene would say. "He said we're a couple of dumb guineas," Or, "Rock. For Chrissake, Rock, that kid's laughin' at ya. He said you're a clumsy jerk."

"Once Rocky was enraged, he was like an animal," Sylvester recalled. "He really punched the crap out of guys, knocked them right down, blood all over the place. I'd he saying to myself, 'Jeez, why'd I send The Rock after this kid. I've got to be careful who I get him mad at. The Rock's really dangerous.' "

But one of Marciano's earliest fights didn't involve Izzy or Eugene, and it was a brawl with no winner.

Rocky and Vinnie Colombo, a neighbor and close friend who later played minor league baseball with Marciano, were ten-year-old fifth-graders on their way home from school.

"Give me that ball, it's mine," Rocky said.

"No, it isn't, it's mine," Colombo said.

Out in the middle of Brook Street, the shoving and name calling went on until finally fists struck out wildly. They punched and wrestled, rolling on the cobblestoned street, until, exhausted and frightened, fighting to hold back their tears, they broke apart and ran toward their homes. The rubber ball lay unclaimed in the gutter.

Rocky stumbled up the front steps, tears streaming down his face.

"Son-a-ma-beetch," his mother exclaimed. "What's the matter, Rocky? Didn't I tell you come right home from school?"

Rocky was humiliated. He sucked blood from his swollen lip. His school shirt was stained and torn, and his knickers were frayed and stuck to the oozing skin of his scraped knee.

"Vinnie Colombo punched me, Ma," Rocky said, standing outside the front door. He spoke in an angelic voice designed to elicit his mother's total sympathy. "He took my ball."

But Rocky hadn't noticed his Uncle John Picciuto, Pasqualena's younger brother, who stood silently behind her.

"What's the matter?" Uncle John said. "Why you gotta run home to your mother, Rocky? Can't you fight your battles?"

Rocky hounded into the house, too embarrassed to face his uncle.

The next morning Uncle John stayed home from his job at the shoe factory. He took an old army duffel bag and stuffed it with rags and wood shavings and hung it from a tree in the backyard.

"Right-left . . . right-left," Uncle John ordered, standing behind his nephew as the boy punched the heavy bag. "You see? Now you can fight. Don't you come running home anymore."

All the while John Picciuto encouraged Rocky to use both hands when he fought. John himself had been handicapped with a withered left arm most of his life, the result of having fallen down a flight of stairs when he was a child in Italy.

"It was a real brawl all right," Vinnie Colombo said. "There was blood all over Brook Street, and most of it was mine. I learned one thing from that fight with The Rock. Whenever there was trouble after that, I always tried to talk my way out of it. I never went looking for fights."

Fighting to a draw with a Colombo was no dishonor. The Colombos were tough and fine athletes. There were so many of them in Ward 2 that Father Jeremiah J. Minihan, coach of the Saint Patrick's Church parish baseball team, once said, "There are enough Colombos here to field a team and send everybody else home."

One of them was Allie Colombo, the organizer, who would later become Rocky's best friend, adviser, and trainer on his rise to the heavyweight championship. But as they were growing up, Allie and Rocky moved in different circles. Allie was almost five years older than Rocky, and although he was not an exceptional athlete himself, Allie was the one who got teams together and planned the games. He was the spark that always kept the spirits high in the little Ward 2 neighborhood.

Uncle John, who was a bachelor during Marciano's youth, was almost like a second father to Rocky. John did many of the things with Rocky that Pierino wanted to do but could not because of his poor health. Also, the job in the factory left him drained and exhausted by the time he trudged up the hill toward home in the evening. Pierino would come inside, flop in his chair, turn on the radio, and pour himself a glass of warm brandy. Often when Pasqualena went to call him for supper he was asleep.

The cottage at 80 Brook Street was Luigi Picciuto's pride and joy. He loved his wine cellar and the grape vineyard and bocce court in the backyard. He took great care keeping the yard clean, the trim painted, and the carpentry and plumbing in good repair. And every spring he planted the garden with zucchini squash, tomatoes, and green beans.

On Friday nights, Luigi's sons Michael and John came home from the factories and placed their pay envelopes on the kitchen table. Luigi opened the envelopes, took the money, and then handed a few dollars back to each of his sons. "Be careful how you spend it," Luigi would say.

His son Michael, who later changed the spelling of his name from Picciuto to Piccento, recalled that the amount Luigi gave the boys varied, depending upon how pressing the household bills were, and the sums ranged from as little as two dollars to ten or fifteen. Occasionally, when one of the boys had displayed his ambition by working longer hours than the other, Luigi rewarded him by giving him more money than he gave his brother. As long as they remained in Luigi's house and did not marry, the boys followed this custom without question. It was also a practice that Rocky

and his father adhered to in the years before Rocky became a fighter.

EVERY FALL, on a Monday evening just as dusk was falling, a dilapidated truck would rattle to a stop in front of Luigi's cottage. It was loaded with bushel baskets of Concord and white grapes.

It was Rocky's job to unload the grapes into Luigi's cellar. To do this he asked his friends to help, close pals like Izzy Gold, Eugene Sylvester, Louie Zipeto, and Jimmy DiStasi. It wasn't easy. There were from 165 to 180 crates of grapes, each weighing more than thirty pounds. The boys had to carry them into the yard, down the cellar steps, and across the dirt floor.

Luigi watched the driver like a hawk, picking through each basket, before the boys hauled it away. "Hey, whatsa matter with these grapes?" Luigi growled. "These grapes are no juicy. You giva me a bad price."

After all the crates were in the cellar, the boys look turns on the masher, squeezing the juice from the grapes.

Rocky loved the way turning the handle made his arms swell with power. He tested himself against the masher, trying to turn the handle one more time after it felt as if his muscles could last no longer. And he always wanted to squeeze more grapes than the other boys.

After all the juice was crushed out of the grapes, Luigi ordered the boys to take everything—leaves, twigs, crushed grapes—and put them into a press. There was very little juice left, but Luigi would let the concoction drip for days. Then he'd have the skins, vines, and leaves removed like cakes of cheese and strewn in the garden for fertilizer. Luigi Picciuto was a man who did not believe in wasting anything.

All Luigi would give the boys was a pat on the back and a few bunches of grapes when the work was done. "Thatsa good work, boys," Luigi said. "Now don'ta you get a bellyache eating these grapes."

It was the way all the old Italian winemakers in the neighborhood paid off the kids. "A few grapes is plenty," the old men figured. "These boys should help for nothing."

When they were grammar school boys, winemaking was fun, and Rocky and his pals figured the grapes were payment enough. But as teenagers the work became a drudgery that took them away from their football games.

"We're a bunch of jerks," Izzy Gold said when they were fourteen. "We've been gettin' screwed on this deal for years."

Izzy was a perpetual schemer. The truck driver was a tall, red-faced Irishman. And part of Izzy's plan took into consideration that Luigi disliked and distrusted Irishmen.

"Lissen, we're gonna steal a crate of these grapes," Izzy said, "Rocky, you take the crate off the truck and hide it inna woods while we keep your grandfather and the truck driver busy."

"I don't know, Izzy," Rocky said. "My grandfather will kill us if he catches us stealing those grapes."

"What're you, yellow?" Izzy said.

"Don't you ever call me yellow," Rocky snarled. "All right. I'll do it. But you'd better be right, Izzy, or I'm coming after you."

"Don't worry, Rock," Izzy said. "Ain't I always right?"

"So we finally talked Rocky into it," Eugene Sylvester said. "Me an' Izzy were a couple of instigators, but Rocky always trusted us."

Izzy diverted Luigi's attention by pretend-ing to try to convince him it would save time if the driver moved the truck closer to the door. Luigi kept arguing that he didn't want the truck to run over his lawn.

Meanwhile Rocky grabbed a crate of grapes and hurried away from the truck. Once he got in back of the house, out of everyone's view, he began running for the woods with the grapes, glancing nervously over his shoulder, expecting his grandfather to suddenly come charging around the corner and grab him. Rocky had almost made it when he tripped on a stump and went sprawling, face first. Grapes flew everywhere.

"*Marana!*" exclaimed Eugene Sylvester, who was posted on guard. "We're finished!"

Rocky was scrambling all over the back-yard, scooping up grapes and stuffing them back into the wooden box. It was the fastest Eugene had ever seen him move, and he disappeared quickly into the woods.

"Son of a whore, you've shortchanged me," Luigi said after he had recounted the crates in the cellar. "This bill is for one hundred seventy-five crates, but there are only one hundred seventy-four. I won't pay."

"You'll pay," the Irish truck driver said. "You counted those crates when they came off the truck. There were one hundred seventy-five."

"Like hell," Luigi said. "I never pay. I pay for one hundred seventy-four crates. That's what I pay."

The boys were crouched at the top of the cellar steps watching Luigi and the truck driver shout angrily, each accusing the other of being dishonest.

"Chrissakes," Rocky whispered. "Now look what's happened. My grandfather's gonna fight that guy."

"Quit worryin'," Eugene said. "He'll kill the Irish son of a bitch."

"All I know is I had one hundred seventy-five crates on the truck," the driver said. "Those kids must have stole one."

"How dare you accuse my kids?" Luigi said. "Here, take your money. I pay for one hundred seventy-four crates, no more. You are the crook, not my kids."

"Imagine the nerve," Luigi told his paesanos at their Saturday night card game. "That Irish bastard tried to tell me my Rocky took those grapes. That son of a whore."

"I told you, didn't I?" Izzy Gold bragged as they sat up in the woods eating the grapes. "See how easy it was? We can do this every time we unload these trucks. Sometimes we'll get two or three crates. Who knows, maybe we could start a little business selling grapes. Whadda you think they'd give for a crate of grapes up onna West Side?"

LUIGI PICCIUTO WAS the neighborhood boot-legger and competed vigorously for the Saturday night trade with Allie Colombo's grandfather. They were archrivals, always scheming on how to get the upper hand.

In the summer, Luigi strung lights over his grape vineyards, where the old Italian paesanos gathered to play bocce. The men gambled for wine, which Luigi sold to the losers. They took the games very seriously, and often late at night they would be drunk and staggering, arguing and swearing loudly in Italian about who won.

During the winter months they went indoors to the dirt cellar, where Luigi hosted card games of *scopa,* similar to cassino or sweep.

The games were always held on Saturday nights, so that the men could relax and work off the frustration of six days in the shoe factory. They knew that on Sunday they could sleep late.

Rocky hid at the top of the cellar stairs and watched. Sometimes the old men shook fists in each other's faces. Whenever Luigi sold a bottle of wine to the loser, the buyer held it up to the light to examine its contents for sediment. If the wine was crystal clear, he kissed his fingertips and said, "Che *bellezza!*" ("How beautiful!").

What Rocky enjoyed most of all were the head-butting contests at the end of the night, when the drunken men argued like soldiers about to charge with fixed bayonets. One old Italian would challenge the other. They'd retreat to opposite sides of the dirt floor and, on a signal, they would rush each other, their heads lowered like rams in the rutting season. The sound of their skulls colliding cracked like billiard balls on a power shot. Then the old men staggered around amid cheering paesanos, cradling throbbing skulls in open palms.

"Wow! You should have seen them," Rocky would tell his friends at the ball park the next morning. "Jeez, what guts those old guys have got."

In the mornings, when he was not delivering a paper route, Rocky practiced running up Saxon Hill near his house. He was determined to increase his speed and to improve his skills as a ballplayer. He exercised secretly to develop his arms and legs.

"I used to come up the house early sometimes and catch Rocky doing chin-ups on a tree in the backyard," Eugene Sylvester said. "It embarrassed him. He never liked the guys to know he was exercising. His Uncle John had a set of stretching coils to strengthen his arm, chest, and back muscles. The Rock used them so much he had them all pulled out of shape.

He wanted to be the strongest kid in the neighborhood, and he was."

If Eugene had any doubts at all about Rocky's strength or fighting ability, they were dispelled that year when the boys turned thirteen.

Rocky and Eugene had walked to Flagg Pond to go ice skating. It was a place where many of Brockton's teen-agers went for winter fun.

"We were just kind of fooling around on the ice when we spotted this nice-looking broad," Sylvester said. "We were just beginning to get slightly interested in girls, but The Rock was still real shy. I was the only one in our gang who could throw the girls a line."

"Euey, see if you can get her to talk to us," Rocky said.

Eugene skated up to the girl and began talking. "So I was wondering if you'd like to meet my friend Rocky," he was saying, so engrossed in the progress he was making with her that he didn't notice her boyfriend skate up and tower over him.

"Who's this?" he said, glaring down at Sylvester.

"Oh, this is Eugene," the girl said. "He's a baseball player."

"Screw, you dumb little guinea," the boy said.

"You and who else is gonna make me?"

They looked comical coming across the ice—skinny little Eugene skating for his life with the girl's enraged boyfriend racing after him.

"Rock, this guy's tryin' to beat me up," Sylvester shouted. "He called me a dumb guinea."

Sylvester saw a fight that "lasted only a couple of minutes." As soon as Rocky heard of Eugene's insult, he charged in and began punching. Rocky connected with a looping right that split the skin above the startled boy's eye. The gash spurted blood onto Rocky's shirt as the boy sprawled over backward.

"It was a nasty cut that wouldn't stop bleeding, and they had to take this kid up to Brockton Hospital for stitches," Sylvester said. "I could tell Rocky was upset because the kid got hurt so bad and the blood got on his shirt. But The Rock didn't say anything. He was still plenty mad because this guy had called us 'dumb guineas.' "

Eugene and Rocky saw the boy around Brockton from time to time after that fight, and years later they noticed that he still had the scar over his eye.

"Even though he was a couple of years older than Rocky and he came after us, we always felt pretty bad about this guy getting marked up like that," Sylvester said. "But later on, when Rocky got his share of cuts and scars too, we realized that, what the hell, that's what happens if you want to be a fighter."

There was a punchdrunk fighter the boys would sometimes pass walking along Main Street in the center of Brockton, near Sylvia Sweets and the pool hall. The fighter had scar tissue over both eyes, a wide, flat nose, and cauliflower ears. He had been a good professional, but in the days of the club fights he had been exploited by managers. He had gone to the ring too often, frequently overmatched by the hungry fight-game sharks, who regarded him as an expendable machine.

"Jeez," Rocky would say. "Didja see the way his head jerks?"

"Guy's punchy, Rock," Eugene or Izzy would reply. "You can't take that many punches. His brains're scrambled."

"Jesus," Rocky said. "See how he has to blink all the time."

Every time Rocky saw the punchy fighter he got very nervous. He had no intention of ever being a fighter himself, but whenever they saw him, Rocky always made comments like, "Nobody should ever let someone hit them in the head. It's the worst thing. It can really screw you up."

"The Rock never thought about being a boxer in those days," Izzy Gold said. "He didn't go to the YMCA or any of those places where they had kids involved in amateur boxing. Rock spent all his time practicing baseball. He never knew it was in the cards for him to be a pro fighter. If Rocky had ever suspected he was going to be a fighter, he'd have been working at it from the time he was ten years old . . . There were guys around Brockton who were bigger and built better than Rock, but they didn't have his determination and guts. The Rock was always first to take a chance at something we were trying to prove we weren't afraid of. He'd jump a river, climb a tree, swim across a lake, fight a kid three years older than him. I always knew he'd be a winner. He was the kind of kid who wouldn't allow himself to lose. But I figured he'd be a winner in baseball."

Their dream was to make a lot of money.

"We were always embarrassed because we figured our families didn't have enough dough," Eugene Sylvester said. "Looking back on it, we were crazy. There was always plenty of food on the table. But things were tight. We wore hand-me-down clothes, and there was never any extra money for the sports equipment and stuff we wanted."

The boys' mothers gave them vouchers to take to the outlet at city hall and pick up surplus food. The public assistance was something that some families were forced to rely upon for brief periods during the Depression, when many men in Brockton were out of work and labored for virtually nothing building roads and stone walls and other municipal projects for the WPA.

"We didn't want to pick up the food," Sylvester said. "We were so embarrassed, we just didn't want to go. We spent most of our time just dreaming and scheming about how we were gonna make money. It was really an obsession."

They often worked hard—mowing lawns, delivering newspapers, doing odd jobs for neighbors. But there was never enough to buy the balls and gloves and Louisville Slugger bats they wanted so much. So sometimes they stole a glove or a pair of cleats from the hardware store or Sears, Roebuck & Company. Like a lot of Depression kids, they were learning how to hustle. And they always dreamed of the "big score" that lay somewhere in that mysterious world outside of Ward 2, Brockton, Massachusetts—a world they longed for but had never seen.

Izzy Gold recalled how they used to plead for hot doughnuts and rolls from the friendly baker at Bob's Lunch on Crescent Street, and then make a fifteen-minute hike to the West Side to steal quarts of milk from the doorsteps of the rich.

"We figured these people got dough," Izzy said. "They ain't gonna mind if we take a few quarts of milk to go with the doughnuts."

In the winter, even before the blizzard stopped howling, they tugged on rubber hip boots and hoisted the old iron coal shovels over their shoulders and trudged to the West Side. Being there first meant the best jobs were theirs. Inside the sprawling brick, ivy-covered houses lived the upper trust of Brockton.

When the drifts were deep enough. Rocky and his pals could earn several dollars each in a morning of shoveling out the long, curved driveways. It was the kind of work Rocky enjoyed, being outdoors, throwing the wet, heavy snow over his shoulder, feeling the sweat rise up cold under his mackinaw, his muscles warm and throbbing. They scraped the drives down to bare tar, dusted off the Cadillacs, sanded the steps, and carved trenches in the ice for the water to drain into the gutters. And when they finished they came away cold and weary, happy to have earned the money, but depressed by what they had seen.

"We knew these people lived a different kind of life," Izzy Gold said. "We knew they had things we didn't have. We saw the houses, the big cars, the fancy clothes. It made us hungry. We'd go home from there and we'd scheme for days about how we were gonna make our big score."

When his mother gave him fifteen cents or a quarter to go to the movies, Rocky plotted ways to avoid spending it. Sometimes Izzy, Eugene, or Nicky Sylvester helped him. Maybe there was an usher at the Modern Theater who was a friend and would let them slip by or a door wedged open at the top of the fire escape at the Rialto. It was a big victory for Rocky when he returned home with the twenty-five cents still in his pocket.

Most of Rocky's time, however, was not spent at the movies, but in James Edgar Playground. Among the teen-agers at the ball park, Julie Durham was "King of the Hill." He was the only black kid in the neighborhood, and he had a reputation for being a fearless, rugged, and skillful fighter.

But Eugene Sylvester never bothered to take those things into account. What was needed was a new baseball to replace the warped, taped ball the boys were using. Eugene had devised a plan to get it, even though he knew it might involve a confrontation with Julie. What the hell, Eugene figured. I can run like a deer, and I've got Rocky behind me.

Julie Durham was the mascot and ballboy for the Taunton Lumber Company's semipro baseball team. He had been hired by Joe Downey, the team manager, who later became one of Brockton's most popular mayors and an ardent fan of Rocky Marciano's. Among Julie's duties was to make certain that all foul balls were returned.

"When one of these guys hits a foul into the woods, we're gonna grab it and screw," Eugene said.

The ball they were waiting for went bouncing into the woods, with Rocky, Eugene, and Izzy in pursuit. Izzy pounced on it and stuffed it under his shirt. They were about to run, when Julie Durham came charging toward them. Izzy dropped the ball and kicked it into the leaves. Then they all began looking, scuffing through the dry leaves, trying to lure Julie away from the spot where the baseball was hidden.

"All right, give me the ball," Durham said.

"What ball?" Izzy said. "I ain't got no ball."

"Yeah," Sylvester said. "We're helping you look for it."

"I'm warning you," Julie said. "If you don't give me that ball I'm gonna bust your head."

"Oh yeah," Eugene said, glancing over at Rocky. "Go ahead and try."

"Why don't you pick on a guy your own size, Julie?" Rocky said.

"Let me get him. Rock," Eugene said, doubling up his fists and pretending to move toward Durham. "I can take him."

And then Rocky said exactly what Eugene had expected him to say, had hoped and prayed he would say. "You stay out of this, Euey. If Julie wants to fight, he'll have to take me."

They began shoving each other, then suddenly Julie reached out with a sharp jab that caught Rocky flush on the nose. In his excitement, Rocky stumbled and slipped to the ground. When he got up, a trickle of blood was coming from his nostrils.

"Get him, Rock!" Eugene shouted. "Kill him!"

But Julie was fast with his fists and accurate. Rocky had both hands up in front of him like a weightlifter curling a barbell. He hadn't thrown a punch.

The bleachers at James Edgar Playground had emptied out, and both fans and players had formed a circle around the fighters.

For a long while they fought in what seemed like a mismatch, with Julie getting all the best of it. Then Rocky suddenly lunged out with an overhead right that caught Julie on the jaw and sent him toppling to the ground.

Julie stayed down, and everybody cheered for Rocky.

Walking home with Izzy and Eugene that night, Rocky felt as proud as he had ever been in his life. He kept going over the fight in his mind, remembering the way they had all cheered him.

"You really showed him. Rock," Izzy said. "Jeez, where'd you get a punch like that?"

"I don't know," Rocky said happily. "I guess it's just a natural."

Rocky couldn't wait to tell his Uncle John about the fight. He made Eugene and Izzy come with him to furnish their descriptions.

"That's great, Rocky," Uncle John said. "Now you're a real fighter. That Julie Durham is a plenty tough kid."

Rocky was so happy that he sat on the steps with Eugene and Izzy until late at night talking about it. It had always been very important to Rocky to make his Uncle John proud. With one punch he had become a big shot in the neighborhood. He was the new "King of the Hill." And it was a sensational feeling.

"Know something?" Izzy Gold said, as he and Eugene were about to leave for home. "Julie Durham ain't such a bad kid."

"No," Rocky said. "Julie's a nice guy. Maybe we'll get to know him better."

Durham did become a good friend, and stayed one until Rocky's death. Julie, Rocky, and Izzy were teammates on the high school football squad. Julie was a scatback, one of the team's biggest stars.

But that hot evening in July belonged to Rocky. He never forgot it.

3.
Living Dangerously

WHEN ROCKY WAS sixteen, the Marchegiano family moved to a two-story wood-shingled house on Dover Street. It was 1939. The new residence was even closer to James Edgar Playground than Luigi Picciuto's home on Brook Street. And, had he wanted, Rocky could have thrown a baseball from his screened-in porch and hit the backstop behind the diamond.

From the time he was thirteen until he quit school at sixteen to go to work, Rocky's reputation as an athlete grew.

The bleachers were full at James Edgar the day Father Jeremiah Minihan's Saint Patrick's Church baseball team defeated a Catholic church team from Cambridge for the archdiocese championship.

With two outs in the final inning, Cambridge had the tying run at second base. The batter hit a sharp single to the outfield. The runner, going on the pitch, rounded third base and headed for home.

Rocky blocked the plate. The throw arrived just as the runner charged home, colliding heavily with Marchegiano. But Rocky held onto the ball, and the umpire called the

Cambridge player out. Pandemonium erupted in the stands. Brockton won the championship.

When he was fifteen and a first-string linebacker on the high school football team as a sophomore, Rocky intercepted a pass in a game between Brockton and New Bedford and ran it back 67 yards for a touchdown. The fans at Eldon B. Keith Field roared. The team is now named the Brockton Boxers. It plays at a new field, Rocky Marciano Stadium.

These were the memories that Rocky savored. He was never a serious student, doing just enough to get by in most subjects. But when he was interested in a course, such as Italian culture, Rocky gave it the same dedication he did to sports.

"I'm going to be a baseball player," Rocky told his friends. "Mathematics won't help me there. I've got to concentrate on hitting the ball."

Father Minihan influenced Rocky's future strongly. He was one Irishman who was always welcomed by the Italian boys in Ward 2.

He often came to James Edgar Playground and encouraged young Rocco Marchegiano's

23

ambition to become a baseball player. You're going to be good, Rocco," Father Minihan would say. "You'll be a fine ballplayer. You've got the power, the determination, and the ability. Someday you'll be a star."

The boys had great respect for Father Minihan, who was an excellent ballplayer himself. He was young, handsome, and forceful, a man to whom they could relate and an athlete they could admire. But Father Minihan did not put up with nonsense, and when the occasion demanded, he showed a brisk Irish temper.

There was a time when gambling threatened to come between Father Minihan and the boys. Snuggled in a shady clearing beyond the thick oaks and elms that bordered Dover Street was the place called "The Gamblers' Woods." Hidden there, young men gathered every Saturday and Sunday to roll dice in what was then the biggest stationary crap game in the city. And Rocky and his friends crouched in the bushes, scheming for ways to get in on the action.

The game was run by a tough-looking, one-legged fat man from Providence nicknamed "Peg-Leg Pete." They played for high stakes, and sometimes the gamblers became very unfriendly.

The Gamblers' Woods was only a minute's walk from Rocky's house and James Edgar Playground. It was here that Izzy, Eugene, and Rocky dreamed of making their big score.

"We'll throw stones at them until they give us some money," Izzy said. "They can't do nothin'. They don't want the cops down here."

Izzy's plan worked a few times. They would pelt the players, mostly men in their early twenties, with small stones. Then Izzy would yell from the safety of the woods, "Give us two bucks and we'll stop."

"All right," a gambler would say, and throw

the money from the pot at them. "Now screw, or we'll bust your asses."

But the gamblers' patience soon wore thin. Peg-Leg Pete's dice games were frequented by unsavory characters who were not amused by three young punks extorting cash and beaning them with stones. They soon came after Rocky and the boys.

"I've got an idea," Eugene said one Sunday morning. "I'm calling the cops on those crapshooters."

"What're you, crazy?" Rocky said. "You'll spoil the game."

"Soon's the cops start comin' through the woods," Eugene explained, "them guys're gonna drop the dough and run. We can jump in just before the cops get there and scoop up maybe fifty, sixty bucks if we're lucky."

"Woooww," Rocky said. "Jeez, we could really make a score on this deal."

Eugene's plan almost worked. The gamblers scrambled for the woods when they saw the police, and they left some money on the ground. But Rocky, Eugene, and Izzy had time to grab only a few dollars before the police were through the trees and upon them, and the boys had to run to save themselves.

"The gamblers never figured out who reported them," Sylvester said. "They let us hang around and watch the games as long as we kept our mouths shut and didn't bother the players. They even paid us to be lookouts and run errands."

It wasn't long before Izzy Gold started getting into the games. He'd bring the five or six dollars that he earned delivering papers, cashing bottles at the corner store, running errands, and playing blackjack on the bleachers at James Edgar field.

The gamblers liked to see Izzy coming. With his small stake, they knew he couldn't win.

"That'll teach you not to gamble," they'd smirk after the little Jewish kid was cleaned out. "Here's a quarter. Go get yourself an ice cream."

Week after week Izzy Gold came back to the crap game, and week after week he lost every penny.

One Sunday, when Eugene and Rocky had skipped Sunday school to go to the Gamblers' Woods, Father Minihan came looking for them. The boys usually played baseball in the morning and then went into the woods to watch the gamblers. They had been skipping church almost every Sunday.

"Heathens!" Father Minihan shouted when he found them.

"Now get away from here, and if I ever catch you skipping church again, you'll play no more baseball for Saint Patrick's."

Father Minihan did not make idle threats, and Rocky knew he could not be bluffed. And playing on the Saint Patrick's baseball team was one of the most important things in Rocky's life.

"That Sunday school isn't so bad," Rocky told Eugene. "Now we're gonna have to start going again every week. It's only a couple of hours anyway. That's no big deal."

The boys went back to Sunday school, but they also continued to attend the crap games faithfully.

On one hot, humid Sunday afternoon in July, Izzy Gold's luck changed. The cocky little fourteen-year-old made five straight passes.

"It's shit luck," one of the gamblers said.

"Seven," Rocky yelled.

"Point," Eugene hollered.

"Chrissakes, Izzy, you're cleaning them out, pal!"

When the game was over, the gamblers trudged off. The Terrific Three stood trembling, their sweaty hands clutching fistfuls of soiled bills—twos, fives, tens, twenties—more money than any of them had ever seen. Izzy Gold had wiped out the crap game.

"Jeez, there must be five hundred bucks here," Izzy said. "What're we gonna do with all this dough?"

"Hide it," Rocky said. "We can't let anybody find out we've got this kind of dough. We've got to bury it."

"Yeah," Eugene said. "We can bury it in the clubhouse. Nobody'll ever find it there."

They ran to Izzy Gold's house on Elm Street, hiding the money under their faded summer shirts. They snuck down the back steps like burglars into the dark, musky cellar.

Inside the tiny clubhouse was a punching bag, a dart game, several warped baseballs covered with black carpenter's tape, a broken bat fastened together with wood screws, and decks of cards that Izzy had marked with barely visible ink dots on the back. The rusty ends of nails protruded from the wall, holding pictures of Babe Ruth, Lou Gehrig, and other famous baseball players, many of them Italians, whom Rocky insisted be displayed more prominently than the others.

"Dig it deep, Rock," Izzy said. "We've gotta be sure nobody finds this dough."

"What a score," Rocky kept saying as he drove the flat-nosed coal shovel deeper into the dirt floor.

They smelled the money, counted it, stuffed it in their wallets, passed it back and forth. When they were finished, they packed it carefully into cigar boxes and tied them together with string. Then they dropped the money into the deep hole Rocky had dug. They had kept out ten dollars apiece to last them a week.

"Don't splurge this dough," Rocky said. "If our mothers find out we've been gambling with these guys, we're in big trouble."

The winnings actually belonged to Izzy Gold, since he had risked his money and had done all the gambling himself.

"But the rules of the Terrific Three were that we shared everything," Gold said. "It was up to me to decide how we'd spend it."

Izzy chose the Brockton Fair, which in those days was a week-long celebration that every youngster in the city keenly anticipated. The fair had a giant midway with dozens of rides, side shows, burlesque, gambling games, horse racing, daredevil drivers, and exhibits. It wouldn't be hard for the Terrific Three to breeze through several hundred dollars in a week at the fair.

But the fair was held in September, more than a month away. Rocky was afraid that something might happen to the money, so every week he snuck into Izzy Gold's cellar and dug the boxes up again.

"I'm just checking, Izz," Rocky said, opening the boxes and counting the bills. "Jeez, what if somebody finds this place? Do you think it's really safe here?"

"Sometimes Rocky dug new holes and changed the burial ground of the dough," Gold recalled. "He was never comfortable about leaving so much cash unguarded."

When the Brockton Fair finally arrived, Izzy, Rocky, and Eugene took the money and went on a wild spree. For seven straight days they rode every ride, saw all the side shows, threw baseballs at metal milk bottles, watched the roulette wheels spin—which almost never stopped on their numbers—had friends place bets horses for them, bought armfuls of souvenirs, and gorged themselves on cotton candy, hot dogs, pizza, candied apples, and soda pop . . . And before the week was finished, before they had satisfied their appetites for the Whip, the Silver Streak, and the Rockets, the money was all gone.

When the gates of the fair closed, the boys went to work, hired on the spot to unbolt the rides, carry the heavy metal parts, and pack them away in the moving crates. It was a good-paying job that lasted into the early hours of the morning.

Rocky was fascinated by the gypsy carnival types, who respected no time clocks and who worked feverishly to pack up the equipment, anxious to move on to another city and new faces.

"They follow the buck," Izzy said. "These guys know when it's time to leave. Next year they'll come back, and everybody'll be waitin' to spend their dough."

When the work was finished, the boys were weary and their muscles sore. The sun was beginning to rise over the chain-link fence that circled the abandoned fairgrounds. Where there had been thousands of people the day before, nothing remained but deserted buildings and mountains of trash, the papers blowing in the dust and piled against the fence. They felt good walking along Belmont Street toward Ward 2. It had been the wildest week in the history of the Terrific Three. And there was a strange sense of fulfillment in the knowledge that for one brief, fleeting interlude they had known what it was like to be rich, to have all the cash they needed to do everything they wanted.

The Terrific Three gambled often after that. They went to crap games in the Gamblers' Woods, to poker, seven-card stud, and blackjack games in the clubs around Brockton; later, when they had quit school and taken full-time jobs, they went to the dog track. But they were never lucky again.

Experienced card players cheated and conned them out of their hard-earned money. The dice rollers nibbled away at Izzy's earnings until they easily recouped the cash he had won in the Gamblers' Woods. Once Rocky rolled the dice for eighty-four dollars and crapped out. They lost repeatedly. But they didn't complain. At least not the way they sulked and grumbled after losing a ball game. They just waited patiently for another payday and went right back to the gamblers, looking for revenge, always believing that someday they would make another "big score."

Once, shortly before they went into the army, Izzy Gold discovered that some gamblers were cheating them. They had suspected it all along, but now Izzy had the proof.

Rocky was furious. That night Rocky and Izzy went to the club where the game was going on. Rocky was trembling with rage. He grabbed the dealer by the shirt and said, "You've been cheating us for years. Now give us back our dough."

"The guy was shocked," Gold said. "He gave us a fistful of bills, but it was nothing compared to what he'd swindled us out of."

Once one of Rocky's friends who had lost heavily in the crap game returned to the Gamblers' Woods a short while later wearing a mask and carrying a gun.

"This is a stickup," he said. "Give me all the money." It was hilarious because everybody recognized him immediately. Rocky and Izzy couldn't stop giggling. "Will you stop it?" one of the gamblers said. "Get lost."

"The guy's crazy," Izzy Gold said afterward. "Even we wouldn't do something like that."

"Yeah," Rocky said. "But what balls he's got. Imagine that? Who'd ever think of holdin' up the crap game?"

As much as he enjoyed the excitement and risks of gambling, Rocky never forgot the bad experiences of being cheated and losing; when he became the heavyweight champion and earned large sums, he avoided gambling almost entirely. He loved to be with gamblers and to watch them, and often friends would bet for him, especially on a fight, to give him added incentive. But Rocky rarely bet his own money except on sure things. He enjoyed living dangerously and taking risks with everything—except money. He would risk his cash for a friend, but nowhere else. For the only fear that ever possessed him was the fear of going broke.

4.
Working

THE FIRST DECISION Rocky made in the spring of 1940 was to quit the Brockton High School baseball team. What happened afterward seemed logical and necessary to Rocky, but it caused much concern and displeasure for his parents.

The coach laid down a policy that varsity baseball players could not participate on teams outside the school.

"This is ridiculous," Rocky said. "I'm not giving up Saint Patrick's."

"I'd rather play for the church myself," Vinnie Colombo said.

"I don't see why we can't play for both," Eugene Sylvester said. "What harm is there?"

Because the Ward 2 boys were intensely devoted to Father Minihan, it seemed a betrayal to abandon Saint Patrick's because of something for which the priest was not responsible. But it was a painful decision, because they had long dreamed of becoming high school baseball stars. They put off making a final decision, hoping that somehow the priest might weave a miracle and the high school coach would rescind his order. But finally Rocky, Eugene, and Vinnie all gave up their schoolboy careers to play for the church.

"If they won't let me be on the team, there's no sense staying in school," Rocky said. "I need experience playing ball."

"What, are you gonna quit?" Izzy Gold said.

"Sure," Rocky said. "Baseball's a lot more important than school. Besides, I want to get a job and help the family out a little."

"Your mother won't go for it," Izzy said.

"Don't worry," Rocky said. "I can convince her."

But when your father trudges home exhausted every night, beaten down by the factory, unable to enjoy many of the simple pleasures of family life—when your father is trapped because he lacks the education and the power to improve his situation—it is hard to convince your mother that education is not important.

"Ma, I'll get a little job, and after work I can practice baseball all the time," Rocky said. "Why do I need to go to school anyway? I'm going to be a pro ballplayer."

"Stay in school, Rocky," Pasqualena pleaded. "You can't do nothing without an education."

His mother remained stubbornly opposed

to the idea for a long time, but Rocky persisted and finally convinced her just enough to
gain reluctant approval. "You're only sixteen,"
Pasqualena said. "You'll see. Someday you'll
be sorry."

"No, Ma," Rocky said. "I know exactly
what I'm doing."

Pierino was easier to convince. He had
great faith in his son's ability as an athlete. "If
you say so, you'll do it," Pierino said. "Just
remember. Don't you ever let yourself end up
in the shoe shops. Now, promise me you won't
do that."

"Don't worry, Pa," Rocky said. "I'll never
wind up in the factory. I'm going to be a big-
leaguer someday."

An uncle got Rocky a job on a coal truck.
The pay was only a few dollars a day and the
work was hard, loading coal onto the truck and
delivering it to cellars all over the Brockton
area. He enjoyed any kind of work that
involved using his muscles, and he liked it
when they were outdoors, traveling around on
the truck but going down into the coal bins
and breathing the dust and getting his clothes
and face and hands smeared with coal dust
bothered him. He wanted a job where he
could be out in the sun exercising, possibly
some type of construction work, but nothing
like that was available.

After a while, Rocky quit the coal truck to
work in a candy factory for higher pay. He
regretted it almost immediately.

"It's like being in jail," Rocky told Izzy.
"They keep the windows closed all day. All you
can smell is that sweet candy. It'd make you
sick."

Every evening he practiced the baseball at
James Edgar Playground. He played for the
church and for local semipro teams. He was
developing as a very powerful hitter, but he
was too slow for outfield and infield positions

and he did not have an exceptionally strong
arm for a catcher.

"Go out on second base," Rocky would tell
one of his friends. "I've got to practice throwing."

He'd throw for hours. He had a strong arm
and could throw accurately, but he lacked the
extra zip that great professional catchers use to
cut down speedy runners.

"I couldn't figure it," said slim Eugene
Sylvester, who never reached 150 pounds. "I
could always throw a baseball harder than
Rocky. But in a fight he'd just knock guys silly.
I used to spend hours wondering where he got
all that punching power. I knew he exercised a
lot, and did everything he could to make himself stronger than the other kids. But a lot of
guys in Ward 2 exercised in those days. So how
come Rocky could belt guys and flatten them
with one punch. *Marana!* I don't think The
Rock even knew."

Rocky would listen to anybody's advice. If
someone told him he should throw in a slightly different way, grip the bat in a certain fashion, or do special exercises to develop his
strength, Rocky would devote himself to doing
it. And it made no difference if the person had
the expertise. A skinny little kid with arms like
toothpicks could give Rocky a method for
developing his biceps and Rocky would try it,
figuring the kid was so self-conscious of his
small arms that he had studied every possible
way of developing them.

When Rocky discovered that an exercise
was not helping him he abandoned it, but he
seldom criticized the person who had suggested it.

"The guy meant well, Izzy," Rocky would
say. "Maybe this worked for him, but it's just
no good for me."

On rare occasions, though, Rocky became
enraged. This was almost always when he

found out that a person who had given him advice had little or no knowledge of the subject, and that the suggested program was actually harmful.

"That asshole," Rocky would say. "Doesn't he know this can screw me up? I've been doing this for weeks, and now I find out that shithead doesn't even know what he's talking about."

But if Rocky even remotely suspected that an exercise was helping him, he invested great reservoirs of dedication and effort in perfecting it.

"You're supposed to do fifteen of these, Izzy," Rocky would say of an exercise routine. "I'm gonna do twenty."

"Won't that hurt you, Rock?" Izzy would say.

"No," Rocky said. "If you don't do enough it'll hurt. But you can't do too many, because you can always tell when you're pushing yourself over the limit."

Even in his late teens, Rocky was still clumsy and slow. He never gave up trying to acquire more speed. In the evenings he ran up Saxton Hill and did wind sprints at the ball park. And he was constantly striving to add power to his legs, arms, and shoulders.

During all these years the family did not have it easy. The Marchegianos had gotten through the hard times of the Depression through Pasqualena's careful management of the household budget and Pierino's steady labor in the shoe factory. Peter was born; now the family was complete, with three girls and three boys. The house on Dover Street was none too spacious for so large a family, but it was their own, and it had been earned through sweat and sacrifice. They thoroughly enjoyed the house, just as they did the companionship of their friends in the Ward 2 neighborhood. The Marchegiano home was full of love and

optimism. And the only regret Rocky ever had was that he was still forced to share a bedroom with his brother Sonny.

The Marchegianos were also a proud family. Rocky as the first son was always very protective of his younger brothers and sisters. He often took Sonny and Peter, who was then just a toddler, to the ball park to watch him play baseball.

"This guy's a great pitcher, Sonny," he'd say. "I'll be trying my best to hit him."

And usually Rocky would hit a double or a triple, or sometimes a home run, and when he came back to the bench it was easy to see how proud he was.

Rocky craved and earned the praise of his uncles John and Mike Picciuto, and he was always pleased when they were in the stands to watch him play ball. All through the years Rocky was developing as an athlete, his Uncle John spent hours almost every day encouraging him and throwing batting practice until well after darkness had settled over James Edgar Playground.

In turn, Rocky devoted much time to teaching his brother Sonny how to play baseball.

"That's not good enough, Sonny," Rocky would shout. "Try it over again. You've got to get that throw over there faster."

He was often critical of his brothers, much more so than he was of friends or acquaintances, but his sharp sense of family pride was clearly evident in the pleasure he took in their achievements.

"The worst thing that happened to Rocky during this time was when he quit the candy factory and went to work in a shoe shop," Izzy Gold recalled. "He was miserable. He'd come home, and it was like he didn't even want to play baseball. All he could do was smell the leather and hear those machines banging away.

I think the poor kid had nightmares about it."

"My food even tastes like leather, Izzy," Rocky said. "I don't know how our fathers can stand it. Imagine if you had to do this the rest of your life."

"The Rock lasted less than two months in the shoe factory," Gold said. "Then he just had to get out of there."

Rocky soon learned that he did not enjoy working in any type of factory where you punched a time clock and were closely supervised by foremen. He wanted a job in the outdoors where he could use his muscles and be left alone. He finally found it with a construction crew, clearing brush for a government blimp base.

"The pay's good, Izzy," he said. "I get to swing a sickle all day. It's terrific exercise for my arms and legs."

When the blimp base project was finished, Rocky went to work clearing land for an army barracks in Taunton, about half an hour's drive from Brockton. Since Rocky didn't know how to drive a car, he relied on friends. But on most jobs he never minded hustling rides—except when he was in a hurry to get home for a ball game.

On Saint Patrick's Day of 1942, they stood in the cold jaws of a northeast wind and listened as the priest delivered his final eulogy at the grave of Luigi Picciuto.

"My father died the same day my daughter Concetta was born," Mike Piccento said. "I went to the hospital that Saint Patrick's Day to see my wife and the baby. Then I went to the cemetery to bury my father. Then I went to work in the shoe shop."

A year later, in March 1943, Rocky was drafted into the army. He was stationed in Wales for a while. Then his outfit was assigned to ferry supplies across the English Channel to Normandy.

It was one of the least enjoyable periods of his life, for, at least temporarily, his dreams of becoming a major league baseball player were sidetracked.

It was not until after Germany had surrendered and Rocky was sent back to the United States for duty at Fort Lewis, Washington, that important changes began to take place. Between the fall of 1946 and the summer of 1948, he was on a course that would eventually lead him to the heavyweight championship of the world.

Book Two

Anatomy of a Champion

1.

The Foul

Rocco Marchegiano arrived home on furlough in the spring of 1946, noticeably overweight in his wrinkled army khakis; he balanced the heavy duffel bag on his shoulder as he climbed the hill from the railroad depot through the center of Brockton toward Ward 2.

It was an emotional reunion, full of hugs and kisses that both pleased and embarrassed Rocky. Pasqualena cooked his favorite *spezzatto*, and Pierino limped to the cabinet and opened the bottle of Strega he had been saving for the occasion.

"Two years," he said, pouring a glass for Rocky. "It's a long time, eh? How you feel, Rocky? Pretty good?"

"Fine, Pop," Rocky said. "Real good."

But Rocky could see that his father's health had been failing. He did not ask him about it because he knew that Pierino was very proud and would never complain.

"I get my inner strength from my father and my physical strength from my mother," Rocky Marciano would one day tell sportswriters when questioned how he had prevailed in the ring.

That Saturday he met Allie Colombo at the ball park. It was the first time the two boyhood chums had seen each other since 1943, and they embraced like brothers.

They walked to the center of Brockton, talking about their families, sports, and experiences they'd had in the military. Then they returned to James Edgar Playground and sat in the wooden bleachers to continue reminiscing.

"Hey, Rock," Colombo said. "I hear you're fighting now."

"That's right," Rocky said. "I've got a good deal going at Fort Lewis. I do a little boxing for the post, and it gets me out of the crap details. I'm on the baseball team, too."

"That's great, Rock," Colombo said. "I'd love to see you fight sometime,"

"Sure, that'd be real nice, Alsack," Rocky said. Alsack was the nickname Rocky often used in addressing Colombo.

Colombo mentioned his friend Dick O'Connor, the former boxer stationed with Allie at Westover Air Force Base, near Springfield.

"He's got connections with the boxing promoter in Holyoke," Colombo said. "Maybe we can get you some fights when you get out of the army, Rock."

"Beautiful," Rocky said. "I could sure use the money."

Colombo, the organizer and leader of all the young athletes in Ward 2, had already begun to allow his Pollyannish mind to drift. Suddenly he was Allie the dreamer. Unknown to Rocky, he was already fantasizing how it would be when his pal won the heavyweight championship of the world.

That evening Colombo went to the Brockton Public Library and read everything he could find on boxing. At home the next day he thumbed through a collection of boxing magazines.

Let's see, Colombo thought. A rough kid like Rock should take about three years to win the title. First we'll get him some fights around Holyoke, then maybe Boston, and then we'll be ready for New York.

But Colombo saw Rocky fight much sooner than either of them had expected. That same evening, Rocky visited his Uncle Mike Piccento, who had for years been interested in boxing.

"Tell me about those fights at Fort Lewis," Mike said, when they had finished dinner and were relaxing with some wine and cigarettes.

Rocky, who had stuffed himself with lasagna, suddenly lost his drowsiness as he began describing the fights. He got out of the chair and began throwing punches at an imaginary opponent. "That's the one that got him, Mike," he grinned, as he finished the story by throwing a very unorthodox, looping, overhand right.

"Why don't I get a fight in Brockton?" Rocky asked.

"Sure," Mike said. "I can fix it. But you ain't in no shape to be fightin' now. You got too much blubber, Rock."

"Aw, don't worry," Rocky said. "Christ sake. I can take care of myself. What's it gonna be, three or four rounds?"

"So you really want to fight," Mike said. "Well, I can arrange it. But be smart and take it easy. Enjoy your vacation. There'll be plenty of time for us to get you some fights later, when you're in better condition. They've got some tough boys fighting in Brockton right now."

"I can handle those fighters," Rocky persisted. "Besides, I really need the dough. I've only got a few bucks to last the rest of my furlough."

"You want some money?"

"No. Just get me the fight."

"See me tomorrow night," Mike said. "They've got some fights going uptown. I'll introduce you to the promoter."

The next day, April 10, Uncle Mike took Rocky to see Generoso "Gene" Caggiano, the promoter of the local "amateur" boxing shows.

"This is my nephew Rocky," Piccento said. "The kid's had a few fights in the army. He'd just as soon fight for you down here. What can he make?"

Caggiano, a tiny, flat-nosed featherweight who had had 138 fights under the name Georgie Dundee, sized Rocky up. He didn't look like much of a fighter. He had a fat rear, thick legs, a flabby gut, and short, stubby arms. But Caggiano needed a Brockton heavyweight. Most of his fighters were from out of town and unknown to many of the local fans.

"Twenty-five bucks," Caggiano said.

"Make it fifty," Uncle Mike said. "This kid's home on furlough. He needs the dough."

"Impossible," Caggiano said. "I couldn't give Joe Louis fifty bucks. I'll give him thirty."

"We'll take it," Mike said. "But don't put him in there with anybody over his head. This kid's only had a few fights."

Caggiano assured them that the fighter who went against Rocky would not have had much ring experience, explaining that it would be better for business if the hometown boxer made a good showing.

"Christ sake," Rocky said, when Caggiano was gone. "I don't care who I fight, Mike. We could've blown the dough arguing over that."

"Let me handle it," Mike said. "Didn't we do all right? Listen, you better lay off the spags and smokes, maybe run and try to get in shape a little bit. This is no joke."

The card was scheduled for April 15, the following Monday night, at the Ancient Order of Hibernians Hall, near Brockton Center.

Word that Rocky was fighting spread through the close-knit Italian neighborhood of Ward 2, and everyone made plans to attend. Nobody knew who he was fighting, but they were all convinced that Rocco would be a big winner.

Rocky ignored his uncle's advice, continuing to enjoy his furlough, gorging himself on the rich Italian food, smoking Camels, drinking wine and beer, and partying long into the night with his paesanos. He was sure he would win. He had never been beaten in a fight.

The most difficult thing was to keep the news of Rocky's fighting from his mother, who Mike and Pop Marchegiano knew would have gone into a tantrum to try and stop it. Nobody in the family mentioned it when she was around.

On Monday night, Rocky arrived at Piccento's house early. He insisted on eating some of the spaghetti and meatballs that Mike's wife was cooking.

"What's the matter with you, Rocky?" Piccento said. "Are you crazy? You can't be loading yourself up with spaghetti. You've got to fight tonight."

"That's all right, Mike," Rocky said. "I've still got three hours to work those spags off before the fight. You watch, I'm gonna be fine in there tonight."

"When we got to the hall, Caggiano came over waving his arms, full of apologies," Uncle Mike recalled. "Caggiano said he had to match Rocky with Henry Lester because he was the only heavyweight available."

Lester had been a Golden Gloves champion three years in succession and runner-up in the New England Amateur Championships the year before.

"Wait a minute," Piccento said. "What's going on here? You told us this would be an easy fight. What're you trying to pull. I ain't gonna put Rocky in there with a guy like Lester."

Rocky was embarrassed. "Christ sake, Mike," he said. "It'll be all right. So what if he's had some fights. This guy's only got two arms and two legs, hasn't he? C'mon, let's go."

Rocky refused to listen to any more of Mike's arguments. The only other comment Piccento could recall was when Rocky saw Lester and said, "Jesus, Mike, I thought I was fightin' a white guy tonight."

Although some of Rocky's friends in sports were blacks, he was raised in a society where the older immigrant Italians considered themselves a notch above the blacks. Italian pride was at stake in this fight. There were Irishmen in this crowded AOH Hall, and these were the ones whom the old mustachioed Italians sharply resented. For the Irish had established themselves in Brockton long before the arrival of the Italians. The Irish were the foremen in the factories, the bosses of the city crews, the politicians, and the police captains. And it was one thing for the Italians to assume a position of superiority over the blacks, and yet another to accept the domination of the Irish.

In the dressing room, Rocky did something that surprised everyone. Minutes after he pulled on his boxing trunks and laced his shoes, still comfortably full of spaghetti, he stretched out on a bench and began to doze.

Rocky's friends were all there: Allie Colombo, Pop Marchegiano, his brother Sonny, the gang from the pool room, the ballplayers from James Edgar Playground, the immigrant Italian factory workers with their stogies and broken English, his uncles, cousins, nephews . . . Rocky did not want to disappoint any of them. And yet he could sleep before a fight.

At the bell for the first round, Rocky charged wildly across the ring and immediately began throwing punches. Lester avoided most of them, but Rocky was so unorthodox and crude that it was like facing a whirlwind that came from any and all directions. There was no way that Lester could employ his usual fighting techniques. He had to join in the slugfest or get blown out of the ring.

When Rocky missed, which was 90 percent of the time, he would grunt and whirl around to slam out another looping overhand right or an uppercut that came up from near the ankles. Every punch was meant to result in instant destruction—and undoubtedly would have had it landed in the right place. Before the first round was over, he had thrown enough punches to last a conservative heavyweight through ten rounds.

The partisan Italian audience was ecstatic. The cries of "Kill him Rock . . . Get him. Get him" rang in Italian through the smoky hall.

But Rocky's offense soon burned up. And while his heart still commanded him to win, his flabby and winded body abandoned him.

Lester was an intelligent boxer, and he soon learned how to move away from Rocky's rushes and counter with hard, well-directed punches.

Midway through the second round, Rocco Marchegiano knew he could not win. He was uninjured and eager to fight, but he was completely punched out and could barely move. It was sadly comical the way Rocky still insisted upon being the aggressor, plodding forward, his arms almost at his sides, unable to protect his face or midsection, while Lester riveted home the punches.

Lester also appeared to be tired from the blistering pace Rocky had set through the first round, but he was in far better condition and had conserved some of his energy. When it became apparent that Rocky was finished, a wave of adrenalin flooded Lester's veins, putting new snap into his punches.

What happened next is debatable—some claim it was intentional, others insist it was an accident.

Lester had begun to throw a right uppercut when Rocky, leaning against the ropes, suddenly brought his knee up hard into his opponent's groin.

A long groan of disbelief rose from the audience, as if someone had just announced that Jack Armstrong, all-American boy, had resorted to kicking the bad guy in the nuts.

Lester doubled over in pain.

Referee Sned McDonald jumped between the two boxers and stopped the fight, indicating that Marchegiano had committed a foul and Lester was unable to continue.

The crowd was at first stunned, then enraged, by the decision to stop the fight. Everyone was jeering as Rocky climbed through the ropes and walked up the aisle toward the dressing room.

"It was one of the worst feelings I've ever had," Rocky said later. "I knew I had to win, but I was exhausted. I couldn't even lift my arms . . . I'd never been so disgusted and embarrassed. I just sort of slipped home quietly that night."

It was also a difficult night for Sonny Marchegiano as he walked back to Ward 2 with some of his seventh-grade classmates.

"Your brother's a dirty fighter," a kid said. "He couldn't win, so he kicked the guy."

"Yeah, he's a dirty fighter," another boy said. "He couldn't beat anybody in a fair fight."

Sonny was so hurt he couldn't get angry with them, even though he was very aggressive by nature and normally would have started fighting at the mere suggestion of such charges.

"Rocky didn't do it on purpose," Sonny said. "It was an accident. He didn't mean to kick that guy."

On his way home, Rocky stopped at Uncle Mike's house. He was depressed and couldn't look into his uncle's eyes.

"You made a real asshole out of yourself," Piccento said. "Right here in your own hometown."

"I wasn't that bad, was I?" Rocky asked.

"Bad?" Uncle Mike said. "You couldn't even lift your arms. I told you I didn't want you to fight."

"Well, I hit him with some good shots," Rocky said. "I know I hurt the guy."

"So what?" Piccento said. "You didn't win."

"Christ sakes, Mike. That guy was a helluva fighter," Rocky said. "Anyway, it was a foul. I didn't really lose the fight."

"You were finished," Uncle Mike said. "You were all burned out. Two rounds and you could hardly stand up. Lester didn't beat you. You beat yourself. In shape you'd murder the guy. Out of shape you're nothing."

Even as he listened to his uncle, Rocky puffed sadly on a Camel. Mike was staring at the flab that bulged at his nephew's belt.

"Either put yourself in condition or forget it," Piccento said. "I've seen too many fighters to let you go in there the way you were tonight. If you want to fight, I'll help you. But only if you work your ass off at it."

That night neither Rocky nor Sonny could sleep.

"Some of the kids said you're a dirty fighter," Sonny said. "You didn't kick that guy on purpose, did you, Rock?"

Rocky sat up in the bed then and stared at his brother.

"I was tired tonight, Son," he said. "Sure I kicked that guy. What was I gonna do, let him beat me? It was the only way I could stop him from coming after me."

"I'm sorry, Rock," Sonny said, trying to hold back the tears. "I didn't know it was that bad."

"Don't you ever be sorry for me," Rocky said, suddenly very angry. "When a man's in a fight, the only thing that matters is winning. Don't you ever forget that. I was disqualified tonight, but I didn't lose the fight. But I'll tell you one thing, Son. I learned something from this fight. And if I ever get into the ring again, you can bet I won't be out of condition."

When Rocky came into the kitchen for breakfast the next morning, there was a thin red welt under his eye.

"Hi, Pa," he said softly. "Gee, I'm sorry I let you down last night."

Pop Marchegiano poured the coffee and placed his arm around his son's shoulders.

"You don't look so bad for one round," he said. "Joe Monte says you know what to do sometimes. Now, you don't tell your mother nothing."

Joe Monte was once a prominent heavyweight who had fought all of the top contenders in the late 1920s and early 1930s. He had waged a great battle before being KO'd by Max Schmeling in 1928 in New York City, and he had lost a ten-round decision to James J. Braddock in 1930 in Boston. But Monte had absorbed much punishment in the ring, including a serious injury to an eye. He had been a judge at Rocky's fight with Lester.

"What'd Joe say, Pa?" Rocky asked. "Did he really think I can fight?"

"Sure," Pierino said proudly. "He said you gotta good punch there. Maybe you could be a fighter sometime. That's what Joe Monte tella me."

But the optimism disappeared as soon as Pasqualena Marchegiano saw her son's eye.

"What'd they do to my Rocky?" she shouted. "Hey you!" she said, pointing a finger at Pierino. "You happy now, my Rocky got hurt. There'sa no more fighting. You understand?"

Pierino was smaller than Pasqualena and by nature much quieter and less given to emotional outbursts. He was nevertheless the master of his household in the strictest Italian tradition. This time, though, he chose diplomacy.

"Okay," he said. "You hear that, Rocky. No more fighting. I'ma tella you no more fights."

"Sure, Ma," Rocky said. "No more fights. I promise."

For Uncle Mike it wasn't quite so easy. Dropping by for a cup of coffee, he had barely had time to unzip his jacket when his sister began her verbal assault.

"And don't you ever tell my Rocky to be a fighter again," Pasqualena concluded with a tone of finality.

When the conversation was finished, it seemed to the men that if Rocky wanted to fight again he was going to have to face two opponents, the other boxer and his mother.

That afternoon Rocky walked across the street to the ball park. Allie Colombo was hitting baseballs to some young boys.

"Hey, Rock," Colombo said. "I saw you down the fights last night. Jesus, where'd you get that experience? You looked all right in there for a while. You was hittin' that guy with some good punches. Did he hurt you?"

"Naw. He didn't hurt me," Rocky said. "I just got tired. I haven't really done any training."

"Well, you looked damn good to me," Colombo said. "Come on, let's take a walk uptown and talk about it."

Rocky hesitated. "I don't know, Allie," he said. "The guys'll all be there."

"So what?" Colombo said. "You've got nothing to be ashamed of. Anybody could accidently foul a guy in the middle of a tough fight. Could those assholes do as good? Come on, let's go."

For the rest of his life, Rocky remembered that walk to Brockton Center as one of his most embarrassing moments.

"It was all over town that I had gotten beat," Rocky recalled. "Every jerk in Brockton was laughing at me."

"Hey, Rock," they shouted across Main Street. "What the Christ ya doin'? How'd you let a guy beat you like that? What'd ya have to kick him inna nuts?"

"I'm going after that son of a bitch," Rocky said. "Don't be crazy," Colombo said, "That's just what those jerks want."

The headline on the sports page of the *Brockton Enterprise-Times* read: JOE FEROLI AWARDED DECISION OVER GEORGE COTE, N.E. CHAMP. The subhead read: Marchegiano, Local Heavyweight, Is Disqualified.

Several paragraphs down in the story it said, "In the only heavyweight bout of the evening, Rocco Marchegiano, of this city, enjoying an Army furlough, lost to Henry Lester, New England championship tourney runner-up, when he was disqualified by referee Sned McDonald. Lester was awarded the bout when Marchegiano forgot himself in the excitement in the second round and fouled his opponent."

The story said that "the main bout of the evening as far as the large crowd in attendance was concerned was the Marchegiano-Lester affair, which made up in spirit what it lacked in finesse . . ."

"Well, Alsack, I've got to be back at Fort Lewis in a few days," Rocky said, as they sat on the bleachers at James Edgar Playground. "I'm going to do a little training when I get there."

"Concentrate on your right," Colombo said. "You've got a helluva punch there."

"Yeah, I'm really gonna try to get in shape," Rocky said.

"What're you gonna do when you get out of the army?" Colombo said. "Have you thought about fighting?"

"I've only got a few months to go," Rocky said. "I don't know yet. Maybe I'll give baseball a try."

"I think I'm going for twenty years in the air force," Colombo said. "I've got six already, and it's a pretty good deal at Westover."

"Well, maybe you'll change your mind," Rocky said. "The service is no life for guys like us."

Using his influence as a master sergeant in charge of flight scheduling at Westover Air Force Base, Colombo got Rocky on a plane heading to Washington State, allowing Rocky to spend a few more days at home and save the cross-country fare, a consideration for which he expressed deep gratitude to his friend.

But in Kansas City, Rocky got bumped off the flight by an officer, and he was fortunate to get aboard another plane which arrived in Washington before his furlough expired.

Meanwhile, after leaving Kansas City, Rocky's original plane developed engine problems.

"The reports kept coming in that the plane was in trouble," Colombo said. "I kept thinking, Holy Christ, I've killed Rocky. I couldn't believe it. They kept saying the plane was in big trouble and would probably have to try a forced landing."

Colombo learned the next day that the plane had landed without incident; when he called Fort Lewis, he was amazed that Rocky knew nothing about it.

At the base, Rocky went on a strict diet and began a program of heavy training. Just about then, he was offered a chance to compete in the Amateur Athletic Union (AAU) championship tournament at Portland, Oregon.

Rocky discovered that there were some very big heavyweights entered in the tournament, some of whom outweighed him by 15 or 20 pounds. He was told that he would have to win three fights to take the title.

With thousands watching, Rocky stormed across the ring to overwhelm his first opponent, KOing the surprised fighter in less than one minute.

The next night, in the semifinals, Rocky duplicated his first performance by knocking out his victim within a minute of the first round. In both instances it had been the looping overhand right that did it.

Caught up in the exhilaration of victory, Rocky had gone halfway down through the cheering crowd before he noticed the sharp pain in his left hand.

"You can't fight anymore tonight," the lieutenant in charge of the Fort Lewis boxing squad said when he had cut off Rocky's bandages. "You've got a dislocated knuckle. That's it for you, Marchegiano."

The fist was swollen, throbbing with pain. Rocky remembered that there had been a twinge of pain when he struck his opponent with a hard blow on the top of the head.

"I've got to fight," Rocky said. "I'm going for the title. Look, it'll be all right. Just bandage it up real tight, and I'll watch out for it in there. You'va gotta let me fight this guy. I can beat him."

Another trainer came over to Rocky and

sprayed "something that looked like Freezone on my hand. It turned all the hairs white and then the hand was frozen. After that, Lieutenant James told me to go ahead if I wanted to win that badly."

With the two first-round KOs fresh in his memory, Rocky believed that if he could land one solid right he would win the heavyweight championship of the tournament.

Joe DeAngelis was a rugged, six-three heavyweight from Boston, an experienced boxer and a terrific puncher, and possibly better than many of the professionals Marciano met later in his career.

Rocky soon discovered that fighting with one hand wasn't easy. The crowd, which had been cheering Marciano, soon shifted its allegiance to the skillful DeAngelis, who was making Rocky look foolish.

"I think they figured I was throwing the fight," Rocky told his brothers. "It was a helluva lousy feeling."

By the third round, Rocky couldn't possibly win without a KO. DeAngelis hadn't hurt him, but he was far ahead on points. Marciano charged and tried repeatedly to land the overhand right. But DeAngelis prevailed, using his superior skills to fend off the challenge and win the championship.

Rocky returned to Fort Lewis that night deeply depressed. There was no solace in the knowledge that he had fought with an injured hand. DeAngelis had won, and winning was the only thing that really mattered.

The next morning Rocky was in the hospital, his arm in a cast, the injured hand raised in traction. A Japanese doctor had experimented with a new technique in an attempt to return Rocky's knuckle to its proper location. The doctor had drilled a hole in the finger and connected a wire traction to gradually move the knuckle back into place.

For six weeks Rocky lay in the hospital, confined to bed, forced to remain in the army beyond his discharge date. It was an extremely uncomfortable period for Rocky, who disliked everything about hospitals: the doctors, the nurses, the smell of medicine and disinfectant, the monotonous routine.

Two months after the DeAngelis fight, Rocky was en route to Brockton. His bandaged hand was still sore and inflamed, although the Japanese doctor had successfully returned the knuckle to its socket. Rocky viewed the powerless hand as a weakness he could not long afford to tolerate, especially if he was to play football and baseball as he had planned.

On the way home, Rocky stopped in Chicago to visit an Italian friend he had met in the hospital.

"Are you serious about fighting?" his friend had asked before they left the West Coast.

"I don't know, Joe," Rocky said. "If this hand gets better, I might try it."

Then you've got to meet my uncle," Joe Cirelli said. "He's a professional trainer. He'll look you over."

Rocky expected the meeting to take place in a gym, and that he'd come away with an offer by the trainer to provide him with a handler in the Boston area. Instead they met in the back of a grocery store owned by Joe's Uncle Louie.

"Take off your clothes," the trainer said.

Rocky stripped to his undershorts, embarrassed by the 15 pounds he had gained during the two months of inactivity in the hospital.

"How old are you, kid?" the trainer asked.

"Twenty-three," Rocky said.

"Then forget it," the trainer said. "You'll never be a fighter. Put you in shape, and you'll be too heavy for a light heavyweight and too light for a heavyweight. You're too old to be starting out. You're not tall enough. Your arms are way too short, and your legs are too thick. Forget boxing. You'd get killed in the pros."

"No kidding," Rocky said, not wishing to offend his pal's uncle. "I'm sure glad you told me that. It's kind of bad news, but I wouldn't want to get started in something I'm not equipped for."

The advice the trainer had given was very logical, but not to Rocky. As the train rolled out of Chicago he was furious.

"Imagine that," Rocky told his brothers later. "Here's this guy, who never met me before in his life, and he says I'll be a failure in boxing. Isn't that ridiculous?"

Rocky arrived home in December. He was unshaven and his muscles were stiff from the long train ride. Snow clung to the leafless branches of the hardwood trees along Dover Street. It was dark, and the children had stopped playing in the ball field.

Walking up the hill beside the old Italians as they trudged home from the shoe factories, he felt the excitement of his new freedom. It did not matter that he had no job, no security, not even a girlfriend to come home to, because Rocky was determined to change all of that. And as he walked with the old men, carrying the empty lunch pails, puffing on the stogies, the frayed collars of their overcoats turned up against the cold, the soldier appeared to be one of them, but he knew that he was not.

2.

Fifty-Dollar Knockout

It was a snowy afternoon in January 1947 when Rocky and Allie Colombo met again in Brockton. Rocky was out of the army, collecting veteran's unemployment checks and receiving weekly diathermy treatments at a VA hospital for his slowly mending hand. Colombo was still a master sergeant stationed at Westover Air Force Base. He was home on a weekend pass.

"Do you think you'll be able to fight again, Rock?" Colombo asked as they jogged in the snow along the golf course at D. W. Field Park.

"Maybe," Rocky said. "I'm hoping the hand will be all right, but it's still awful sore."

"You've sure got the potential, Rock," Colombo said. "I'd hate to see anything spoil it."

"Don't worry, Alsack," Rocky said. "It'll be all right. What're you always worryin' for? It's gonna be great."

For the next month Rocky concentrated on restoring the strength to his injured hand. He followed a routine of light exercises and went faithfully for the diathermy treatments.

Rocky was still shy about asking girls for dates, but he sometimes went to stag dances in West Bridgewater and Holbrook with Nicky

Sylvester and his other Ward 2 pals. He was a clumsy dancer, and usually remained on the sidelines chatting with his buddies. Then one night he was introduced to a tall, athletic, dark-haired Irish girl for whom he felt an immediate attraction.

Barbara Cousins was a fun loving nineteen-year-old, who was a very good dancer and enjoyed all sports. She lived in Brockton, and worked during the summers as a lifeguard at the local pools and beaches.

Rocky began following Barbara to the dances, and soon he was spending more time with her than he was with his pals.

But whenever they danced, he kept stepping on her feet.

"I'm not a very good dancer, Barbara," he said. "But maybe you can teach me. It'll help me with my footwork for boxing."

Rocky visited Barbara at her home and took her to occasional movies and sporting events. But he still didn't have a job, and had very little money to spare.

When Rocky had regained some of the strength in his injured hand, Barbara's father, Lester Cousins, who was a policeman in the city, helped him get a job with the Brockton

Gas Company. He was assigned to a pick and shovel crew, digging trenches to install new gas lines.

"Hey, look at poor Rock," his buddies, who were still unemployed, would say as they drove past. "Poor guy's workin' his ass off."

"How's the hand, Rock?" Colombo said, telephoning from Westover.

"Great," Rocky said. "I think it'll be as good as new pretty soon."

"Terrific," Colombo said. "Rock, I've been talking to my friend Dick O'Connor. He'll get you a fight in Holyoke. Fifty bucks for four rounds."

"Beautiful," Rocky said. "When do I fight?"

"March seventeenth," Colombo said, "It's a Saint Patrick's Day card."

"Good, Al," Rocky said. "We'll teach those Irishmen some respect for the Italians."

"Try to get in great shape, Rock," Colombo said. "It's only a few weeks away, and Dick said there're some pretty fair fighters up here."

"Don't worry," Rocky said. "I'll be in shape. I'll start working out right away."

For the first time since returning from the army Rocky was excited again. Finally he was faced with an immediate goal he considered worthwhile. He ran in the park every morning and evening, and embarked on a strenuous routine of exercises at the YMCA. He forced himself to eat only rare meat and fresh green vegetables.

Remembering the humiliation of the Ted Lester fight, he spent more time in training than he did on his full-time job at the gas company. But there were no experienced trainers or sparring partners for Rocky. He had no way of judging his progress. Nor could he get any actual boxing experience.

"Hey, Rock," one of Marciano's baseball-playing friends said. "We're going down to try

out for the Chicago Cubs. You want, you're included."

"Everything's breaking for me," Rocky told his brother Sonny that night before supper. "My hand's all right, and now I've got offers in both baseball and boxing."

Marciano stepped off the Boston-Springfield train wearing baggy work clothes and carrying his boxing equipment in a faded canvas bag. Colombo drove him to Dick O'Connor's house on the fringe of Holyoke.

"Who's this guy I'm fighting tonight, Allie?" he said.

"He's a good heavyweight," Colombo said. "How's the hand, Rock?"

"Don't worry," Marciano said. "It's fine."

But Colombo did worry. It was his nature, and he persisted in asking Rocky questions about how hard he had trained, what kind of condition he felt he was in, and what he planned to do in the fight.

"For Christ sake," Rocky said. "Will you stop worrying? I'm gonna ruin this guy."

Mrs. O'Connor prepared a large rare steak and a salad of fresh greens. Rocky inhaled them like a shipwrecked sailor.

"I'm kind of tired," Rocky said after the meal. "Do you think I could catch a little nap?"

And for the next two hours Rocky slept on O'Connor's bed.

"How can the guy do that?" O'Connor said. "This is his first pro fight. Isn't he nervous?"

"It's a funny thing about The Rock," Colombo said. "He can just put it out of his mind."

At the weigh-in, Rocky scaled 190 pounds. His opponent, Lee Epperson, looked rugged and confident.

Epperson's handler seemed smug and relaxed, convinced of their superiority as they glanced disdainfully at Rocky in his crumpled work clothes and Allie in an army air force uniform.

"They think they've got a soft touch," Allie whispered to Rocky. Rocky grinned but said nothing.

Allie and Rocky had agreed that Marciano should change his name for this fight to protect his amateur status, should he decide against pursuing a professional boxing career.

"It's Saint Patrick's Day," Colombo said. "Why don't we give you an Irish name?"

"Me an Irishman?" Rocky giggled. "That's funny."

"Why don't we call you Rocky Mack?"

"Good thinking, Allie," Rocky said. "I sure don't want Ma to find out I'm fighting. She'll murder me. Rocky Mack is fine."

O'Connor had hired trainer Red Kinsella to prepare Rocky. While Kinsella was wrapping tape around Rocky's hands, five minutes before the fight, Colombo went to promoter Orielle Renault to confirm the fifty-dollar purse.

"Are you kidding?" Renault said. "Four-rounders only get thirty-five dollars. What're you trying to do, hold me up at the last minute?"

Colombo was stunned. He didn't know where the confusion over the fifty dollars got started. But he did know how Rocky would react to receiving less money than he expected.

"I promised Rocky fifty," Colombo said. "If we can't get that there's no sense fighting."

"If you don't want him to fight, go home," Renault said.

"No hard feelings then," Colombo said, and he went back into the dressing room, followed by the promoter.

"Rocky, get dressed," Colombo said. "We ain't fightin' tonight."

"What?" Rocky said. "What's going on here?"

"We're not getting the fifty."

Rocky began taking off his boxing trunks.

"How much do you want?" the enraged promoter growled.

"Fifty," Colombo said.

"All right. Get him ready."

Epperson, a local favorite, received a roaring cheer as he entered the ring. But Rocky, unknown by the fans, was greeted by mild token applause that came from O'Connor's friends at the Valley Angler's Club.

Epperson was a skillful boxer whose best punch was a crisp left jab. The jabs, thrown in rapid succession, rattled off Rocky's head like machine-gun bursts.

Rocky was an easy target, wading straight in, but soon it was clear that Epperson's punches only annoyed him, and it was impossible for the Holyoke heavyweight to hurt him.

Having had no professional training, Rocky threw punches at random almost as if he were in a brawl at James Edgar Playground. They were looping overhand rights and wild upper-cuts, but never any jabs or hooks to keep his opponent off-balance. It was a repeat of his performance in the Ted Lester bout, only this time Rocky was prepared and he had more than enough stamina to go the distance.

By the second round, Colombo saw that Rocky had command and was hurting Epperson. Then, at the beginning of the third round, he threw a right that crashed into Epperson's midsection and dropped the local hero to the canvas.

"It's all over!" Colombo shouted. "Chrissake, you knocked him out, Rock! You knocked him out!"

Rocky's face was puffy and sore from Epperson's sharp jabs, but he grinned broadly as Colombo led him through the crowd.

"Jeez, you looked great in there, Rock," Colombo said proudly, once the trainer had finished cutting the tape off Rocky's hands. "You couldn't have done much better."

Rocky grinned. He was flexing his left hand, which he noticed was slightly swollen and had begun to throb. "Better collect the dough, Allie," he said.

While Rocky got dressed, Colombo went to the office. The cashier handed him a folded twenty-dollar bill.

"What's this?" Colombo said, shoving the money back. "This isn't right."

"The pay's thirty-five," the cashier said. "But I took out fifteen for the license."

"Rock, they're only giving us twenty bucks," Colombo said in the dressing room.

"What?" he said. "Those assholes. I'll kill them."

"Take it easy, Rock, I'll get the dough," Colombo said. "I'm going to get Renault."

When Renault came to the dressing room and saw how furious Rocky was, he said, "Wait here. I'll be right back," according to Colombo.

The promoter returned with two police officers.

"We were supposed to get fifty bucks," Colombo pleaded.

"Calm down and get out of here, before you get yourselves in big trouble," a policeman ordered.

"But we don't even have the lousy twenty," Colombo shouted. "I turned it back in."

"Then go to the office and get it, and then get the hell out of this arena," the officer said.

Colombo rushed to the cashier's office while Rocky, fully enraged by then, continued to argue with the police.

"I just saw Renault and he okayed the extra fifteen," Colombo told the cashier.

"Okay, here's thirty-five. I'm still taking fifteen out for the license," the cashier said. "But I've never heard of a fighter getting paid fifty for a four-rounder."

When Colombo returned to the dressing room, Rocky was involved in a heated argument with the police.

"He was really burning up," Colombo recalled. "I kept mumbling, 'Let's go, Rock,' but he wasn't listening. All he could think of was that we were getting screwed out of the money. I thought for sure he was gonna be locked up."

"I'm gonna get that dough," Rocky kept saying. "Somebody's gonna pay it."

When Colombo finally convinced him to go outside, Marciano said, "What's wrong with you, Allie? Why didn't you let me go after those guys?"

"Rock, I've got the dough," Colombo said.

Rocky immediately began grinning. "Imagine that," he said. "Jeez, Allie, how'd you do it? You really know how to handle these guys."

Bruised and sore from Epperson's sharp jabs, Marciano accompanied O'Connor and Colombo to a private club where the fight crowd gathered. O'Connor suggested it would be a nice gesture if Rocky bought a round of drinks.

Marciano went directly to the bar and bellowed, "Set them up."

With the train fare, the hotel expenses, and the cost of buying the drinks, Marciano barely broke even on the fight. He had spent hundreds of hours training, had given up his holiday, and had been stung and bruised by Epperson's jabs.

"Jesus, Allie," he said, when they were alone in a room at the Roger Smith Hotel in Holyoke. "With all these expenses and setting up the bar, I'm not making a thing. Isn't this ridiculous?"

That was the first and last time that Marciano ever spent money buying drinks for customers after a fight. When he became heavyweight champion of the world, wine flowed freely in the name of Rocky Marciano, but it was not bought by Rocky. There were wealthy men who made huge sums of money betting on Rocky's fights and who harbored a great desire to be included in his entourage. And these people paid gladly.

"Well, don't be discouraged, Rock," Colombo said. "You did great in there tonight. Any guy who can punch like you can make plenty of dough in boxing. You're gonna stick with it, aren't you?"

"I don't know, Buddy," Rocky said. "It's a tough way to make a buck. My hand's sore again just from this fight. Besides, I've got a chance to try out for the Cubs."

"Go ahead and take a shot at baseball, Rock," Colombo said. "I know how much you love it. But remember, Rock. You could be a tremendous fighter. You can be a champ."

"Come on, Allie," Rocky said, embarrassed. "I win one pro fight, and already you've got me beating Louis for the title."

"You've got it, Rock," Colombo said. "I know it."

"I know I can fight, Allie," Rocky said. "It's just something I feel real comfortable with. But it isn't an easy business. You saw how we got screwed tonight."

"Sure it's cutthroat," Colombo said. "That's why you've got to have a good manager with all the right connections."

"Well, I'm going to give baseball a try first," Rocky said. "I think I can make it. But if anything happens, and I decide to become a fighter, you'll be with me, Alsack. I guarantee you that."

3.
The Failure

CARRYING HIS WARD 2 PALS on the most important mission they had ever known, on a raw, windy day in late March 1947, Vinnie Colombo headed his old, gray, two-door sedan down the highway toward Fayetteville, North Carolina.

Rocky, Vinnie, Eugene Sylvester, and Ray Gormley had prepared and dreamed of becoming major league baseball players since grammar school. Now they were on their way for a tryout with the Chicago Cubs' farm system, the steppingstone to the majors. Already in their mid-twenties, they knew only too well that this might be their only chance.

Eddie Colombo, Allie's older brother, had introduced them to Ralph Wheeler, a Cubs scout, who worked as a sportswriter for the *Boston Herald.*

"Rocky wants one fling at baseball," Colombo had informed Wheeler. "If he doesn't make it, he'll be a fighter."

"I can't make any promises," Wheeler said. "He'll get a tryout, but he'll have to prove himself."

"How do you impress these guys?" Rocky kept asking Eugene Sylvester in the car. "What're these managers looking for?"

"Gee, I don't know, Rock," Sylvester said. "You've just got to play good ball. They're always looking for power hitters and classy fielders."

"I'm giving it my best shot," Rocky said. "Don't worry about that."

After stopping overnight in New Jersey, Colombo drove straight through to Fayetteville. Six boys from the Brockton area made the trip together, but they had gotten a late start and arrived a day late for camp.

"The manager didn't like it at all," Red Gormley said. "It seemed like we got off on the wrong foot right away."

Gormley had talked baseball with Rocky constantly, before and during the trip to North Carolina.

"I had no idea Rocky was fighting," Gormley said. "He never mentioned it once. We both were confident. We figured we were as ready as we'd ever be for making it in baseball."

But the Ward 2 hopefuls soon discovered that there were tremendous differences between semipro ball at James Edgar Playground and the fierce competition for positions on the Fayetteville Cubs.

They were only in camp a few days when Rocky's arm problems began. He couldn't make a hard throw to second base. But he was hitting so well that the coaches decided to try him out as a first baseman.

"Jesus, what'm I gonna do?" Rocky said. "Just when I need it, my arm's gone dead."

"Don't worry, Rock," his pals said. "The way you're hitting, you'll make it."

"The Rock was getting his hits," Vinnie Colombo said. "He belted one shot to deep center that really opened up the coach's eyes. But Rocky ran so slow he only got a double out of it. Still, if it wasn't for the arm, I think he might have made the team."

They roomed at Mrs. Brown's boardinghouse in Fayetteville, a city of about forty thousand, which was much more quiet than what they were accustomed to in Brockton.

"We didn't care that it was a dead town," Gormley said. "We were obsessed with making the team. The only thing we went overboard on was food. Mrs. Brown served terrific home-cooked meals for fifty cents. It was put out on platters and you could take all you wanted. Rocky and I ate and ate and ate."

By the end of the first week, they were convinced it was going to be very difficult if not impossible to get on the Fayetteville roster. Eugene Sylvester had been throwing well, and they generally felt that he had the best chance of staying with the Cubs' farm system.

For Marciano it was a frustration of the highest order, since he sincerely believed that without his lame arm he could easily make the squad.

"Gee, Euey, this is what we dreamed of all our lives," Rocky said. "We've got to give it everything we've got."

"We can make it, Rock," Sylvester said. "You'd be a cinch if it wasn't for that bad arm."

Vinnie Colombo moved on to try out for another team. Rocky, Red, and Eugene struggled to survive with the Cubs, playing in company that was much tougher than they had ever expected.

"Rocky didn't smoke," Gormley said. "But I noticed, after a bad practice, he'd light up a cigarette. I don't think anybody ever wanted something as much as we wanted to make that team."

Rocky and Red shared a room at Mrs. Brown's, and in the evenings Rocky did exercises on his bed. He'd have the bed shaking from the strenuous routine. Then one night the bed collapsed on one side.

"I'll have to sleep with you, Red," Rocky said.

"That's all right," Gormley said.

When it was time to go to sleep, Rocky climbed in with Gormley.

"The next thing I know he's giving me a little jab," Gormley said. "I said, 'Rock, what's this?'"

"Just a little jab," Rocky said. "Don't worry, I won't hurt you."

"The next thing I know, we're goin' at it full steam, and the Rock knocks me right out of the bed."

"Jeez," Rocky said. "You're all right, ain't you?"

"He was practicing on me," Gormley said. "And I don't even know he's a boxer yet."

The Fayetteville Cubs were paying them expenses and from $200 to $250 a month in salaries. Some very good ballplayers had already been cut from the squad. Rocky and his friends knew they had to show the coaches something soon or it would be all over.

Rocky was in the midst of trying to impress the coaches when a southern player, who was competing for the first base job, hit him a grounder.

"The Rock bobbled the ball, and this rebel

beat it out," Gormley said. "The ball had skipped behind Rocky, but not far enough so the guy could advance. The next thing I knew, I heard this rebel say, 'Pick it up, you nigger-loving Yankee.' "

"Rocky hit him with a left that broke his nose," Gormley said. "One punch and the kid went down. He was grabbing his nose, and the blood was spurting all over the place. They helped this kid from the field, but the manager didn't say a thing. Nobody blamed Rocky. The guy deserved it."

After the third week, the manager called Rocky and Red aside. "That's it," he said. "I'm going to have to cut you fellows."

"I can't go home a failure," Rocky said. "There must be some other team we can play for."

Tully Colombo was on the Goldsboro (North Carolina) Bugs in the Class D Coastal Plain League, so Rocky and Red went to see him about getting a tryout. But they didn't make the team.

"I remember we tried out in Macon, Georgia, too, where they got you a job days and you played ball at night," Gormley said. "But we were only there two or three days when the coach said, 'Forget it. Go back home.' "

"We gave it our best shot, Rock," Gormley said. "We'd better go home."

"Why don't you get me a few fights down here," Rocky said. "I'll be the fighter, and you can be my manager. We'll really make some dough. I can beat these guys."

"I think we'd better forget it, Rock," Gormley said. "I don't know anything about being a fight manager. We haven't got any connections. I wouldn't even know how to get you a fight. Let's go home."

"I thought Rocky was just depressed and didn't want to go home failure. Even when he

insisted, and told me about the fights he had won, I wasn't that impressed. If only I'd known then what I know now. I thought his spirits were down, just like mine, and he was grabbing for straws."

"It wouldn't be hard to get me a fight, Red," Rocky persisted. "Any of these big cities have fight clubs. We'll just look up some promoters."

"No," Gormley said. "Fighting's not my game. Let's go home. It'll be all right once we get back to Brockton."

"Well, I guess I can always go back to work for the gas company," Rocky said sadly. "But what the hell are we gonna tell them?"

"Stop worrying," Gormley said. "It'll be okay. We're not the first guys who didn't make it to the big leagues."

THE CHICAGO CUBS PROVIDED transportation home for players who failed to make their farm system. Rocky and Red reluctantly hitchhiked back to Fayetteville and boarded a train for Providence.

"We were really dejected on that train," Gormley recalled. "We didn't talk much at all. The closer we got to Brockton, the more we realized we didn't want to go home. We just stared out the window. There I was sitting beside millions and I didn't know it. I'd talked my way out of becoming Rocky Marciano's manager."

For Rocky, returning to Brockton a failure was even more depressing, because he knew his dream of becoming a big league baseball player was finished.

4.

Turning Pro

IT WAS THE MOST DISMAL homecoming Rocky ever knew. He didn't want to go into the house to face his father or his brother. He dreaded having to explain the failure to his uncles Johnny and Mike, and to the other athletes in Brockton.

Allie Colombo sensed Rocky's disappointment and embarrassment as they sat on the bleachers at James Edgar Playground.

"I should start getting into shape for fighting," Rocky said. "My hand feels good. I don't think it'll give me any more trouble."

"Beautiful, Rock," Colombo said. "Don't waste any time. You should really concentrate on boxing now."

It was already fall, but Colombo, who had just gotten out of the army, hadn't seen much of Rocky, who had gone back to his old job of digging trenches for the Brockton Gas Company.

On weekends, Rocky played center and linebacker for a semipro football team. Colombo sat in the stands at O'Donnell Playground and watched Rocky make jarring tackles and envisioned his friend in the ring.

"I got chills up and down my spine just thinking about it," Allie wrote later.

"Everything I remembered Rocky had done as a kid—the fight with Julie Durham, the time he was eight and I put him in the ring with a twelve-year-old kid, five inches taller and thirty pounds heavier, in my uncle's backyard. Rocky had stayed right in there and slugged it out. I just knew he had to be a champion."

Gene Caggiano, the local boxing promoter, began working with Marciano and asked him to enter the Golden Gloves in Lowell.

Rocky began the tournament with three straight KOs that January of 1948. Observers recall that Rocky was an animal, superbly conditioned, punching, clawing, mauling his opponents to the canvas.

Charlie Mortimer, an outstanding nineteen-year-old top amateur from Lowell, had two first-round KOs before he met Marciano for the title. In the navy, Mortimer had sparred with Freddie Beshore, a top heavyweight pro.

"I'd had twelve amateur fights and won them all," Mortimer said. "When I met Rocky, I was in good shape and was coming off two quick knockouts. I was boxing good against Marciano, and I thought I won the first two rounds. The local fans all wanted me to knock Rocky out. So I chased him across the ring in the third round. He came off the ropes, with twenty seconds to go in the fight, and hit me with a right uppercut. It was a tremendous punch. I was really knocked out. After that, I never fought again. I figured if you can't win them all, forget it."

The three KOs at Lowell qualified Rocky to go to New York as the New England representative to the Golden Gloves All-East Championship Tournament.

Colombo, Caggiano, Mike Piccento, and Lester Cousins, Rocky's future father-in-law, drove to New York in Piccento's sedan and checked into the Park Central Hotel, headquarters for the New England boxing team. Rocky had made the trip with the team and was already at the hotel when they arrived.

The next morning, March 1, 1948, they went to the *New York Daily News*, sponsors of the tournament, and learned that Rocky had drawn Coley Wallace as his first opponent. Rocky's friends immediately began inquiring about Wallace's fighting ability.

"We soon heard he was being touted as the new Joe Louis," Colombo said. "The New York trainers were very high on Wallace. He had been in seventeen fights and won them all by knockouts. We were all pretty worried. Not Rocky though. He didn't even want to hear about Wallace."

Rocky swarmed after Wallace at the opening bell. He was throwing wild but heavy punches that landed everywhere—on the arms, the shoulders, the top of the head.

The crowd at Ridgewood Grove Arena in Brooklyn was on its feet cheering. They sensed an upset, and even though Coley was a local favorite, they abandoned him.

But Wallace was an excellent boxer for an amateur, and he soon adjusted his style to cope

with Rocky's bull-like rushes. It was the classic boxer versus slugger contest that fight fans crave.

Wallace had been scoring points with his slick style, but he did not have a punch to hurt Marciano. As the fight ended. Rocky was battering Coley against the ropes.

Wallace had been stylish, but Marciano had carried the fight to him throughout all three rounds and had delivered all of the punishing blows.

When the judges announced Wallace the victor, the fans, who believed Marciano had won easily, were indignant. They booed and threw soda bottles into the ring.

"They booed so loudly, I couldn't hear myself talking to The Rock as we left the ring," Colombo said. "Everybody in the place wanted to pound Rocky on the back. We could hardly get through the crowd to the dressing room."

Wallace went on to become a very mediocre professional. His biggest moment came not as a real boxer, but as an actor, when he played the role of Joe Louis in the fabled Brown Bomber's life story.

Rocky was disgusted with the judges but felt he had most certainly won the fight, so he was not depressed over the decision.

"The first thing we did after we left the arena was eat," Colombo said. "The Rock was hungry. And we were all very pleased by his performance."

"I want another shot at that Wallace," Rocky said, munching on a steak. "Next time there isn't going to be any decision."

Both Rocky and Allie figured that if Marciano won the New England AAU tournament, scheduled to take place in Boston in less than a month, he'd be certain to face Wallace again in the All-East tournament.

Caggiano decided to cash in on Marciano's

popularity by featuring him in an amateur show at Canton Hall in Brockton.

"Rocky and I worked for Caggiano selling tickets, setting up the ring, and arranging the seats," Colombo said. "We put in a full week and sold seven hundred dollars' worth of tickets, enough to fill the hall with people."

Rocky KO'd his opponent, Joe Sidlaskis, in the first round, barely working up a sweat. But when he went to collect from Caggiano, Rocky was enraged.

Rocky claimed that Caggiano offered him $100 and tried to pay him $40. Caggiano maintained that Rocky got everything that was coming to him. And when Rocky continued to refuse the money, the promoter sent it to his mother in an envelope.

The incident marked the beginning of differences between Marciano and Caggiano, then Rocky's trainer and handler; differences that would keep them apart until Rocky was killed in 1969. Caggiano died in March 1975.

"Jesus, we worked hard for that dough, Allie," Rocky said. "And what'd he give us, a lousy forty bucks. I'm telling you, he'd better come up with the rest of that cash or else."

In the first bout of the evening, Rocco Marchegiano hammered his way to a two-round knockout over a bobbing and weaving heavyweight named Fred Fischera. Rocky was never in trouble, but he looked awkward and clumsy, and threw many wild punches, because of Fischera's deceptive style.

"In the dressing room, waiting for the next fight, I saw the Rock flinch when he took his left glove off," Colombo said.

"What's the matter, Rock?"

"The hand hurts a little. It's nothing."

"Let me take the bandages off and look at it," Colombo said nervously. "You can't fight if the hand's hurt bad."

"I'm the fighter, Allie," Rocky snapped. "Leave the bandages alone. The hand's fine. I'm gonna fight."

"Let's go, Marchegiano," a trainer shouted. "You're on."

Colombo saw Rocky rush across the ring with his left hand tucked safely along his side, protecting it, not using it to either throw punches or block them.

Rocky never used the left once throughout the entire fight, but he was banging his opponent around with his right, and in the third round he bludgeoned the kid with rapid-fire rights, knocking him down twice. Rocky got the unanimous decision.

"It was the first time I watched Marciano," Silverman said. "But I didn't really see him. He didn't impress me. I don't even remember how he fought. All I know is he won the AAU Heavyweight Championship from a short, fat, dumpy-looking kid from Belmont named George McGinnis."

"We were all impressed with a couple of 126-pound class kids," Silverman said. "A young kid from Providence named George Araujo beat a tough dago from the North End of Boston, Tony DeMarco, in a terrific fight.

IN THE SPRING OF 1948, a stocky, ruddy-faced fight promoter named Sam Silverman sat ringside at the AAU Olympic tryouts in Boston Garden. The gravel-voiced, cigar-smoking Silverman was the busiest promoter in New England, with more than five hundred shows a year in Providence, Boston, Fall River, and New Bedford, and throughout the state of Maine. Like a hawk in search of carrion, Silverman was at the AAU trials to find new and younger blood to draw the crowds to his boxing shows.

We all came away talking about what a drawing card these kids would make. But nobody saw Marciano."

Araujo was later defeated in a bid for the professional lightweight title, and DeMarco won the welterweight championship of the world.

Colombo's worst fears were confirmed when he unwrapped the bandages from Rocky's left hand following the McGinnis bout. Rocky was grinning broadly. He was the new champ. But the troublesome left thumb was swollen to twice its normal size, and the knuckle was out of place.

"The thumb's broken," a doctor said when Rocky went for an examination.

Marciano was forced to withdraw as New England's representative in the National AAU Tournament. It was a bitter disappointment, since Rocky had dreamed of beating Coley Wallace and fighting for the United States at the Olympics.

"What'm I gonna do with this fuckin' hand?" Rocky asked Colombo, "I've got to toughen it up. Now I can't fight for at least two months."

Not only was Marciano temporarily out of the ring, the injury was so severe that he couldn't hold a shovel and had to quit his job at the gas company.

Colombo was very worried. He knew that Rocky would be twenty-five in a few months, an old man to be starting out in the prizefighting game. Colombo wanted Marciano to turn pro. But he had to do it soon or it was going to be too late.

"I didn't realize it then," Colombo said. "But the injury was a blessing in disguise. Now that The Rock couldn't work at the gas company, we could concentrate full-time on getting him ready for boxing."

THE MCGINNIS KO was Rocky's final amateur fight. He'd been in a dozen fights, losing four: to Lester, DeAngelis, Wallace, and Bob Girard.

Girard was a rugged six-foot-plus heavyweight from Lynn, Massachusetts, who worked in a hot tannery wrestling big slabs of leather and then went out at night to fight for twenty-five or thirty dollars. Girard had won the Massachusetts Amateur Heavyweight Championship two years in succession.

Rocky had just KO'd another opponent in the tournament and had injured his bad hand. The hand was swollen and the knuckle was pushed back.

"You can't fight," Mike Piccento told his nephew. "That's it."

"Don't worry, Mike," Rocky said. "I'm fighting. Look at the guy I'm going up against. He's afraid of me. I'll ruin him."

Girard was known as a courageous fighter and was confident of winning. But Rocky was beginning to believe he was invincible and that every fighter must fear him.

Girard boxed Rocky stylishly to win the decision, but he was very modest about his victory.

"How do you think I beat Rocky?" Girard said. "I beat him because it was three rounds. There were a hundred guys who might have stayed three rounds with The Rock. But no man in the world was gonna beat Rocky in fifteen rounds; not Dempsey, not Ali, not anybody. I knew he was going to be the champ. I don't think anybody could hurt Rocky. Every time he hit you, you saw a flash of light. You either grabbed him or you moved back, because if he hits you twice you're gone."

IN THE SPRING OF 1948, there were many people in Brockton who laughed at Rocky's ambitions. He was almost twenty-five, his broken hand had been in a cast for five weeks, and yet they saw him with Colombo every day, wrapped in a sweat shirt and towels and running in D.W. Field Park.

Rocky's romance with Barbara Cousins was becoming serious. But he had no job and was embarrassed, because he couldn't afford to take her to nice places or contribute to the support of his family.

A meeting was held in the parlor of the Marchegiano home to determine Rocky's future. Rocky, Colombo, Mike Piccento, Dom Prosper, Caggiano, Lester Cousins, and Pierino Marchegiano attended.

Colombo and Caggiano engaged in a heated argument over the sixty dollars Rocky still claimed was owed him for the Canton Hall fight. By then Marciano was very disenchanted with Caggiano as a manager and trainer.

"He wanted me to get rid of my overhand right," Rocky said. "It was my best punch, but he wanted me to jab, short and crisp. I tried, but I didn't like it."

Both Eddie Boland, an acquaintance of Colombo's who had been associated with boxing for thirty years, and Joe Monte, the respected former heavyweight from Brockton, advised Colombo to take Rocky to New York, where the managers had the best connections and there were many excellent trainers who could polish Rocky's crude style.

Boland gave Colombo a list of managers that included Al Weill. Rocky and Allie liked Weill because he had handled Lou Ambers, who beat Tony Canzoneri for the lightweight title in 1936. As Italian champions, Canzoneri and Ambers (Louis D'Ambrosio) had been among Rocky's boyhood idols.

"We'll get in touch with Weill," Colombo said. "But let's wait for your hand to heal first. You've got to be in shape to really impress this guy."

In May, Rocky's cast was removed. The thumb was completely healed, and he could punch hard without pain.

An excited Allie Colombo wrote the following letter:

Dear Al Weill:

Your name was recommended to me by a Mr. Eddie Boland, in regards to your handling a future heavyweight champion.

Rocco Marchegiano is 23-years-old [Rocky was actually twenty-four, almost twenty-five] 190 pounds and one of the greatest prospects in the country. Although we are close to Boston we are dissatisfied with a Boston contact and would much prefer New York handling.

I have known Rocco all of my life being a next door neighbor, and I know his background. He is rough and tough and has shown in his amateur fights a tremendous punch in either hand. He has the necessary foundation to become a great fighter.

If you are interested contact me soon. My address is Al Colombo, 76 Brook Street, phone 3956-W, Brockton, Mass.
Sincerely, Al Colombo

COLOMBO AND MARCIANO were in the midst of a game for the Ward 2 Memorial Club baseball team when the call came from New York.

"Can you bring the fighter to New York on

Saturday for a tryout?" Weill said.

"Sure I can," Colombo said. "We'll be there."

⚜

ARMAND "AL" WEILL SAT behind a cluttered desk in his upstairs office at 1585 Broadway, puffing on a stubby cigar. Grinning from a chair beside the squat, white-haired manager was his top heavyweight, Arturo Godoy, the Argentinian brawler who had fought well against Joe Louis twice in losing bids for the heavyweight championship.

Colombo, Marciano, and Mike Piccento had made the five-hour drive from Brockton to New York in Piccento's sedan.

"What makes you think you can fight?" Weill's foghorn voice grunted. They soon learned that Weill believed in being blunt and was always in command of a conversation.

"He's never lost a fight," Colombo said smugly, hoping Weill didn't know Rocky had lost four.

"That don't mean nothin'," Weill said. "Who'd he ever fight? Amateur fights don't count. How many fights you had?"

"A dozen," Colombo said,

"I'll have to see you in the gym, Rocky," Weill said. "If you can punch like Colombo says, maybe you've got something. Twenty-three's pretty old to be starting out though, kid. Fighters win championships before they're twenty-three."

The office phones rang constantly. Weill bounced nervously in the chair, chewing on the cigar holder as he answered them. At fifty-four, he had managed fighters most of his adult life. He was short, with a round face and eyes that shifted in every direction. Insiders in

the fight game called him "The Vest," not because he wore one, but because he "always came home with the gravy." He was shrewd, knew all of the right people, and was not afraid to use them.

"Don't ever take your eye off the guy," Piccento had warned Rocky before they left Brockton. "Because if you do he'll steal the eyeballs right out of your head. Don't trust him. But if you play your cards right, you'll make more money with Weill than anybody. He's got the right trainer and the right connections."

Piccento did much of the talking for Rocky, who spoke to Weill very seldom.

"What can you do for the kid?" Piccento said. "Where will he be training? How much help can you give him?"

"Not so fast," Weill said. "If he's got potential, we'll see what can be done."

Considering the possibility that Weill and Rocky might not agree on a contract, Piccento had arranged to meet with Joe Vella, manager of the lightheavyweight champion Gus Lesnevich, after Marciano's session in the gym.

When Piccento told Vella that Rocky was going to sign with Weill, the manager said, "The kid won't do any better than Weill. He's a good manager, and he knows how to move a fighter."

Weill had managed three world champions: Joey Archibald (featherweight), Lou Ambers (lightweight), and Marty Servo (welterweight). But the big prize, the heavyweight championship of the world, had always eluded him. That title carried with it wealth, prestige, and power far in excess of that attained by champions in any other weight divisions.

Weill had come closest to realizing this dream with the powerful Godoy. As they started for the CYO Gym on West Seventeenth

Street, he envisioned no such potential in Marchegiano.

Weill was becoming irritated because Piccento had done most of the talking for Rocky.

"Who the hell is this guy?" Weill asked Rocky.

"He's my uncle," Rocky said.

"Well, I don't deal with him," Weill snapped. "He's not in the picture. Do you owe him any money?"

"Yeah," Rocky said. "I owe him a lot."

"Well, if I decide to manage you, pay him off," Weill said. "He ain't part of the deal. I manage my own fighters and nobody else is in the picture."

"What about Allie?" Rocky said.

"The same goes for him," Weill said. "He's out."

"Allie's my trainer," Rocky said. "If I fight for you, he's gonna be with me."

"I've got my own trainer," Weill said. "The best in the business. If you want Colombo with you, you'll have to pay him."

"Don't worry. He'll be with me," Rocky said.

GNOMELIKE CHARLEY GOLDMAN bounded across the CYO Gym floor on sixty-year-old legs that defied their ancient origins. Just over five feet tall, he had the broad, flat nose and thick, misshapen hands of a bantamweight who had been in more than three hundred fights.

Goldman had trained his first champion nine years before Rocky was born. He was a manager-trainer for Al McCoy, who took the middleweight title with a first-round KO over George Chip in 1914. Little Charley had handled three champs and several hundred fighters, many of them first-rate and contenders for crowns. But, as with Weill, Goldman too longed for his first heavyweight champion.

Charley peered over his thick, black-rimmed glasses at Marchegiano. Goldman and Weill both spoke with the heavy accents of less than affluent Bronx and Brooklyn Jews, their conversation sprinkled liberally with words like "dis" and "dat" and "dese."

"Is dis the fighter, Al?" Goldman said. "He don't look like no heavyweight ta me."

"Fix the kid up with some equipment, and let's see how he goes," Weill ordered.

The gym was on the second floor, stuffed in behind big, dirty windows. It smelled of cheap cigars, hot liniment, dirty socks, and sweaty jock straps. There were dozens of fighters of all sizes, shapes, and talents, punching bags, skipping ropes, exercising, shadowboxing, and sparring in the ring.

"Dint ya bring anything?" Goldman asked.

"Sure," Rocky said, holding up the bag that contained his trunks, socks, and shoes. "All I need're the gloves."

"Let's go then," Goldman said.

In the dressing room. Rocky began to pull on his boxing trunks over his Jockey shorts.

"Where's your cup?" Goldman said.

"I didn't bring one," Rocky said.

Goldman went to the equipment bag, pulled out a metal protector, and tossed it to Rocky. "Put it on," he ordered. "A fighter should always wear a cup. Next thing, you'll be telling me you ain't got no mouthpiece."

"I never wear a mouthpiece," Rocky said. "I can't get used to them."

"You should," Goldman said, knitting his brow so the wrinkles shot up into the large, oval, bald crest of his receding hairline. "The mouthpiece is for your own protection."

Goldman bandaged Rocky's hands and told him to get in the ring.

Weill was near the ropes talking to Frankie Genaro, the former world flyweight champion. Genaro had brought a good heavyweight prospect named Wade Chancey up from Florida.

"Put on your headgear," Goldman told Rocky.

"I don't want it," Rocky said.

"You've got to wear it," Goldman said.

Just as Goldman was calling them out of their corners. Rocky turned to him and said, "Real fight?"

Goldman was stunned. "Yeah, kid," he said. "It's a real fight."

Rocky waded in, throwing punches in his typical whirlwind fashion. Chancey was stinging him with jabs. Then Rocky crashed a looping right to the head and Chancey fell back into the ropes, dazed.

"Time," Goldman shouted.

As Marciano was getting out of the ring, he glanced at Colombo and said. "How'd I look?"

Colombo grinned. "Terrific, Rock," he said.

Weill had a scowl on his face. He was talking to another fight manager by the ring apron.

"Forget it, Al," the manager said. "The guy got lucky. He's got no chance."

"Maybe," Weill said. "Maybe not."

"If you done anything right, I didn't see it," Goldman told Rocky.

Weill came over and took Goldman aside. "What about it?" Weill said.

"He's no boxer," Goldman said. "But the kid can punch. That's the most important thing."

"Bring him down to my office in an hour," Weill said.

As they were approaching Broadway

Rocky was confident, despite Goldman's comment. He was wondering how much Weill would pay him to sign a contract. It was important that he be put on a salary so that he would not have to work and could concentrate completely on boxing.

"You're a good prospect, kid," Weill said. "I want you should stick around here. You'll stay with Charley at Ma Brown's on Ninety-second Street."

"Do I get expenses?" Rocky said.

"What expenses?" Weill grunted. "I can't give you no expenses. You ain't done nothing yet."

"Well, he doesn't have a job," Colombo said. "And he has to help out at home."

"That's too bad," Weill said. "I wish I could do something."

"If I can't get paid I won't stay here," Rocky said.

"Do you live near Providence?" Weill asked.

"Yeah," Colombo said. "About thirty miles away."

"All right, then go back to Brockton and get yourself in shape," Weill said. "Manny Almeida runs the boxing shows in Providence, and I do a lot of business with him. Let me know when you're ready to fight, and I'll get you fixed up with a match down there."

After much persuasion, Pasqualena Marchegiano had reluctantly agreed to Rocky's trip to New York. But by the time he returned to Brockton she had already changed her mind.

"No, Rocky," Pasqualena said. "I no want you to fight, *figlio mio.*"

"Gee, Ma, I thought you said it would be all right. I told that manager in New York I'd be fightin' for him," Rocky said, already decided that he would go ahead with his plans to become a fighter, but very concerned about gaining his mother's approval.

"No," Pasqualena said. "It's no good you fight. You're gonna hurt somebody, and somebody's gonna hurt you. You tell that manager you won't fight."

"It's the only thing I can do, Mom," Rocky pleaded. "I promised Pa I wouldn't end up in a shoe factory, didn't I? Anyway, boxers don't get hurt. Nobody's gonna hit me that much."

"I don't like it," Pasqualena insisted. "If you want me to get sick, then go ahead and be a fighter."

The day after Rocky's return from New York, Pierino came into the kitchen for Sunday breakfast looking tense and forlorn. "Maybe it's not so good you fight. Rocky," he said. "Isa no easy business, this fighting. Why don't you getta yourself a good job?"

"What's the matter. Pa?" Rocky said. "Are you turning against me too? I thought you wanted me to fight. What about the way we were gonna show the Irish who the best athletes are in Brockton?"

"You know what's the matter," Pierino said. "Your mother's stubborn. She made me promise to tell you not to fight. But I can't do it. If you want to be a fighter, then you be a good fighter, Rocky."

"I will, Pa," Rocky said. "Don't you ever worry about that."

ON MONDAY MORNING, Colombo called Brockton Mayor Joseph Downey and explained Rocky's ambition to become a professional boxer. "He could sure use a little job to tide him over until he gets a few fights," Colombo said.

Mayor Downey put Rocky and Allie to work as laborers for the city highway department. It was an easy, outdoors job that left Rocky refreshed enough to follow a rigorous training schedule in the evenings.

They ran before work in the morning and again in the evening, often more than seven miles a day. In the afternoons, they went to the YMCA gym. With no experienced trainers or sparring partners available, Rocky concentrated entirely on developing stamina and power. They stuffed an old navy sea bag full of wood shavings to make a heavy punching bag. It weighed more than a hundred pounds, much heavier than the standard heavy bag used by professional boxers.

Rocky worked for hours every day pounding the heavy bag, but he refused to go near a speed bag, which he was awkward at punching. He was convinced it was of no use to a heavyweight.

Months later, Goldman insisted that Rocky work out on the speed bag in order to form the habit of holding his hands high. He attacked it clumsily and hit it hard as though be were using the heavy bag, but Goldman didn't care so long as his hands stayed up where they would protect his face.

Rocky always followed his heavy bag workouts at the Brockton YMCA by going into the weightlifting room and pressing and curling barbells for an hour. He was convinced this would help develop his strength as a fighter.

One afternoon, a huge, powerfully built man came in and began working out on the weights with Rocky.

"I'm getting in shape to be a fighter," Rocky said. "What would you recommend?"

"If I was you, I'd be careful," the big weightlifter said. "You've got to know what you're doing with these things. If you don't, you could get musclebound. Lifting weights the wrong way could ruin a guy like you for boxing."

"That's it, Allie," Rocky said. "No more weights for me. I'll just stick to the exercises."

After punching the heavy bag and going through his exercise routine. Rocky finished his workouts by wading shoulder-deep into the YMCA swimming pool and throwing rapid and powerful uppercuts until he could barely move his arms through the churning water.

"This is really gonna do it for me, Alsack," he said after the first session in the pool. "I can feel it. This'll be one of my best exercises for power."

A few days before Joe Louis KO'd Jersey Joe Walcott on June 25 to retain his heavyweight title, Colombo wrote to Weill, informing him that Rocky was ready to fight.

"Get in touch with Manny Almeida and he'll make arrangements for a four-round bout," Weill wrote to Colombo. "Good luck to Rocco."

On July 12, Rocky's Ward 2 paesanos made the first of many Monday-night trips to Providence to watch him.

Rocky's opponent was twenty-one-year-old Haroutune "Harry" Bilazarian, of Boylston, Massachusetts, who had been the U.S. Army light heavyweight champion in Sapporo, Japan, in 1947. He had been a teammate and sparring partner of Rex Layne, who later had an important fight against Marciano.

"I really didn't enjoy fighting," Bilazarian said. "When I got out of the service in nineteen forty-eight, work was bad. That's the only reason I decided to go into it."

Bilazarian, whose name appears in most record books as "Balzerian," had lost two of his first three professional fights. His manager assured him that Marchegiano was inexperienced and crude and would be easy to beat, so Harry trained hard and was confident of victory.

Pasqualena Marchegiano felt sick that Sunday night, before Rocky's fight. "Tell me you won't fight. Rocky," she said. "Promise you'll give this crazy idea up."

"What's the matter with you?" she said to Pierino and Rocky's Uncle Mike. "You men think money's the most important thing. What's gonna happen to my son?"

"I won't get hurt, Ma," Rocky said. "I promise."

"Promise?" Pasqualena said. "Who could promise such a thing? If you don't fight, then you won't get hurt. Promise me that."

Then she glared at her brother Mike Piccento. "You," Pasqualena said. "Out of my house."

"I'll promise you this, Ma," Rocky said. "If I ever get hurt bad in a fight, I'll quit."

"And I'm gonna check you after the fights," Pasqualena said sternly. "If you got a big bruise, big cut, big bump, then you're gonna quit this fighting."

Sonny Marchegiano was listening to the conversation, thinking all the while, My brother can't lose. There's not a man alive who can hurt Rocky.

"All right, Ma," Rocky said. "I promise. But remember, a guy can scrape his back against the ropes or get a little bruise on his arm or face, and it's nothing. If I get a real big cut or something, I'll quit."

"You'd never quit, Rock," Sonny said, when they had left the house. "Would you?"

"What do you think?" Rocky said. "That's our mother in there. I don't think anybody's going to hurt me, but what's the sense of letting her worry?"

They arrived in Providence shortly before the 2 P.M. weigh-in, at which Rocky scaled 185. Tony "Snap" Tartaglia, a Ward 2 chum, and Colombo were going to be in Marciano's corner, but neither had had any experience at handling a professional fighter. Colombo had barely reached the stage of learning how to wrap bandages on a fighter's hands, and Snap was there mostly to carry the water bucket. Since neither Weill nor Goldman had made the trip from New York, they had to find someone who knew the business to work Rocky's corner.

Almeida sent Colombo to Frank Travers, whom he said was the best cornerman in Providence. Fortunately for Rocky, Travers had his own fighter George Araujo making his pro debut at the Providence Auditorium that night, and he agreed to be in Marchegiano's corner.

Araujo, who won a four-round decision, later lost a bid for the world lightweight title when Jimmy Carter KO'd him in the thirteenth round in June 1953.

After the weigh-in, Rocky took a two-hour nap at Tartaglia's sister Alvina's house in Providence. When he awakened at about five, Alvina began cooking his rare steak. Rocky followed this routine through many of his early fights in Providence.

The loud echo of the Hammond organ ringing out over the rows of empty seats sent shivers of excitement through Sonny as he sat ringside, waiting for his brother to emerge from the dressing room. There were fewer than a hundred people in the stands when Rocky entered the ring, and many of those were Rocky's own loyal band of followers from Ward 2.

The fight lasted 1 minute and 32 seconds. Rocky hit Bilazarian twice with the overhand right and knocked him to the canvas.

"The first time he knocked me down, he broke my tooth," Bilazarian said. "When I got up I was afraid I'd swallow it. Then he knocked me down again. Then I don't remember anything."

"See, Ma," Rocky said the next morning. "Not a scratch on me."

Pasqualena made him take off his shirt. "So you didn't get hurt this time," she said. "I go to Mrs. Parziale, and she took away the *malocchio*. I go to Saint Patrick's and light the candles and pray you don't get hurt and you don't hurt nobody else. How many times can I do this? God doesn't like you to fight."

5.

Winning

THAT SUMMER ROCKY'S GOAL was to fight as often as possible, and to register some impressive victories so that Al Weill would begin to notice him.

Sam Silverman and Manny Almeida were partners promoting the Providence Auditorium boxing cards. Almeida had the Rhode Island license, and was closely associated with Al Weill. Silverman, who disliked Weill intensely, supplied fighters from the Boston area.

"At the beginning of the summer of nineteen forty-eight, we were stuck eighteen thousand dollars on our fight shows in Providence," Silverman said. "Then a couple of guys named Rocco Marchegiano and George Araujo came along and bailed us out."

One week after his victory over Bilazarian, Rocky KO'd an average heavyweight named Jack Edwards, of Hartford, in the first round. It was an overhand right again that did the damage, and it took him 16 seconds less to finish Edwards than to KO Bilazarian.

Despite Rocky's two first-round KOs, Sam Silverman was still very unimpressed with him. Rocky was short, clumsy, and couldn't box. Silverman had no qualms about doing his

pal Jimmy O'Keefe a favor at Rocky's expense.

O'Keefe, a prominent Boston restaurant owner, controlled the contract of a promising young light heavyweight, Bobby Quinn. He was grooming Quinn for the big time, bringing him along very slowly. Quinn had won fifteen of his sixteen fights, losing only to Mad Anthony Jones, a solid ten-round fighter. But Bobby hadn't fought for a long while when O'Keefe called Silverman to set up a match.

Silverman assured O'Keefe that "this Marchegiano kid's got nothing. He can punch all right, but I've never seen a fighter as clumsy. The kid doesn't know what he's doin' out there. Quinn won't have no trouble with him."

Rocky had asked Silverman to let him fight every Monday night regardless of the opponent. He needed both the forty dollars per fight, the victories, and the experience. He was angry that he had been kept idle for two weeks because Almeida supposedly could not find anyone for him.

"This guy's got fourteen KOs," Colombo said nervously when Almeida called to offer them the bout. "He's got too much experience."

"What's the matter with you, Allie," Rocky

said. "Take the fight. What do we care about Quinn?"

Before he left for Providence that Monday, Rocky had a long talk with his Uncle Mike Piccento.

"Watch this Quinn," Piccento said. "He's a sharp boxer and he's got a terrific right. Be careful with the right."

Colombo was tense, pacing around the house as if Rocky were going into a championship fight. Not Rocky, though. He took his usual two-hour nap, and then had a rare steak.

Rocky weighed 185 to Quinn's 180, and he was more powerful than the Boston Irishman. But instead of rushing across the ring after Quinn, as he usually did, Rocky shuffled out of his corner, as if to size his opponent up. Quinn seemed content just to stay out of Marciano's reach. It was a very dull first round.

But in the second round Quinn launched an all-out attack on Rocky. He came in low, bobbing and weaving and delivering solid left hooks and powerful rights. The Providence fans cheered for Quinn to KO Marciano.

At the bell starting the third round, Quinn charged after Rocky. Marciano threw a short right that crunched against the left side of Quinn's jaw, jerking him off his feet. It happened so fast, the crowd was stunned. Seconds later, a tremendous roar thundered up from the stands. There was an electricity in the auditorium, a sense of discovery, as the audience suddenly realized that Rocky Marciano was no ordinary heavyweight.

Silverman shuffled into Quinn's dressing room, chomping on the ever-present cigar. "You put me inna middle with O'Keefe," he said, "I told Jimmy you'd beat this guy easy. This kid can't fight to knock you out."

"I know," Quinn alibied. "I wasn't in shape."

When Rocky saw Mike Piccento after the fight, he confronted his uncle. "Don't ever tell me how good a guy is, Mike," he said. "I don't want to know. I've got to beat them all."

Before the Quinn fight, Rocky's roadwork had consisted of running in James Edgar Playground and around the lakes and golf course at D.W. Field Park.

"It was getting monotonous," Colombo said. "We finally decided to get a football and throw long passes for about two hours a day."

Doing roadwork with a football became a regular part of Rocky's training, which he retained throughout his entire career. Since Rocky was right-handed, he started throwing left-handed passes. This made him feel more comfortable when he used his left in a fight, and Rocky always felt it made his left-hand punches as strong as the rights.

Rocky also began going on long hikes with Nicky Sylvester, Colombo, and others, often from ten to fifteen miles a day. He particularly enjoyed Sylvester's company and humor on these marathon walks, which he took faithfully every day regardless of whether he was in serious training at the time or not. He always believed the hikes were responsible for much of his great stamina.

Once they were going to a high school football game in Quincy, more than twenty miles from Brockton.

"What time do you want to leave, Rock?" Nicky said.

"We'd better get started about six," Rocky said.

"But the game's at one," Sylvester said.

"I know, but I figured we'd walk over," Rocky told him.

Another time Rocky and Nicky walked thirty-three miles to Manny Almeida's bar outside Providence just to visit. They stayed an hour and started back to Brockton.

"Rock, we're not gonna walk back, are we?" Sylvester pleaded.

"Oh, all right," Rocky said, watching his pal struggle along the highway. "I guess we better hitchhike."

Still fuming over Rocky's win over Quinn, Silverman matched him against Eddie Ross, an undefeated heavyweight from Montreal.

"Ross was classy," Silverman recalled. "He had twenty-six wins and twenty-three knock-outs. He was fighting for me in New Bedford, and I was looking to keep him around for the summer. I figured Rocky was bound to get beat, and Ross was the kid to do it. I threw Rocky in to give this kid another win and keep his popularity up in New Bedford."

It took Rocky exactly 1 minute and 3 seconds to hand Ross his first defeat. He threw a hard right that Ross tried to duck. The punch parted Ross's thin hair, cut his skull, and flattened him.

After the fight, Almeida told Colombo that Rocky was the hardest puncher he'd ever seen—and he'd seen them all, including Louis and Dempsey.

With each knockout Rocky registered, Colombo's dream of seeing his Ward 2 pal win the heavyweight title became more compelling, and soon it dominated his entire life.

"We've got to go to New York, Rock," Colombo said. "It's the only way. You're gonna be fighting tougher guys all the time. You've got to have some sparring partners and a top trainer like Charley Goldman."

Colombo and Rocky were both concerned because neither Weill nor Goldman had attended any of the fights. It was as if Rocky was completely on his own, and the shrewd New York fight sharks would not even waste a train fare until he had completely proven himself.

Then they learned that Weill was in the hospital, recovering from surgery. He also had diabetes and had to take insulin injections daily. Almeida told them that he had spoken to Weill on the phone, and that the Vest was very enthusiastic about Rocky's victories. Rocky and Allie wondered: if he was so enthusiastic, why he didn't at least send Goldman or Chick Wergeles, a trainer-manager and associate of Weill's, to protect his interest in Marciano?

Although Marchegiano's KOs were spectacular, the pay was still forty dollars for four-rounders. Rocky had quit his job to concentrate entirely on boxing, and he was hungry for two things—the heavyweight championship and money.

"From the very beginning we had only one real goal—the greatest prize in sports, the heavyweight championship of the world," Colombo said. "We knew the sacrifices Rocky had to make, but we also knew the rewards."

They were living partly on the money Colombo had saved in the service, but that would soon run out. Rocky knew he had to become a main bout fighter soon in order to earn adequate pay or find some other way to augment his income that would not interfere with his training.

"Right after the Ross fight, this kid Marchegiano came up to me and said, 'I know how we can make some big money, Sam,'" Silverman recalled. "'I know quite a few people in Brockton, and I can sell a lot of tickets.' I hardly knew Rocky, and I was still plenty mad at him for beating Ross. So I didn't pay any attention to him. I still figured Rocky was just a lucky fighter."

Generoso Caggiano had spent the month of July being treated for a back injury in a Boston hospital. When he returned to Brockton in August and discovered that Rocky had begun a professional career, he took legal action to try to gain control of Rocky's contract.

On August 23, the day Rocky fought Ross, lawyers for Caggiano filed a bill of complaint in Plymouth County Superior Court, seeking to restrain Rocky from engaging in any further fights until the matter was resolved. The restraining order was not allowed. The case lingered in the courts until July 1951, when Rocky was already a top contender for the heavyweight title.

In a brief filed by his attorneys with the court, Caggiano said he telephoned Rocky in August 1948, and recalled the following conversation:

"Rocky, this is Gene."

"So what?"

"Remember, we have a manager-fighter contract which I want you to live up to."

"Wipe your arse with it," Rocky supposedly replied. "I've got a big wheel for a manager now, Al Weill of New York, and when I see you on the street, I'll bounce one off your jaw."

In an admission-of-facts paper, requested by Caggiano, Rocky denied making the statements.

Since amateur boxers are not allowed to sign contracts, Caggiano felt the written agreement he had signed with the fighter on February 27, 1948, entitled him to be Rocky's manager. It said, in part:

In consideration of the time, efforts and teachings of Gene Caggiano to Rocco Marchegiano in the art of boxing, the said Rocco Marchegiano agrees with Gene Caggiano that in the event the said Rocco Marchegiano should turn professional and enter the professional field within the next five years, the said Rocco Marchegiano will enter into a contract with Gene Caggiano to retain Gene Caggiano as his manager.

The agreement was witnessed by Rocky,

Caggiano, and Vincent Pereira, who is married to Rocky's sister Alice.

Caggiano also alleged in his brief that, on March 22, 1948, at the New England Amateur Boxing Tournament in Boston, Marchegiano said, "I'm going to show you what I can do, and get through tonight's fight as fast as possible. Then I'm going to turn pro after the nationals in April. You can make as many plans and contacts for me regarding my pro fights as you are able to. I am going out after the fast buck, and pretty soon we'll both be wearing diamonds, because I'll knock them all out, and become the heavyweight champion of the world."

AFTER FOUR SPECTACULAR knockouts in less than two months, the fans were finally beginning to notice Rocky. They no longer giggled and laughed at his ambitions as he and Colombo ran along the narrow, winding roads of D.W. Field Park. Many of them actually leaned out the windows and waved, and shouted words of encouragement, "Thataboy, Rocky. You'll show them." And Rocky loved it.

"There were two schools of thought right from the beginning," Colombo said. "One group, including everybody in Ward 2, figured The Rock was the greatest puncher of all time and one of the toughest fighters ever. The others thought The Rock was just a lucky bum who couldn't fight and would get knocked out as soon as he faced a fairly good opponent."

"Even after quite a few knockouts, I still seen Rocky as a real lucky fighter," Silverman said. "I didn't figure him to keep winning. Nobody did. But I begun to notice something, As awkward and clumsy as the kid looked, he could deliver an accurate punch. The kid was hitting guys right on the button."

There was a reporter for a weekly newspaper near Brockton who constantly belittled Rocky and played down his victories.

"That asshole," Colombo would say, clenching the newspapers. "I'd like to show him who can fight."

"Fuck 'm," Rocky said. "What does he know?"

Rocky pretended to ignore the stories, but Colombo could sense that they enraged him. It showed in the intense dedication he poured into training. Rocky always hated to be criticized.

"At least the *Enterprise* is behind us," Colombo would say. "That other asshole. I hope I never meet him."

The *Brockton Enterprise-Times* was the major daily newspaper in the area. Reporter Vic Dubois wrote accurate accounts of Rocky's fights under banner headlines. The *Enterprise* also solidly supported him in editorials.

Following the Ross fight, Rocky was introduced to Russ Murray, a wealthy sportsman who was an owner of Raynham Dog Track, near Brockton.

"I've got a place all equipped for training," Murray said. "Use it anytime you want. I'll be happy to have you."

Murray's estate was in South Easton, twelve miles from Rocky's home. There was an outdoor gym with a ring, a heavy bag, and a swimming pool. Murray had built the boxing facilities for his friend Johnny Shkor, a Boston heavyweight who Rocky would eventually knock out.

"We loved the solitude of this beautiful country estate," Colombo said. "Russ Murray was a wonderful, generous man, and meeting him was really a lucky break. Because of Russ, we had our own private training camp. It was a setup usually enjoyed only by champions and contenders."

Rocky's brother Sonny often helped him train. Every evening after supper they'd go to James Edgar Playground, and for two hours Sonny would throw football passes to Rocky. But Rocky always tried to make it seem as if it were for Sonny's own benefit.

"This is gonna be good for you. Son," Rocky said. "You might be a quarterback sometime. It's important that you learn how to throw these passes. Now I'm gonna keep running, and you throw the ball way out ahead of me."

"I'm gonna need someone to spar with," Rocky said to Sonny shortly after he had begun training at Murray's estate. "There's nobody around Brockton, and I can't afford to hire a guy, so you're gonna have to go with me."

"Sure, Rock," Sonny said. "I've never boxed before, but that's all right."

Sonny was fifteen years old and weighed 150 pounds. He had a reputation among the teen-agers for being an aggressive, rough-and-tough athlete, but it was asking a lot of the boy to go into the ring with a 185-pound heavyweight, especially his brother Rocky, who he knew was likely to become so engrossed once they began fighting that he would completely forget to pull punches.

Snap Tartaglia was about Marciano's age, but he was shorter than Rocky and a middleweight. He was Rocky's paesano and, when he was asked, he also became a sparring partner without hesitation.

Along with Allie Colombo, they drove to Russ Murray's estate every evening in Mike Piccento's sedan. Rocky spent hours sparring with Sonny and Snap and punching the heavy bag, and he always devoted at least half an hour to punching underwater in the pool, more convinced than ever that it was helping his leverage and punching power tremendously.

Fortunately for Rocky, both Sonny and Snap were good boxers and tough fighters who were not afraid to mix with him. They were fast, and they could deliver hard punches.

"I knew both of them had the potential to become great middleweights," Colombo said. "But Snap didn't want to be a fighter, and Sonny's mother wouldn't let him."

For the most part, Rocky exercised great control in the sparring sessions. He refused to hit Sonny or Snap with hard punches to the head, but he held back nothing in attacking their midsections. They knew how Rocky hated to be hit to the head himself, but it was almost as if he commanded them to do so. Once Sonny hit Rocky with a solid right to the chin as his brother was advancing upon him. Rocky's eyes blinked, and for an instant it looked as if he might go out of control.

"Time," Colombo shouted, jumping into the ring between them.

A few seconds later Rocky was grinning. "Wow," he said. "You can hit as hard as most heavyweights, Son."

"It looked like Rocky was coming after me," Sonny recalled. "But when his tongue didn't come out, I figured he was all right. Whenever Rocky really lost his temper, his tongue always came out between his front teeth and kind of curled upward. Then you really had to watch it or he'd ruin you."

They were excited that Monday, August 30, 1948, when Rocky faced Jimmy Weeks from New York, because Weill had finally sent Charley Goldman to Providence to watch Marchegiano fight.

"This is it, Allie," Rocky said. "We're finally on our way. If Weill sent Goldman, we must be ready for New York."

But little Charley was more cranky than friendly when he stepped off the train in Providence. Goldman almost always wore a smile. But now the bowler hat was tilted to the back of his balding head, and he was frowning as he chewed on a stubby cigar and peered out over horn-rimmed glasses at Rocky. Charley could still humor Al Weill's fantasies and chase rainbows, but only if he glimpsed the gold on the horizon. He saw no such treasure in the clumsy, overstuffed middleweight who stood before him.

As usual, Colombo was worried. "He looks like Joe Louis," he whispered to Snap Tartaglia, glancing across the ring at the huge, powerfully built Weeks. "I'm telling you, Weill and Goldman must have sent this guy down from New York to give the Rock a real test."

"Stop worrying," Tartaglia said. "The Rock will murder this guy."

"We'll show that Goldman something," Rocky whispered to Colombo just before the bell. "I'm gonna get this guy real fast."

Goldman came a long way to see a short fight. In the first round, Rocky crashed a short right to Weeks's jaw. The referee could have counted to thirty.

In the dressing room, reporters Vic Dubois of the *Brockton Enterprise-Times* and Mike Thomas of the *Providence Journal* asked Goldman about Rocky's potential as a heavyweight.

"I can't give no opinion," Goldman said. "The fight was too short. How do I know if the kid can box? But he's got a punch. That's important."

Colombo, bubbling with enthusiasm after the fight, resented Goldman's apparent lack of interest. "I don't believe this guy, Rock," he said. "He could have said something better than that. I don't care how great Goldman is. He never saw such a beautiful punch."

"How about joining us for a bite to eat, Charley?" Rocky said.

"I've got to get right back to the city," Goldman said. "Got a kid coming to the gym early inna morning. Al wants you should come to New York and begin training with me, Rocky. I'll see what I can do to show you something. But remember, there ain't no short cuts. It takes years to make a fighter."

"I want to learn it all," Rocky said.

"Yeah, kid," Goldman said. "I think you do. Well, just get down to New York foist chance you get. We got plenty of sparring partners at the CYO Gym, and I'll do my best to bring ya along. But I want you should know, you ain't any too young, and you got an awful lot to learn, kid."

6.

Moving Up

IT WAS THE MORNING before Labor Day, and the people were coming home from mass at Saint Patrick's, when Rocky and Allie walked to Brockton Center and boarded the Greyhound bus for New York.

"I trust you, Alisay," Pasqualena Marchegiano had told Colombo. "You watch out for my Rocky. Make sure they don't cheat you. And don't let my Rocky get hurt. If everything's not pretty good, you packa your bags and come right home."

"Don't you worry, Mama, The Rock is gonna do just great," Colombo said. "But if I ever think he can't make it, I'll bring him right back to Brockton."

They were really gambling now. Colombo had drawn his savings out of the bank. They would need money for hotel rooms, meals, and transportation. Weill would pay for nothing.

"If the fighter wants to come down and learn the business under the best trainer there is, that's fine," he had said. "But I don't pay no expenses."

They were greeted at the door of the drab brick rooming house by the owner's daughter, Ethel Brown.

"I'm sorry," she said. "I was only expecting Rocco. There's just one vacant bed, but there's a couch in Charley Goldman's room."

"The couch is fine for me," Colombo said quickly. He didn't stop to wonder why no provisions had been made for him. If it was Weill's way of telling Colombo he wasn't needed, Allie didn't recognize it.

"Central Park's less than a block away," Goldman said at eight the next morning. "You'll do your roadwork around the reservoir, then take a rest and meet me at the CYO Gym about three."

Goldman then explained how to get to the gym by subway. "But he could have saved his breath," Colombo said, "because the Rock was sure to walk it."

They were half an hour late at the gym.

"Where ya been?" Goldman grunted. "Didja get lost onna subway or something?"

"Gee, I'm sorry, Mr. Goldman," Colombo said. "We decided to walk, and we must have timed it wrong."

Goldman stared at them in disbelief. "Seventy-five blocks with the temperature almost ninety degrees," he said. "Youse must be nuts. Well, let's go. We ain't got all afternoon."

For the next five days, Goldman had Rocky working out on the heavy bag, shadowboxing, skipping rope, and doing everything except sparring, which was what Rocky wanted to do.

"You've got so much to learn it ain't funny," Goldman told him. "You don't do nothing right."

Goldman scribbled notes—wild punches, no balance, legs too far apart, stride too long, no defense, stands up too straight, needs to get more body into punches, not enough leverage, doesn't know how to use combinations, relies too much on the right, no left hook . . . The list was endless.

"The kid's got nothing as a boxer," Goldman reported to Weill at Polyclinic Hospital. "But he's got a helluva punch and plenty of determination. And he listens to everything I say. He puts out more than a hundred percent. To me that's pretty important."

"See what you can do," Weill said. "Maybe he can learn something. The kid's got five straight knockouts. He can't be all bad. But remember, we don't pay him no expenses. I've got enough broken-down fighters already."

Allie and Rocky loved the excitement of the big city and the bright lights of Broadway. They spent hours walking up and down the street past the theater district, and when they were walking back to the rooming house they were always very hungry.

"Finding good food for Rocky was one of my toughest jobs in New York," Colombo recalled. "He had a tremendous appetite, and I wanted to be sure he got the right foods to keep off the fat. But in most places the food was either lousy or too expensive. It was nothing like what we were used to at home. We finally found a little combination bar and grill that featured nice lean roast beef at cheap prices. This place became a regular stop for us."

They'd arrive in the vicinity of Ninety-second Street at about 9:30 P.M. and always stop at a fruit stand to buy grapes and apples. Then they'd sit on the steps of the rooming house for about an hour, discussing their futures in boxing. There were many broken-down fighters at the end of their careers staying at Mrs. Brown's because the rates were very low. Rocky liked to question them about the fight game, but most of the fighters were South American and could speak very little English. There were fighters on their way up and fighters on their way down, but nobody of any fame. The only well-known boarder was little Charley Goldman, a curmudgeon who never spent a nickel unnecessarily. Charley liked the cheap rent.

"We've got to change your name," Weill informed Rocky when they visited him at the hospital. "Marchegiano is too long, too hard to pronounce."

"I'd rather not," Rocky said.

"I said it," Weill bellowed. "We change the name. It needs a ring, something the fans will really go for."

"How about Rocky Mack?" Colombo said.

"That stinks," Weill said.

"I don't like it," Rocky said. "It isn't Italian. It's got to sound Italian."

Weill talked with Manny Almeida on the telephone. "What's the matter with 'Marciano'?" Almeida said. "The fans all love it."

The ring announcer in Providence, having trouble pronouncing Marchegiano, had shortened it to Marciano.

Weill scribbled the name on a piece of paper: Marchegiano. He crossed out the *heg*: Marchegiano. "That's it," he said. "Marciano. Rocky Marciano. That's flashy."

"I don't know," Rocky said, "I guess if it's got to be done, Marciano will be all right. It's

Italian, all right. It's almost my real name."

But on the way back to the rooming house with Colombo Rocky was more apprehensive. "What a fucking business," he said. "Who'd have thought they'd make me change my name. How do you think Pop's gonna feel?"

Rocky's next fight was a first-round KO over a fat, sheepish heavyweight from the Bronx named Jerry Jackson. Weill's increased interest and caution in handling Marciano was clearly evident in this 254-pound victim, who posed no threat to Rocky and was pounded to the canvas by looping rights in 1 minute and 28 seconds.

The day after the fight, Rocky and Allie strode into George's Cafe in Brockton, a few minutes' walk from Marciano's house.

"Step right up," shouted Snap Tartaglia, who was tending bar for his brother George. "The drinks are on Rocky."

It was a joke they shared. Rocky never bought any drinks. They were poured free of charge by Tartaglia. They always felt it made Rocky look like a big, free-wheeling heavyweight such as the great John L. Sullivan. Rocky enjoyed the image as long as he didn't have to pay for it.

"They're going to criticize you if you blow all your dough in bars on fast living, and they're gonna criticize you if you hold onto it," Rocky told his brother Sonny after he became champion. "Well, I'd rather keep the money and let them knock me that way. I'm the only one who knows what I went through to get it."

Rocky returned to New York for more training with Goldman before his next appearance in Providence. This time it was a first-round KO over Bill Hardeman of Boston, who crumpled under the looping overhand right.

They traveled to Washington for the next bout. Al Weill was out of the hospital, and it was the first time he saw Marciano fight.

"I don't have to tell you what this means, Rock," Colombo said. "There'll be a lot of important people here. If we look good for Weill, we're on our way. Next thing, he'll have us fighting in Madison Square Garden."

"You know something, Allie," Rocky said. "I'm really hungry."

They walked the streets of Washington in torrential rain that afternoon. The fights, scheduled for an outdoor arena, were postponed for two days because of the rain. Finally it was decided to hold the bouts indoors, at the Uline Arena.

The two days' wait had unnerved Rocky's father and his Brockton paesanos, who seemed very worried. Rocky's only concern was to win in a style that impressed Al Weill.

Rocky's opponent was a sad-faced Puerto Rican, Gil Cardione. They talked before the bout, and Cardione explained that he was having a rough time supporting his family, and that was the only reason he was a fighter.

"It's too bad a poor kid like this has got to fight," Rocky told Colombo. "He hasn't got the heart for it. I'm gonna ruin him."

"That's exactly what you're supposed to do. Rock," Colombo said. "Don't forget it."

With Weill in the audience, Marciano demolished Cardione in exactly 36 seconds. The punch surprised everyone. Cardione was coming in when Rocky threw a left uppercut that jerked his head violently upward and collapsed him in a heap on the canvas. Cardione was unconscious for almost ten minutes.

"It was the first time I got frightened, and felt that the man may have been badly hurt," Colombo recalled. "When Cardione finally began to move his head and legs, I felt a shiver rush through me. We were both standing beside him. Rocky refused to leave the ring until they brought him back to full consciousness."

Weill and Goldman had been shouting ecstatically at ringside. Rocky was paid $200 for the fight. And on October 1, 1948, when they returned to New York, both Rocky and Allie figured the big money lay just ahead so long as Rocky continued to win.

"The Rock had no intention of losing," Colombo said. "We had heard they paid six-round fighters five hundred dollars at Madison Square Garden. Rocky really wanted some of that dough."

But Weill had other ideas. When they arrived at his office on Friday, the manager told Rocky he had just three days to get ready for another fight in Providence.

"That son of a bitch," Rocky said, as he and Colombo were walking back to the rooming house. "How'm I gonna make any money if he keeps me in Providence?"

Rocky easily unhinged his next opponent, Bob Jefferson, with a second-round KO, but the fight ended his boxing career for almost two months.

When Rocky woke up in Brockton the next morning, the middle knuckle on his right hand was swollen to twice its normal size.

"I can't bend the finger," he said. "I think it's broken."

"We've got to tell Weill," Colombo said.

"I don't think we should," Rocky said. "What if Weill says I've got to lay off? I don't want to stop fighting now."

But that afternoon Weill called from New York.

"Goldman says you flinched pretty bad when he took the bandages off," Weill said. "I want you should get down here right away. I want my doctor to see that hand before you fight again."

"You've got water on the knuckle," the doctor said. "I can drain it, but it will be blown up again in twenty-four hours."

"Drain it anyway," Rocky said. "There's nothing to lose."

"It feels good," Rocky told Colombo that night, "Tell Weill to get me a fight for next week."

But the next morning, when he woke up at Mrs. Brown's rooming house, the fist had ballooned still more.

This time Weill called Dr. Vincent Nardiello, the New York State Boxing Commission doctor.

"You'll have to rest it at least a month," Nardiello said. "There's no other cure."

Rocky returned to Brockton disgusted. He knew he had to rest the hand but he continued training, doing his roadwork faithfully and chasing Colombo and Sonny around the ring throwing lefts.

Armed with the immediacy of the injury, Pasqualena Marchegiano launched another campaign to convince her son to quit boxing.

"You promised," she said. "You say you quit this fighting if you get hurt. Why you no quit?"

"She put up a pretty good argument for a while," Sonny recalled. "But we could all see that Mom's heart wasn't in it anymore. She still wanted Rock to quit, but she knew now he never would, and he was determined to go all the way."

"If only we had a whirlpool machine, the hand might heal a lot faster," Colombo said.

A few days later. Rocky was watching his mother stuff dirty laundry into the washing machine. "You know something. Ma," he said. "That's a whirlpool."

Rocky began pouring Epsom salts into the washing machine and soaking his hand in the hot, swirling water. In the afternoons he went to Al Norling, the Brockton YMCA's physiotherapist, for massages. Norling was one of Rocky's favorite people. He advised the fighter on how to exercise, rest, and use his muscles to their fullest advantage. And he never charged for his services.

"I like the kid," Norling said. "Why should I take his money. The poor guy hasn't got any."

After five weeks the hand finally responded, and the swelling and inflammation disappeared. Colombo called Weill to say that Rocky was ready to fight.

"Come to New York," Weill said. "Don't use the hand. Do ya understand? Don't do nothing."

Rocky was broke. He didn't even have enough cash for a one-way ticket to New York. In the three months he had been fighting, Weill had not taken any cut from his purses. But Marciano had only made $700, and most of that had gone for living expenses in New York.

"Allie, I've got a beautiful deal for us," Rocky announced one afternoon. "I met some truck drivers who said they'll give us a free ride to New York."

They rode in dilapidated old trailer trucks that traveled by night from a Brockton firm. Colombo and Marciano boarded separate vehicles shortly after midnight on a cold November 15, 1948.

"It was free, and that was important," Colombo said. "But that ride to New York was anything but comfortable. The cab was always vibrating, and we had to yell at each other if we wanted to talk. After a while I got drowsy. I didn't want to fall asleep because I felt it wasn't fair to the driver. But pretty soon I had a tremendous headache. I remember thinking what a horrible way it was for a fighter to travel. A trip like that could upset you for a week."

Rocky became very friendly with his driver, Bill O'Malley, and Colombo did the same with Roy Cavanaugh, both of Brockton. "Now I want you to promise you'll try to make it down to Providence to see me fight," Rocky said, when the truckers dropped them off about 5 A.M. at the corner of Second Avenue and Ninety-second Street.

Rocky was limping as they walked the few blocks to Mrs. Brown's rooming house.

"What's the matter. Rock?" Colombo asked.

"It'll be all right, Allie," Rocky said. "I guess my back must have gotten a little stiff from riding in the truck."

"You sure?" Colombo said. "Maybe we should have someone look at It."

"Naw, it's fine," Rocky said. "It's getting better already."

⚔

"LET'S GO, MARCIANO," Charley Goldman shouted. "Cesar here is gonna spar wit ya. I hope you've got the mouthpiece this time."

Cesar Brion looked over at Goldman and Rocky and grinned. A rugged heavyweight from Cordoba, Argentina, Brion had just been brought to the United States to fight professionally in New York. Charley Goldman was his trainer. And in Cesar Brion, a seasoned veteran but a year younger than Marciano, a polished boxer who possessed both style and power, shrewd little Charley saw visions of his championship.

"I got my piece," Rocky told Goldman. "I'll just be a few minutes warming up on the heavy bag."

"This guy's a helluva fighter," Colombo said. "He's won twenty straight pro fights and over a hundred amateur bouts. What a sparring partner!"

"Beautiful," Rocky said. "This is exactly what I want, Allie."

All that week, Marciano and Brion had wars in the ring at the CYO Gym. Brion outboxed Rocky, but the Brockton slugger bullied him and drove him into the ropes. Yet every time Rocky began, pounding Brion with the overhand right, Goldman would panic. "Time!" Charley shouted. "Time!"

Despite his desire for perfection in the ring, Charley Goldman was low-key and friendly. He wore a perpetual grin, and he had the patience necessary to train a fighter like Marciano, who possessed the rare gifts of power, courage, and determination, but was uncommonly clumsy and had almost no formal training as a boxer.

"Don't worry, he's coming along good," Goldman assured them. "I'm not gonna fool with him much. When a fighter's winning big, a trainer's got to be careful he doesn't do nothing to foul him up. But he has to learn to fight onna inside. His arms ain't long enough. A good boxer'll murder him at long range."

"But The Rock's a great long-range puncher," Colombo said. "How do you think he scored most of his knockouts?"

"Sure," Goldman said. "I'll tell you how. Because he ain't fought nobody yet. When we go for the big guys, he'll have to get inside and take advantage of those short arms. We're gonna want more leverage on those punches."

For the next few months, Goldman concentrated heavily on teaching Rocky how to use more leverage in his punches, take shorter strides (he even tied Rocky's legs together to get him accustomed to this), and develop a left hook.

"The kid always listened," Goldman told reporters later. "You never had to tell Rocky anything twice. The thing I liked best besides his right hand was that he was always trying to improve."

Rocky's next fight was an eight-rounder against Irish Pat Connolly at Providence. It was billed as the co-feature.

"Connolly was dying to fight Marciano," Silverman said. "I figured he might do something with Rocky. He had handled Rocky well in the gym, and had a pretty good pro career going for himself. He was a big, six-foot-five, red-headed, freckle-faced Irishman."

Rocky craved revenge on Connolly for an embarrassing session in a gym near Brockton, where some of his paesanos had seen the much larger and smoother Irish boxer punch Marciano with authority while Rocky was hard-pressed to defend himself against the long reach. Marciano had KO'd Connolly in the amateurs, but still had not forgotten the sparring session.

On Thanksgiving morning the air was crisp. They stood outside Mrs. Brown's rooming house talking with Charley Goldman, who was on his way to the coffee shop for breakfast.

"I'm going to the park to do some roadwork," Rocky said. "Then I want to get some sparring in. You got anybody around?"

"Jeez, kid," Goldman said. "What are you doin' here? Ain't you got no family? How come you didn't go home for the holiday?"

"I got a fight Monday," Rocky said. "I gotta get some training in. How about it? You got anybody for me to spar with?"

"Yeah," Goldman said. "I guess I can dig a guy up. You'll have ta go ta Stillman's, though. The CYG is closed today."

"That'll be all right," Marciano said. "I'll head right over there as soon as I finish my roadwork."

The fog was still rising in gray clouds from the surface of the reservoir in Central Park as Marciano, bundled in heavy sweat shirts, ran along the shoreline with Colombo at his side. For the first time since they had begun training in New York, there were no other fighters around doing roadwork. And there were just a couple of trainers and three or four fighters working out when Marciano and Colombo arrived at Stillman's Gym.

"Get ready," Goldman ordered. "You're gonna go a couple rounds wid Gene Gosney."

Gosney was a huge and powerful heavyweight, who was training for a bout with Roland LaStarza, a stylish boxer from the Bronx, undefeated in twenty-seven pro fights. (LaStarza would knock out Gosney on December 10, 1948, in six rounds.)

"We were watching LaStarza very closely," Colombo said. "We knew that someday he and Rocky would be in together. But on this Thanksgiving Day, Gene Gosney was our problem. He was a slugger just like Rocky, and from the minute Goldman began the fight they went after each other. There were no knockdowns with the big gloves, but the few people that were in Stillman's got a real kick out of the way these fighters went at it. When the bell rang to end the second round they were still punching, and Charley Goldman and myself had to jump into the ring and break them up."

After the workout at Stillman's, Colombo and Marciano took a long walk along Broadway.

"About five clock we stopped at a little restaurant to have our Thanksgiving dinner," Colombo said. "We had big, rare steaks, salads with oil and vinegar, and bowls of turkey soup. Everybody else in the place was eating the traditional roast turkey with stuffing, mashed potatoes, cranberry sauce, hot rolls, and gravy. It looked pretty good, but I knew it wasn't for us. Rocky gained weight so easy, he couldn't eat any of that fattening stuff. And I had already made up my mind that whatever sacrifices he had to make, I was going to try to make too."

The next day they did their roadwork in Central Park and went to the CYO Gym in the afternoon. At four o'clock they boarded a train at Pennsylvania Station for Providence. Uncle Mike Piccento was waiting for them at the depot to drive them to Brockton. This became the normal Friday-night routine during the first year that Marciano was fighting in Providence.

Monday morning was gray and cold. Snow mixed with sleet pelted the windshield of Snap Tartaglia's brand-new, 1948 DeSoto sedan. Rocky had to be in Providence by two in the afternoon for the weigh-in for the fight. Otherwise Snap would not have gone out in the weather with his shiny new car. Tartaglia's brother George, the owner of George's Cafe, was sitting in front with him. In the back seat were Marciano, Colombo, and a friend, Joe Fedele.

They had just started from a traffic light and were crossing a bridge into East Providence when the car began to skid on the ice and snow.

"The car was completely out of control," Colombo said. "The next thing I knew, we smashed into the side of a truck coming the opposite way. The two front doors flew open and Tony [Snap] and his brother George disappeared."

"I was stretched out on the pavement watching the car skid crazily down the street toward the bridge abutment," Snap Tartaglia said. "It looked like it might go right over into the river."

"We had been jolted and slammed against the seats in back," Colombo said. "But now we were just hanging on, waiting for a crash. I finally realized that we had lost our driver and that there was no one in the front seat."

Colombo leaned over the seat back and grabbed the emergency brake. The car skidded on the ice, slammed into a guard rail at the side of the bridge, then struck a patch of dry pavement and jerked to a stop.

George Tartaglia was staggering down the street fifty yards behind the wrecked automobile. Colombo and Marciano ran toward him. The cafe owner was incoherent, stumbling, and babbling to himself. A thin stream of blood trickled down his forehead.

"He must have a concussion," Colombo said. "We've got to get him to a hospital."

Snap Tartaglia had rushed to his brother's side. He seemed miraculously unhurt after having been jarred from the driver's seat face-first onto the pavement. "I'm okay," Snap said. "We've got to get George to a doctor."

Within five minutes the police arrived. They drove George to the hospital in a cruiser ambulance. Colombo had been right, George had a concussion and had to be admitted.

"We're late for the weigh-in," Colombo said. "I'd better call and tell them Rocky won't be fighting tonight."

"You will like hell," Marciano said. "I'm fighting tonight."

"Are you crazy, Rock?" Colombo said. "You don't know what might've happened to you in that crash."

"I'm all right," Marciano said. "I'm not hurt. I'm warning you, Allie, don't interfere. Call Almeida and tell him we're gonna be late, but I'm all right and I'm ready to fight Connolly tonight."

When Colombo called Almeida, the promoter said, "Get some rest for Rocky and the boxing commissioner will have him examined at seven tonight at the auditorium."

The police had called for a tow truck to haul Snap's new DeSoto away. It was completely demolished.

Traffic was backed up for several hundred yards at the entrance to the bridge, and, fortunately for the Ward 2 group, one of the motorists who had stopped to look at the acci-

dent was going into Providence and offered them a lift.

"We went right to my sister Alvina's house," Snap Tartaglia said. "Rocky had a big steak and a salad and then he went into the bedroom and took a two-hour nap."

"Everybody was still shaken up over the accident," Colombo said. "I was worried. I didn't want to let Rocky fight. But it didn't seem to bother him at all. He insisted he was all right and was going ahead with the fight."

When Charley Goldman arrived at the Providence Auditorium that night, Colombo described the accident and pleaded with him to convince Rocky not to fight.

"The doctor examine ya?" Goldman asked.

"Yeah," Marciano said. "He says I'm okay."

"Then we go ahead with the fight," Goldman said.

A half-hour before the fight, Marciano took his customary warm-up in the dressing room. This time, however, he confined himself to shadowboxing. Usually Colombo would put his palms on Marciano's shoulders and try to hold him back while Rocky kept charging like a lineman on a football team. It was an unorthodox method of warming up, and it had Goldman and almost every fighter and trainer who saw it for the first time scratching their heads. But Rocky liked it, so they did it.

"Do you think he's hurt?" Colombo asked.

"Stop worrying," Snap Tartaglia said. "The Rock is fine."

Fifty-eight seconds after the bell signaling the start of the first round, big, six-foot-five, 210-pound James Patrick Connolly was stretched out flat on the canvas, a victim of Marciano's overhand right.

Rocky's Ward 2 paesanos were screaming for joy as the handlers used smelling salts to revive the red-headed Irishman from Boston. "Bring on Louis! Bring on Louis!" they chanted.

7.

Going the Distance

"HOW DO YOU LIKE NEW YORK?" Roy Cavanaugh shouted to Colombo over the roar of the truck's engine.

"Great," Colombo said. "But we're walking too much. It's seventy-five blocks each way from Mrs. Brown's to the CYO Gym."

"Why don't you take a bus?" Cavanaugh said.

"Are you kidding?" Colombo said. "Rocky won't take a bus. He'd walk if it was ten miles."

"Well, then move downtown," Cavanaugh said. "Some of the truck drivers stay at the YMCA on West Thirty-fourth Street. It's not bad. Nothing fancy. But for a buck-seventy a night, you can't go wrong."

"Eighty-five cents apiece," Rocky said, when Colombo told him about the YMCA. "That's cheaper than Mrs. Brown's. We'll go there right now."

The Sloan House, as the YMCA on West Thirty-fourth Street was known, suited their needs perfectly. It was cheap, it was close to the CYO Gym, Weill's office, and Broadway, and it had a gym Rocky could use if rain postponed his roadwork, since the CYO Gym was closed mornings. There was even free stationery for writing letters home.

"What's wrong?" Charley Goldman said, when they arrived at the CYO Gym the following afternoon. "Don't you like my joint?"

"We're at the Y on West Thirty-fourth Street," Colombo said. "It's cheaper and we like the location better."

"That's up to you," Goldman said. "Just so's you get to the gym on time. That's all I care about."

But Weill was furious. He sent word for Rocky to report to his office.

"It's none of Weill's business," Rocky said. "He's not paying any expenses. I'll stay wherever I get the best deal."

When they got to Weill's office, he said, "Since when do you move without my permission?" as he bounced up and down in his seat with anger. "Now I want you should go right back to Mrs. Brown's, where I sent you inna first place. Don't never do nothing like that without my permission. Remember, I'm the manager, and you're only the fighter. Don't you forget it. I do all the thinking."

But when Rocky explained the situation and asked Weill's permission to move, the manager softened his stance.

"All right," he said. "You've got my permission to stay at the YMCA. Now I've got important news. You're fighting in Philly ten days from now. Godoy goes against Louis in an exhibition that night. I'm expecting some important people. I want you to look very good that night."

After moving to the YMCA, Allie and Rocky had to make some adjustments in the training schedule. They were too far away from the reservoir where Rocky had been doing his roadwork, so they shifted to a playground in Central Park. As usual, Colombo threw the passes and Rocky ran after the football for one and a half to two hours without resting. They also needed a new place to eat and were lucky to find Schiavoni's Italian Restaurant on Thirty-third Street, where they became very friendly with the family; Rocky enjoyed the heaping bowls of minestrone they prepared especially for him.

"Rocky really loved the spags and pasta dishes and rich foods with spicy sauces, but he always gained weight so easily that even though he'd work out ten or twelve hours a day sometimes we knew he couldn't touch it," Colombo said. "He wanted to be around a hundred eighty-five pounds because he felt stronger and quicker at that weight, and it was a tremendous sacrifice for him just to eat rare meats and salads to keep the weight down."

He'd be up at daybreak for roadwork, then at about 9 A.M. they'd walk to a cafeteria at Columbus Circle for a poached egg, a dish of fruit, a glass of juice and a cup of tea. At noon he'd have just the bowl of soup, and for supper a steak and salad. He ate no fried foods or desserts other than fruit and drank no coffee.

After breakfast, Rocky always took a two-hour nap. Colombo was like a sentry when Rocky slept, refusing to allow anybody to awaken him. Marciano felt very strongly about the naps and claimed he was sluggish and "felt lousy" whenever he was forced to miss one.

"Just give me a couple or three minutes, I've got to catch a little nap" was one of Rocky's most common expressions.

"To the body. To the body," Goldman screamed at Marciano in the gym. "We all know ya can punch to the head. Just remember, someday you ain't gonna be able to unless you get the body first."

Balance, leverage, body punching—these were the things Goldman stressed.

A roly-poly sparring partner named Jimmy Gambino, who looked slow but had extremely fast hands, was very helpful to Rocky. He could absorb tremendous punches to the body through the layers of fat, and yet his hands were so quick that he had no problem hitting Marciano. Whenever Rocky and Gambino fought, everybody stopped training to watch them. Outside the ring, Rocky and Jimmy were the best of friends. But between the ropes they hated each other.

There was a kid named Angelo Dundee, who followed Charley Goldman around the gyms of New York. Angelo was a bachelor, hungry to learn the boxing business, and he had chosen Goldman as his teacher. Dundee worked the corners, carried the buckets, "did anything I could to learn the business."

"Every night Charley and I went out to eat at a little home-cookin' joint around Ninth Avenue and Forty-ninth Street," Dundee said. "The price was right, and we didn't have no scratch. Then one day Charley tells me, 'Ange, you gotta come look at a guy. He don't look like nothin', got two left feet, don't know nothin', but oh, can he punch.'

"We used to go to Stillman's every morning and work with the fighters there," Dundee continued. "But this afternoon, Charley takes me over to the CYO Gym to see his new kid, Rocky conies walking in about three o'clock carrying a little canvas bag, wearing an old pair of coveralls and a pair of them big, clodhopper shoes. He don't look like anything. He's too short, got them stubby arms, big, thick, football player's legs, and he ain't really big enough for a heavyweight. But then he gets in and spars a few rounds. Man, I was really impressed. I mean the guy had bad balance, but what a puncher."

"I got him punching with leverage," Goldman said. "He's the only kid I've got can dip and punch onna way up."

Dundee watched Marciano charge across the ring against the more experienced sparring partners, taking their best punches, always on the offense, never retreating.

"That great desire to win was so evident in the guy," Dundee said. "I could see it right from the beginning. And I could see the progress. Rocky came along remarkably well, because he had a great teacher. In each trainer's life there always come a greatness with one certain fighter. For Charley Goldman it was Rocky Marciano. Rocky and Charley were fortunate they had each other, because these two guys just jelled right from the start. In my opinion, Marciano was the most underrated heavyweight of all time. He had so much more than they ever gave him credit for. He was capable of getting these bigger, heavier guys and destroying them."

Following Goldman around the gym, watching Rocky develop into a champion, Dundee learned his lessons well. His own greatness with a fighter was only a dream in a business immersed in dreams. For who could predict that a young kid in Louisville named

Cassius Clay would sit by a radio and feel the shivers up his spine as the announcer said, "And still heavyweight champion of the world—Rocky Marciano," and that, years later, Dundee would take what he had learned from Goldman and others and as trainer-manager use his skills to help mold another truly great heavyweight champion, Muhammad Ali.

Jack Dempsey, the famed Manassa Mauler, strode into the CYO Gym smoking a fat cigar and looking tanned, trim, and fit. Dempsey had with him an Austrian heavyweight named Joe Weiden, and he told Goldman he wanted the fighter to work out with Marciano to see if Weiden could take a punch.

Rocky was getting dressed for his final gym session before taking his customary two-day rest in preparation for the Philadelphia fight.

As Colombo was putting the gloves and headgear on Rocky, Dempsey came to the corner and said, "Watch yourself. He's a pretty good puncher, but he's got a bad habit of keeping his chin up. If you spot it, hit him right on the button."

"Watch yourself. Rock." Colombo said. "I don't know about this guy. Don't take any chances."

Weiden was big and weighed 215. They came at each other and fought toe to toe. Then Rocky threw a left hook that ripped a gash over Weiden's right eye.

"Time," Dempsey shouted. "Come here. I want to look at that eye. I think we'd better go see a doc."

They never saw Dempsey in the gym again, but Weiden returned as soon as his eye healed and sparred many more rounds with Marciano.

With Chick Wergeles, Weill's business partner, driving and Colombo, Goldman, and Marciano in the car, they left New York early on the morning of December 14.

"A lot of big guys are gonna be here," Wergeles said. "Harry Markson [press agent for the 20th Century Sporting Club, which promoted the fights at Madison Square Garden] and a lot of other important people."

"Once they see The Rock, we'll be a cinch to get some fights in the Garden," Colombo said.

"Don't worry, Allie," Rocky said, "I'm gonna show 'em what I can do, and then we're going after the big money."

Wergeles had managed the popular world lightweight champion Beau Jack, but the fighter was retired and broke.

"What happened to Beau Jack's dough?" Rocky said. "How come he's not rich? He was the champ."

"Beau Jack blew his dough," Wergeles said. "That's why he ain't rich."

"You mean everything?" Rocky said. "He blew it all?"

"Hey, Rocky," Wergeles said, "What're ya makin' a big thing of it for? Lots of champs piss their dough away. Most of 'em do. Beau Jack made plenty with me. But he gave it away."

"Wow," Rocky said. "That's really something, Chick. What you're telling me is Beau Jack fought for nothing."

Al Weill was nervous at the weigh-in, and he was shouting orders at everyone.

"He was like a wild man," Colombo said. "I couldn't believe a guy that jumpy had already managed three world champions."

Joe Louis, the heavyweight champion of the world, came in. He was immaculately groomed, wearing an expensive overcoat and a stylish hat with a bright feather.

"Hey, Joe," Weill shouted. "Shake hands with my new heavyweight."

"What a big guy, Allie," Rocky said, when Louis had gone. "Did ya see those clothes? The hat alone must've cost fifty bucks. Imagine all the dough that guy's got."

The spectators at Convention Hall didn't realize it that night, but they were watching four fighters who would hold world championships: Louis, Marciano, Percy Bassett (featherweight champion, 1953), and Harold Johnson (light-heavyweight champion, 1961).

Rocky had taken his afternoon nap, but his practice of resting on the table in the dressing room before a fight was completely disrupted by the nervous Weill.

"Remember, go to the body," Weill said. "Louis said this guy's a smart cookie. You've got to box this guy. I've got a lot of important people here tonight. I want you to look good."

Weill was so nervous that Rocky, who was usually very calm before a fight, began to get excited. He was thinking more about his manager than the opponent.

The fight had barely begun when both Weill and Goldman were shouting at Rocky from the corner.

Marciano was charging Gilley Ferron, a huge heavyweight, who towered over Rocky and outweighed him by 20 pounds. Rocky wasn't boxing; he was throwing punches one after another. He was aiming strictly for the head, and some of his roundhouse rights missed Ferron completely and sent Rocky off-balance and stumbling.

Ferron, who had sparred with Louis, was a heavy puncher too, but he also applied some science to his attack.

"No! No!" Weill screamed. "To the body. To the body. What's he trying to do? Rocky!

Rocky! Listen to me. Go to the body."

But Rocky didn't need the advice. In the middle of the second round, he was landing vicious shots to Ferron's head. The fighter was reeling, unable to defend against the assault, and the referee stopped the bout

"You looked like an amateur," Weill said in the dressing room. "You didn't do nothing I told you to do."

"As long as you take them out of there, don't worry about how you look, Rock," Colombo said when Weill was off getting Godoy ready for Louis. "It's a lot better to look bad winning than to look good losing."

"What the hell does that guy want?" Rocky said. "I won, didn't I?"

Colombo began cutting off the bandages.

"Hey," Rocky said, flinching. "Watch out for the hand."

One of Rocky's wild punches had missed and the top of his right hand had landed full force on Ferron's skull. The instant the bandages came off, the hand began to swell.

"We'd better have a doctor look at it," Colombo said.

"It'll be all right," Rocky said. "I want to watch Louis fight."

Colombo filled a towel with ice and wrapped it around Rocky's hand, and they watched the final two rounds of the Louis-Codoy exhibition from the wings of the stage.

"He's a helluva fighter, Allie," Rocky said. "The guy's a real champion."

Al Weill was not in good humor when Rocky and Colombo arrived at his office the next morning. Before the Ferron fight, the cocky little silvery-haired manager had been bragging to the New York fight crowd that they were about to see "the next champeen of the world."

"Are you kidding?" they said after Rocky's brawling exhibition. "That kid trips over his own feet. He's nothing."

Now Rocky stood before him with a swollen hand that was obviously more than just bruised.

"Get over to the University Hospital and see Dr. Ritter," Weill ordered. "Don't do nothing else until he looks at the hand."

"It's a bad break," the doctor said after examining Rocky's X-rays.

"When can I fight again?" Rocky said.

"You'll have to lay off fighting for at least two or three months," Dr. Ritter said.

"Jesus, can you believe these hands?" Rocky said disgustedly as they left the hospital.

"Don't worry, Rock. It'll be all right," Colombo said. But already Colombo's brain was spinning and clouding with doubt. He'd read everything there was about fighters. And he knew that "fragile hands" had ruined some very promising ones.

"Forget it, Allie," Rocky said, when they were walking toward the YMCA. "I must have caught that guy wrong with the punch. I'm not letting this stop me. We'll keep right on training."

"Yeah, Rock," Colombo said. "We'd be crazy to quit training, even for a week. We're too close to the big time now."

But there was a cast on Rocky's hand when they caught the train out of Pennsylvania Station for Providence, and as they headed home to Brockton for the holidays, Colombo was thinking, It wasn't a very good Christmas present, but it was a challenge we had to accept and overcome if The Rock was going to become a champion.

No matter how cold it was, they walked from five to ten miles every morning that winter. In the afternoons they held long boxing sessions in Rocky's backyard on Dover Street. Colombo and Sonny Marciano spent hours dodging Rocky's left hooks and jabs as he chased them around the makeshift ring. They could not punch back since it would risk damaging Rocky's injured right hand.

There were some swirling blizzards between December 1948 and February 1949, and the snows were deep in the playground and along D. W. Field Park, but they did the roadwork faithfully.

"We left the house at eight every morning, even when it was snowing so hard you couldn't see the road," Colombo said. "And in the afternoons we shoveled out the yard and boxed. The Rock was keeping in top condition."

Pasqualena Marchegiano had renewed her efforts to get Rocky to stop boxing. "See, you hurt yourself and you hurt somebody else," she said. "You don't make much money. It's crazy this boxing. Now tell me you're gonna quit."

And whenever fifteen-year-old Sonny put on the gloves to spar with Rocky, Pasqualena became furious. "Oh, no. Oh, no," she shouted. "You get in the house right now, Sonny. You're no gonna fight. One fighter is bad enough. You want me to get sick? Then just keep it up. It's not bad enough my son breaks his hand, now you want my Sonny to fight, and he's just a baby."

Mike Piccento was a most unpopular brother then. "See," Pasqualena said. "Sonamanbeetch. What I tell you? You happy now? My Rocky's got a broken hand. Sonamanbeetch you! Get outta my house."

"I'd just pick up my hat and kind of ease out of there," Piccento said. "It was no time

for reason. What the hell, I figured, if a brother and sister can't argue once in a while, who can?"

In February, the cast was removed from Rocky's hand, and the doctor said, "That place is stronger than the rest of the hand now, and if you break it again it probably won't be there."

"I want a fight as soon as possible," Rocky told Weill.

"Go back to Brockton," Weill said, "I don't want you to use the hand yet. Better to play it safe. Give it a couple more weeks."

"Safe?" Rocky said. "Lissen, Al. I need the dough. I can't afford to be loafing. I want some fights."

"Go to Brockton and do roadwork," Weill ordered. "Don't even use the hand to blow your nose. Remember, I'm the manager and you're only the fighter. I know what's best. Just stick with what I say, and you won't be sorry."

"What's the matter with him?" Rocky said as he walked with Colombo along Broadway. "He isn't paying us any expenses. For Chrissake, I need some fights."

"You have to respect Weill's judgment, Rock," Colombo said. "The guy's managed three champions. He must know what he's doing."

"Yeah," Rocky said. "You're right, Allie. We'll do it his way."

It was almost a month later when Weill finally said, "Go to the gym and see Goldman. Don't do nothing unless Goldman tells you. Don't aggravate that hand. Your next fight is in two weeks. It's a ten-rounder, so train to go the distance."

Goldman carefully tested Rocky's mended hand by having him throw hundreds of punches of gradually increasing power into the heavy bag. When he was satisfied, the flat-nosed little trainer returned Marciano to his sparring sessions. For the next two weeks Rocky sparred six rounds a day with Weiden, Gambino, and Harry Bernstein.

"You throw an awful lot of punches, kid," Goldman said. "Maybe you'll have to pace yourself. You could get plenty tired in a ten-rounder."

"Don't worry about that," Marciano told him. "I'm in better condition than any of them. I can go as many rounds as I have to go."

"OH, LOOK AT HIM! Oh, look at him!" Al Weill giggled hysterically. "He's a sucker. He's ready to go!"

Marciano was battering the veteran Johnny Pretzie all over the ring in the third round of their scheduled ten-rounder at Providence. He was hitting the journeyman heavyweight almost at will, but strangely, Pretzie remained on his feet

"It was the third time that Weill was in our corner, and once again he raised havoc with things," Colombo said. "Two or three times I thought Pretzie was finished. Then Weill would start his screaming, ridiculing the guy, and somehow Pretzie would come back with a flurry."

Pretzie, a converted southpaw with plenty of power in his left hand, was at the tail end of his career.

When he came back to the corner after the third round, Pretzie said, "Jackie, I'm tired," according to Jackie Martin, who was Pretzie's manager at the time.

"You can't quit, we won't get our money," said Martin, who was one of a number of Bostonians who, it has been claimed, could have managed Marciano for a price but refused.

In the fifth round, the referee stopped the one-sided slaughter, with Pretzie swaying helplessly as Marciano battered him.

In the dressing room, Colombo was concerned that Rocky may have been holding back on Pretzie, still favoring the right hand. Since the fight had been so one-sided, he decided against discussing the possibility with his pal.

"I had a lump in my throat when I cut the bandages off, though," Colombo said. "Then Rocky flexed the hand and grinned."

"It feels great," Marciano beamed, obviously very pleased. He had another KO, a $250 payday, and was unmarked. After three months of inactivity and frustration, it was a satisfying way to return to the ring.

THE FOLLOWING MONDAY NIGHT Rocky ended all apprehension about whether the broken hand had healed properly when he flattened Art Donato, of Red Bank, New Jersey, in 33 seconds. At the bell beginning Round One, Donato rushed across the ring and began punching furiously. Rocky crouched, threw his favorite overhand right, landed it flush on Donato's chin, and the fight was over. The Rock had thrown just one punch, and he wasn't even sweating when he left the ring.

Ironically, it was not Marciano's brittle hands but his ailing back that eventually posed the most serious threat to his chances for success as a fighter.

It was the first week in April, and they were getting ready at 7 A.M. for roadwork in Central Park when Colombo noticed Rocky was having trouble bending over to tie his shoelaces.

"What's the matter. Rock?" Colombo said. "You catch a cold or something? Maybe we should skip the roadwork today."

"It'll be all right," Rocky said. "It's been stiff in the morning lately, but as soon as I begin working out and start sweating it's okay again."

"Maybe you pulled a muscle," Colombo said. "You could aggravate it in the gym."

"Stop worrying," Rocky said. "It's nothing."

But when Marciano started chasing Colombo's football passes that morning he limped and ran very slowly. Within five minutes, though, he was running as fast as ever and the stiffness was not noticeable. He even ended the session with his customary series of hundred-yard dashes.

"I don't want you telling Weill or Goldman about this," Rocky said. "All I need is them telling me I can't fight again."

But a worried and nervous Colombo couldn't resist taking Goldman aside and asking him about the stiff back.

"You've got to see a doc," Goldman said. "I don't want you to do any more training until that back's checked out."

"Chrissake," Rocky said, as they followed Goldman's orders to go to an osteopath in upper Manhattan. "Now look what's happening. They'd better let me fight. That's all."

The osteopath took X-rays and gave Rocky leg exercises to do, and he showed Colombo how to pull Rocky's legs to relieve the tightness in his back.

After that, Colombo tugged on Rocky's legs every morning before he got out of bed and again in the dressing room at the gym before his workouts.

But both Goldman and Colombo were worried that Rocky had lost some of his mobility in his sparring sessions. Marciano kept insisting he was fine, so another fight was

scheduled for Providence. At the weigh-in they met a friend, Dr. Vincent Oddo, Jr., a Providence dentist who had just invented the double-hinged mouthpiece that became very popular among fighters and football players. Oddo suggested that Rocky be examined by his father, a prominent surgeon.

Dr. Oddo, Sr., diagnosed the problem as a pinched nerve and said the condition would take about two years to correct itself. He recommended that Rocky continue to exercise and fight, because the condition might get worse if he failed to remain active.

"The diagnosis was correct, but further complications came along later when Rocky seriously injured the back again," Colombo recalled. "From the way it crippled him sometimes, I knew The Rock must be going through hell. The trouble was, I could never really tell how bad it was, because The Rock would never complain."

But that night, April 11, 1949, there didn't seem to be much wrong with Marciano's back.

"That's it," Goldman shouted when Rocky fired the overhand right at James Walls, of Englewood, New Jersey. "Suzie Q. The fight's over."

Goldman had stopped trying to analyze Marciano's unorthodox right. He knew it was nowhere to be found in the fighter's manual, but with that rare skill possessed by a few trainers he instinctively knew that the punch was good for Rocky and he never discouraged the fighter from using it.

"What the hell is that, Charley?" the trainers in New York often asked.

"It's the secret weapon," Goldman chuckled. " 'Suzie Q,' I call it. Now don't ask me to teach it to your guys. It's a natural punch, and you either got it or you ain't."

Until Marciano began fighting main bouts, Weill had not taken a cut from any of the fighter's purses. But after his ninth or tenth straight knockout, Weill finally decided to have him sign a contract, the details of which were not made public. Whenever he could not personally attend one of Rocky's fights, he sent Chick Wergeles or his stepson Marty Weill to collect the money.

"It's like he doesn't even trust Goldman with the dough," Rocky said. "The guy really treats Charley like a dog. I don't know how he takes it sometimes."

"Charley's happy," Colombo said. "As long as he's got good fighters and a place to train them, Goldman will always be happy."

Mike Piccento said Rocky indicated to him that Weill and Marciano each gave Colombo 5 percent and took 45 percent each for themselves. Weill had not wanted to give Colombo anything, but Marciano insisted, Piccento said.

"Later, when the big-money fights started coming, Colombo went on a flat rate at Weill's insistence," Piccento said. "They paid Allie a salary just like Goldman had always been paid. I think Goldman and Colombo got ten thousand dollars apiece for each championship fight."

Persons close to Marciano said, however, that the actual written contract called for Weill and Rocky to receive 50 percent each. Colombo and Goldman were not on the contract and could be dropped at any time, even though it was inconceivable that Rocky would allow that to happen to Colombo.

ROCKY'S BACK CONDITION kept worsening, and finally the exercises and leg-pulling routine no longer seemed to help. It was taking him half the morning to get fully loosened up, and after his noon nap the back would he stiff again.

"After a while we decided Rocky should stop taking the naps even though he felt sluggish without them," Colombo said. "We started going for long walks during the time when Rocky would otherwise be napping."

They were walking along Broadway one day when Colombo spotted Willie Pep coming out of a hotel with a showgirl on his arm and wearing an expensive suit and shiny black shoes. A champion who had won 137 fights, with only 2 losses and 1 draw, he had just won the featherweight title back from Sandy Saddler.

Rocky watched Pep with great admiration. Here was a true paesano, William Papaleo. A great champion and a *spaccone*, with plenty of class and style.

"Let's follow them," Rocky said.

"Yeah," Colombo said. "But don't let them spot us."

"Don't worry," Rocky said. "Besides, Willie wouldn't know us from a hole in the ground."

Dressed in faded khakis and Ward 2 baseball jackets, Marciano and Colombo followed Pep and the beautiful girl along Broadway.

Everyone Pep passed smiled and said something like, "Hi, Champ. Great fight."

Willie stopped at a florist's, bought a corsage, and pinned it on his date, kissing her on the forehead.

"Imagine that," Rocky said. "What a classy guy, huh, Allie?"

A few minutes later Pep and the showgirl ducked into a theater that featured reruns of Humphrey Bogart films, a perennial favorite of Willie's.

"Did you see that broad, Allie?" Rocky said. "And how about the way everyone kept calling him 'Champ'? Wasn't it beautiful?"

Two weeks after Rocky KO'd Jimmy Evans in the third round at Providence for his fifteenth straight knockout victory, Weill ordered him to report to the New York State boxing commissioner's office. There Weill's fighters, including Marciano, Godoy, Buddy Holderfield, and Jerry Mekler, were given releases from their contracts with the stocky manager.

"I'm taking over as matchmaker at the Garden," Weill explained. "I'm turning your contracts over to Marty [Weill's stepson]. If anything happens to the job, I'll be returning as your manager."

HARRY MARKSON OF THE INTERNATIONAL BOXING CLUB had stumped to get the matchmaker's job for Weill. The job paid less than two hundred dollars a week, but Weill enjoyed the security and prestige. Meanwhile, as matchmaker, he could no longer actively manage a fighter, according to boxing commission regulations. Weill had no intention of getting rid of Rocky or his other fighters, but he had to transfer them on paper to make things legal. He was always the real manager behind the scenes.

"This is beautiful. Rock," Colombo said, "With Weill calling the shots, how can we miss fighting at the Garden?"

"We're finally gonna start making some of that big money," Rocky said. "It's all beginning to fall our way."

MARCIANO SAT DEJECTEDLY in the dressing room. For the first time in his professional career the letters KO would not appear beside

his name in the record book. Don Mogard, a journeyman heavyweight who could box well but was a weak puncher, had withstood Rocky's battering fists and forced the Brockton Blockbuster to go the ten-round distance. The unanimous decision did little to soothe Rocky's wounded pride.

"It done you good, Rocky," Sam Silverman said. "Every good fighter has to go ten rounds sometime."

"I should have had him, Allie," Rocky kept saying, "I really thought I was going to get the guy."

"Aw, don't be so downhearted," Colombo said. "You won, Rock. That's what counts. You showed them you could go ten and win the decision."

"I should have knocked him out," Rocky insisted.

"Okay, have it your way," Colombo said. "I still say it was a helluva fight, and you got plenty of experience. Now, how about getting something to eat?"

Rocky grinned for the first time. "Yeah," he said. "I guess I am a little hungry."

ROCKY'S FAMILY PHYSICIAN in Brockton tried treating his sore back with a series of shots and heat therapy, but nothing seemed to be helping and the stiffness continued to get worse.

"Maybe you should lay off for a while," Colombo suggested. "Maybe you need a long rest."

"That's ridiculous," Rocky said. "The doctor said I should keep active. Besides, I want another fight right away."

Rocky craved another KO after being held to a decision by Mogard. He got it by decking a hapless New York heavyweight named Harry Haft in the third round. But there were only 1,655 fans at Providence Auditorium, the smallest crowd Rocky had drawn in a dozen fights, and his back was hurting very badly that night.

On August 16, Silverman took Marciano out of Providence to fight a main bout in New Bedford.

"That was one of the worst days Rocky ever had with his back," Colombo said. "Our friend Johnny Jantomaso drove us from Brockton for the weigh-in at two. The Rock was so stiff and sore he had to keep walking all day. We kept trying to convince him to call off the fight, but he insisted he wanted it."

Weill had sent Jack "Doc" Moore as a substitute for Goldman, who was on the West Coast with Arturo Godoy. Moore, a sixtyish promoter and trainer, took one look at Marciano and agreed with Colombo and Jantomaso that he should not fight.

At the Page Arena, Rocky could not lie down on the table to take his customary rest before the fight.

"This is bad," Colombo said. "The Rock always rests before a fight."

"Hey, Alsack. Come on, let's go for a walk," Rocky said. "Maybe it'll loosen up."

"Call the fight off," Colombo said as they walked the streets of New Bedford. "It's foolish to risk it."

"I'm not calling off any fight," Rocky insisted. "What's it gonna be, a couple of rounds with this guy? The back's gonna be fine."

Rocky's opponent, Pete Louthis, an experienced heavyweight from Cumberland, Rhode Island, was aware of Marciano's record and popularity with the fans and knew that a win against the Brockton fighter could put him in a position to command some well-paying fights in Providence.

Marciano could barely get through the ropes to enter the ring, even with Colombo bending the lower strand almost to the canvas and stretching the middle rope as high as possible.

When the bell rang, Rocky came out very slowly. But Louthis also was cautious. There was very little action.

"Toward the end of the first round. Rocky bent down to get under a punch," Silverman recalled. "The round ended, and Marciano walked back to his corner like the hunchback of Notre Dame. The next round Rocky came out low, all crouched down. I thought he was trying to get smart. If he kept it up, Marciano was ready to be taken."

The crowd was booing. Rocky wasn't throwing the punches he usually did, but Louthis failed to take advantage of the situation. It was a dull fight.

Between rounds, Rocky stood hunched in his corner. He removed his mouthpiece, and his teeth were clenched from pain.

"You can't fight like this. Rock," Colombo said. "What're we gonna do?"

"I'm all right, Allie," Rocky said. "Don't worry."

"The next round, Rocky came out real low," Silverman said. "But Louthis did a choke. He was backing away. He was petrified of Marciano because he came from Rhode Island and he had seen Rocky's knockout fights in Providence."

Marciano hit Louthis with a left hook to the jaw that crumpled him to the canvas. It was Rocky's first good punch of the fight, and it gave him his eighteenth KO in nineteen fights.

"What're you trying to do, become a cutie?" Silverman asked him in the dressing room. "How come you was missing your shots and getting down so low? You're gonna stink joints out like that."

"I hurt my back," Rocky said. "I don't know how it happened."

"For Chrissake," Silverman said. "That's too bad, kid. But you shouldn't be fighting like that. Get it taken care of right away."

"We've got to see a specialist in Boston," Colombo argued as they drove back to Brockton that night. "We can't take any more chances."

"Aw, for Chrissake," Rocky said. "It's just a pinched nerve or something. It'll work itself out. Haven't we already been to enough doctors? You know how much a specialist costs?"

"Promise me. Rock," Colombo said. "I won't stop worrying until we find out."

"All right," Rocky said. "If you're that worried, we'll go."

"You've got a slipped disc," Dr. Thomas B. Quigley informed Rocky after examining a series of X-rays. "It'll require an operation."

"How long would I be laid up?" Rocky said.

"What do you do for a living?" the doctor said.

"I'm a fighter."

"Well, I'm sorry, but you'll be out for at least a year, and it's very likely you'll never be able to fight again," the doctor said.

"That's it then," Rocky told Colombo when he had limped out of the doctor's office. "I'm just gonna keep on fighting, and we're gonna forget about the back."

"The Rock wasn't going to let anything stand in the way," Colombo recalled. "But I could tell it was a real bombshell. On the way home in the car we hardly spoke. I kept thinking, what will Rocky do if the back suddenly goes in the ring and he can't move when some big, tough heavyweight is coming after him? We had to do something to fix the back. But I knew The Rock would never let any doctor operate on him now unless it got so bad he was

completely crippled."

Rocky could put the pain out of his mind, but it was the loss of mobility that bothered him more than anything. He went faithfully to the chiropractor and had Al Norling at the YMCA massage his back. Colombo continued the leg-pulling to relieve pressure, and Rocky halted all exercises that involved lifting or placed heavy strain on his back.

Five weeks later, when Rocky knocked out Tommy DiGiorgio of Schenectady in the fourth round, the stiffness in his back was barely noticeable.

Two weeks later, Sam Silverman brought in Tiger Ted Lowry, a tough, ringwise heavyweight from New Bedford, to face Marciano. Lowry had a record of 56 wins and 45 losses, but he was usually involved in close fights and almost never got knocked out. He had fought to a draw in 1947 with Lee Savold, a respected heavyweight contender, and had been decisioned by Archie Moore in 1948.

"I thought Lowry was gonna lick Rocky," Silverman said. "I was disgusted with Al Weill, and wouldn't have minded getting rid of him. Weill wanted too much money. He was getting twenty-five percent of the gate, but the greedy guy wanted thirty. And Weill was looking to get Rocky soft fights now that he thought he had found something in Marciano. But I had to protect my club. Rocky's fights were all legitimate, good, hard fights. A lot of people were talking about how he was being fed setups. Marciano could have lost any number of times in his early fights."

Lowry was a defensive fighter; he didn't throw many hard punches but seldom took any. Rocky kept battering Tiger to the body, trying to bring his defenses down, but he knew how to take the punches and held on for the ten-round distance.

"It was good experience," Colombo told a

disconsolate Rocky in the dressing room, "You won the decision easy. You just can't expect to knock everybody out. Nobody knocks everybody out."

"I should have had him," Rocky kept saying, and he was almost as disgusted as if he had lost the fight.

"You know that dago looks like another Johnny Risko," Silverman told trainer Al Lacey as they were driving back to Boston, "He's a tough son of a bitch. He's gonna beat a lot of good fighters. The kid gave Lowry a bad body beating."

Lacey laughed. "Are you kidding?" he said. "He'll never be a fighter."

"Why, because he ain't a fan dancer or somethin'?" Silverman said.

"No, because his ankles are too thick," Lacey chuckled.

"I never knew what Lacey meant by that remark," Silverman said.

MIDDLEWEIGHT CHAMPION MARCEL CERDAN often watched Rocky box at the CYO Gym.

"Tony. He don't know how to fight, but his heart, she's so big, she does not believe in defeat," Cerdan told Colombo. "He'll fight anybody, and he bleed and bleed and bleed, but always he comes back."

Cerdan, who called all Italians "Tony," had no idea who Marciano was, and he did not live to see Rocky become a champion. Cerdan himself was killed in a plane crash in the Azores in October 1949, en route from France to New York for a chance to reclaim the championship he had lost to Jake LaMotta.

AFTER AN EASY KO VICTORY over Joe Dominick in Providence, Rocky's undercover manager Weill finally booked him for a fight in Madison Square Garden.

But Charley Goldman devoted very little time to preparing Marciano for his Garden debut. The tiny trainer was busy with Cesar Brion, who was scheduled for the main event against Roland LaStarza, a flashy, undefeated heavyweight from the Bronx, who with thirty-six straight victories was already being touted around New York as the new White Hope to take the title from Ezzard Charles. Goldman knew that an impressive win over LaStarza would catapult Brion to stardom as a ranked contender for the heavyweight championship.

"Brion shouldn't be fighting LaStarza," Rocky said as Colombo was massaging his back in the room at the YMCA. "I should, I can beat them both."

"Sure, Rock," Colombo said, "It's ridiculous. But we've got to be patient. At least Weill got us into the Garden."

"In the semi-final, listed for eight rounds, a heavyweight with a remarkable knockout record will make his New York debut," a story in the New York Times said on December 2, 1949. "He is Rocky Marciano of Brockton, Mass. Marciano with a record of twenty-three knockout victories will see action against Pat Richards, former Ohio State athlete." The figures on Rocky's record were incorrect in the story, since Marciano actually had 20 KOs and 2 decisions at that point in his career.

Irish Pat Richards was a handsome, inexperienced heavyweight who had neither the toughness, determination, nor ability to challenge Rocky Marciano. From the opening bell, Marciano battered his opponent. When the referee stopped the slaughter shortly after the beginning of the second round, Richards was pushed through the ropes, a look of bewilderment on his face as he sat, head bowed, his gloves pulled together above his knees as if he were praying.

"He didn't even look like a fighter," Sam Silverman said, "Weill wasn't doing Marciano no good by putting him in with a guy like Richards."

The next morning Colombo rushed to the newsstand. The *New York Times* banner headline ran eight columns across the top of the sports page: UNBEATEN LASTARZA OUTPOINTS BRION AT GARDEN FOR 37TH STRAIGHT TRIUMPH. Beneath the headline was a picture of Brion and LaStarza in action and a long story describing a dull fight. At the end of the story was a single sentence, "Rocky Marciano, 181, Brockton, Mass., knocked out Pat Richards, 187, Columbus, Ohio, in 0:39 of the second round in the scheduled eight-round semifinal."

"What the hell do they want, Rock?" Colombo said dejectedly. "You could have beaten any fighter in the Garden last night"

"Don't worry, Allie," Rocky said. "It won't be long before I'm fighting the main bouts, and then I'll get all the headlines."

8.

The Gladiators

On the night before New Year's Eve, two proud and confident young Italians prepared to do battle in Madison Square Garden.

Eleven days earlier Rocky Marciano had demolished Phil Muscato, scoring a fifth-round knockout in a scheduled ten-rounder at Providence Auditorium. Rocky was in peak condition and his back was feeling fine. By now championship fever was rampant in Brockton, and many of Rocky's Ward 2 paesanos had made the trip to New York.

Carmine Vingo was the hero of his depressed Italian neighborhood in the vicinity of 152nd Street in the Bronx. "Bingo," as he was called by his paesanos, was a fearless fighter who had just turned twenty a day before the scheduled bout with Marciano. He was planning to get married in February, and was looking forward to the victory and the big purse from the ten-rounder at the Garden.

Carmine had known poverty in his youth and had walked the streets of New York without a dollar in his pockets. He had a beautiful girlfriend, Kitty Rea, and boxing was a way to give them "a little better chance in life." For, unlike Rocky, Carmine had "never believed I was good enough to become a champion."

Vingo knew nothing of Marciano and didn't even consider possible dangers in facing him.

"Half the guys I fought, I don't recall their names," Vingo said. "When I got inna ring, as long as the other guy had two arms and two legs I didn't care who he was. When I went into the ring against Rocky that night, the only thing on my mind was that I hoped I had enough in me to go the limit if the fight had to go that far. I wanted to put on a good show, like I always wanted to do. I figured the most that can happen is you knock the guy out or the guy knocks you out, but I never considered it could be anything more than that."

Vingo had been fighting since he was seventeen and had won all but three of thirty fights, half of them by KOs. He was six-foot-four and 187 pounds, and he had a much longer reach than Marciano.

Trainer Whitey Bimstein had worked with Vingo at Stillman's Gym, trying to impress upon him the importance of the fight and warning him that Marciano had power in both hands and usually overwhelmed his opponents, but that he was vulnerable to a good boxer who moved in and out fast.

Meanwhile, at the CYO Gym, Goldman

was saying, "Vingo's young and tough and the kid can punch. But he fights flat-footed, and stands up straight. If he don't make no changes, he'll be all right for Rocky,"

Matchmaker Al Weill had scheduled three ten-round bouts for the Garden. Strangely, Marciano was not the feature attraction. Even the newspaper columnists questioned Weill's choice of light heavyweights Dick Wagner and Nick Barone as a feature over ten-rounders between Marciano and Vingo and Lee Sala and Ruben Jones.

"The magnets on the card are Sala and Marciano, each of whom has performed favorably in this city in the past," a story in the *New York Times* said.

Excitement rippled through the little Italian neighborhood in the Bronx. To his friends, Vingo was every bit as dynamic as Rocky was in Brockton's Ward 2. They had bet heavily on the fight, and even Carmine himself had sent a hundred dollars with his cousin to bet on himself. Kitty Rea had baked a cake for her fiancé and placed it on the table. They were planning a combination victory and birthday celebration.

Forty-five minutes before the fight Colombo awakened Rocky, who had been resting on the dressing room table. Rocky shadowboxed. Then Colombo placed his palms on the fighter's shoulders while Rocky bulled forward like a football player to get his blood flowing and warm his muscles. He weighed 180¾, a few pounds lighter than his average fighting weight, but he was trained to a razor's edge.

From the opening bell Vingo and Marciano were upon each other in a steady rain of punches. Then Marciano sent Vingo crashing to the canvas with a left hook that echoed off his jaw.

Vingo blinked and shook his head and finally heard the referee's growl cut through the roar of the crowd. He came up at the count of nine and snorted like a wounded boar. Who could say what went on in the caverns of his spinning brain? Vingo himself could never recall. There was no retreat to the sanctuary of fear. No caution or boxing sense was applied. For, driven by his own animal instincts to survive, Vingo charged forward, carrying the attack to Marciano.

It was Rocky's own game, and he loved it. They stood toe to toe, and Marciano's punches thumped on Vingo's skull. Then Carmine's right crunched against Rocky's chin and shook the Brockton Blockbuster all the way to his ankles. Marciano raged back. They were like Roman gladiators, and the carnage was more than the crowd had ever dared to hope for.

They came out punching in the second round and stood in the center of the ring, exchanging whirlwind volleys of brutal punches. Marciano's tongue protruded between his teeth in anger. He was hitting Vingo with punches that shook the Bronx battler. But Carmine effectively blocked the overhand right with his long left arm and countered with powerful rights. The "Suzie Q" that so often ended a fight did not land solidly.

Then Rocky whipped a left hook to the jaw that floored the stunned Vingo. Again Carmine got up at the count of nine. Again, instead of being cautious, he rushed to the attack. And almost immediately Vingo crashed a right to the jaw that staggered Marciano. The Garden erupted in pandemonium.

James P. Dawson summed up the next few rounds in the *New York Times* the following morning: "torrid slugging during the third, fourth and fifth rounds, until it seemed human endurance could stand no more; one or the other must drop from the combination of punches and exhaustion."

In the fifth round, Vingo staggered Rocky with a savage right that sent him stumbling half a dozen steps backward. But Carmine made no attempt to follow it up; instead he stood flat-footed in the center of the ring, too weary, battered, and beaten to take advantage of the windfall. His glassy eyes searched blankly for Marciano. And an instant later Rocky came roaring after him.

In the sixth, Marciano mauled Vingo like a lion torturing its prey. Vingo was finished. Manager Jackie Levine said he would have thrown in the towel but for a New York Boxing Commission rule that forbade it. The referee could have stopped the fight but did not. Vingo had been too valiant, game, and determined. He would go down fighting.

Vingo's heart slammed against his ribs. Blood ran in dark rivers from his mashed-in nostrils. He blinked repeatedly and held his arms too low.

A short left hook sprawled Vingo over backward, and the back of his head thudded on the canvas. He came up to his elbows, trying to rise—the heart willing, but the body unable to respond to its command. His face was masked in blood, his eye and nose gushing.

The referee counted to three, waved his arms, and signaled the end of the fight.

Dr. Vincent Nardiello rushed to Vingo's side. By now he was ashen and unconscious. The crowd fell silent. Marciano had already left the ring.

Reverend Paul Gallivan of Boston gave Vingo conditional absolution while Nardiello called for an ambulance. But there were none available, so Vingo was wrapped in the blankets, robes, and overcoats of his friends and handlers and carried on foot through the cold December night the two blocks to Saint Clare's Hospital.

In the dressing room, Rocky was happy and excited as he greeted reporters. It had been his toughest fight, but he was unhurt, and the record book would read KO-6.

"Rocky, you'd better get over to the hospital," a reporter said. "They say Vingo isn't in very good shape."

Marciano was stunned. It was the first he knew of Vingo's serious injury.

Carmine's father, Michael, brother Jimmy, and sister Stella were already at the hospital when Rocky arrived. They had been at the fight. Their eyes clouded with tears, but nobody blamed Rocky.

"We know it's not your fault," Jimmy Vingo said. "I used to fight. It's something that can happen to any fighter."

The Catholic chaplain had given Carmine the last rites of the church. Vingo was in a coma, and would lapse in and out of consciousness for the next several days.

"How is he?" Rocky asked when he saw Dr. Nardiello coming from Vingo's room.

"He's under intensive care," Nardiello said. "He's critical. Got a fifty-fifty chance of making it. I'm sorry, but everything that can be done is being done."

Vingo's mother was sitting in a chair in the waiting room, sobbing.

"I'm sorry," Rocky said.

Mrs. Vingo did not answer him. Then Carmine's brother came over and began talking to Rocky.

Allie Colombo paced the floor outside the waiting room. Colombo could not hold back his emotions the way Rocky could. He could not mask his apprehensiveness.

"Everything's gonna be all right," Colombo kept telling Vingo's family and friends. "It's got to be."

Charley Goldman stood quietly, holding his derby and puffing on a cigar. Charley had seen tragedy and near tragedy in the ring. He saw it as an unfortunate but ever-present hazard that loomed darkly over the violent business. Surely Goldman recalled the fight in which Al Weill's lightweight Lou Ambers KO'd Tony Scarpati just six months before Ambers won the title from Canzoneri. Scarpati died from injuries received in that fight. For a boxer there is always that risk.

Beyond his concern for Vingo, Goldman was worried about Marciano. Charley had seen fighters ruined by the psychological impact of causing serious permanent injury or death to an opponent. He had seen them pull their punches, losing the killer instinct.

"You didn't hurt him, the ring did," Goldman said. "The kid hit his head. It might have happened no matter who knocked him out."

"I know that," Rocky said. "Don't worry. I'll be all right. Let's just think about Vingo now."

"Yeah, kid," Goldman said. "You will."

"There's no change," Nardiello said, at about 1 A.M. "Why don't you go back to the hotel, Rocky? There's nothing you can do here."

Nardiello informed reporters that Vingo's X-rays showed a brain contusion, a slash or tear on the surface of the brain.

"It's much more serious than a concussion," he said. "But we're still hoping he'll pull through."

In his room at the Belmont Plaza, Rocky spent a restless night discussing the fight and Vingo's injury with his family and friends. There was a great deal of sadness, yet there was also optimism. Vingo's injury had dulled their enthusiasm over Rocky's victory, but everyone knew it meant that Marciano would emerge as a heavyweight the public craved to watch. For when a fighter destroys an opponent the way Rocky destroyed Vingo, the fight

crowd becomes a vampire, lusting after the taste of blood.

The sun was creeping up between the buildings as Allie and Rocky went out of the hotel for a walk. They had not been to bed, and Rocky's back was stiff because he had gone to the hospital still sweaty. Clouds were beginning to grow larger and turn gray, promising rain or snow before Times Square began to bristle with the frenzy of a New Year's celebration. They walked like zombies, impervious to the world around them, halfway between the agony of Vingo's tragedy and the glory of a great triumph. Colombo stopped at a newsstand and bought all the New York papers.

The eight-column headline on the *New York Times* sports page read: BRONX BOXER PLACED ON CRITICAL LIST IN HOSPITAL AFTER KNOCKOUT AT GARDEN. The subhead read: Vingo Collapses in Marciano Bout. There was a picture of a lean Marciano with Vingo crumpling before him.

The lead of James P. Dawson's story said, "The heavy hand of near tragedy hung over the boxing last night in Madison Square Garden . . . Vingo's collapse ended a hurricane battle that overshadowed the feature bout in which Nick Barone, light heavyweight, decisioned Dick Wagner in 10 rounds.

"They fought at a pace which would have done credit to lightweights, in a slam-bang, knockdown and drag-out battle that provided the best heavyweight action seen here since the rise of Joe Louis."

Before they returned to the hospital, Rocky and Allie visited Mike Piccento at the Times Square Hotel.

"These things happen in the fight game," Piccento said. "It's too bad. But you can't be soft, you can't worry about an opponent. Remember, he's in there to destroy you. It's either you or him. When you start worrying about what happens to an opponent, you might as well get out of the boxing business."

"He could have done this to me, Mike," Rocky said. "I could have been in his shoes. Don't worry. I'm going for the title, and nothing's going to stand in my way."

At Saint Clare's Hospital, Dr. Nardiello was grim and bleary-eyed. He had remained at Vingo's side through the night

"Rock, we've got good hope," the doctor said.

"You've got to pull him through for me," Rocky said.

When the New Year's Eve celebration erupted in Times Square, Rocky and Allie were sound asleep. They had gone without sleep for two days, talking of nothing but the fight and Vingo, eating only sandwiches and coffee. Everyone else had gone back to Brockton. Alone at the Belmont Plaza, they had crawled into the beds at 11 P.M., exhausted. The sounds of blaring horns and shouting crowds at midnight never reached them, and it was late the next morning before they finally awakened. When they got dressed, they walked through the drizzle to visit Vingo at the hospital.

"Go back to Brockton," Dr. Nardiello said. "There's nothing you can do here. I'll keep you informed of Carmine's progress."

A dark shadow hung over the Marchegiano home in Brockton. Rocky's mother never watched or listened to any of her son's fights, but she had learned of Vingo's tragedy.

"I can only be happy if Rocky no gets hurt and he no hurt anybody," Pasqualena said. "When a nice boy gets hurt I'm very sad. It's not worth it."

"But Mom had given up on trying to get Rocky to quit boxing," Peter Marchegiano said. "She knew that boxing meant everything to Rocky now. And he just couldn't give it up."

It rained every day that week in New York while the newspapers maintained a death watch on Vingo. Then, on January 4, the *New York Times* published its first encouraging news: "Vingo improved, eating solids, no more lapses of unconsciousness, had eggs for breakfast."

Three days later the *Times* reported: "Vingo still on critical list but showing very satisfactory progress in improving his condition."

When Rocky returned to New York he had not trained at all for two weeks. He went directly to the Saint Clare's Hospital.

"I don't remember anything about the fight, Rock," Vingo said. "The last thing I know is being in the dressing room."

"It was a helluva fight, Carmine," Rocky said. "It was my toughest fight. One punch you hit me so hard, I was just waiting for another one. If you hit me another one then, I think that would have done it."

"The best man won, Rock," Vingo said. "Don't worry about anything. It was nobody's fault."

Rocky left the hospital that day feeling comfortable for the first time since the fight, grateful for the knowledge that Vingo was finally improving.

But it was a long, hard road to recovery for Carmine. When he had first regained consciousness he couldn't remember things. Every day Dr. Nardiello would come into the room and say, "What's my name?" and Vingo would stare at him blankly.

Finally, one day, when the doctor came through the door Vingo said, "I know you. You're Dr. Nardiello."

"We all laughed," Vingo recalled. "It was a good feeling,"

"I'll fight again, won't I?" Vingo kept asking.

"No. You can't," the doctors said.

When he left the hospital, Carmine knew his fighting career was over. It would take all he could do just to survive.

Carmine and his childhood sweetheart Kitty Rea were married. They had grown up in the same broken-down neighborhood in the Bronx. When Carmine first wanted to get acquainted with Kitty, they were standing by the hot dog cart in front of his stoop.

"I didn't have the quarter to buy her a hot dog," Vingo said. "Later, when we wanted to get married, I figured the boxing would give us a start. We didn't want much, just a little something out of life."

And in his deepest crisis Kitty Rea stood by Vingo. She couldn't eat and lost weight, but she came to the hospital every day.

"I was very lucky to have such a wonderful girl," Vingo said. "Maybe I couldn't have done it without her. I couldn't walk. I had to learn all over, like a kid. I had to go to Bellevue Hospital for therapy. I couldn't fight, I couldn't work, I couldn't do anything. It was the most depressing thing. For a whole year I couldn't work, and Kitty supported me."

More than twenty years after his tragic fight with Marciano, Vingo spent a few days with Peter Marciano. He was working in New York as a security guard. He still lived in the dilapidated house in the Bronx, but it was soon to be razed for urban renewal and Carmine and Kitty were preparing to move their family to a project.

Peter and Carmine drove to Camden, New Jersey, to meet with Jersey Joe Walcott, which was a thrill for Vingo and a relief from the drudgery of his night watchman's job. Vingo spoke with a heavy Bronx accent, but his mind was clear and there was no slur or incoherence. He was tall and rugged and looked like a man who had once been a fighter, but when he got out of the little Chevy Nova after being cramped in it for more than an hour, he walked with a noticeable limp.

Vingo's entire purse from his bout with Rocky went toward his hospital bill. He received $1,500 for the fight, but the medical expenses totaled $3,000.

"There was some insurance from the Garden, and that went on the bill too," Vingo said. "I don't know how the rest of the bill got paid. I don't know if Rocky paid anything, but I think he must have. If he did, he never told me."

Rocky and Weill always promised a benefit for Vingo to get him started in business.

"Every time I went to see Rocky at the training camp, we'd talk about it again," Vingo said. "But Weill always said, 'Not right now. Rocky's got an important fight coming up. After this fight, come back and see us.'"

It went that way right up until Rocky's last fight against Archie Moore. Vingo came to Grossinger's a few weeks before the fight, and Weill said, "Sure, Carmine. We'll talk about it right after this fight."

"Over the years. Rocky acted like he really wanted to do something for me," Vingo said. "But he never did. I figured there was something, some reason why he couldn't. But I didn't ask any questions."

About a year before Rocky died, a man came to Vingo's house on 152nd Street.

"Rocky said if I was ever near the Bronx to look up Carmine Vingo," he said. "What do you think about living in Florida? Rocky might have something for you to do."

Carmine and Kitty agreed it might be best for the family if there was a good job for him in Florida. They were anxious to learn more about it, but the man Vingo knew only as "Sam" never called again.

Once his own career was ended, Vingo followed all of Rocky's fights and always rooted for him. Rocky often gave him tickets to the fights and occasionally visited him.

Once, when Vingo and his fourteen-year-old son were at home watching Rocky fight on television, the boy said, "Is that the man you fought?"

"Yeah," Vingo said.

"He's not such a big guy," the boy said.

"Well, if you feel the way this guy hits, he doesn't have to be as big as you want him to be," Vingo said.

9.

The Undefeated

THE TWO FIGHTERS CAME to the Garden that night undefeated, each dreaming he was destined to be heavyweight champion of the world.

At twenty-two, Roland LaStarza had everything going for him. The handsome college kid from the Bronx had won thirty-seven straight fights since turning pro in July 1947. He was the darling of the New York fight crowd, a smooth, intelligent boxer who usually went the distance but had shown power in registering seventeen knockouts.

Rocky Marciano was the animal, a block of granite, who took everything a fighter had and then went on to destroy him. There was an awesome image about Marciano since his annihilation of Carmine Vingo. It had been almost three months, and he had not been in the ring since. The fans lusted for his savagery.

James D. Norris and the International Boxing Club had forced a reluctant Weill to make the match between Marciano and LaStarza.

At forty-four, Norris was a handsome six-footer with wavy black hair and dark, probing eyes. He was always immaculately groomed and wore expensive custom-made suits. He was a smooth talker who cultivated an image of the suave sportsman, who dabbled in thoroughbred race horses, and who was quick to help a friend in need. He flattered reporters and others who could assist in projecting the facade while insiders cringed at his craving for authority and power. He came from a family worth more than $200 million, so he had never known hard times. He gambled on sports and was drawn to the underworld characters that cast their seamy shadows over the world of professional athletics. His name was linked closely with those of Frankie Carbo and others. He controlled Al Weill, the Garden matchmaker. And Weill controlled Rocky Marciano. James D. Norris was a man whom Marciano would grow to despise, and was a definite influence in Rocky's decision to retire from boxing.

When Sam Silverman heard that the Marciano-LaStarza match had been made for Madison Square Garden, he was furious.

"What's going on here?" Silverman asked Weill over the telephone. "You didn't want no part of Rocky and LaStarza when I tried to book them in Providence."

"Norris forced me to take it," Weill reputedly said. "It's my job."

"What's that mean?" Silverman said. "You

can't risk losing a lousy two-hundred-dollar-a-week job?"

When Mike Piccento and his Ward 2 pals arrived in New York, they discovered that everyone wanted to bet on LaStarza; Rocky was the underdog.

"That was the first time I bet on Rocky," Piccento recalled. "I bet five hundred dollars. Then I bet every fight after that. I just let the money stockpile. I kept betting what I won."

The fight they saw in Madison Square Garden on March 24, 1950, was a Sunday afternoon taffy pull compared to the violence of the Marciano-Vingo affair.

Marciano did not launch his customary relentless pursuit of his quarry but instead boxed carefully, as if he were suddenly more concerned about looking good on television than meting out the punishing blows necessary for LaStarza's destruction. Somehow Rocky appeared more awkward than he did boxing in his usual style.

LaStarza was outboxing Rocky, landing some jabs, but unable to hurt Marciano.

After three rounds of waltzing, the fans began to jeer the fighters.

Charley Goldman was nervous in the corner. He had seen LaStarza decision Brion, and Charley considered Brion a much more polished boxer than Rocky. The little trainer felt that Rocky would have to KO LaStarza to win. But Rocky wasn't punching with power. Charley couldn't help but wonder if Rocky might still be spooked by the specter of the Vingo tragedy. But he wasn't, and Colombo, Piccento, and the others knew it. He was trying to be a fancy boxer instead of a slugger, and it just wasn't his style. And after the third round he forgot about it.

In the fourth round, Rocky began to bully LaStarza, landing some hard punches. Then he crashed a looping right to LaStarza's head, and

the Bronx heavyweight crumpled to the canvas.

LaStarza struggled up to one knee and rested. The fans bounded out of their seats and roared. The count had reached eight when the bell rang, ending the round.

LaStarza stayed at long range in the fifth round and cleared his head. He jabbed effectively and forced clinches whenever Rocky managed to get in close.

Roland dominated the sixth and seventh rounds with crisp boxing that scored points but only annoyed Marciano.

In the eighth, Rocky rushed at LaStarza, punching wildly. In his eagerness to gain the advantage Marciano threw a low punch. The round was awarded to LaStarza on a foul. The two judges and the referee later agreed that without the illegal punch Marciano would have won the round.

They fought furiously in the ninth and tenth rounds with Rocky forcing the action, seemingly inexhaustible in his ability to continually deliver hard punches. LaStarza was still boxing well and scoring with his jabs. And when the fight ended, the fans gave them a standing ovation.

Each fighter thought he had won; both were nervous as they awaited the decision. Undefeated records hung in the balance.

Because of Marciano's foul in the eighth round, the fight was very close. The judges were split, one voting 5-4 and one round even for Marciano, the other 5-4 and one even for LaStarza.

"Referee Jack Watson scores five rounds for Marciano, five for LaStarza," ring announcer Johnny Addie barked into the microphone. There was a long pause. The crowd was roaring. "In points," Addie shouted, "he scores six points for LaStarza, nine for Marciano. The winner . . . " Then the crowd erupted like a volcano.

In the gloomy dressing room of the defeated, LaStarza's manager, Jimmy "Fats" DeAngelo, was enraged. He, along with some others, felt the decision had been influenced against his fighter by Al Weill's role as IBC matchmaker. DeAngelo's fists were clenched. He stood to lose prestige, vast sums of money, and perhaps an eventual chance at the heavyweight championship of the world.

When Al Weill opened the door to congratulate LaStarza on having made a great fight, DeAngelo slammed it in his face. For "Fats" it would prove a costly display of temper. For a great young heavyweight prospect like LaStarza it was a grave injustice.

Weill's pride was hurt. Nobody treated The Vest with such disrespect. DeAngelo would pay dearly.

The crowd of 13,658 had paid $53,723 to watch Rocky beat LaStarza, the second largest gate for Madison Square Garden in 1950. (Only Rocky Graziano and Tony Janiro's gate of $80,000 eclipsed it.) The public craved a rematch and the IBC envisioned a tremendous gate. Norris argued for it. Rocky wanted it for the big money involved and to prove he could knock LaStarza out. But, in a rare stance against the wishes of the IBC, Weill would have no part of it.

It wasn't only Weill's pride that made him balk. Roland was an excellent boxer who had waged a tough, intelligent battle against Rocky. But now Marciano was undefeated and LaStarza was not. Rocky was at full steam, bucking the stormy seas that led to the heavyweight championship. Another fight with LaStarza would prove nothing and, to Weill's cautious mind, could be disastrous. Weill was never a man who risked millions to make thousands.

For LaStarza it was a discouraging setback in an outstanding ring career. Of his next ten fights, only two were in New York, and those were not at Madison Square Garden. The others were against journeyman heavyweights in such obscure places as Holyoke, Massachusetts, and Waterbury, Connecticut. He also went to Providence for three straight wins. In his remaining two years as the Garden matchmaker, Weill only booked LaStarza for one fight, and that night Roland lost a decision to Dan Bucceroni. But even though it appeared that he was being sidetracked at the peak of his earning potential as a fighter, LaStarza kept winning. By Christmas 1952, Marciano was the heavyweight champion of the world, and LaStarza, the only controversial decision in Rocky's unblemished career, had won all but two of his seventeen fights after being defeated by Marciano. There did come a time when the big money meant more than pride, and Weill finally relented to give Roland his chance at the title.

10.
Injuries

That fall of 1950, Rocky was still a long way from becoming the heavyweight champion. Freddie Beshore, Nick Barone, Lee Oma, and Jersey Joe Waicott were all ahead of Marciano in contention for Ezzard Charles's NBA title. Weill wanted Rocky to gain more experience, but he was also being very careful in selecting his opponents.

During the summer, Rocky had easily defeated a couple of worn-out heavyweights, Eldridge Eatman and Gino Buonvino. Eatman fell in three rounds, but, surprisingly, Buonvino had escaped Rocky's KO punch until the tenth.

"Buonvino was just an ordinary Italian heavyweight," Sam Silverman recalled. "It was the first chance I had to bring Rocky to Boston, and I put them in a small telephone-booth ring in Braves Field, where they couldn't move and had to fight toe to toe. Rocky figured to knock this guy out easy. Buonvino had a bad jaw. But amazingly Gino fought a tough fight and avoided getting nailed until the tenth round, when Rocky hit him a good shot that cut his eye, and the referee stopped the fight.

"What people didn't know was that Marciano could have as much trouble with an ordinary fighter as he did against the very top guys," Silverman said. "Rocky never cared who he was fighting. He fought them all the same way."

Silverman had tried several times to match Rocky against Johnny Shkor, but Weill had refused. Shkor was a six-five, 225-pound giant from Boston who had a reputation for being a rough-and-tough fighter.

But Shkor was on the downhill slope. He had recently been KO'd by Jersey Joe Walcott in Philadelphia. He was easy to hit and would be mincemeat for a slugger like Marciano. Silverman mailed Weill a picture of Shkor being KO'd by Jersey Joe.

"Johnny looked like a big oak tree falling," Silverman chuckled. "I waited a few days, then I put Shkor's manager Johnny Buckley onna phone with Weill."

"This guy can't fight anymore," Buckley said. "I'm just looking for a pay night. I want him to quit. I don't care about the guy no more."

"All right, we'll take it," Weill said.

But as soon as the match was made Buckley's attitude changed. He put Shkor into a heavy training program and told everyone around Boston his fighter was going to win.

The old curmudgeon Buckley was a shrewd operator; he had been around the boxing game for many years and had managed former heavyweight champion Jack Sharkey and other top-ranked fighters. Two years earlier Buckley had made a serious error in judgment. He claimed he could have become Marciano's manager for $1,000 but turned it down because Rocky was nothing as a fighter. With Shkor he hoped to prove it.

"I've got Johnny in good shape, Sam," he said. "He'll beat Marciano."

"Rocky'll break him in two," Silverman laughed. "Shkor's got no chance."

Rip Valenti, another of the Boston fight managers' "in" crowd, was at Providence that night.

"What're you gonna bet on Shkor?" Silverman said. "The guy's gonna get knocked out. Save your money."

From the opening bell. Rocky battered Shkor around the ring. So brutal was the slaughter that there was never any doubt about the outcome.

"Rocky was demolishing Shkor and Buckley was going frantic in the corner," Silverman chuckled. "Buckley was a very frugal guy. Very, very frugal. He had bet two hundred dollars on Shkor. 'Get him, Johnny! Get him! Hit him inna balls! Hit him inna balls!' Buckley kept shouting. The old guy was so excited, he was jumping up and down like a kid. Then Buckley's false teeth flew out, and he was crawling around under the ring looking for his teeth. Rocky was murdering Shkor. He beat him so bad it finished the guy's career."

Then, as Rocky was coming in, Shkor lowered his head and charged. The sound of bone against bone rang dully across the ring. Blood spurted from a gaping wound above Rocky's left eye, where the top of Shkor's skull had butted the thin, tight flesh. By the time he KO'd Shkor in the sixth, the gash had puckered and widened, and the gore was spilling down his face.

In the dressing room, Rocky was furious and disgusted. Goldman and Colombo paced nervously while a doctor stitched the puffy wound. After emerging victorious from twenty-eight straight fights with barely a mark on him, Marciano had finally received a serious injury. There would always be the danger of an opponent banging open the scar tissue over that eye and the referee stopping a fight.

THERE WAS MORE BAD NEWS for Marciano that fall of 1950. On November 3, Justice Frank E. Smith ruled in Plymouth County District Court that the contractual agreement between Rocco Marchegiano and Generosa Caggiano was valid. The written agreement, signed in 1948 before Rocky turned professional, bound him to fight exclusively for Caggiano. Justice Smith stated that Rocky had earned $29,624 as a fighter up to this point in his career, and decreed that he must pay one third of that amount to Caggiano. The justice further ordered that Marciano refrain from fighting for anybody but Caggiano. He then ordered the two men to execute a contract between them. Attorneys for Marciano immediately appealed the decision and the case was then referred to the Supreme Judicial Court of Massachusetts.

"It was because of this case that I couldn't bring Marciano into Boston to fight anymore," Sam Silverman said. "I could've got a lot of money for him in Boston at this time. But Weill was afraid to come to Massachusetts again after the decision."

On July 16, 1951, Judge Swift in Supreme Judicial Court in Boston reversed the decision and dismissed the case against Marciano. Caggiano no longer had any control over the fighter. A month later, on August 27, Marciano was fighting Freddie Beshore in Boston Garden.

On November 13, Rocky fought Tiger Ted Lowry in Providence, and was again forced to go the distance. Rocky battered Lowry with body punches; in his efforts to protect his head from a KO punch, Tiger Ted did very little offensive fighting. It was an easy decision for Marciano but a disappointing one, since he had so wanted to KO Lowry.

"I think Lowry would have gone the distance if we had fought a hundred times," Marciano said, assessing his career after his retirement. "I could never get used to his style of fighting."

For months, Al Weill had been dodging Rocky's requests for permission to marry Barbara Cousins. "Not yet" was Weill's familiar response. "Be patient. Fighters' wives hurt fighters. I want you and Barbara should get married, but I'll tell you when it's time."

But Rocky was a main-bout fighter now, beginning to earn large purses. Barbara was pressing him to force Weill's hand, and Rocky himself was eager to get married.

"All right," Weill said reluctantly. "Have one more fight. Then you can get married."

Rocky demolished six-two, 229-pound Bill Wilson, who Sam Silverman described as "a big bum from South Carolina." Halfway through the first round, he smashed Wilson's left eye open with a hard right, injuring the fighter so seriously that the referee stepped in and stopped the contest.

Rock had been concerned that he not receive any cuts or bruises that would show during the wedding ceremony. He emerged from the fight without a mark.

"It was a completely one-sided murder," Silverman said. "We were running out of cannon fodder. Rocky had beaten every good heavyweight around Boston."

About a week before the wedding, Al "Sonny Boy" West, a lightweight managed by Chick Wergeles, was critically injured in a fight with Percy Bassett at Saint Nicholas Arena in New York.

An article in the *New York Times* said, "West, a promising boxer, who had scored forty-six victories in forty-eight fights, never before had been counted out. He is married and the father of a year-old daughter."

West died the following night at Saint Clare's Hospital, the same place Carmine Vingo had been taken after his KO by Marciano.

The day before his wedding. Rocky and Nicky Sylvester went to New York to buy a ring.

"Rocky wanted to get a good ring, and he was willing to pay a decent price but not too much," Sylvester recalled. "He figured he'd get a better deal in New York. We walked all over the jewelry district trying to find the right ring for the right price. We spent so much time, we were an hour late getting back for the wedding rehearsal at Saint Coleman's Church in Brockton. Everyone was a little mad because we were late, even Father Cooney. But Rocky was happy, because he got the ring."

It was December 31, 1950, Rocky's wedding day. Ushers Duna Cappiello, Allie Colombo, and Nicky Sylvester soon discovered there were not enough seats in Saint Coleman's Church to accommodate the crowd. On one side sat the Irish, their gazes all fixed proudly on the bride. On the other side were the Italians, equally preoccupied with admiration for the groom.

Ten-year-old Peter Marchegiano stood beaming in the doorway wearing the miniature tuxedo he had donned for his role of junior usher. His brother Sonny, the best man, nervously kept fidgeting in his pocket to be certain the ring was still there.

Following a horn-blaring procession of cars through the center of Brockton, the reception was held at Cappy's, a nightclub just outside the city.

"It was a very unusual wedding reception," Nicky Sylvester recalled. "It was the wops against the micks. First the Irish got up and danced. Then the Italians got up and danced. The band didn't know whether to play 'Volare' or 'Danny Boy.' You could have cut the tension with a knife."

But the wine flowed freely, and soon the party was happy and boisterous. Everyone wanted to meet Weill and Goldman, who were making their first visit to Brockton. And the manager and trainer shook their hands and grinned happily, secretly concerned that perhaps they were about to be forced to relinquish part of the important control they held over the fighter.

Carmine Vingo was treated like a celebrity at the reception. Many of the guests viewed the tall, rugged athlete in astonishment and awe.

"Some of the guys there thought I had been killed in the fight against Rocky," Vingo recalled. "They couldn't believe they were meeting me. When they realized who I was, they couldn't do enough for me and Kitty. They were great people, plain and simple, and nothing phony about them. They even wanted us to stay in Brockton for a long visit, and I really wanted to, but Kitty had gotten sick from all the rushing, getting ready to come to the wedding, and we had to go back to New York."

Weill had not called Vingo until the evening before the wedding to inform him that he was invited, and so the experience had been hectic, and one that Kitty viewed with considerable suspicion.

"I thought we were being invited because it was good publicity," she said. "But I could see how much it meant to Carmine. But then when we got there, everybody was wonderful. They really made us feel wanted. Mrs. Marchegiano was a truly wonderful lady. She reminded me so much of my own mother, a really old-fashioned Italian mother, who enjoyed so much the simple family things."

When they first saw Kitty Vingo, with her flaming red hair, the old Italians from Ward 2 thought she was Irish. So they were pleasantly surprised when she began speaking to them in fluent Italian.

Charley Goldman drew happy applause when he proposed a toast and informed Barbara that she had a fine husband who was easy to control, always listened, and was eager to do whatever was right. "And Rocky, you've got a sweet, understanding girl," Goldman said. "So here's wishing the best to both of you."

But then Weill got Rocky's hackles up as he proceeded to steal the show. The Vest cleared his throat to draw the attention of the crowd, held up his wineglass, and croaked in his bullfrog voice, "Remember, Barbara, Rocky's boxing future comes first. This marriage has to play second fiddle, because he'll have to pay strict attention to me. And Barbara, honey, I'm going to make him the next champeen. I promise you that."

For years afterward, Rocky would refer to Weill's speech as a source of great embarrassment. And even though the crowd had cheered and roared with laughter, Rocky had always known that Weill was very serious. But, in truth, Rocky himself placed fighting second to nothing.

Rocky's Ward 2 paesanos had pooled their money and bought the couple a new DeSoto for a wedding gift. Marciano had never owned a car; he didn't even have a driver's license.

"Rocky was the world's worst driver," Sonny Marciano said. "He drove just like he fought, straight ahead. Stop signs, road-lane markers, red lights didn't mean a thing to him. I don't think Rocky even knew where reverse gear was. He just put his foot on the gas, and everything was supposed to get out of his way. Guys were afraid to ride with him. Fortunately, he didn't get a chance to drive that much."

After the reception at Cappy's, they drove to Boston to continue the celebration at a hotel. It was quite a different New Year's than they had spent the year before while Vingo lay in critical condition at Saint Clare's Hospital. And the year 1951 held the promise of an even brighter future.

They honeymooned in Miami. Weill had promised them ten days of uninterrupted vacation, but within two days the nervous manager was on the phone to Rocky at the Dempsey-Vanderbilt Hotel.

"How do you like it?" Weill said.

"Great," Rocky said. "We're having a terrific time."

"Watch yourself," Weill cautioned. "Remember, no late hours."

Weill sent Rocky to the Roney Plaza Hotel to look up his friend Jack Wertz, who was called the "Diamond King," because he was an authority on jewels and had owned so many of them, reputedly including the precious "Vanderbilt Diamond." The wealthy Dayton, Ohio, businessman immediately took a liking to the Marcianos and was their host during the remainder of their honeymoon. They went to nightclubs, parties, dinners, and all of the exclusive places around Miami. It was Rocky's first real view of how the wealthy lived, and he enjoyed it immensely.

But within a few days Rocky began to feel guilty about the soft living he was enjoying. He'd done some underwater punching at the hotel pool, but no other training. So in the morning he slipped out before breakfast without telling Barbara and went to a golf range to run. The next morning, Barbara followed in a convertible they had borrowed and watched him.

"You don't have to sneak out to do your roadwork," she said. "I understand."

But within a week Weill cut the honeymoon short and ordered Rocky back to New York to prepare for a fight in Providence.

Barbara had to travel from New York to Brockton alone while her husband of less than two weeks returned to his dingy room at the YMCA and prepared to spend his days sweating in the CYO Gym.

Charley Goldman was not taking Keene Simmons lightly. He had seen the big heavyweight from Bayonne floor Cesar Brion in a hard-fought bout a few months earlier. Simmons could deliver a hard punch and take a hard punch, but he could also be hit easily, and with Rocky's durability and punching power he did not figure to go the distance.

Once again, it was an injury that almost turned the tide against Marciano. In the second round, Simmons slammed two jolting rights to Rocky's head. The skin above Rocky's left eye blew open and began spewing blood.

It was a large gash, and Simmons made it a target. For the next five rounds both fighters threw heavy punches, but there were no knockdowns. Rocky had never been off his feet in a fight, and Keene had been KO'd just twice in a lengthy career. The cut over Rocky's eye widened.

"Referee Sharkey Buonnano told me later he could have stopped the fight anytime after the second round," Mike Piccento said. "He didn't want to because Rocky was undefeated and a big attraction in Providence. He didn't want to stop it unless it was absolutely necessary."

When Rocky returned to his corner after the seventh round, a doctor examined his eye. Rocky appeared to be pleading to allow the fight to continue. When the bell rang, he ran across the ring after Simmons.

"Marciano threw a thousand punches, missed five hundred and almost tore Simmons's head off with the other five hundred," said Silverman. "This guy Simmons was a tough, experienced fighter."

In his own mind, Rocky knew that the fight could not go another round. He kept punching and punching until it seemed as if every ounce of energy would surely be sapped from his body, but Simmons would not go down. Then, just as the round was about to end, Rocky battered Simmons against the ropes and slammed an overhand right to his jaw.

Simmons's face showered sweat and twisted like the image of a carnival's funhouse mirror. He sagged forward, and his eyes went glassy and vacant. Marciano punched furiously. But Simmons refused to fall. Then the referee stepped between them and stopped the fight.

For Rocky it was a disappointing way to start his marriage: his eye reinjured, his coming perhaps as close to losing a fight as he had in any contest other than the LaStarza bout. Rocky would have clearly been declared the winner had the fight gone the distance, but it seemed that injuries were beginning to dictate his fate again.

Russ Murray had loaned Rocky and Barbara the use of his estate in Easton until they had a chance to get settled and find an apartment or house of their own. They spent two days together, and then Rocky headed straight back to New York.

With a stitched and taped eye, he could do no sparring for at least several weeks. But Goldman worked constantly on developing Rocky's crouching style, combination punching, leverage, and the perfection of a powerful left hook, which was becoming one of Rocky's deadliest weapons.

"No matter how well I do, they never give me a compliment," Rocky complained of Weill and Goldman. "They never give me credit for anything."

"If he wins the fight, that's reward enough," was little Charley's philosophy.

Rocky was idle for two months after the Simmons fight—partly because Weill wanted to be certain the gash was completely healed, and partly because the Vest was biding his time and being very selective in choosing opponents. When Weill finally decided to test the eye, it was against a very unimpressive heavyweight from Atlantic City, Harold "Kid" Mitchell. There was no conceivable way that Mitchell could hurt or defeat Marciano, and should he happen to open the cut Rocky could swiftly finish the contest before there was any danger of a referee stopping it.

"This kid's nothing, Rock," Mike Piccento said as they were driving to Hartford. "Get yourself a workout."

"You're right, Mike," Rocky said. "Maybe I'll go eight or nine tonight."

Rocky did very little heavy punching in the first round. He danced around his opponent, working on the crouch and trying a few ineffective left hooks. Mitchell did not display an offense.

"Rocky's gonna carry this guy a while," Piccento explained to his puzzled friends.

"He's rusty. He needs the work."

But in the second round, Mitchell delivered a light jab that grazed Rocky's vulnerable eye. The punch did no apparent damage, but it sent Marciano rushing into wild assault. A left hook floored Mitchell for nine. He rose, wobbly, and Rocky immediately swarmed all over him. A hard right pole-axed Mitchell for another nine-count. When Mitchell struggled up again, he was instantly floored by another right. The fight was over.

"What happened, Rock?" Piccento said. "1 thought you were going to get yourself a good workout."

"I don't know," Rocky said. "I wanted to, but I just couldn't."

11.

The Contender

"COME ON, ARTHUR," ROCKY PLEADED. "Get back in the ring."

Arthur Thayer, a lanky, then undefeated middleweight, had just leaped out through the ropes at the CYO Gym as Marciano stormed after him during a sparring session.

"Not if you're going to hit me," Thayer said. "You don't know your own power, Rock."

Rocky and Colombo had discovered Thayer working out at the Brockton YMCA. They were very impressed at the way the kid just out of the marines hit the speed bag; and Thayer explained that he had been undefeated in his fights in the service.

"You won them all?" Rocky said. "Gee, that's great. Well, you sure look pretty smooth in there. I'm a fighter too. My name's Rocky Marciano, and this is my trainer, Allie Colombo. How'd you like to come to New York with us? We know a lot of people there and could kind of get you started."

Thayer, who had recognized Rocky immediately, jumped at the opportunity. He soon found himself sharing the room at the YMCA in New York, splitting a weekly rent of $11.35 three ways with Colombo and Marciano. Thayer fell into the pattern of working out in Central Park every morning and then walking all over the city with Marciano.

One afternoon before his workout at the CYO Gym, Rocky was taking a long walk when he saw Mario Lanza's name on a marquee.

"Mario's one of my favorites," Rocky told Thayer. "Let's go see this movie."

But just as they were about to buy their tickets, Rocky discovered that it was cheaper if you went before 1 P.M.

"Why don't we wait and go tomorrow, before they change the prices?" Rocky said.

"That's fine with me, Rock," Thayer said, recalling that he welcomed the suggestion because he "didn't have any money to waste in those days."

Rocky always wanted Thayer to spar with him because Thayer was tall and fast and had long arms. Thayer could give Rocky a good workout, but he was afraid to hit Marciano. He thought that, even though they were friends, Marciano was always vicious in the ring and would forget himself once he was hit by a hard punch.

"Come on, Arthur," Rocky kept pleading. "Open up. I won't hit you."

"I just didn't like to fight him," Thayer

said. "I was always concerned about getting hit by him, because it hurt so much and he could hit me almost any time he wanted to. You have no idea how vicious he was. That time when I hung a real good one on him, it was unbelievable the way he came at me. That's when I jumped out of the ring."

ROCKY AND BARBARA DID NOT YET have their own home, but they had moved from Murray's estate and were staying first with Barbara's parents and then with Rocky's family. Most of the time Rocky was in New York training, and Barbara was with her own family. Rocky had some important fights coming up, and his manager would not tolerate any distractions.

Cautious Al Weill wanted no part of the Mormon fighter Rex Layne. He complained to Norris, but the IBC boss saw big money in the match. He placated Weill by giving Marciano 30 percent to 25 percent for Layne in a purse that might easily have been split even.

Layne was a mammoth country boy from Lewiston, Utah, who had overpowered most of his opponents by brute strength. At twenty-three, he was five years younger than Rocky and had an eight-inch reach advantage. He had a record of 35 wins in 36 fights, including 24 KOs. His only loss was a decision to an average heavyweight named Dave Whitlock, which he later avenged by knocking Whitlock out. Layne had beaten Jersey Joe Walcott and Goldman's protege Cesar Brion. He had also KO'd a very impressive light heavyweight named Bob Satterfield.

Word was traveling around the inner boxing circles of New York that the winner of the Marciano-Layne bout was in line for a shot at Ezzard Charles's heavyweight title as soon as the Cincinnati Flash defended the championship against Joe Louis in September.

Al Weill was worried. He sent Rocky to his first training camp, at Greenwood Lake in the Ramapo Mountains of New York State. It was a great thrill for Rocky to have his own gym, private sparring partners, a cook, and special menus. He had a few close friends, like Nicky Sylvester, with him for companionship. There were weaving country roads and hills to challenge his stamina during roadwork and fresh, crisp mountain air to breathe. But more than the ideal training conditions, being in a camp was a symbol to Rocky. He was finally making it to the top. He was a contender. And nothing was going to stop him.

Charley Goldman had noticed that, when Brion fought Layne, the big Mormon slugger had a weak belly.

"You can slow this guy down by going to the midsection," Charley told Rocky. "Cesar couldn't do it, but you're stronger. I want you to get inside and pound his gut until he's ready to be taken."

Apparently Weill wasn't quite so confident, according to Sam Silverman, who had dinner with Weill the night of the fight in Jack Dempsey's Restaurant on Broadway. Silverman recalls their conversation as follows.

"You screwed me," Silverman said. "I never made a decent payday with this kid. I could have made you fifty thousand dollars with this fight in Boston."

"I know it," Weill said. "I don't even want the fight. They made me take it."

"What for, the lousy two-hundred-dollar-a-week matchmaker's job?" Silverman said. "I could draw two hundred and fifty thousand dollars for this fight in Boston."

"I should quit the job," Weill said. "What do I need it for? Why should I be sacrificing this kid? I'll make more money with him. I know it's no good."

One of Layne's sponsors was Peter Fuller, son of the late Massachusetts Governor Alvin T. Fuller and a wealthy sportsman whose horse Dancer's Image once won the Kentucky Derby but was later disqualified. Fuller had been a top amateur boxer in New England when Rocky was also an amateur, and he had always supported Marciano in his other fights.

"I'll have to be going against you in this one, Rock," Fuller said when he visited Marciano before the fight

"That's all right," Rocky said. "That's life, Pete."

Despite Goldman's advice, it was Layne who went for the body from the opening bell. The fighters stood toe to toe in the center of the ring, neither willing to give ground. Layne, who seemed slightly flabby around the midsection, tried to bully Rocky by leaning on him and throwing heavy but cumbersome punches to the ribs.

But the punches barely seemed to bother Rocky, who, being much faster than Layne, rifled some solid blows to the Utah strongboy's head.

In the second round, Rocky went into a deep crouch, determined to remain at short range. He slammed an overhand right that opened a gash over Layne's left eye.

The fighters continued to crowd each other in the third round, Layne leaning on Marciano and concentrating on the body. Rocky threw a left uppercut and a hard right that staggered Layne. Then Rocky moved back and rammed home a sizzling right that buckled Layne's knees and forced the big heavyweight to grab Rocky and hold on.

From then on Layne was slow, showing the effect of Rocky's heavy blows to the midsection and head. Less than half a minute into the sixth round, Rocky ended it with a sledgehammer right that "sheered Layne's front teeth off at the nubs," according to Fuller, who saw Layne afterward.

Layne appeared to hesitate as if he were stunned but might recover and continue. Then he suddenly crumpled and pitched forward like a slaughtered steer, almost landing on Rocky, who bent at the waist and flung his arms wide apart to maintain his balance. Layne fell heavily to his knees, his right arm braced stiffly against the floor. Then he collapsed and lay motionless, his head resting on the canvas.

"I heard the count from one to ten," Layne said later. "I kept telling myself I had to get up, but I couldn't move. It was the strangest feeling."

It was the first knockout Layne had suffered in his career, and bedlam erupted in Madison Square Garden as Marciano danced around the ring, his right hand held high. Colombo rushed to Rocky's side and kissed him, and Rocky went to the apron and greeted his wildly elated friends from Brockton. It was impossible to hear the ring announcer giving the official proclamation of victory.

The impressive win over Layne on July 12, 1951, established Rocky as a top contender for the heavyweight title. Ezzard Charles was scheduled to defend against Jersey Joe Walcott in six days, and, if victorious, he planned to fight Joe Louis in September. But Rocky was the fighter the fans were watching now, and it could not be long before he would have his chance at the championship.

The following Sunday night Rocky appeared on *The Ed Sullivan Show* and received a warm welcome from the fans. When he and Barbara returned to Brockton, they were met by a motorcade in Providence, where they rode in the back seat of a shiny new convertible, escorted in style back to the Shoe City. There were celebrations in the streets of Brockton, and the Cosmopolitan Club sent a band. Mayor Melvin B. Clifford gave Rocky a huge cardboard key to the city.

Everywhere he went now, whether it was for a walk amid the bright lights of Broadway or along the main street of an obscure town in Massachusetts, the people recognized Rocky. They all wanted to congratulate him and shake his hand. He was a contender and it was a heady experience, one that he would not soon forget.

But the excitement diminished slightly a few days later, when Jersey Joe Walcott knocked out Ezzard Charles in the seventh round in Pittsburgh to win the heavyweight championship.

Walcott would have to give Charles a return bout. And then there was Joe Louis, in the midst of a successful comeback, waiting for a shot at the crown. Rocky's aspirations for a title bout could be stalled for a long time.

On July 23, Colombo and Marciano took Art Thayer to Boston for his first professional fight. It was an important fight for Thayer, but he was upset when Rocky named his opponent.

"This guy's been around a long time," Thayer said. "They tell me he's got a record of twenty wins and no losses."

Thayer was extremely nervous before a bout; he couldn't sleep the night before and he always threw up just before the fight. "Once the bell rang for the first round, I was fine. There was never any problem in the ring," Thayer said. "But before the fight I was always really on edge. But Rocky had ice water in his veins before a fight. He couldn't understand why I was upset about fighting Wilfred Tinker Pico."

'This is the only guy the promoter had available," Rocky said. "You've got to get a

fight under your belt so we can get you started in New York."

Colombo and Rocky were working Thayer's corner. "Go out there and hit this guy on the potato," Rocky said. "He's nothing. You'll ruin him."

"Just having a guy like Rocky in my corner gave me so much confidence that I did it," Thayer said. "I went out and knocked out Wilfred Tinker Pico in the second round. It was a great feeling. Pico was so upset he never fought again."

Just before Marciano had left for Greenwood Lake to train for the Layne bout, Al Weill had visited their room at the YMCA.

"This place is a dump," Weill said. "What's the matter with you? You're a main-bout fighter. Get over to the Belmont Plaza and get yourself some sharp clothes. You're a contender. Don't let me hear of you staying inna dump like this again."

"Gee, Al was really upset," Rocky told Thayer afterward. "I guess I'd better get over to the Belmont Plaza." Thayer didn't see much of Rocky after that.

Then one day Colombo and Rocky asked Thayer to come to the hotel. They had a contract for him to sign.

"You're going to be champ of the world, Rock," Thayer said. "What time would you guys have for me? I want a manager who can really devote some time to bringing me along."

"Sure, Arthur," Rocky said. "I understand. You do whatever you think is best. And I wish you the best of luck."

Occasionally Thayer would see Charley Goldman at Stillman's Gym. "Rocky wants to know how you're doing," Goldman would say. "He's always asking me how Art Thayer is doing."

"It really made me feel pretty good," Thayer said.

On July 29, 1951, Allie Colombo married attractive, blond Lilly Kirel at Saint Patrick's Church in Brockton. His brother Eddie was best man, and Rocky, Nicky Sylvester, and John Jantomaso were ushers. Some of Marciano's newly acquired friends in the boxing fraternity thought it strange that Rocky was not the best man.

"I thought Rocky should have been the best man myself," Eddie Colombo said. "But the custom in our families was always for the older brother to be given that honor."

On August 15, Joe Louis, in the midst of a successful comeback, was unimpressive in jabbing his way to a ten-round decision over Jimmy Bivins in Baltimore.

The IBC wanted Louis to fight Rocky, but Weill was avoiding the match. Instead, arrangements had been made for Rocky to fight Freddie Beshore, who had been KO'd by Ezzard Charles in a bid for the NBA title a year earlier. It was considered a low-risk match for Rocky to keep him in shape and before the public eye during the shifting heavyweight championship situation.

"We took the Beshore match with the condition that Rocky wouldn't have to fight too hard," Chick Wergeles said. "Frankie Carbo came out to Boston to make sure that things went all right."

But Beshore's manager, Champ Segal, said nothing was done to insure an easy victory for Rocky. He claimed Beshore was in poor condition and had not trained hard.

Rocky had spent the entire month after the Layne fight in Brockton with Barbara. It was to be about the longest continuous stretch he would be with her during the rest of his career. He later figured they were together about one year out of the six that they were married while he was fighting. While he was champion, for four years between the Walcott and Moore fights, "we only saw each other on a hundred and fifty days."

Beshore was a year older than Marciano but had been fighting professionally since 1942. He had an unimpressive record of 29 wins and 12 losses, but had lost against tough men like Charles, Lee Oma, and Joe Louis. In his last 11 fights before meeting Rocky, Beshore had lost 8 times. The victories had been over comparatively unknown heavyweights, but the losses fattened the records and coffers of the champion and some top contenders. Some speculated that Beshore was "company owned," controlled by a closed circle of opportunists who manipulated boxers, and was not supposed to beat the money fighters. But it was all conjecture, and either way few would argue with those who claimed Beshore was no match for the powerful fists of Marciano.

It was a Boston match, promoted by Silverman, and it ended in the fourth round with Beshore flat on his back, his arms extended fully across the canvas like rabbit ears on a television set. It was Marciano country, and the fans went home happy, convinced that the Brockton Blockbuster was on his way to the title.

ROCKY MARCIANO AND FRANKIE CARBO were friends. In fact, Carbo was one of the few men with known underworld connections that Rocky was often seen with in public despite the obvious tarnish it gave to his image. The association had begun through Carbo's close relationship with Weill and Goldman, and it had flourished, strictly on a friendship basis, as time went by.

"Rocky always admired a guy who had balls or was talented in sports," Sonny Marciano said. "It didn't matter if it was a guy like Carbo, or an astronaut like John Glenn, or a ballplayer like Joe DiMaggio. But he usually leaned toward Italians. He took a special interest in and helped out a lot of guys who probably never would have gotten to know him if they had not been Italian."

Carbo was a split personality. He had a black reputation for his undercover activities in professional boxing and had been accused of many acts of violence including murder. This was the Frank Carbo who had come up through the slums of New York and had learned at an early age that in order to succeed he would have to fight in any way possible, and that in his world the powerful always defeated the weak, and only the strongest and most arrogant or the weakest and most timid were able to survive.

Men like Carbo did not consider traveling the hard road to rise legitimately under the corrupt civil and political system that oppresses underprivileged Italians, Irish, Greeks, and blacks. Carbo was a man who would never allow himself to wallow in poverty and obscurity, whatever the price to escape it.

The other side of Frankie Carbo shows a very basic, emotional, almost peasantlike, simple Italian who was capable of sincere, warm compassion toward his countrymen. It is perhaps most eloquently described by sports columnist and author Barney Nagler in his book *James Norris and the Decline of Boxing*. He says:

It is easy to describe the face and form of Carbo and achieve a good likeness, but it is impossible to get a perfect image of him as overlord of boxing in the United States. Of necessity, his labors were hidden under a black cloak and not even the other mobsters who were in conspiracy with him to control boxing in the United States can, each of himself, offer a total picture. Carbo spoke in circles, rambling on by design to give the impression of uncertainty, and nobody ever came away from a conversation with him certain of what he had heard. He was more than one-dimensional.

He was, for one, a sort of Broadway Robin Hood, and in this guise he handed out alms and largesse to needy serfs. He was a soft touch for anybody with a tale of sorrow and melted in the presence of a guy who was down on his luck and in need of room rent. When he was drunk he ran a rambling verbal course, from sentiment to cruelty and arrogance, and mumbled words intended to convey the impression that he was a misunderstood adult who, as a boy, had stolen an apple and had never been forgiven by society. He was gallant in the presence of women, who were charmed by his soft voice and good manners, and he regarded motherhood as being more sacred than money.

THERE WERE MANY THINGS ABOUT Frankie Carbo that appealed to Marciano. He had an aura of mystery, danger, and excitement about him that fanned Rocky's lust for adventure. He was, to Rocky, a class guy who dressed well, enjoyed the best of everything, and knew how to move. He could command respect, admiration, and even obedience from a shrewd, arrogant man like Weill, and yet he never seemed to push or abuse or intimidate the little guy, the guy who could not defend himself. In Rocky's eyes, Carbo's tough-guy tactics were reserved to his own violent world where tough-guy tactics were the accepted way of doing business and only the toughest could survive. And that he did not forget his Italian paesanos was very important to Marciano.

On numerous occasions during World War II and afterward, Carbo furnished the talent for shows at Fort Hamilton in Brooklyn and other military bases around New York. Neither Carbo nor the entertainers were paid. And Marciano was often among them.

But there were some things about Carbo that Rocky abhorred: foremost was "Mr. Gray's" abuse and control of many fighters.

On December 2, 1961. U.S. District Judge George H. Boldt sentenced Carbo to twenty-five years in prison and a $10,000 fine for muscling in on the earnings of welterweight champion Don Jordan. There were many other instances alleged in testimony before Senator Estes Kefauver's Committee on Antitrust and Monopoly where Carbo was involved in shady dealings or manipulations with contenders or champions. For example, Jake LaMotta testified that the underworld had forced him to take a dive in a 1947 bout with Billy Fox in order to be allowed a shot at the title. Carbo made a $35,000 killing betting on Fox with the big bookmakers, according to John C. Bonomi, assistant district attorney of New York County. Carbo's name was linked closely, through testimony, with Al Weill, James Norris, Truman Gibson, and Blinky Palermo.

While many felt that Carbo controlled Weill, and hence had a piece of Marciano's action, Gibson also testified that "Felix Bocchicchio was one of the managers controlled to some extent by Carbo." If true, when Marciano, managed by Weill, and Jersey Joe Walcott, managed by Bocchicchio, met for the title, Carbo could not lose.

There are many examples of Carbo's close relationship with Al Weill.

In 1964, Paul B. Zimmerman, sports editor of the *Los Angeles Times,* wrote a letter to Judge Boldt. Zimmerman said that on November 11, 1945, he had been a lieutenant colonel in the army and, along with another officer, had found himself stranded in New York without a room.

"Hotel reservations were impossible to get since the Army-Notre Dame football game at Yankee Stadium the next day had brought an influx of people," he said.

"As a last resort I telephoned Al Weill, a fight manager whom I had known before the war. He called back in a little while and said, 'Frank Carbo will let you have his room at the Forest Hotel.'

"As a newspaper man, I knew who Carbo was, but had never met him. Mr. Weill met us at the Forest, and in a short time Mr. Carbo arrived and was introduced. 'Stay as long as you like,' he requested, and seemed genuinely pleased that he could do us a favor.

"When we checked out on Monday the cashier refused to accept our money. 'Mr. Carbo gave specific instructions that you were his guest,' the man insisted.

"Although I saw Frank Carbo on several occasions from that time on he never requested nor even hinted for any sort of editorial favor for himself or any of his friends," Zimmerman said.

On the other side, there were people who lived in terror of Carbo, a man who had five times been charged with murder. And, because of the close relationship between Mr. Gray and the Vest, some were actually leery of offending Al Weill.

In Carbo's trial, Jackie Leonard, a Los Angeles boxing promoter, testified that he got on Carbo's bad list because he was not giving

Al Weill's fighters enough work at Hollywood Legion Stadium. Leonard said he was at the Robinson-Basilio fight in Chicago in March 1958 when Jim Norris told him that Frankie wanted to see him. When he ignored the message, Al Weill came and took him to Carbo's suite at the Palmer House.

"They held a trial for me, more or less," Leonard testified. Leonard, whose real name was Leonard Blakely, was later the matchmaker placed in the middle when Carbo and Palermo wanted half of Don Jordan's action if he was to fight for and win the title from Virgil Akins. He was sick with fear.

The Norris-Weill-Carbo association was a merry-go-round. Norris controlled the IBC, and therefore literally owned the heavyweight championship and dominated boxing in New York and other major cities. Weill worked for Norris as his matchmaker and was subject to the playboy millionaire's whims. And Carbo was linked closely with both of them.

Even Rocky's family does not know how much, if any, influence Carbo forced upon Weill during Marciano's rise. It is common knowledge that Weill was supercautious concerning Marciano and had to be prodded into taking some of the bigger matches of Rocky's career. Rocky's brothers are convinced that Rocky liked Carbo and hated Weill and Norris. Some of that was because Carbo was Italian and had the smooth personality of a paesano as opposed to Weill's domineering arrogance and Norris's built-in superiority complex. But much of it was because, toward the end of his career, Marciano felt certain that Weill and Norris were cheating him out of money.

Carbo himself said that his relationship with Rocky was strictly confined to mutual respect and admiration. But he was in no position to elaborate, since he made his comments in letters from the federal penitentiary at Marion, Illinois.

"Al Weill was a very capable and shrewd manager," Carbo said. "Since Rocky was a green kid, Weill made the right decision by turning him over to Goldman for training. It's questionable how far Rocky would have gone without Weill or Goldman, for many a good prospect was ruined by mismanagement, improper training, and many other reasons.

"Time after time I would meet Rocky, and on one occasion while in Boston, Rocky invited me to visit with his mother and father, who are lovely people, and they were very proud of their son Rocky," Carbo said. "I met his mom and dad again in New York City while they were visiting Rocky.

"For his honesty, courage, determination, and all-around fighting ability, I think it would be almost impossible to find Rocky's equal," Carbo went on. "He was always ready and willing to appear at all charitable events, and he appeared in many a benefit for me. Rocky went on to prove himself a great champion and a credit not only to his family, but to the sports world and his friends. He belongs with the greatest heavyweight champions of all time. Other than a good mutual friendship, I knew nothing of Rocky's business or personal affairs." Carbo died in a civilian hospital in 1976 after a lengthy illness.

The name of Dominick Mordini, alias Billy Brown, also has been linked with Carbo in the past. Brown, in his seventies, got into the fight business when he was fourteen. He was an assistant to Weill and took over the IBC matchmaker's job when the Vest was forced out after the Marciano-Matthews fight.

"There was never any inside stuff with Marciano," Brown said. "Everything happened aboveboard. Marciano could fight. He didn't need anything. The Rock did it all on his own, with no help from anybody.

"Weill didn't want a lot of fights," Brown continued. "He was cautious. We, Jim Norris and myself, had to bring him around. He was always looking for a little more time. 'Get someone else,' Weill would say. Joe Louis, Ezzard Charles, and Joe Walcott in the beginning were some that Weill had to be pushed on. But any good manager does the same. They want to get the best possible deal and be as sure as they can of a win. Weill was a good manager. He knew what he was doing.

"With Al Weill you never knew. Sometimes he'd say yes to a match, and the next day he'd change it. He watched out for Marciano like a mother hen. He worried about everything Marciano did, just like it was him and not Rocky that was going to fight.

"In my opinion, Rocky was the best of them all, the best fighter of any era," Brown concluded. "I've been around the fight game for almost sixty years and watched every great fighter who came up, and Marciano was positively the best I ever saw."

But in the summer of 1951, not too many shared that opinion.

With his crushing knockout over Layne, Marciano had caught the fancy of the New York fight fans and established himself as a top contender for the heavyweight title. But there were still plenty of sports columnists and self-appointed experts who ridiculed his awkward style of fighting. Rocky had gained some important ground, but there remained a long, uphill road to travel. And, just ahead, the great Joe Louis was blocking his path.

12.
The Death of a King

WHEN JOE LOUIS DEMOLISHED MAX SCHMELING in the first round at Yankee Stadium on June 22, 1938, fourteen-year-old Rocco Marchegiano and his pal Izzy Gold were listening to the fight on the radio at a carnival in Brockton.

"We had about fifty cents in our pockets," Gold said. "And we were thinking about all that money that Louis made. We never dreamed that someday Rocky would be fighting Louis in Madison Square Garden. We had wild imaginations in those days, but not that wild."

In 1951, as Rocky prepared to fight him, Louis was a boxing legend. He was thirty-seven years old, had been champion for twelve years before vacating the crown to go into temporary retirement in 1949, and had defended his title an unprecedented twenty-five times. Louis had been defeated only twice in seventy-two professional bouts, a knockout by Schmeling in their first encounter and a fifteen-round decision lost to Ezzard Charles when he launched a comeback in 1950. But after losing the title bid against Charles, Louis won eight fights without a loss, four of them by KOs.

Even though Louis was winning, he had not been very impressive in recent bouts when Norris and the IBC finally convinced the cautious and reluctant Al Weill to take the fight. When the Vest finally did agree to it, Marciano came out on the short end of the deal.

"Rocky was the attraction, not Louis," said Sam Silverman. "Louis was the opponent. But Louis got forty-five percent of the gate and Rocky only got fifteen percent. It was a ridiculous deal. Norris had the TV and was cheating Rocky and everybody else on that."

Just before Rocky left for Greenwood Lakes to begin training, Eugene Sylvester met him doing roadwork near the sewer beds at Brockton Heights. It was a good place for hunting, and Sylvester had been conditioning his beagles by running them on rabbits prior to the October opening of the gunning season.

He recalls the following conversation with Rocky about the approaching fight. Sylvester had recently gotten married and had purchased a new Plymouth for $1,700. He had put $100 down and borrowed the rest from the Lafayette Credit Union in Brockton. He was broke and wanted to bet on Rocky, but, like many people, he was in awe of the great Joe Louis and needed reassurance.

"Rock. Are you gonna fight him?" Sylvester asked.

"Yeah," Rocky said. "It's all signed, Euey."

"Rock, this guy's awful big and plenty tough," Sylvester said. "But I know you can beat him. Right?"

"I'll never lose to a nigger, Euey," Rocky allegedly said.

"Rock, I ain't got any money, but I'm gonna bet my car," Sylvester said.

"Go ahead and bet it," Rocky said. "And if I lose I'll give you your money back."

"When you win I'm gonna bite your ass," Sylvester said.

"I won't forget that," Rocky laughed. "You better not bite hard."

Rocky trained at Greenwood Lake in the mountain solitude. He was a contender now, and each approaching fight was more important than the last. He respected Louis but did not fear him. It was a thrill and an honor for Rocky to be facing the immortal Brown Bomber. He wanted to be in the best possible condition to win the fight impressively, so he forced himself to the brink of human endurance—running the hard, grueling miles along the hills of lonely country roads, sweating and bleeding in the gym—dedicated to a program designed to develop the ultimate in physical power and endurance.

In the evening, Rocky, Allie, and Nicky Sylvester would play Ping-Pong and cards and tell stories around the training camp table.

The cook prepared the steaks very rare, and Rocky chewed the pieces, swallowing the juice before discarding the pulp on his plate. He ate a large green salad every night and a bowl of minestrone, a glass of blended carrot and celery juice, and sometimes a baked potato. But he never used pepper or ate any fried food. The evening meal was his only large meal of the day, and he was always ravenous, but he forced himself to eat slowly and to chew the food over and over again.

By the time they broke camp, Rocky was lean and tough. He had sparred 110 rounds, more than for any other fight. He was almost overtrained. And even Sylvester, who could always make him laugh, avoided him as an unarmed man shies from a jungle cat.

"I could always make Rocky laugh until three days before a fight," Sylvester recalled. "After that he was something else. He was like a tiger waiting to attack. He didn't want to hear anything. The man was unbelievable."

Louis had always had quick reflexes and tremendous power. During his prime he was an excellent boxer with a sharp killer instinct, and could knock an opponent out with either hand. But the Brown Bomber was also vulnerable. He did not have good balance and was easy to hit. He had been KO'd only once, but knocked down many times. Schmeling, Walcott, Buddy Baer, Two-Ton Tony Galento, and others had floored him. In his first amateur bout, Louis was overmatched, and an Olympic boxer named Johnny Miler put him down seven times in two rounds. But as Louis progressed, he became a fighting machine that always moved forward and seemed indestructible. He forced his opponents to fight defensively, and many of them were paralyzed by fear long before they entered the ring.

But Marciano was fearless. No fighter could stalk him, because he was a brawler always on the offense. He had KO'd 32 of 37 opponents and had never been defeated as a professional. He was very confident of a victory over Louis.

"Are you worried?" a reporter asked Rocky.

"No. I'm not worried," Rocky said. "It's just another fight."

"Do you think you'll win?"

"Win?" Rocky said. "Yeah, I think I'll win."

"By a knockout?"

"I'll be trying for one," Rocky said.

Public bragging was not Marciano's style. He was proud and confident and would always predict victory to his friends, but he never liked people who blew their own horns in front of strangers. His favorite Italian saying, which he tried to live by, was *"Fa i fatte e no parole,"* which means, simply, "Do it. Don't talk about it."

"THAT WAS A DUMB QUESTION the reporter asked today," Rocky told Colombo when they were alone that night. "If I didn't think I was going to win, why the hell would I be fighting?"

But Louis was also confident. At thirty-seven, he was fighting because he needed the money desperately. But he was a champion, and champions seldom consider defeat. He was balding and puffy, but, even though his jab had lost some of its quickness and sting, Louis banged his sparring partners around the ring at Pompton Lakes, New Jersey, with power and authority. A few days before the fight, the aging Brown Bomber decked sparring partner Holly Smith. It was a confident Louis who told reporters he expected to KO Rocky.

Joe had the size, six-two and 212 pounds, to Rocky's five-ten, 187. He had a nine-inch reach advantage and far more experience than his younger opponent. But Rocky had youth, stamina, power, and hunger on his side. It was a critical match for both fighters, and one that might easily determine who would be the top contender for the heavyweight championship.

When he arrived at Madison Square Garden, Sonny Marciano discovered that Al Weill had given him a seat so far away from the ring that he could barely view the action. Sonny rushed to the box office and tried to exchange the ticket, but there were no more ringside seats.

"Jesus, Al, I can't even see from up there," Sonny pleaded. "Can't you get me closer to the ring?"

"What are you complaining about?" Weill snapped. "You should be grateful you've got any kind of a seat. We've got a big house tonight. Take what you've got and be happy."

"Christ sake, I'm willing to pay," Sonny said. "Just get me closer to the ring. My brother's fighting Joe Louis tonight. I want to see it, Al."

"We ain't got any more ringside tickets, kid," Weill said. "I can't do a thing for you."

"You cheap son of a bitch, you sold my ticket," Sonny Marciano said. "You're gonna be sorry for this."

"I take care of the tickets," Weill snapped. "You'll go where I tell you to go."

Before major fights, both camps were customarily given blocks of complimentary tickets, tickets that could be scalped for good profit. Weill guarded them in miserly fashion.

"Weill never gave Rocky his fair share of tickets," Sonny Marciano said. "Rocky complained to me many times that he couldn't even take care of his close friends because Al was scalping the tickets. Rocky felt he deserved at least half of them, but how the hell could he keep tabs on a guy like Weill? The guy was a shrewd Jew. This was just one area where my brother felt he was really getting screwed."

A crowd of 17,241 fans at the Garden and millions watching on national television saw an unusual fight. For the first time in his career Joe Louis was not the aggressor. From the opening bell Rocky pursued him; the Brown Bomber relied on his famed left jab to keep his younger opponent at bay.

For five rounds Rocky came in and Louis retreated. But Joe's left jab was very effective, and Marciano had to take it to deliver his own punishment. Joe's left cheek was raw and swollen and there was a mouse under his eye. There was a trickle of blood coming from Rocky's nostrils and a slight cut at the corner of his eye. It was a good fight, and Rocky was slightly ahead in the eyes of the judges.

Louis's superior experience showed when the fighters came at close range, but although he ripped Rocky with uppercuts and used his jab frequently, Joe seemed to conserve his once-devastating left hook. This was possibly out of respect for Marciano's looping overhand right, which had accounted for many of his KOs and could be delivered over an opponent's left.

By the end of the sixth round Louis appeared weary. Rocky pursued him, willing to absorb the unavoidable jabs. And in the seventh Rocky continued the pressure. Louis was slow and flat-footed but far from accepting defeat. Rocky slammed two hard lefts and a right to Joe's jaw. But he came back with a savage left hook that crashed into the right side of Marciano's jaw.

Rocky was winning. Referee Ruby Goldstein had it four rounds for Rocky, two for Louis, and one even; Judge Joe Angelo had Marciano ahead, 5-2; and Judge Harold Barnes favored Rocky, 4-3.

In the eighth round Rocky went headhunting. He forced Louis toward the ropes and a short left hook collapsed the Brown Bomber to the canvas. The fans leaped from their seats, roaring. Louis was flat on his back, but he rolled over almost immediately and rose to one knee.

The crowed prayed for the legendary hero to come off the canvas. Sentiment glazed their powers of reasoning, and many felt that old Joe could actually recover and win the fight.

Louis took a count of eight and began to rise. His eyes were cloudy and his head bobbed instinctively as Rocky came directly for him, like a shark with the taste of blood. And the old champion waited, not with fear—although surely he knew the inevitable—but with pride and determination. For Louis had been a great champion, and great champions could be destroyed, but their hearts would not accept defeat.

And now the shark began to devour him, and there was nothing gentle about it. Rocky forced Joe to the ropes and ripped him with two savage left hooks. Joe's eyes went vacant, and his arms hung down at his sides. The King began to sag, alone and helpless, unable to prevent his own annihilation. Rocky's eyes were wild with frenzy. In a split second he aimed the devastating right that rang against the bone of Joe's jaw, like a bell declaring a moment in history.

Louis fell over backward through the ropes and sprawled awkwardly onto the apron, with one leg remaining inside the ring.

Goldstein began the count, but when he reached three or four he waved his arms, signaling that the fight was over. Then he hurried onto the apron to assist his old friend Joe, who appeared as if he might roll off the apron into the press rows.

When Rocky's left hook sent Louis to the canvas for the first time in the fight, Sugar Ray Robinson, the great welterweight and middleweight champion, left his seat and began moving toward the ring.

Louis was trying to rise, rolling his bruised face from side to side in bewilderment.

Robinson climbed up onto the apron and

cradled his idol's head in his arms, fighting back tears, oblivious to the roar of the crowd.

"Joe, Joe, you'll be all right, Joe," Robinson said. "You'll be all right, man."*

"For many people it was a sad affair," said Referee Ruby Goldstein, who had been on tour with Joe during World War II. "A great sports figure like Lou Gehrig or Babe Ruth is finished. People idolized Louis. They didn't want to see him when he was not himself. It wasn't easy for me. We were friends. But when you're a referee, you've got to steel yourself. You've got to be a little hard. You've got to realize there are two boys in the ring, and they both are trying very hard to win the fight, because it means a lot of money to them."

"Why'd you stop it? Why didn't you complete the count?" Goldstein was asked by people who believed in the invincibility of Louis.

"Louis was finished," Goldstein told them. "I stopped it to give the men in his corner five or six extra seconds to administer to him."

Maybe when Louis was young and in his glory as a champion Goldstein would have had second thoughts. But he had noticed early in the bout that Louis's left jab was not the same anymore. "But I figured Louis might find himself. Only he never did, because Marciano just doesn't give you a chance. He just keeps you going back all the time. I remember Joe Louis went down [the first time] and he went down not like a young boy goes down. When a young boy goes down, he still has that hustle, that feeling inside like 'I gotta get up,' but Joe went down with a thud. Still, he did get back up. Joe was knocked down a lot of times in his career, but he always got up because he had a heart. People like Louis don't stay down. Sometimes they stay down because it's physically impossible to get up, but their heart doesn't stay down."

Asked if he felt Rocky was ever in trouble during the fight, Goldstein said, "It would be hard to tell if Rocky was ever in trouble, because hitting him was like hitting a stone wall. If he was ever hurt, he didn't show it. He was a rough, tough, game guy who came to fight and came to win."

It's unfortunate when a great champion at the end of his career has to be defeated by an emerging great champion, but that is the essence, the heart and soul, of competitive sports. There were those who were bitter over Louis's defeat, claiming Marciano wouldn't have stood a chance against Joe in his prime. And there were those who belittled Louis and claimed he was never really great. They were all wrong. For true champions almost always have a chance against other true champions. And Marciano and Louis were both giants among the heavyweights.

After this momentous fight, which ended Louis's career and toppled him onto the path toward oblivion while vaulting Marciano nearer the shadowy pinnacle of Mount Olympus, the fighters showed more class than many of the fans.

"You were just too old, Joe," someone said in Louis's dressing room.

"He hits harder than Max Schmeling," Louis told reporters. "The better man won. It was a beautiful left hook that started it. This kid is tough enough to beat anyone."

In his dressing room. Rocky took time out from his victory celebration to write a note to Louis. He had tremendous respect for Louis's fighting ability, and he envisioned how the old champ must be feeling.

"It was an awful good fight," Rocky told reporters. "He kept hitting me with those jabs, and I just had to take them."

"When Rocky won, the boys from Ward 2 went crazy," Eugene Sylvester said. "We all bet heavy, and after we collected the dough,

*As recalled by Robinson in his autobiography, *Sugar Ray*.

we got it all over the beds in the hotel room and began counting it. What a night! It was one of the greatest.

"When I got my cash all counted and stashed away, I went to the room where Rocky was staying," Sylvester continued. "Al Weill and a couple of sportswriters were in there. Rocky was lying on the bed with just his undershorts on. He was grinning, and his eyes were a little puffy. 'Roll over, Rock,' I said. He laughed. Then he rolled over onto his belly, and I bit him on the ass."

Back in Brockton, five thousand cheering fans had spilled out of homes and taverns and clubs where they had been watching the fight on television. They were shouting, driving along Main Street blasting their horns, wanting to tell the whole world what had happened. Never in the history of the city had there been such a hero.

While Louis had recognized Rocky's ability and admitted it, there were still some sportswriters in New York who refused to give him any credit. Before the fight some of them had been ridiculing Marciano and scoffing at his chances. Now that he had defeated Joe, they still withheld their praise.

Arthur Daley's column in the *New York Times* said the next morning, "The Louis of 10 years ago would have felled Rocky with one punch . . . Louis losing is more important than Marciano winning."

"That asshole," Colombo said. "It might have been an easier fight ten years ago. Louis would have been coming in then instead of backing away. Rocky might have gotten to him sooner. How can he say what would have happened? One punch my ass."

"Forget it," Rocky told him. "What does he know? Has he ever fought Louis?"

"I can't figure some of these guys out," Colombo said. "What do they expect of you?"

"Fuck 'em," Rocky said. "Who needs them?"

But he did not really mean that, for Marciano was very concerned about his image. Later in his career he went to great lengths to protect and enhance the profile he projected to the public.

As much as he enjoyed good publicity and a favorable public image, Rocky took even greater pride in the faith his friends showed in his ability. He was honored when men who worked hard every day in the factories would bet far more than they could afford to lose on his fights.

"I'll never let them down, Allie," he would tell his friend when he heard of the exceptionally heavy bets that were being placed on him. "There's too much at stake."

But he was very disturbed when he heard of a friend betting against him. It was totally unacceptable and he never forgot it. He could never bring himself to be friendly with that person again.

On Saturday, a Times photographer took a picture of Rocky picking up his check for $49,605 from Jim Norris. It appeared in the Sunday edition, with Rocky grinning and flanked by Norris and Marty Weill.

"Rocky couldn't stand to have his money tied up in checks," Sonny Marciano said. "As soon as possible he had it converted into cash. He got a little more than twenty-four thousand dollars after the split with Weill."

"Handing Rocky his first big purse was like feeding blood to a tiger," Weill used to joke. "He just couldn't get enough."

"As soon as he got his hands on the cash. Rocky packed it into paper bags and we took it up to his room at the Belmont Plaza," Sonny said. "He spread it out on the bed, and then told me to count it while he went into the bathroom. I couldn't believe all that money, thousands of dollars. It must have taken me half an hour to count it. When he came back, he asked me how much there was. I forget the figure I gave him, but it came to just a few dollars less than Rocky expected."

"Count it again," Rocky ordered.

"But, Rock, it's only a few dollars off," Sonny pleaded.

"Never mind," Rocky said. "I'll count it myself."

He sat down on the bed and began counting his money. "It's all there," he said, grinning at Sonny. "You must have made a mistake."

One night when they were in the hotel room together, Rocky went into the bathroom and locked the door behind him. He was in there almost an hour when Sonny became suspicious. He tried the door and then knocked on it. "Hurry up, Rock," he said. "What are you doing in there?"

"Chrissake," Rocky moaned, "Can't a guy even take a crap in peace?"

When Rocky finally came out of the bathroom he had a sheepish look on his face. He had not flushed the toilet. Sonny was still suspicious but did not say anything. Later, when Rocky was gone. Sonny went into the bathroom and looked around. Out of curiosity he lifted up the top of the toilet's water tank. There was Rocky's money, taped inside the tank in several large plastic bags.

Rocky and Barbara remained in New York for a week after the fight, enjoying the limelight and the social whirl of fancy restaurants and Broadway shows. The destruction of Louis had confirmed Rocky as the Great White Hope among the heavyweights. Wealthy fans argued among themselves for the pleasure of his company. Some of them were sincere admirers, who respected all great athletes, but among them also were the hypocrites, those who pretended to be unprejudiced, but who would never have socialized with a black fighter. Rocky savored the attention, but he soon began feeling guilty. Fighting was more important. It was the only thing that was important. And he had to return to his training.

There was turmoil at the Marchegiano household in Brockton. Rocky's mother had received a letter saying that if her son came home for the celebration he would be shot.

"Stay away from here, Rocky," Pasqualena said when Rocky called her. "I don't want you to come home." But Rocky seemed more intrigued than disturbed by the threat.

"Imagine that, Son," Rocky said. "Some guy wants to get me."

"Rock, this is serious," Sonny Marciano said. "This guy may be a real nut. I'd like to get the son of a bitch."

"Fuck 'em," Rocky said. "You're not gonna worry about a jerk like that, are you? When it's your time, it's your time. Nothing's ever going to happen until then."

Police later traced the letter to a thirteen-year-old schoolgirl who had been dismayed by the beating Rocky had given Louis.

"Gee, imagine a little girl like that thinking so much of the guy," Rocky said. "That's really great."

On November 10, 1951, it seemed as if the entire population of Brockton lined the streets for the parade honoring Rocky. The mayor led the caravan along Main Street as thousands showered their hero with confetti and shouts of praise.

Before the speeches and the wild celebration that concluded the parade at James Edgar Playground, Rocky walked across the street and went into the old two-story house where he had spent much of his youth.

Pasqualena Marchegiano was in the kitchen. She had not seen her son fight the great Joe Louis, nor had she heard them on the radio. She still did not completely accept her son's fighting career. But she was relieved because Rocky was happy, safe, and unhurt.

"You must be hungry Rocky," she said, after they had embraced. "Sit down. I'll make some soup for you. Outside they're gonna wait. It'll only take a minute."

While thousands waited in the playground, Rocky wolfed down a bowl of his favorite *spezzatto*. Then he strolled across the street to where the crowd was roaring. Rocky grinned and waved a clenched fist over his head. In Brockton, Marciano was the local boy who made good.

13.
The Final Hurdles

FOR ROCKY MARCIANO, the winter of 1952 was the beginning of the longest mile. There were few obstacles remaining between him and the heavyweight championship. The public was already clamoring for the Brockton slugger to be matched against the crafty champion, Jersey Joe Walcott.

But Jim Norris and the International Boxing Commission held a stranglehold on boxing. The IBC had an exclusive contract to promote Walcott's fights, and its officials insisted that Jersey Joe defend his title against Ezzard Charles, even though the two had already been involved in three unspectacular fights.

After his knockout of Joe Louis, Rocky told reporters that he wanted Walcott next. He wanted nothing less than a chance for the heavyweight title.

But Norris was in control, and when he pulled the strings the puppets danced or they were soon cut loose. Marciano versus Walcott would have made much more money than Charles versus Walcott. But the IBC bosses didn't want it. They pulled Al Weill's strings, and Weill pulled Rocky's.

Publicly Marciano said that Charles was entitled to a return bout for the title and that

he would not fight Walcott unless Ezzard waived his contract for the match. But privately he was furious. He disliked Norris almost as intensely as he disliked Al Weill, and he felt that Norris was taking advantage of him again.

That January, Weill had gotten into trouble as IBC matchmaker. After middleweight Ernie Durando was awarded a TKO over Rocky Castellani at Madison Square Garden, an argument erupted in the center of the ring. Castellani's handlers didn't think the bout should have been stopped, even though Rocky was groggy and being pummeled against the ropes. There was a shouting, name-calling scuffle in the ring, and some people, including the referee, got pushed around.

Afterward Weill went into Castellani's dressing room and confronted his handlers. He was promptly knocked to the floor, where he was kicked, punched, and mauled by several persons, according to later court testimony.

Weill's face and ribs were bruised, but not nearly as much as his ego. The matchmaker's job was becoming more and more of a drag to the cocky and ambitious manager, who secretly controlled the destiny of the next heavyweight champion of the world.

THE CHICAGO BOXING WRITERS AND
BROADCASTERS ASSOCIATION had chosen
Marciano as the winner of the McFarland
Award, for the man who did the most for box-
ing in 1951. Sugar Ray Robinson was the run-
ner-up.

Rocky had proven himself as a top contender for the title. But Walcott was biding his
time, making money off his crown through
exhibitions and public appearances. Almost a
year would pass from the time Jersey Joe won
the championship until he made his first
defense against Charles in June 1952.
Meanwhile, Rocky had to fight to remain
sharp and stay in the public's view. Weill was
looking for opponents tailor-made for
Marciano's brawling offense. Lee Savold
seemed a perfect victim, and the bout was
scheduled for February 13.

The fight figured to be easy for Marciano.
Savold was an old warhorse who had battled
the best heavyweights of his era as a contender and challenger for the championship.
But Lee was tired, and he could no longer
hold his own against the class fighters of his
division. Joe Louis had found him a slow, easy
target when he won every round and battered
Savold to the canvas for a sixth-round KO
nine months earlier.

Rocky had been training at Greenwood
Lake and was in excellent condition. Then,
about a week before the fight, he began to get
sluggish and lose his appetite. A few days later
he was in bed with a virus that raised his temperature to more than a hundred degrees.

"You've got to call the fight off," Mike
Piccento told his nephew. "You can't take shots
and medication and expect to go in there and
fight."

"We can't call it off," Rocky said, as they
sat in his room at the Bellevue-Stratford Hotel
in Philadelphia. "They've got the TV and
everything all committed. I'm feeling better
now. Don't worry, I'll be okay."

"You're crazy," Piccento said. "Call it off.
You want to take a chance of blowing everything so these guys can make a few lousy
bucks?"

"I'm telling you I'm all right," Rocky said.
"There's no way we can call it off now, so don't
even talk about it."

For the first time Piccento noticed that
Rocky had stopped listening to him. "He had
his mind made up and that was it," Piccento
recalled. "I was mad as hell, but what could I
do? For a long time I never gave Rocky any
advice after that."

Sonny Marciano was worried too. He had
been with Rocky for two days before the fight
and noticed that he was weak, pale, and sweaty
and had constant diarrhea. But Sonny was disturbed even more by a rumor he had heard.

"It was going around that Rocky's handlers
were trying to make a deal with Savold's
camp," Sonny said. "They'd get paid extra for
every round Lee didn't last. I'd heard it was
done like that sometimes. I don't think Rocky
knew anything about it. If he did he never
mentioned it, and I'd never ask him. I knew
that even sick Rocky would ruin Savold. But a
lot of guys were worried, including big shots
like Jim Norris, who was looking to make plenty of dough with Rocky in the future."

It was Rocky's clumsiest fight since amateur days. He was in constant pursuit of Savold
and rarely stopped punching, but he had not
had a fight in almost four months and few had
ever seen him as awkward. He missed punches by feet instead of inches, and even when he
landed a solid blow the power seemed to be
missing.

But while the fans were laughing at Rocky's wild lefts and roundhouse rights, Savold was on the receiving end of what was described in the *New York Times* as the "worst beating in his 17 years of boxing."

Savold's face was a gory mess. In the first round his nose had been smashed and bled profusely. His lips were split open in the third, his left eye cut, and his right eye badly gashed in the sixth.

"It was evident by the fourth round that Savold was helpless to defend himself against the power of Marciano," the *Times* story said.

In the sixth, Rocky threw a punch that missed Savold by two feet and sent Marciano sprawling to the canvas. On his knees, Rocky grinned as he clutched the top strand of the ropes. Savold, covered with blood and gore, stood over him menacingly. He was snarling as if Rocky had not slipped but had been dropped to the floor by one of Savold's own punches.

Embarrassed by the slip, which had brought bursts of laughter from the audience, angry with himself for not having KO'd Savold in the few rounds that it had taken Louis to dispose of the thirty-six-year-old Paterson, New Jersey, brawler, Rocky stormed after his opponent. Marciano's white trunks were covered with Savold's blood as he hammered the beaten heavyweight with both fists, trying desperately to put him down.

When Savold returned to his corner at the end of the sixth round, his manager, Bill Daly, began waving a towel. Lee sat on the stool, head nodding, eyes vacant, apparently unaware of what was happening. His face looked like it had been hit by a truck and dragged over cement—the eyes swollen, blood bubbling in a dozen cuts and scrapes. Daly told the referee the fight was over because his man could not continue.

In the record books the consecutive notations under Savold's name read "Joe Louis KO by 6" and "Rocky Marciano KO by 6," although under NBA rules when a man cannot answer the bell, the KO occurs in the round that is coming up.

Savold had paid the price that old fighters pay when they are fed to the young lions. His teeth had been smashed into his gums. He was urinating blood. And he had to be hospitalized for observation and treatment.

After seeing how defenseless Savold had been against Marciano's attack, Pennsylvania Boxing Commissioner John "Ox" DaGrossa suspended him indefinitely for his own protection, thus barring him from fighting within NBA jurisdiction. Lee's name was never in the news as a boxer again. Like many other gifted fighters whose abilities had taken them near the top of their violent profession but who had fallen short of the championship, Savold drifted into oblivion. Once he had become a broken-down ex-pug, Lee worked on the docks, in the factories, as a bartender. Then, in the spring of 1972, Savold suffered a stroke and died in a New Jersey medical center.

14.
Brothers and Enemies

In January 1952, Jersey Joe Walcott had gone to Maine on an exhibition tour. Now the Maine fans wanted to see the explosive New England contender they had been hearing so much about. Although Marciano regarded exhibitions as useless and seldom participated in them, always preferring to have something at stake in a fight, in March he welcomed the opportunity to earn some easy money and remain near home while waiting for his chance at the title.

"I'll take it," Rocky told the promoters. "I can get some great amateurs, Peter Fuller and Tony Zullo, to make the tour. We'll give you a terrific show."

"Peter Fuller would love to go with me," Rocky told Chick Wergeles, who represented Weill's interests on the tour. "Pete's the ex-governor's son and a damn good boxer. He'll be a big drawing card up there in Maine."

But when Rocky finally got around to calling Fuller, there was little time remaining before the first fights were scheduled. "Listen, Pete, I've got this exhibition tour in Maine and I thought it'd be nice if you could make it with me," Rocky said.

"Gee, I'd love it, Rock," Fuller said. "You

and I never did get in the ring together."

"We're all set, Chick," Rocky said. "Tony Zullo can't make it, so it's gonna be me and Pete Fuller."

But meanwhile Fuller had checked into the matter further and decided to decline Marciano's offer.

"The only problem is, I'm still hoping to make the Olympics," Fuller explained to Rocky. "If I went on the tour I'd lose my amateur status. Not that I think I'll ever make it, but the Olympics is important to me."

"Sure, Pete," Rocky said. "I understand. That's all right. Good luck, and I hope you make it."

But on the morning of March 19, Rocky was in Lewiston, Maine, with a fight scheduled for that night and no opponent.

"I'm going to call my brother Sonny," Rocky said. "We've done a lot of sparring together, and he's tougher than most of the heavyweights anyway."

"Are you sure we can get away with it?" Wergeles said. "Sonny's just a kid, and he's only a sixty-five[165]-pounder."

"Don't worry, Chick," Rocky said. "We'll give them a helluva show."

Sonny Marciano was in good condition, having already begun working out for spring baseball, but it had been months since he had done any boxing. He was an eighteen-year-old high school senior, and scouts from several major league teams were watching his progress as a hard-hitting third baseman.

"Son," Rocky's voice came through the phone with the familiar urgency that told his younger brother that he was about to be called upon to perform a service. "You have to help me out up here. Bring your gym equipment. You're gonna have to go with me tonight."

"But, Rock, I haven't done any boxing lately," Sonny pleaded. "What's the matter?"

"Never mind," Rocky said. "Don't ask any questions. I'll explain it later. Just bring your gear and get up here. Don't let me down now, kid. And don't mention this to Ma."

Sonny packed his fighting equipment into Eugene Sylvester's old gray DeSoto and, along with Eugene, Barbara Marciano, and Allie Colombo, drove through snow and sleet to Lewiston. He had been searching for an excuse to skip a few days of school and follow his brother on the tour, but he had never expected it to happen this way. He had a perfect excuse, but he couldn't tell his mother. He had to pretend he was staying with friends for a couple of days, even though he knew it wouldn't work. When Pasqualena found out her two sons were fighting each other before thousands of people for money, he didn't want to be anywhere near the house on Dover Street.

"What am I supposed to do in there, Rock?" Sonny asked in the dressing room. "I mean, what do you expect of me?"

"Just do whatever you can," Rocky said. "Give it your best shot. Try to go for a knockout. It'll be good for me."

"That's fine. Rock," Sonny said. "But what are you gonna do to me?"

"I'm gonna punch pretty good too, kid," Rocky said. "We've got to give them a show. Besides, I don't know how to pull punches very well. But don't worry, I won't be going for the knockout."

When he found out about the scheme the promoter was going to call off the fight, Sonny recalled, but faced with the prospect of refunding the ticket money he allowed them to continue.

Sonny danced in his corner as the announcer introduced him as Peter Fuller, the top New England amateur boxer. He entered the ring wearing a sweat shirt to conceal the obvious weight difference between them. But the brothers were very similar in their features, and anyone who saw them standing side by side should have known there were two Marcianos in the ring.

As far as the boxing was concerned the fans were not cheated. The two brothers put on a rough-and-tough exhibition of punching that had the crowd cheering. Several times in the four-round bout, Rocky hurt his younger brother, but Sonny didn't complain and always kept coming in.

"Rock could sense when I was hurt," Sonny said. "He'd back off then and not throw as many punches. Naturally he didn't go for the knockout."

Sportswriters told the story of a rugged fight between heavyweight contender Rocky Marciano and Peter Fuller, the talented Boston amateur, in the morning papers.

The Associated Press story headline read MARCIANO STRONG IN MAINE EXHIBITION.

"A City Hall fight crowd of less than 1,000 saw heavyweight Rocky Marciano of Brockton, Mass., put on a power exhibition in a four-round sparring duel with amateur Peter Fuller of Boston last night.

"Heavy-muscled   Marciano   and   the

unawed Fuller, son of a former Massachusetts governor, gave a satisfactory show and drew a respectable round of applause . . . "

On March 22, the brothers fought again in Rumford, Maine, billed as Marciano vs. Fuller. The crowd went away happy with the slugging exhibition. In the several matches that followed, Sonny alternated between being Peter Fuller and Tony Zullo.

One evening the owner of an Italian restaurant called Rocky's hotel room. Chick Wergeles answered the phone.

"I'd be honored if Rocky could come to my restaurant for dinner tonight," the owner said.

Wergeles's mind spun into motion. They had no plans and an Italian meal was appealing, but there were many people with Rocky.

"Yeah, The Rock would enjoy that," Wergeles said. "But I think we've already got a commitment to go to another restaurant." He quickly named the only other Italian restaurant in the area.

"But I'd really like to have you as my guests," the owner insisted. "I know you'll enjoy the food tremendously."

"Well, I don't know," Wergeles replied. "Let me check."

"Hey, Rock," Wergeles shouted so the owner could hear him clearly over the phone. "Is there any way we can get out of that deal tonight? Fellow here's a great fan of yours and he'd really like to have us go to dinner at his place."

Rocky was lying on the bed with his hands folded behind his head, grinning. "Well, I think we could arrange it," he shouted.

"Say, that's wonderful," the restaurant owner said. "I'll expect you about eight, and believe me, you won't be sorry you chose my place."

"The only problem is we've got a few friends with us," Wergeles said.

"Don't worry about a thing," the elated owner said. "Bring them right along."

"We showed up that night with about fifteen people," Wergeles recalled. "The owner laid out the golden carpet, all the best wines and food in the place. Rocky stuck with his steak and salad, but the rest of us gorged ourselves with all that terrific Italian food. It was all on the house, and the guy even picked up the cab fare back to the hotel. We used New York tactics on this Maine hick, and it worked beautiful."

By the time the tour reached Portland, Sonny had acquired some tender bruised ribs, a cut lip, and red welts on his arms and midsection. After the first fight in Lewiston, he had discarded the sweat shirt and wore no headgear. He had a natural ability to punch hard and was an aggressive fighter, and by then he felt he could hold his own as long as Rocky didn't unleash his heavy artillery.

"How'm I doin', Rock?" Sonny asked after a good session.

"Great," Rocky said. "You hit me as hard as any heavyweight."

But Sonny was getting too cocky. He wanted to prove to Rocky that he could punch even harder.

In the second round of the next exhibition, Rocky got careless and dropped his left hand. Sonny smashed a right over Rocky's guard that was thrown with all the power he could summon. The punch exploded in the center of Rocky's jaw.

Rocky's head snapped back. His eyes blinked and he hunched his shoulders and pounded his gloves together against the sweaty matted hairs of his chest. Then he spat the bloody mouthpiece onto the canvas, and his tongue protruded between his teeth.

Sonny backed away. He saw the wildness in Rocky's eyes and the tongue coming out and he realized what was happening, but it was too late to stop it.

Rocky swarmed all over Sonny with a steady barrage of punches that drove him into the ropes. The blows hit Sonny on the jaw, the top of the head, the arms, the shoulders. His knees began to buckle. The fans were cheering for Rocky to finish him, and he knew his brother planned to do exactly that.

"I saw the killer come out in Rocky," Sonny recalled. "I knew he wanted to murder me. But there was nothing I could do."

Sonny fell forward and clinched. "Rock! Rock!" he shouted. "Take it easy. I'm your brother. I'm your brother, Rock!"

Rocky pushed him roughly out of the clinch. He backed off several steps and snorted like a bull. He was still raging as he blinked and hesitated, trying to comprehend what was happening. Then he moved back in toward Sonny, flicking lighter punches now, giving his brother the opportunity to recover.

Eventually the Maine Boxing Commission learned of the charade the Marcianos had played. The commissioners suspended Rocky and the promoters for thirty days.

In a story published in the *Lewiston Journal*, promoter Sam Michael was quoted. He said he knew Peter Fuller would not appear and that Sonny would be fighting in his place, but he did not change the name on the marquee because "Sonny could fight under any name he wanted." Michael claimed he never advertised Sonny as "Peter Fuller of Harvard."

"Let them suspend me," Michael said. "I'm not going to put anybody in the bag."

Michael and Johnny Rogers were co-promoters of the four fights. Sharing the blame for the masquerade were promoters Chick Hayes of Portland, William Cyr of Bangor, and Albert Parent of Rumford. Sonny had been introduced in Lewiston as Peter Fuller and in Rumford and Bangor as Tony Zullo.

"We gave them a very good show," Rocky told the commissioners. "I punched Sonny as hard as I punched Joe Louis."

The commissioners asked why Sonny's identity had been concealed.

"Because my mother doesn't want him fighting," Rocky said.

A Maine district attorney called Peter Fuller and asked him to press charges against Marciano. Fuller refused.

The promoters appealed the suspensions and succeeded in getting court action to force the boxing commission to remove the blemishes from their records.

But Rocky never formally appealed. The blot remained for years as the only bad mark on his record. In 1960, State Representative Louis Jalbert failed in an effort to have the commission reverse the suspension. Jalbert finally filed a bill in the state legislature that was approved and cleared Rocky's name.

When Sonny returned to Brockton, he discovered that he had been stripped of his amateur status and would not be allowed to play for the high school baseball team. Rocky had paid his brother nothing for the tour, but the athletic directors felt Sonny had participated in a professional activity and could no longer qualify as an amateur.

It was a serious setback for Sonny, who was eager to impress the major league scouts. He was forced to miss the first two games while further deliberations were being made.

"What the hell's the matter with them?" Rocky said. "You didn't get paid. Tell them you were just doing something for your brother."

Fortunately, Sonny was reinstated and finished out the season at third base. He had a very good year and received offers from several major league teams.

AFTER THE JOE LOUIS FIGHT, Rocky had visited his father at the shoe factory. Things were different now. But there was still the drudgery of working all day at the bed laster. Rocky believed the machines could defeat a man, could ruin his body and his spirit, and make him old too soon. And they were doing it to his father. Only now Pop Marchegiano was a hero. He was no longer the tired-looking, little old Italian immigrant who for forty-six years had labored in the shoe shops, obeying with gritted teeth the orders of the Irish foremen. Rocky's victories over Layne and Louis had made quiet, inconspicuous Pierino a celebrity among his fellow workers. Nobody was going to push him in his job anymore.

It seemed hard for them to believe that Pierino Marchegiano, who was slight of build and seldom boasted or asserted himself among his fellow workers, could be the father of so devastating a fighter. But there he was, a very popular fellow. The attention Pierino received had progressed since Rocky had first begun fighting in Providence. In the beginning, when many scoffed at Rocky's chances, old Pete received little notice. Then, as his son continued to win, more and more people wanted to get close to him. Pierino welcomed the friendship. Finally, he had so many friends that it was impossible for him to recognize all of them.

But Rocky was neither impressed nor satisfied by his father's newfound popularity. Pop was fifty-seven years old and in very poor health. He still had to get up very early every morning and force his pain-racked body to trudge down the hill to the drudgery of his job. No matter how popular he was, it was impossible to slow down the production pace of the bed laster machine. The job was still killing him.

"Pretty soon I'll be going for the championship, Pa," Rocky told him one day shortly after the Louis fight. "I'm earning good money now. I want you to be with me. From here on I'm gonna need you in the training camp. So I want you to go down there and quit your job."

Getting his father out of the factory was a goal that Rocky had set for himself when he first began fighting. Accomplishing it was a source of extreme satisfaction for him. He also gained new responsibilities. With the retirement of his father, Rocky became the patriarch of the Marchegiano clan. He was now to his mother and father and unmarried brothers the Luigi Picciuto of his youth. He would take care of their expenses and their needs, but in his own curious fashion. He would look out for them and protect them and see that they were not uncomfortable. He would see that the bills were paid and that there was always heat in the radiators and food in the refrigerator, but he would do it his way. And nobody would ever question him about it.

IN THE SUMMER OF 1952, James Norris and the IBC were being investigated by the United States Senate on charges that the IBC monopolized boxing championships. A prime instigator was a crusty West Coast fight manager named Jack Hurley.

As the manager of Harry "Kid" Matthews, Hurley claimed the IBC was blocking his chances for a light-heavyweight title bout against champion Joey Maxim.

Hurley didn't stop with Norris but bandied Al Weill's name around, complaining to everyone who would listen that Weill was involved in a blatant conflict of interest and violation of boxing commission regulations by secretly managing Marciano while he worked for Norris and the IBC as matchmaker at Madison Square Garden.

A New York grand jury began an investigation of the IBC. Norris was worried. His private kingdom was being invaded. The IBC pressured Maxim's manager, Jack Kearns, to offer a title match to Matthews to convince everyone that the IBC conducted its business fairly. Surprisingly, Hurley refused the chance. He knew he had the IBC on the defensive, and he was shooting for bigger stakes now. He wanted the heavyweight championship.

After Hurley turned down the Maxim title bout, the Senate committee called a halt to its investigation. The IBC offer had seemed reasonable. But Hurley kept the pressure on. And Norris knew the IBC could not stand up to close scrutiny.

Norris went to Weill and insisted upon a fight between Marciano and Matthews, with the winner to challenge Walcott for the heavyweight title. He tried to convince Weill that Rocky would easily defeat Matthews, the fight would draw a big gate, and, most important to Norris, the outspoken Hurley would finally be silenced forever.

"Forget it," Weill said. "Get yourself another fighter. I don't want it."

"Think it over," Norris said. "We need this fight."

But Weill knew that Rocky was the top contender for the title. He had no intention of risking him against Matthews, an unknown quantity who could do nothing to enhance Marciano's position in the heavyweight ranks.

In April, Rocky had KO'd Gino Buonvino in the second round in Providence. Then in May he knocked out Bernie Reynolds, who

had a record of 52 wins and 9 losses, in the third round. Rocky was tired of waiting. He wanted to fight for the title.

On June 5, Walcott had retained his championship in an unimpressive fifteen-round decision over Charles.

The fans were overwhelmingly in favor of a Marciano-Walcott bout. The only obstacle was Jim Norris and the IBC.

As usual, Weill succumbed to the IBC's wishes. He accepted the match against Matthews, and it was set for July 28 in Yankee Stadium.

Marciano was furious when he learned he was to fight Matthews, not Walcott. It enraged him even more that Weill had told him nothing until the fight was agreed upon and it was too late for Rocky to enter the discussion. He was convinced that no light heavyweight, regardless of his boxing skills, stood a chance of going the distance against him. But it meant he had to wait again. It meant Norris and Weill were screwing him to solve their own problems.

Harry "Kid" Matthews was a paper tiger. He had an enviable record of 77 wins, 3 losses, and 7 draws, with 57 KOs. But he was from Seattle, Washington, and had fought almost exclusively on the West Coast. He had had only one bout in New York, when he won a ten-round decision over Irish Bob Murphy in 1951. A few weeks before the fight, the word in the fight crowd was that Hurley had nurtured Matthews with a steady diet of stiffs, and that Marciano would take him apart.

Hurley himself feared it. He argued for a direct shot at Walcott, insisting to Norris that he wanted no part of Marciano. But Norris had Hurley exactly where he wanted him. Rocky was the number one contender. He could not be expected to wait around while Matthews had a shot at Walcott. So Hurley was trapped. But it was worth taking the chance.

Thunder rumbled overhead as Marciano and Colombo took their traditional walk along the streets of New York that hot, muggy morning of the fight.

"This is it, Allie," Rocky said. "After this guy, who the hell can they put in my way? They've got to give me a title shot."

"We've waited a long time, Rock," Colombo said. "It's almost too good to be true. In a few months you'll be the champ."

Rocky and Allie went to Madison Square Garden early for the noon weigh-in. Matthews, who still had time, had not yet arrived.

"Where's Matthews?" Weill was asked.

"How should I know?" Weill said. "All I know is my fighter's here."

It was that slip of the tongue that sealed Weill's fate as IBC matchmaker. Robert K. Christenberry, chairman of the New York State Athletic Commission, was disgusted with the rumors and bad publicity Weill's dual role had received in the newspapers. That afternoon he summoned Harry Markson to his office and ordered him to terminate Weill's job with the IBC.

Four days later, on August 1, Weill told reporters that he was resigning as IBC matchmaker, effective September 1, to resume full-time management of Rocky Marciano. The sportswriters chuckled. The Vest had finally spilled some of his gravy.

It had rained in the afternoon and dark clouds were still threatening as Marciano entered Yankee Stadium that night to fight Matthews. He wore an old pair of rubbers into the ring to prevent the soles of his boxing shoes from getting wet.

Matthews was a year older than Rocky and, at 179 pounds to Marciano's 187, was one of the few opponents ever to give Rocky a weight advantage. Rocky was absolutely fearless, but it was obvious from the tense expression on Matthews's face that the reverse was not true.

Matthews won the first round with effective jabs that kept the aggressive Marciano at bay. But in the second round Rocky chased Matthews across the ring toward his corner and, punching out of a crouch, delivered two sweeping left hooks that banged off the right side of Harry's skull. His head jerked violently as each punch landed. His mouthpiece flew out, and as he sank to the canvas his head struck the lower rope in his own corner. He struggled to his knees by the count of eight, and it appeared as if he might try to get up, but then he fell backward. His head rested against the ring post, his eyes closed and his arms spread flat over the canvas.

Marciano danced around the ring, grinning and holding his arms high overhead. Colombo rushed to Rocky, wiped his face with a towel, and then hugged and kissed him. Rocky was unmarked, unhurt, and not even slightly tired. The heavyweight contender Matthews had been easier to defeat than most of the mediocre club fighters Rocky had met early in his career at Providence.

"Did ya see them left hooks?" Charley Goldman was shouting, "Who said Rocky didn't have no left? Didja see them?"

Hurley was bitter. After the fight, he publicly ridiculed Matthews for not having followed his fight plan. He even seemed to be admonishing Matthews in the corner before the kid had recovered his senses. It was a big loss for Hurley in more ways than one. He would never again invade the IBC's kingdom. His fighter had no further chance for a title shot as either a heavyweight or a light heavyweight. Harry "Kid" Matthews was no longer

the bright star Hurley referred to affectionate-
ly as "my athlete." Like so many other good
but not great boxers, he had been unable to
rise to the occasion when the opportunity was
golden.

"Do you think you can beat Walcott?" a
reporter asked Rocky in the dressing room.

"I can lick anybody I get in there with,"
Marciano said.

The reporters went away happy, as did
most of the 31,000 fans, the majority of whom
had come to see Marciano destroy the myth of
Harry "Kid" Matthews. The Marciano name
was gold. He was even much more popular
than the champion, Jersey Joe Walcott. The
size of the crowd Rocky had lured to Yankee
Stadium was unheard-of for a nontitle fight.
The largest crowd to attend a bout in Madison
Square Garden in 1952 was under 9,500, with
the average only 4,000 persons. Norris and the
IBC looked greedily toward the fortune that
would be made in a championship bout
between Walcott and Marciano.

15.
The Prize

AND NOW IT WAS ROCKY MARCIANO'S TIME and he knew it.

He came to Grossinger's in the summer of 1952, lean and hungry, obsessed with but a single purpose of mind and spirit—to become heavyweight champion of the world. Mesmerized by the fast approaching climax of his personal crusade, he retreated from the world, carrying in the inner sanctums of his soul a reverence and dedication equal in magnitude, if not motivation, to the religious zeal of a Trappist monk.

It's curious, but understandable, how the great athletes of any sport never allow themselves to consider the possibility of defeat. Ted Williams expected to get a hit whenever he went to the plate. Jack Nicklaus is convinced he can win any golf tournament he enters. And Marciano was the same way, always certain that he would win. Defeat was an ugly specter, made to remain invisible somewhere in the shady caverns of the fighter's subconscious. Even in the three decisions and disqualifications that had gone against him as an amateur, Rocky believed that he had really won. He was as convinced as any man could ever be of his own infallibility. It was one of his most impor-

tant assets. For, as if governed by some fundamental natural law, the fighter who dwells upon losing will eventually do just that.

Despite the critics who claimed he was too slow, clumsy, a brawler unskilled in the finer points of his craft, Marciano's sheer stamina and overwhelming desire to win more than compensated for any shortcomings in his boxing style. He trained, not sometimes casually like Muhammad Ali, George Foreman, and other modern heavyweights, but as if every fight was going to be his last. And in his obsession to win he had an almost non-human ability to resist destruction. It would be seen that September night in Philadelphia, when, as the fight wore on and even close friends had given up on him, it was Marciano's undefeated heart, more than anything else, that carried him from the edge of obscurity to the heavyweight championship of the world.

And so that summer he was a Spartan. He lived in a house on the mountain near the airport, a hermit of sorts, isolated from the glamour of the bright lights and celebrities that beckoned amid the sizzle of excitement in the posh resort below. And, like the good gladiator locked in the dungeons of the Colosseum, he forfeited sex, food, parties, and anything else that manager Weill and trainers Colombo and Goldman felt might dull the killing sharpness of his fighting machinery.

Prehistoric in its simplicity, his purpose was to punish, torture, submerge his body and his soul, until all traces of flab and gentleness were exorcised and all that remained were the basic instincts of survival possessed by an animal.

"There's only one reason to be here, Alsack," he told his friend. "I'm going for the title. Then it'll be all over."

"All over, Rock?" Colombo said.

"That's right," Marciano said. "We'll have it made. There won't be a thing we can't do once I've got the title."

BUT IN ATLANTIC CITY there was a man who had different ideas. Jersey Joe Walcott, whose career already spanned twenty-two years, was publicly critical of the challenger.

"He can't fight," Walcott told John Webster of the *Philadelphia Inquirer*. "If I don't whip him, take my name out of the record books."

In retrospect, long after his retirement, Walcott told me, "In Atlantic City I had just trained hard and conditioned myself. I was just going in there to win. I knew he was a rough, tough, strong, good puncher, and I knew it was going to be a rough, tough fight for me. I just planned to go out there and win. If the opportunity presented itself, I'd go for the early knockout. But, if not, I was trained to go the whole fifteen rounds.

"Rocky had perfected his style very well," Walcott said. "But a guy that has skill could use little twists and little moves to keep him off-balance. I discovered later that Rocky was easy to hit, but not to get at with effective punches."

On September 13, Walcott knocked out sparring partner Pete Nelson. Everyone who saw him that day was impressed. Jersey Joe seemed to be working harder than ever to bring his aging body into trim. He was thirty-eight, the oldest man ever to hold the heavyweight championship, but somehow he had managed to retain the good legs and quick reflexes of a much younger fighter.

Arnold Raymond Cream, known as Jersey Joe Walcott, began fighting in 1930, when Rocky Marciano was seven years old. It had taken him twenty-two years to win the heavyweight championship. He was as reluctant to give it up as Marciano was determined to take it from him.

For a champion, Walcott's record was not impressive. He had 48 wins, 15 losses, and 1 draw. But Walcott was known as a skilled and tricky boxer who could counterpunch and hit with power. He had been involved in some great battles, including five title bouts. He had fought Joe Louis twice, losing a controversial fifteen-round decision in 1947 after decking the Brown Bomber and seemingly outfighting him; then he was knocked out by Louis in the return match a year later.

Jersey Joe had beaten Joey Maxim (former light-heavyweight champion) two out of three times, and had defeated other good fighters including Lee Oma, Jimmy Bivins, Harold Johnson, and Joe Baksi. He had won the title on July 18, 1951, with a seventh-round knockout over Ezzard Charles, and he had outpointed Charles in a return match just four months before.

"I'm going to beat him," Walcott kept insisting in Atlantic City. And although Jersey Joe was the underdog, those who had come to watch him train went away believing in him.

M<small>EANWHILE, IN THE</small> C<small>ATSKILL</small> M<small>OUNTAINS OF</small> N<small>EW</small> Y<small>ORK,</small> Marciano continued his relentless training program. There would be no living with the humiliation should he lose, although he never considered that. The recognition, the money, the security—everything that mattered to Rocky depended upon winning.

By mid-September, Marciano had sparred eighty-five rounds to Walcott's thirty. Rocky was approaching the peak of condition. His back did not bother him, and there were no other injuries.

A reporter asked one of Joe Louis's former sparring partners, who was now in Marciano's camp, to compare the two fighters.

"Louis is faster with a barrage of punches," he said. "But Rocky hurts more with one punch than Joe did with four. Rocky hurts you every time he connects."

Early in the negotiations for the Walcott-Marciano fight, there had been problems between Jim Norris of the IBC and Felix Bocchicchio, the champion's manager. Norris wanted to have the fight in New York, where the IBC controlled the action. But Bocchicchio had a criminal record, and couldn't get a license there.

"We can get the biggest gate in New York," Norris insisted.

"No deal," Bocchicchio said. "Walcott doesn't fight anywhere I can't be the manager."

"I don't care where they hold it," Marciano said. "As long as I fight him and the money's there, what difference does it make?"

Bocchicchio was in control. He had the champion.

They finally agreed to hold the fight in Philadelphia's Municipal Stadium. The site was in Walcott's backyard, Jersey Joe being a resident of Camden, New Jersey. Bocchicchio demanded forty percent for Walcott to Marciano's twenty, which was not unreasonable since Joe was the champion, but he also insisted on a return-bout clause calling for the same percentages should Walcott be defeated.

What can I do? Weill figured. I don't take the deal, we don't get a title shot.

Marciano stayed out of it, but those closest to him sensed how he felt. For Christ sake, he thought. I'm going to be champ, and I still get the short end. Can't they do something with those guys?

Sonny Marciano could see the tension that was building between his brother and Weill. It involved much more than money, although that was an important part of it.

"Weill was becoming paranoid," Sonny said. "He was jealous, like a guy with a broad. I'd come up to the camp, and he'd try to boss me and my friends around like he owned us. He didn't even want me to be around my brother. A few times I wanted to go after Weill myself."

"It's getting so this guy wants to do all my thinking for me," Rocky told Sonny. "I can't do anything on my own. He's got his nose stuck into my marriage, my personal friends, and everything else, He's like a fuckin' wild man. The guy's becoming a real pain in the ass."

But in those days Marciano was like the trained circus lion who, hating his master, still moved obediently to the crack of the whip. Weill was the boss. He had the connections and the savvy in the fight game. And if this was part of the sacrifice necessary to become a champion, Rocky was willing to absorb the mental punishment, although it inflicted more permanent wounds than any physical beating ever could.

There are dozens of anecdotes from a variety of sources—however unreliable they may sometimes be—which support the claim that Marciano was disenchanted with his manager long before he became champion.

One such incident, told by his brothers and several friends, involved Marciaino's father, and took place shortly before the title fight.

They claim that one night Rocky's father got hungry and went into the kitchen to make a snack. Apparently the chef, Alfred Reinaur, on loan to the camp from Grossinger's and later a very good friend of Marciano's, had received orders from Weill not to let anybody in the kitchen.

"Get out of my kitchen and stay out," Reinaur ordered.

Pierino went to bed hungry.

When Marciano found out he was furious. "I don't care what the rules are," he told Weill. "Nobody bosses my father around. If he wants to go into the kitchen or anyplace else, he can. If the cook doesn't like it, you'll just have to get rid of him."

"Sure, Rocky," Weill said, according to the story. "I don't want you should get so excited. You know we can't take any chances. You've gotta be very careful with the food in a training camp. Something bad could happen."

"Not my father, you asshole," Marciano said.

It was strange, Rocky's friends felt, the way Weill never really did understand the Italian ethic.

When Marciano had first begun training at Grossinger's, his wife, Barbara, had visited the camp. But while she was around, Weill was extremely nervous.

"Fighters' wives hurt fighters," Weill kept reminding Rocky.

And Charley Goldman concurred. Weill and Goldman made it so uncomfortable for

Barbara that she soon returned to Brockton. And in the final two weeks before the fight Marciano was not even allowed to talk to her on the phone, although that did not disturb him so much, since by then he was completely preoccupied. "I don't want he should get any letters or phone calls," Weill ordered. "It might upset Rocky."

For a week before the fight, Marciano was not allowed to shake hands or even go for a ride in an automobile. He was interviewed by reporters and filmed for television, but he was not allowed to read newspaper stories dealing with the fight. Some writers were criticizing Marciano. Arthur Daley of the *New York Times* belittled Rocky's ability in several columns, calling him crude and even questioning his power, implying that he was not good enough to be a champion.

Picture Muhammad Ali minus his entourage. A championship fight without Howard Cosell television spectaculars. Instead a sequestered monk, alone on the hill, running and sweating and punishing himself, with no poetry, no dancing girls, no social, religious, or racial revolutions to command.

IN 1952, RACISM KEPT A LOW PROFILE in America. It had always been there, dormant so long as the blacks and Puerto Ricans and other minorities remained passive and did nothing to question the system of white superiority, prejudice, and segregation that had gone unchallenged since time immemorial. Racism then was not found echoing in the bars and streets of middle-class America as it would in the late 1960s and 1970s. But the country still had a sizable group of real "nigger haters."

And so, that summer, Marciano had emerged as the Great White Hope, a serious contender to become the first Caucasian to reach the pinnacle of boxing since 1937, when Joe Louis knocked out James J. Braddock in the eighth round in Chicago.

Louis had been an awesome fighter and a national hero, who held chits of gratitude from every patriotic American for undermining Hitler's pride by destroying the German superman Max Schmeling. He had more respect than perhaps any black athlete in American history, and yet like all great blacks of his period—the Satchel Paiges, Billie Holidays, Charlie Parkers—there were times when Louis was forced to the back of the bus.

Charles and Walcott were drab by comparison to Louis, and shared none of the Brown Bomber's popularity with white America. Unquestionably there were those who would cheer for Marciano on the basis of skin color alone. There were doors that would be opened for Marciano as heavyweight champion that had always been closed to Walcott.

SINCE RESIGNING AS MATCHMAKER for the IBC, Weill no longer had to pretend he was not Rocky's manager. When he had been managing the fighter behind the scenes, he had stayed away from the training camp. But now he spent all of his time there. His nervousness was irritating Marciano, who had trained himself to an explosive edge for the approaching fight.

"He's unbelievable, Allie," Marciano said. "The guy's got sugar diabetes. He's got to take the needle every day. It's got him on edge."

"He's always been a wreck," Colombo said.

"Christ, remember the Cardione and Pretzie fights."

"I'm gonna talk to him," Marciano said. "I don't even want the guy near me during this fight."

A few days before the fight, Marciano asked Weill if he'd mind staying out of the corner. "I want Colombo and Goldman there," Rocky said. "I seem to do better when they're in my corner."

Weill was shocked and then incredulous with anger. "Absolutely not," he said. "You don't think I'm gonna bring you all this way and then not be in your corner for the big one."

"All right, Al," Marciano said. "I just thought you should know how I feel about it."

IT WAS THE FINAL DAY OF TRAINING, and Allie Colombo was reading the sports pages of the morning newspaper.

"Hey, Rock," Colombo said. "Bivins knocked out Coley Wallace last night."

"No kidding," Marciano grinned. "Beautiful, beautiful." He had never forgotten the night in Brooklyn when the judges had awarded the controversial decision to Wallace in a fight Marciano always felt he won.

They broke camp that Monday in a drizzle and fog so thick that all flights were canceled.

Weill's mood matched the weather. He had discovered that he was missing two of his complimentary tickets to the fight, ringside seats worth forty dollars apiece.

"What'd you do with those tickets, Sylvester?" he asked Rocky's pal.

"What tickets?" Nicky Sylvester asked. "I don't know anything about any tickets."

"Don't get funny," Weill said. "One of youse has got my tickets, and somebody better come up with them."

"Weill kept insisting that either Colombo, Rocky, or me had the tickets," Sylvester said. "He was calling us every name in the book. I didn't know anything about it, but until the day he died Weill thought I stole those tickets."

Marciano's friend Steve Melchiore, the Philadelphia police detective who was in charge of the detail to protect Rocky during his stay, led the caravan of cars down through the fog out of the Catskills.

The skies were overcast when they arrived in Philadelphia at about 5 P.M. Weill had planned to stay at the Warwick Hotel but had been told that Bocchicchio might be there, so he went instead to a suite at the Bellevue-Stratford.

That night Colombo and Sylvester walked the streets in the rain.

"Yeah, we're nervous," Colombo said to a reporter from his hometown newspaper, the *Brockton Enterprise-Times.* "But The Rock's upstairs, sleeping like a baby."

Meanwhile Ox DaGrossa, of the Pennsylvania Athletic Commission, was on television that night, saying, "If only poor Rocky can take the punches . . . "

When Marciano woke up in the morning of the fight, there was a slight stiffness in his back. It had rained and the skies were gray. He went with Melchiore and Colombo and jogged in the park across from the stadium. They talked of baseball and general subjects, but did not mention the fight.

After breakfast, Colombo and Melchiore walked across the street to a promoter's office to pick up some complimentary tickets.

"When we walked into the office, I was amazed to see Blinky Palermo [a boxing figure

with known underworld connections, who was later sentenced to a prison term for illegal activities involving the fight game], Felix Bocchicchio, Ox DaGrossa, and Charley Daggert [referee for the fight]," Melchiore said.

"They wouldn't give me any answer when I asked them what they were doing there before the fight," Melchiore said. "The promoter said they just happened to drop in. Having been a policeman and a detective most of my life, I didn't buy it. I figured there had to be something more.

"Colombo didn't like it either," Melchiore went on. "As we were walking back to the hotel, he asked me to try to find out what was going on but not to mention it to Rocky."

Marciano showed up at 11:45 for the weigh-in, but Walcott didn't arrive until 12:35. Rocky's handlers were nervous and angry. They figured Bocchicchio intentionally had the champion show up late to rattle Rocky. But Marciano himself was relaxed. He spent the time chatting with friends and reporters.

Rocky's uncle Mike Piccento was having trouble finding bets. He had forty thousand dollars with him, his own money and cash from Marciano's friends in Brockton.

"I finally bet the whole thing at Lou Tendler's restaurant," he said. "Then I went back to the hotel."

There were people from Brockton who had bet thousands on Marciano. Some already believed that Rocky was unbeatable. They had sold cars, taken out loans, pawned their watches, and, in one instance, even mortgaged a house to make the easy money that would come from Walcott's defeat.

"I wasn't going to let anyone down," Rocky told Nicky Sylvester after the fight. "There was too much at stake."

Meanwhile Weill and Colombo were upset because Charley Daggert was to be the referee. They felt Daggert was too closely associated with the Walcott camp. It was a point that had been argued by Jake Mintz, one of Ezzard Charles's managers, at the Charles-Walcott title bout in 1951.

🥊

It is two hours before the fight. The tempo quickens. A strange exhilaration sweetens the air, mystical and haunting, sensual as love notes soaring from a jazz saxophone. People are arriving, as if siphoned through some great global funnel, sensing the destiny of the night. The suspense and tension grows, and rumors sprout like mushrooms in an autumn rain.

Colombo is concerned with only one.

"There was a strong rumor around that Rocky couldn't win unless he knocked Walcott out," said Sam Silverman. "I don't know where it came from, but I heard it, and so did a lot of other guys."

The crowning of a heavyweight champion is a supreme occasion in sports. The fight that creates the new King is important in its most infinite detail. People who have no interest in boxing attend because it is the most chic place to be. For those who love the sport it is an eternal orgasm. Its celebration sizzles like a rare champagne that intoxicates the world. It is the ultimate in charisma, excitement, suspense. And nowhere else is victory so consummately rewarding and defeat so inconsolably agonizing.

There is not anywhere near the same intensity in mood and atmosphere when the little men, the middleweights, lightweights, and featherweights, risk their hearts and titles upon the canvas. Nor can it be found in the Masters Golf Tournament, the Super Bowl,

the Indianapolis 500, or the World Series.

In a world that claims to abhor violence and yet immerses itself in it, the heavyweight champion is a symbol, the very image of power and survival. The toughest man alive. Most violent of the violent. An idol in a generation that no longer recognizes idols.

🥊

Marciano arrives early and goes directly to the dressing room, beneath the outdoor stadium. Friends are there, offering their final encouragement. Nicky Sylvester has loaned Rocky a pair of suit pants to wear down to the ring. The challenger will also wear rubbers to make absolutely certain that the soles of his boxing shoes do not get wet after the rain. Sylvester, always the camp jester, is solemn now. He and Colombo are the two who can sense when and when not to provide humor for Marciano. Everyone in the locker room knows that now is not the time.

The preliminary bouts begin. The room is cleared except for Rocky and his handlers. Colombo and Goldman are tense as they review the fight plan.

"You've got to bully him. You've got to take him right over," Goldman says. "Don't let this guy think he can handle you, but don't get careless either, because Walcott can hit."

Thirty minutes to go.

Marciano dozes on a table in the dressing room. He has listened to his handlers and thought the secret thoughts that every fighter must consider and filter out, relegating some to the subconscious while holding others near the surface in sharp focus, ready to be used as the need arises. He has done all of this, and now nothing remains but the countdown. And so he rests and closes his eyes, and somehow, during this most difficult time, when minutes can be measured as days, he blocks out the impossible and commands his body and mind to relax completely. And he waits.

Colombo is supposed to awaken him in time to warm up, clear his head, and flush his muscles with a quick burst of shadowboxing. But now the word has been passed to bring Rocky into the stadium. Colombo realizes that his watch is slow, although he is certain, at least as certain as he is of anything now, that he had set it at the correct time when he awakened in the morning.

A detail of eight uniformed policemen leads Rocky into the stadium and down the aisle toward the ring. He has on the black and red robe, the colors of Brockton High.

Steve Melchiore commands the police detail. He walks at Marciano's side. Melchiore is still suspicious of situations surrounding the fight. He is especially concerned because of a rumor that the odds favoring Rocky have fallen sharply.

"Rocky. I want you to lissen an' lissen good. You're gonna have to knock him out to win," the detective said as he led Rocky to the ring. "Don't ask me why. I've still got to find that out myself."

And then Marciano is in the ring, and the crowd is roaring, but he does not hear it. He is alone, and it is his time, and he knows it.

In the center of the ring, Marciano did not look into Walcott's eyes. There was no emotion now, only the need to get on with it. Darkness fell over the stadium. And then the fighters were in their corners, ready to begin.

How do you gauge how a fight will begin? Who could have speculated that in such an important contest there would be none of the preliminary sizing up by the opponents?

They came together almost immediately.

Walcott lashed out with a volley of lefts and rights that landed but did no damage. Then suddenly he connected with a hard left hook to the jaw that dropped Marciano to the canvas.

The hook collided with Rocky's chin like a torpedo that explodes on contact. He was barely aware of it before he was dumped on the seat of his trunks. It was the surprise, the embarrassment, that shocked Marciano more than the physical effect. ("I wasn't hurt by the punch," Rocky said later. "Not even dazed.") He quickly rolled to his knees. Only a minute had gone by, and he was on the canvas for the first time in his career.

Cameras flashed from behind the ring apron. The crowd was on its feet, delirious.

Marciano was enraged. "You son of a bitch," he said. "I'll get you."

Weill and Goldman screamed at Marciano to take an eight-count. He ignored them, bounding up at three. Walcott came for him. But Marciano waded in punching. Walcott smashed him, and blood trickled from Marciano's lips. Rocky swung wildly. Walcott continued to hit him. When the round ended, Marciano's left eye was swollen.

In the corner, Weill looked like a ghost. He tried to caution Marciano, but the words came out like garbled gibberish.

"I'm all right," Marciano said. "For Christ sake, I'm all right."

Marciano kept bringing the fight to Walcott, taking the punishment in order to press the attack. It was the only way he knew. But Walcott was two inches taller, ten pounds heavier, and had a seven-inch reach advantage. He was a superior boxer who knew how to get the most out of every move, and he was using Rocky's style as a springboard for some very sharp counterpunching.

Just before the bell ending the third round, Walcott slammed an ungodly right to

Marciano's head. The punch could have shelled a coconut. Marciano blinked but kept coming. He snorted like a Brahma bull that feels the spur. Then he unleased a right, left, and a hard right that hurt Walcott. They were still smashing each other after the bell.

Weill was jabbering nervously in the corner. Rocky didn't want to talk. He gave Weill a push with his glove.

"That's it, Al," said Colombo. "Stay out of the corner. Me and Charley will handle it." (This was according to Marciano and Colombo long after the fight.)

Marciano was thinking that he had to get in some heavy punches to take Walcott over. But it wasn't happening. Rocky did deliver some hard blows, but Walcott shook them off, danced away, and ripped the challenger with counterpunches. Sometimes Marciano drove Jersey Joe to the ropes. They battered each other in close, and once Rocky staggered the champion, forcing Joe to grab hard. But mostly it was Walcott who was in command, hitting more often and punching with plenty of authority.

There is an implied guarantee that the audience will see a good fight when a straight-ahead slugger meets a shrewd boxer who can also punch. Witness Frazier and Ali. It's wild and exciting but not the same when two brawlers stand toe to toe seeking instant demolition. And only the purists enjoy watching two Fred Astaires with marshmallow punches waltz their way through an evening.

In Marciano and Walcott the fans had the best of all possible worlds: Rocky, the relentless slugger who would never be defeated and would knock out 43 of his 49 opponents for the highest percentage in boxing history; and Jersey Joe, a consummate boxer, unafraid to move in on the Brockton Blockbuster, with tricky moves and a punch that had been strong enough to knock out 30 opponents.

In the sixth round, as Marciano charged Walcott deep in his familiar crouch, the fighters' heads collided. The top of Rocky's skull rammed the thin-skinned bone above Walcott's left eye. Blood and gore began spewing from a deep gash in the thin hair above Marciano's forehead, and the flesh around Jersey Joe's eye was ripped open. They fought like injured savages.

Rocky wanted to make Walcott's cut a target. But blood from his own wound was streaming down his forehead into his eyes, so he couldn't see Jersey Joe clearly enough to deliver accurate punches.

"There's something in my eyes," Marciano told Colombo in the corner. "They're burning."

Rocky's handlers had squeezed a sponge over his head to clean the gore from his cut so they could treat it. They put medication on it to stop the bleeding.

"My eyes are getting worse," Rocky said at the end of the seventh round. "Do something. I can't see."

Freddy Brown, the expert cut man Weill had hired just before the fight, Goldman, and Colombo washed the eyes with small sponges soaked in cold water. They were red and misty.

"We suspected it was some kind of medication used on Walcott," Colombo said. "But we didn't know what to do about it. We just kept trying to wash the stuff out of his eyes, but they seemed to be getting worse all the time."

"What're they doin'? What're they doin' to Rocky?" Weill screamed at Referee Daggert as he ran beside the ring apron. "Check his gloves. Check his gloves. They've got something on his gloves" (according to Detective Melchiore, who was standing next to Weill).

"That's when Ox DaGrossa told Weill to sit down or he'd throw him out of the stadium,"

Melchiore recalled. "I took over for Weill after that. He sat down and told me what to holler.

"Then Ox told me to sit down or I'd get thrown out too."

Melchiore said he replied, "You or nobody else is gonna put me outta this stadium. I'm assigned to Rocky Marciano to guard him and see that he's not harmed."

But Marciano was being harmed. In fact, he was being battered. Only not into submission. For he kept coming forward relentlessly, always bringing the fight to Walcott.

"It seemed like Walcott had some stuff between his neck and shoulder where I rested my head when we got in close," Rocky surmised after the fight. "Every time we came together, my eyes would start smarting again."

But other eyewitnesses, knowledgeable about the fight game, thought Marciano was blinded by his own handlers.

"No question. They blinded him in his own corner," said Sam Silverman. "I was sitting ringside, right next to them. I think it was poor work, a mistake by his own handlers, that blinded Rocky. Whatever they used on his head got into his eyes.

"Weill had everybody crazy in the corner," Silverman continued. "Walcott had the legs of a twenty-year-old. He was having the best fight of his career. He must've put Rocky into two hundred head-on-collisions. It was one of the worst lickings I ever seen a guy get. Weill was a maniac, hollering and screaming. Everybody got nerved up. Instead of getting towels and pads, they hit the kid with a sponge and the cut stuff went right into his eyes. They blinded him. The poor kid couldn't see. He was getting the shit punched out of him."

But Marciano kept on coming. Possessed by something too intense for description—determination, killer instinct, courage—all of these and something more. For Marciano had to win. It was all that mattered.

But Walcott was unaware of the problem. He was concentrating on just one thing, winning the fight, and as the rounds wore on he was doing exactly that.

"If there was anything in his eyes," Walcott said, "it had to be medication. I didn't know it."

"He was too wrapped up in the fight," Marciano said. "You don't notice what the handlers are doing to you between rounds, you're too busy concentrating on the fight. They could have put it there and Joe never would have known. He was too great a champ to go along with something like that. They wouldn't tell him. But somebody did it, because I know what was happening to my eyes."

"Rocky believed he was blinded intentionally until the day he died," Peter Marciano said. "He spoke of it often."

Long after the fight, Rocky would become so convinced that there had been foul play that he accused Bocchicchio of rubbing a hot, irritant salve, a capsicum ointment, on Walcott's gloves and upper body. He made the charges in a story published in the *Saturday Evening Post* in October 1956, and the Curtis Publishing Company was promptly sued by Bocchicchio. But, based largely on testimony by Rocky's paesano Melchiore, a Pennsylvania jury believed the allegations and found in favor of the *Post* . . . But right now Rocky was fighting for his life. He didn't know why it was happening. He only knew he was almost blind, and everything he'd ever dreamed and hungered for was slipping out of his grasp.

"What's happening to your pal," a reporter asked Nicky Sylvester, who sat pale and silent at ringside.

"What do you think's happening?" Sylvester snapped, "He's getting his brains knocked out."

"What's going to happen if he loses?" the reporter asked in typical journalistic jugular fashion.

"I'll tell you what's going to happen," Sylvester said. "Fifty thousand Italians are going to commit suicide."

By the end of the ninth round, Marciano's eyes were clearing up. He chased Walcott around the ring in the tenth. The exchange was furious.

"How'm I doing?" Rocky asked Colombo.

"You're doin' all right," Colombo said.

But he wasn't. And in the eleventh round Walcott landed a right to Rocky's heart. The impact, assuming proper placement, might have killed a two-year-old buffalo. The punch stopped Marciano in his tracks. Walcott smashed him with a barrage of lefts and rights to the head. A nasty gash opened over Marciano's right eye. Jersey Joe was battering him at the bell.

It didn't seem possible, but with only four rounds remaining Walcott was looking fresher, stronger, more confident than ever. Where was the mass of gelatin that an old man's legs were supposed to contain after he had gone the equivalent of a distance runner's marathon in the ring? Where were the spasms and cramps in the arms that forced an ancient fighter to lower his defense, leaving his jaw exposed to the coup de grace? Or was it just that Walcott had such a pride and desire to keep his beloved championship that the laws of nature no longer applied?

"I'll never forget it," Marciano's boyhood chum Izzy Gold said. "Rocky was taking a helluva pounding. He didn't look like he could win. There were guys from Brockton who had bet everything, gone in hock way over their heads, to make a fast buck on this fight. They looked sick, like they was gonna puke all over the place any minute. These were guys who knew Rocky,

so-called friends, and now all they were thinkin' about was trying to lay off the bets and save their dough. They didn't give a crap about Rocky, not as long as their money was at stake. I was saying to myself, 'Go ahead, I hope you get rid of those bets, because Rocky's gonna win. There's no way he's gonna lose this fight.' "

In the eighth round, the fight had become too much for twelve-year-old Peter Marciano.

"I was sitting with a priest from Providence," he said. "Suddenly I couldn't stand watching it anymore. I wanted to get out of there. I started crying and running up the aisle. But the priest came after me and grabbed me and told me to sit down. He said to have faith and pray for my brother, and if I did that everything was going to be all right. So I say there crying and praying, and I didn't want to watch it, but I did anyway, because I couldn't help myself."

Near the ring Sonny Marciano was seated behind his cousin Duna Cappiello. The look of death was upon his face.

"I had on a light blue Windbreaker," Capiello said. "Sonny was pounding me on the back. He had bitten his fingernails down to the nubs. At the end of the fight, I had blood all over my jacket."

Inside the ring, Walcott's white boxing trunks were covered with blood. Marciano looked like he had crawled through the windshield of a cracked-up Volkswagen.

"In this fight I did something I never did before," Walcott said. "In the eleventh round I hit Rocky a tremendous left to the body. The bell saved him. In the twelfth I thought I'd go out and finish him, but he made it through the round. In the corner after the twelfth I planned to go out and set him up real good with two left jabs . . . "

"How'm I doing?" Rocky asked Colombo after the twelfth.

"You're losing," Colombo said. "You'll have to knock him out to win."

They came out for the thirteenth, each determined to finish the other, although by this time Walcott was well ahead and might, had he been cautious, have shuffled and feinted his way to certain victory. No doubt he has thought of this many times since. Times when his mind was clear, free of the narcosis that sends a fighter spinning toward the primitive.

Frank Sinatra turned to say something to Barbara Marciano, seven months pregnant as she sat cheering her husband to victory. He missed the action that gave his friend the title.

Marciano hooked a left to the body. Walcott backed off, retreating toward the ropes. Then Rocky delivered the punch that canceled his trip to obscurity and placed him ten seconds away from the throne.

It was a tremendous short right that distorted Walcott's jaw and sent sweat beads of destruction raining from his skull. The hollow thump of leather on bone announced the end.

As Walcott crumpled, Marciano came around with a looping left that grazed his head. But the punch was not needed. The champion sank to one knee, his left arm hooked behind the middle rope strand, his head resting on the canvas.

Marciano ran for his corner. But the fight was over. Daggert could have counted to one hundred. Walcott never moved. And finally, when it no longer mattered, he had to be helped to his corner.

"I was going to set him up real good with two left jabs," Walcott said. "He was finished. I jabbed the first jab, a straight stiff jab. The jar of the jab gushed the blood from my cut into my left eye. I couldn't see his right side. He had started the knockout punch, but I could only see the left side. If I had only thrown the right instead of the left jab, if I

could have seen the punch, and stepped back, he would have fallen down from the force of the punch. He was worn out, beat, and he might not have been able to get up."

These are the dreams that live in the memory of a fallen King, and should not, cannot, be denied.

"He was starting to throw his left," Rocky told reporters later. "My right was inside of it. I saw my chance, and that was it."

Marciano's paesanos from Brockton almost tore the ring down trying to get to him. Rocky was bouncing up and down, his hands high above his head. Colombo tackled him with a bear hug and kissed him, his eyes full of tears.

When they had finally pushed and shoved their way back through the wildness of the crowd, the Marciano dressing room erupted. Celebrities poured in like flowing wine.

"You fought a helluva fight. Champ," Humphrey Bogart said, clasping Rocky's hand. "You just fought one helluva fight."

Sonny Marciano sat on top of the lockers, the tears streaming down his cheeks, overwhelmed by the current of brotherly compassion and pride.

Sportswriters clamored for his attention. "Magnificent fighter" . . . "Devastating puncher" . . . "An animal, unbelievable endurance" were the kinds of superlatives they enshrined the new champion with now.

Rocky had risen high in the esteem of the former champions who attended the fight.

"Marciano is the hardest hitter and gamest heavyweight I've ever seen since Dempsey," said Barney Ross.

Rocky was grinning, greeting them as they came, unselfish in his praise of the great fight that Walcott had made. The happiness on the new champion's face clashed with the unrepaired gore like ice cream on pizza.

In another universe, Walcott's dressing room was the high school gym after the dance, a hospital ward for terminally ill millionaires. Walcott was old and battered and alone despite the people who insisted differently. The cut above his left eye would require eight stitches, a thin, puckering scar like the brand on a steer.

"I felt the great, deep hurt of losing a fight that was so one-sided," Walcott recalled, still amazingly fit years after his retirement. "No fight that I ever fought did I ever feel better or more confident. But after a few days of thinking it over, I realized that I was very fortunate to have had the title and to have lost to a guy who proved to be a great American and champion."

Marciano sat on the bed in his hotel suite, sore and weary. From beyond the door, the party sounds rained like confetti. Adrenalin boiled like gasoline in Rocky's veins. He had earned the right to collapse. But he knew that no amount of exhaustion could defy the exuberance that awaited him.

For a while he was alone in the room with Nicky Sylvester. Rocky was grinning, shaking his head from side to side as if he didn't believe the way it had happened. He walked to the mirror and glanced at his battered face.

Once before they had gone to a fight and seen a courageous Italian boxer pummeled by the quick, unforgiving fists of a more experienced opponent. The fighter had been viciously pounded and cut but gamely resisted defeat, his heart refusing to let him go down. Nicky and Rocky had been so impressed, they had spoken strongly of it in Italian.

Now, as Marciano stared at his own macabre image, he began to repeat the words. "Gee, *Nitch*," he said. "*Sango . . .*"

But Rocky never finished. For all at once, the lonely clown's fortress of humor fell apart and, unable to hide any longer, out staggered the stranger, a bruised and naked soldier, armed with nothing but his love and devotion to the champion.

Sylvester was suddenly overcome by a hurricane of emotion. His body shook, and tears rolled down his face. He tried to speak, but could not. And Rocky went to him and gathered him in his arms and consoled him.

Dr. Vincent Nardiello began repairing Rocky's wounds—fourteen stitches to close the gashes on the champion's scalp and above the bridge of his nose at the corner of his left eye. Thick slabs of adhesive tape pressed over the cuts. Ice packs for the purple lump under his eye. Linament to salve the ribs.

Machine-gun bursts of laughter ricocheted off the walls from the room outside.

A friend from Brockton, concerned about Marciano's injuries, came into the room.

"How's it feel, Rock?" he asked.

"Beautiful," Rocky said. "Beautiful."

It was 1 a.m. when Marciano finally called his mother, the latest he had ever phoned her after a fight. As was her custom, Pasqualena had seen or heard nothing of the fight, although she certainly knew the results. By the time the call came through, Brockton was in a state of bedlam.

For four hours horns blew, firecrackers exploded, banners waved, barrooms rang with music, mobs ran in the streets, automobiles screeched back and forth laying tributes of rubber and smoke. It was the ultimate party of a city claiming its King, a festival of spontaneous joy never seen before or since in the usually drab Shoe City.

"Are you all right, Rocky?" Pasqualena asked.

"I'm all right. Mom," Rocky said. "I'm fine."

"Are you sure you're all right?" she said. "Do you feel like a champion?"

"And how I do," Rocky said.

"All right, let's get happy now," Pasqualena told friends who had gathered at the house on Dover Street. "Rocky's fine. He'sa champeen now. Everybody be happy."

16.
The Kingdom

"IT's UNBELIEVABLE, SONNY. It's like they want to give me the world," Rocky said. "Millionaires, athletes, celebrities—they all want to be with the champ."

All of his life Rocky Marciano had dreamed of becoming a wealthy sports hero, but when it finally came true he had to reach out and touch it before he was convinced it was real.

After the fight, Rocky and Barbara spent a week in New York doing the town. He had a legion of new friends who fought for his attention and waved his banner in every vestibule of society and prominence in the city. He did not ignore any of them, but he always favored the Italians.

"Someday you're going to win the title and then a lot of guys you never saw before will be coming around," Mike Piccento had told him long before. "If they want to be with you, let them pay. They've got the money. They can afford it. They don't want to be with just plain Rocky. They want to be with a champion. If you were nobody they wouldn't give you a second look. And if you go downhill, they'll drop you like a hot potato. So let them pay,"

It was good advice, even though Rocky didn't need it. He had no intention of spending his money foolishly. He had seen what happened to other champions, and the way they were treated by the once-adoring public when they were broke and finished as fighters. Rocky was scheming for ways not only to hold on to his money but to earn much more. He didn't spend a dime on the Johnny-come-latelies that squired him around New York.

"If a champion spends his money foolishly, they ridicule him for that, and if he doesn't spend it, they call him cheap," he told Sonny. "Well, I'd rather have them criticize me for not spending it and wind up keeping my money."

Meanwhile, Al Weill was ecstatic. He was already plotting tours, nightclub appearances, guest spots on television, and refereeing jobs for Rocky. He claimed offers from Las Vegas, Chicago, Reno, New York, and foreign countries. "We're gonna make hundreds of thousands before next year," he told Rocky. "And you won't even have to throw a punch." But he never gave Marciano any of the details.

Fifty thousand people lined the streets of Brockton to welcome Rocky home on October 2, 1952. They had been standing there on a muggy, overcast afternoon for almost two hours without a sign of him or any word, but the enthusiasm did not wane.

Rocky's plane had been unable to land at Logan Airport in Boston because of heavy fog and was forced to return to Bedford, about an hour's drive from Brockton.

"I hope they won't think I'm getting stuck up because I'm so late," Rocky said.

"Don't worry," Charley Goldman said. "You're the champ. Everybody waits for the champ."

The champion came into the city shortly after 4 P.M., grinning from the back seat of a Cadillac convertible that had a large golden crown on its hood. He was very proud and happy, even though his face still bore the signs of Jersey Joe's punishment. His eyes were slightly puffy and bloodshot, but he was grinning broadly as the car inched along past showers of confetti and rice and shouts of "Rocky! Rocky! Champ! Champ!"

An airplane trailed a WELCOME HOME ROCKY banner while hundreds of police held back the excited mobs that pressed forward to shake hands with the champion. Police said later the ovations surpassed those accorded to Presidents Roosevelt and Truman when they campaigned in the city.

There were special ceremonies at James Edgar Playground and at Eldon Keith Field, where the high school played its football games.

"I thank all you good people for wishing my son well and praying with me for his success," Pasqualena Marchegiano said, greeting the crowd in broken English.

That evening forty of Rocky's friends, who had won almost fifty thousand dollars on the title fight, honored him at a dinner in a local supper club. He was surprised by the gift of a brand-new Cadillac with special plates that

had, instead of numbers, the letters KO.

"Rocky was still the world's worst driver," Sonny chuckled. "But now he owned two automobiles."

Rocky wanted to spend time with his wife and family in Brockton, but Al Weill had different plans. There was plenty of money to be made and Weill had the tours all scheduled. The first was an appearance at the Kid Gavilan-Billy Graham welterweight title bout on October 5 in Havana, Cuba.

Rocky soon discovered that there would be very little time for his wife and family, and almost none to spend with his old friends in Brockton. There was important money to be made, people to meet, new horizons to conquer.

He was supposed to come to Brockton for Nicky Sylvester's wedding, but never made it, sending along a very warm recording of his friendship for Nicky instead. When the Marcianos' first baby, Mary Anne, was born at Brockton Hospital on December 6, 1952, Rocky was in California. He was forced to spend another seven days fulfilling commitments before finally arriving home to see his wife and daughter. He would miss many other important weddings, birthdays, holidays, christenings, and births.

"Sometimes I think you're only the champ, not my son anymore," Pasqualena said sadly. "Why don't you stay home? Spend more time with us."

"Gee, Ma, I've got to make a living," Rocky said. "You know I'd rather be here with you and the family."

*

"HE LEARNED TO HANDLE MA better than any

of us ever could," Peter Marciano recalled. "She was very proud of him, and he knew just the right things to say to her. He always wanted to do things for Ma and Pa and make them happy, but he had to live his own life too."

In November, Rocky sent his parents on a trip to Italy to visit the villages where they had been born. The night Rocky won the title were great celebrations in the streets of Italy. The mayor of Ripateatina, where Pierino was born, sent a telegram of congratulations to Brockton. This made Rocky very proud. He had always wanted to be able to send his parents back to Italy to see their relatives and friends. But the trip was a disappointment, and the Marchegianos cut it short when Rocky's daughter was born.

"Everywhere we went we saw the sadness and poverty," Pasqualena said. "They were all poor and everybody looked to us for what we can do for them. It was too sad, too much lonely."

Within a few weeks after the tour began, Rocky's patience with Al Weill began to wear thin.

"The guy's ridiculous," Rocky told Sonny. "He tells me when to be in my room, who I'm going to see, when to come downstairs, when to go to bed. He never tells me where we're going or what I'm making. I think the guy's cheating me. I'm not putting up with it much longer."

But Weill knew what he was doing. The money was coming in from all directions, and there were more offers than they could accept.

On a tour of the Pacific, where Rocky fought exhibitions, they visited Hawaii, the Philippines, Japan, and Okinawa, and everywhere they were welcomed with great enthusiasm.

"They love us," Weill said. "There's not a place in the world where we can't make out."

In the Philippines, Rocky was asked to appear at a leper colony. He was warned not to come in close contact with the lepers. But Rocky mingled with them and shook their hands.

"They're people, aren't they?" Rocky said. "I'm not going to treat them like outcasts. If you're gonna get something, you'll get it. There's no sense worrying about it."

And yet he always wiped off the silverware and glasses with a napkin before he ate in a restaurant.

"He was a strange one," a friend once said. "Nobody ever knew Rocky except Rocky, and that was exactly the way he wanted it."

In Tokyo, Rocky became upset with Weill again. Rocky wanted to spend several days sightseeing and shopping for souvenirs in Japan.

"We got there one night, trained the following day, then boxed that night and left," Rocky said. "I didn't get a chance to see anything. Al had us booked for two days later someplace in Kentucky."

It was a frantic game of hopscotch, running for the money with no tomorrow. They lived out of suitcases in planes, taxis, hotels, restaurants, and fancy country clubs. But this would end. For Rocky was becoming edgy to resume his training. He knew that the windfall of easy money was there only because he was the champion. And somewhere Jersey Joe Walcott was plotting to regain his title.

17.
The Defender

THAT JANUARY, ROCKY returned to the Catskills to train, determined to make a better showing in his return match with Walcott, to avenge the only knockdown of his career.

They lived in a cottage in the valley at Grossinger's main resort, unable to take advantage of the isolation of the house by the airport because of the heavy snows that covered the mountains, and restricted access to the airport training camp.

Barbara was with Rocky for the first two weeks, but then went back to Brockton to care for their infant daughter and leave Marciano to the serious business of preparing to defend his title. By now she realized that Rocky's thoughts were dominated completely by boxing, even more so than before, when he was still a challenger. And if she blamed Weill outwardly for taking her husband away from her, she must have secretly known that Rocky would have given everything over to fighting then, regardless of the manager. It was a lonely life for Barbara, one that was not likely to change.

In the morning Marciano and Colombo bundled up in sweat shirts and parkas and went out into the hills to run. Often the skies were overcast, and sometimes it was snowing.

It was very cold, with the wind raw in their faces, but Rocky did not complain. He would run long after the pain and cramps had forced Colombo and his other friends to stop, always willing to go the extra mile, knowing that someday, alone and facing the lion, he could call upon it.

"This wind's not so bad," he told Colombo. "It toughens up my skin. It'll make me harder to cut."

Marciano's preoccupation with physical conditioning cannot be overstressed. He was eager to train every day before a fight, and, unlike most heavyweights, he sometimes went to camp months before there was even a fight scheduled for him.

Even Joe Frazier, the former champion who also prided himself on being fit, a slugger who, like Marciano, relied heavily on stamina and strength to bull his way through the defenses of an opponent, did not train with anywhere near the same dedication that Marciano devoted to it.

"I've been to camp eight weeks," Frazier said before his title bout with Muhammad Ali in Manila (September 1975). "The longest in my life, and I feel I'm ready."

It is safe to speculate that eight weeks of

training would not have satisfied Marciano had he been scheduled to fight Ali. He had often trained for four or five months to go against far less skilled opponents. For he truly believed that there was something about long-distance training that increased a man's endurance, just as a slow, sensible diet trims off the fat more evenly than a dramatic crash program. And, although one can never be certain, there is reason to doubt whether Ali or any other fighter could have worn Marciano down and destroyed his defenses the way Muhammad did to Foreman and Frazier.

In the middle of his training, Rocky changed camps and traveled to Holland, Michigan, to accept the hospitality of Ted Cheff, the wealthy, middle-aged president of Holland Furnace Company.

Cheff was a dedicated fan of Marciano's and a man who enjoyed showing his appreciation. Sonny Marciano remembers him as "a guy with a lot of class" and one of Rocky's close friends. The days spent in Michigan were some of the happiest in Sonny's memory, and Rocky and his friends returned there many times.

Barbara joined Rocky in Michigan and remained in camp for three weeks, leaving for Brockton about six weeks before the fight. Scrapbooks filled with pictures show the Marcianos relaxing at Cheff's sprawling estate. There were trips in the yacht on the lake, afternoons by the pool, elegant meals in the dining room.

But despite the relaxed atmosphere, Marciano was like a politician romancing a crowd, always aware of his purpose and the dangers of unprotected intimacy. The memory of having been knocked down by Walcott was more than enough to keep him at the punching bags.

There were things that Rocky had to do over and over again: study the fight films,

learn to adjust to Walcott's deceptive style of moving off and jabbing. Mostly he had to concentrate on overcoming Jersey Joe's six-inch advantage in reach.

"I'm going after him right away this time," Rocky told Colombo. "I'm gonna try to get him real quick. I know I can do better against this guy."

But to the press Marciano was more conservative. He never tried to psych out an opponent. He also stayed away from predictions, regardless of his own confidence.

This time, however, he told reporters, "I'll be trying for a knockout. I think I'll get him midway in the fight."

Marciano's pride was another factor that made him more dangerous than ever after he had become champion. In December he had been awarded the Boxing Writer's Association Edward J. Neil Memorial Plaque as fighter of the year for 1952. He also received *Ring Magazine*'s Annual Merit Award, including the Gold Medal as Fighter of the Year and the Championship Belt. Then, in January, he was awarded the $10,000 Ray Hickock Belt as Professional Athlete of the Year.

Everything was going well until shortly before the fight was scheduled to take place, when one of his sparring partners injured Marciano's nose. The damage impaired Rocky's breathing, which had always been something of a minor problem. The sound of Rocky's nostrils blowing out air during a fight was usually much more noticeable than the breathing of most fighters. "Hhffft . . . hhffft . . . hhffft . . . " like the snort of a wart hog, it seemed to add to Rocky's tenacity as he crouched and came toward an opponent. But, with the injury, the fight had to be postponed from April 10 to May 15.

IF A FIGHTER COULD PREDICT with some accuracy the way a match would come out, oceans of self-denial and emotion might be saved. For had Marciano known how it would be that night in Chicago, he probably would not have spent the better part of four grueling months preparing for it. And yet there was no way he could know.

"As a fight it was a joke," said the late Nat Fleisher, editor of *Ring Magazine*. "As a requiem for a heavyweight who had been champion of the world, it was a sad affair."

And so it seemed to many that dismal night in Chicago. It was a black eye for boxing. As damning, it appeared, as later was the Liston-Clay fiasco in Lewiston, Maine, when Clay's "phantom punch" floored the Ugly Bear in the first round. But the comparison is not really fair. Because Marciano did hit Walcott, and those close to the action saw it. He not only hit him, he hit him very hard.

It was planned that Rocky would come on fast in this fight. He spent much more time in the dressing room warming up than he had previously.

"We can't take any chances this time sending him out cold," Charley Goldman said. "He's got to go in hot. We don't want him on the canvas again in the opening rounds."

A reporter asked Goldman why Marciano was such a slow starter.

"Because he's absolutely without tension before a fight," Goldman said. "He can sleep in the dressing room, just like Louis used to."

What little there was to describe of the fight went about like this:

Walcott appeared tense as he came out of his corner. Marciano seemed cautious, but then he charged the challenger, showing absolutely no fear or respect as he fired a series of punches that exploded in Walcott's face. Rocky bounced a hook off Walcott's head and the challenger held on. They separated, but Marciano kept the pressure on. Walcott held him off briefly with his tricky shuffle and some pretty jabs.

Then came the punches. Rocky threw a left, which he followed quickly with a short right uppercut that landed squarely on Walcott's jaw. The force of the punch lifted Walcott off his feet and toppled him over backward, and he landed with a thud on his back, his legs kicked up stiffly like a gymnast completing an exercise.

Walcott rose quickly to his haunches and sat glassy-eyed in the corner as Referee Frank Sikora began counting. Midway through the count, it appeared as if his head was clearing and he had shaken off the dizzyness. Everyone assumed he would get up and continue the fight.

Because Walcott's back had been to the camera, television audiences did not see Rocky's punches. The knockdown appeared to come from a shove rather than a solid blow. Even many of the fans at the stadium failed to see the uppercut.

They couldn't believe it when Sikora waved his arms to signal that the bout was over.

Jersey Joe bounced up from the canvas and stomped around the ring, protesting to Sikora that he had beaten the count.

"Let them fight. Let them fight," the enraged fans shouted.

The knockout had come at 2 minutes and 25 seconds of the first round, one of the swiftest endings ever to a heavyweight championship fight. It was a proud addition to Marciano's record, but the fans did not like or believe it.

Joe Louis, who watched the fight on television, told reporters that the match, "came out bad for the fight game."

The officials and 15 of 17 sportswriters polled felt that Walcott had received a fair count and had not gotten up in time. Most thought the knockout was the result of a solid punch.

"I hit him with a left hook and followed it up with a right uppercut," Marciano insisted. "I think it was a better right than I got him with in the first fight."

For Walcott it was the last stop. He promised his wife and family that he would retire if he lost to Marciano, and he kept his word.

Years later, in Camden, New Jersey, I asked Walcott why he waited so long to get up when it was obvious from the way he protested that his head had cleared and he still possessed plenty of energy.

Walcott said the punch that Marciano hit him with was "a real good right, but not as good as the one in the first fight."

"I didn't hear the count from one to three," Walcott said. "Then I heard it from three to seven, but I blacked out between seven and ten. I didn't hear it at all. And when I jumped up, I couldn't believe I was counted out. That was my last fight. I told myself that right then. I realized that when you can't recuperate from a punch, it's time to retire."

But on the night of May 15, 1953, the enraged fans could not have known Walcott's explanation. And even had they been aware of all the facts, it would probably have made no difference. They felt cheated, anticipating a savage brawl and getting a taffy pull.

The uproar of the crowd gained momentum, becoming so intense that as people shoved their way through the corridors police were concerned for their safety.

"Calm down. Calm down," the officers shouted. "Take it easy before someone gets hurt."

"All I know is that Walcott really got hit," said Roland LaStarza, a logical contender for Marciano's title. "He went down and he didn't get up in time. That's all there is to it!"

But the controversy lingered. Thousands of fans did not see any punches and in some of their minds Walcott had either taken a dive or the referee had given a quick count. Even Marciano's image was muddied by suspicion.

"For Christ sake," Rocky told his brother Sonny. "I hit this guy a terrific shot, and now they want me to apologize because he didn't get up. First Norris screws me on the money, and then these assholes start complaining about the knockout. Can you believe it?"

MARCIANO WANTED TO GET BACK in the ring as much as Norris and the IBC wanted to put him there to erase the stigma. LaStarza and Ezzard Charles were the opponents under consideration.

Rocky preferred LaStarza, because he wanted a chance to prove he could defeat the Bronx college boy far more decisively than was indicated by the split decision in their first encounter.

Some fight fans were convinced that LaStarza had won that first fight against Marciano and had been victimized by Weill's influence as the IBC matchmaker. Time had faded their memories of Rocky knocking LaStarza to the canvas, losing a round because of a low punch, and coming on to batter Roland during the late rounds. Some were convinced that Marciano was trying to avoid a rematch.

Weill wanted LaStarza for different reasons. The fight would draw a bigger gate than one with Charles, who was an excellent boxing stylist but not flashy or explosive enough to be a crowd pleaser. It would also be a much easier fight for Rocky, since LaStarza was not nearly as experienced or skillful as the former champion. Beyond that, Weill knew that he could dictate much stiffer terms to LaStarza's handlers, who were starving for a shot at the title.

LaStarza hadn't fought any top heavyweights except Marciano and Cesar Brion. He had been in the ring frequently since his bout with Marciano, but only against mediocre opposition, and although he had won more than fifteen fights against average heavyweights, LaStarza had lost to light heavyweights Dan Bucceroni and Rocky Jones.

Weill and Goldman were convinced that Rocky had improved as a boxer much more than LaStarza. They viewed the fight as a minimal risk. Marciano himself refused to acknowledge any risk at all.

When they signed the contract, Weill got his revenge on LaStarza's manager, Jimmy DeAngelo, for slamming the dressing room door in his face after that first bout. The terms were 42.5 percent for Marciano to 17.5 percent for LaStarza—not good for Roland compared to the 20/40 split Rocky got when he challenged Walcott for the title. De Angelo had to take it or give up a title bout.

Marciano returned to Grossinger's to train. He was still disturbed about the criticism of his knockout of Walcott and about the money he had been paid for that fight.

He received a total of $166,030, almost $100,000 less than the challenger.

"Norris took advantage of me," Weill moaned. "We got screwed."

"How the hell could you let this happen?"

Marciano said. "You're supposed to watch out for these things."

No matter what Weill said, Marciano could not understand how his manager could accept terms that would give the challenger so much more money than the champion. By now Rocky's feelings toward Norris were bitter.

"He's got all the fighters tied up and he thinks he's a fucking King," Rocky told Sonny. "He's been screwing me ever since I started fighting in New York. But someday I'll get him back."

The big percentage advantage over LaStarza went a long way toward salving Marciano's wounds, but as time went on he became more and more convinced that both Norris and Weill had taken advantage of him. They would learn that cheating Marciano out of money was as dangerous as stealing flies from a tarantula.

One of Rocky's dearest friends was Ernie Clivio, a middle-aged businessman from Stoneham, Massachusetts. He was a frequent visitor to Grossinger's, and he always tried to help Rocky in every way possible.

A proud Italian and boxing fan, Clivio had taken an avid interest in Rocky's career. They had met briefly after one of Marciano's early fights in Providence. Then, more than two years later, a mutual acquaintance had suggested that Clivio travel to New York with him and watch Rocky training for his fight with Carmine Vingo.

Despite the lapse of time and the casual way in which they had met, Rocky recognized Clivio instantly.

"Hi, Ernie," Rocky said. "Good to see you, pal. I'll be right with you."

It amazed Clivio that Rocky remembered him, but he learned that Marciano had a phenomenal memory for names and faces, and once he met someone he rarely forgot him.

They had gone to a corner of the gym and had a long conversation, soon discovering they had much in common. They were both first sons of immigrant Italian parents. There were three boys and three girls in each of their families. They had both been through the hard times of the Depression and struggled to achieve their success.

It was a fortunate day for both men, because Rocky and Ernie were good for each other. A low-key person who seldom forced himself upon anyone and usually remained in the background, Clivio was one of the few in Rocky's entourage that remained on friendly terms with Al Weill. For the Vest regarded him as a good influence and no threat to his control over the champion.

Clivio recognized Rocky's obsession for training immediately. He wanted to earn Rocky's friendship and tried to relieve him of responsibilities so he could concentrate completely on boxing.

"Rocky, I'll take care of Barbara," Ernie said. "You just think about the fighting. I'll give her the money for the rent, groceries, and whatever she needs every week, and you can settle up with me whenever you want."

"Wow, Ernie," Rocky said. "That'd be great. It'd really mean a lot to me, buddy."

"After that I handled the bills at home and Rocky paid me about twice a year after his fights," Clivio recalled. "I just told him what he owed me and he wrote a check."

Rocky had that personal touch that made average people feel comfortable and welcomed. And almost everyone who met him went away with an increased sense of pride and self-importance.

"I MET ROCKY FOUR TIMES IN MY LIFETIME, and he was my idol," said Frank Butera of Seekonk, Massachusetts. "I have a photo of Rocky, myself, and some of my friends taken at the Saint Lawrence Church gym at a church smoker in North Providence in March 1952. I was twenty-two years old and I remember it like yesterday, because it was one of the greatest moments in my life. Rocky and I went outside to get some air because the smoke was bothering him. We were sitting on the wall outside the church, just he and I, discussing some of the local fighters.

"Rocky knew I was a true fight fan, and had a scrapbook of his fights," Butera wrote in a letter praising Rocky. "There was a young, undefeated heavyweight coming up named Willie Wilson. He was fighting six- and eight-round preliminaries."

"What do you think of Willie?" Rocky asked Butera.

"I think he hits hard, but I don't know if he can take a punch," Butera said.

"Here's a guy who had just beaten Joe Louis and Lee Savold asking me, a nobody, about a certain fighter," Butera wrote. "And to top it all off, Rocky used this fighter, Wilson, as a sparring partner for the second Walcott fight. Like I said, Rocky was my idol."

Peter Marciano recalled many occasions when he went to fancy restaurants with Rocky and groups of wealthy businessmen or celebrities.

"I want you to meet the manager," someone would say to Rocky.

But often Rocky would already be talking to a waiter or he'd turn to one of the rich men and say, "I'd like to go out in the kitchen and meet the cook."

As the LaStarza fight drew closer, Rocky crept deeper and deeper into the cocoon of determination and pride that sealed him off from his family, friends, and socializing, and left room only for the rigors of training.

His diversions were brief. Conversations with friends who visited the camp. A game of softball with some of the New York Yankees who often came to Grossinger's. A flight in an airplane piloted by his pal Frank Gengler.

Rocky loved to fly. He'd go up in anybody's plane on a moment's notice. Weill was nervous and always tried to keep him out of the planes, but apparently to no avail.

'This is my pilot, Frank," Rocky would say when introducing Gengler. "Maybe we'll fly down sometime to see you."

Often they would go off on flights with no particular destination in mind. It was like a narcotic for Rocky, completely relaxing. He loved it when they flew high above the cities and he could look down and see dwarfed shadows of the buildings and the traffic inching like snails over the highways. There was a strange sense of detachment, even power, in being high above the earth, and Rocky felt it and savored it.

"Rocky always went to sleep in the plane," Sonny Marciano recalled. "It relaxed him tremendously. Once with Frank we flew into a bad storm. The plane was bucking like mad. I thought it was gonna fall apart. Frank was pale, like he was getting sick. I got worried and woke Rocky up."

"Hey, Rock," I said. "This doesn't look good. Maybe we're gonna crash or something."

"Is that all you're waking me up for?" Rocky said. "What's the matter with you? What are you worried about? If it's your time, it's your time, and there's nothing you can do about it. If it isn't, then there's nothing to worry about."

"I guess Rocky figured it wasn't his time, because a few minutes later he was sound asleep again," Sonny said. "But I wasn't that sure about it."

Years later it was Frank Gengler's time. He was killed with most of his immediate family when that same small plane crashed into the side of a mountain.

Marciano had other friends who flew him around in their planes. One was Ben Atwood, who sometimes hired out for cropdusting jobs over the cranberry bogs near Brockton. Rocky enjoyed swooping down low over the trees and bushes to spray the lethal chemicals. Unfortunately, Atwood was another friend who was killed when his plane crashed.

Managing the large sums of money Rocky was earning through fights and public appearances continued to concern him. He had no faith in lawyers and was leery of conventional banking methods. He wanted his money matters kept completely secret. Even his family and close friends should not know how much he had amassed. He had already begun to squirrel the cash away in unconventional places, some of which are yet to be located by his heirs.

"Once I came into the room at Grossinger's and Rocky was lying on the bed, reading an article entitled 'How Champions Lost Fortunes,'" Sonny Marciano said. "He was always thinking about the way some of those guys blew their money, and he was determined it wasn't going to happen to him."

He would still listen to almost anyone's advice, convinced that even a small piece of information might prove useful sometime.

A few days before the LaStarza fight, a reporter came into the room and was amazed to see Rocky sprawled on the bed reading *A Fighter's Manual on How to Fight*, by Lyman Rawson.

If Marciano seemed secure and unemotional about the approaching fight, it all changed when word drifted into camp that LaStarza had said, "A guy like Rocky's got to get punch-drunk. He takes too many punches."

"This really burned Rocky up," Uncle Mike Piccento said. "It changed his whole attitude toward the fight. He forgot the strategy. He was bullshit."

"I'm not gonna knock this guy out, Mike," Rocky said. "I'm gonna punish him."

"They finally stopped the fight," Piccento said. "But I really think Rocky could have knocked LaStarza out anytime."

"Just the sound of the word 'punchy' made Rocky cringe," Peter Marciano said. "Anytime he saw a punch-drunk fighter he became upset. He never feared pain or injury or any man in the ring, but to see some guy walking on his heels made him sick to his stomach."

But you couldn't prove that Marciano was upset based on the findings of Dr. Vincent Nardiello as he examined the champion before the fight.

"This guy doesn't need a doctor," Nardiello said. "He's in the finest condition of his career. Ice water, that's what he's got in his veins. He's the coolest thing you'd ever want to see."

As 44,562 persons came to the Polo Grounds on September 24, 1953, it seemed as if the fans had completely forgotten how close the decision was the last time the two fighters met. Marciano was a solid 5 to 1 favorite. Most were giving LaStarza little chance to go the distance.

But in the early rounds Marciano was not sharp. He carried the fight to LaStarza, forcing the challenger to retreat, but he seemed listless. He failed to storm out of his corner for the early KO, and there was no devil's agent of misery and punishment in his fists such as he had promised his Uncle Mike. Rocky was awkward, missing often, not throwing as many punches as usual.

LaStarza was a textbook boxer, avoiding Rocky's wild swings and taking most of the punches on his body and arms. He jabbed and counterpunched effectively, and occasionally showed brief flurries of aggressiveness, although his punches were not nearly powerful enough to hurt Marciano.

In the second round, Marciano lowered his head and butted LaStarza. He was warned by Referee Ruby Goldstein. Then Rocky delivered a hard left hook that opened a cut over LaStarza's right eye.

In the third, LaStarza jabbed Rocky and landed some sharp punches. Marciano hit him after the bell and was loudly jeered by the crowd.

There was nothing friendly or clean about Rocky in this fight. He was warned six times by Goldstein for butting, low punches, and elbowing. He seemed to lack the killer instinct, content to merely maul his prey like a cat playing with an injured mouse.

LaStarza was ahead on points, even though he was obviously the only fighter absorbing any punishment.

Then, in the sixth, Marciano punched low and the referee took the round away from him.

"What's the matter with you, Rock?" Colombo said in the corner. "You could lose this thing if you're not careful."

From then on the crowd saw a different Marciano. In the seventh, he charged LaStarza wildly, throwing lefts and rights as if there were no exhausting the supply. He went for the head, arms, body, anywhere the punches would fall.

LaStarza retreated, powerless to contain the assault. He took a hard right to the temple and staggered but did not go down. Rocky never stopped punching. LaStarza looked groggy, almost defenseless, but he did not fall.

The eighth and ninth rounds brought more of the same. Rocky punished LaStarza, badly gashed his upper lip, split open the bridge of his nose, bruised and battered his arms and ribs. The challenger no longer had an offense. Time after time his knees buckled under Rocky's painful punches, but still he did not crumple. It was clear to everyone in the stadium that LaStarza could not win. The puzzle was why Marciano, who was noted for his powerful knockout punching, could not dispose of a man who floundered so helplessly.

Rocky had spent months preparing for this fight. He was in superb condition. Why, then, didn't LaStarza fall? Had Marciano overtrained, perhaps leaving his knockout punch in the gym? Or was he, as Uncle Mike suggested, "punishing LaStarza" for implying that Marciano might someday go punchy?

In the tenth, he looked like the old Marciano, charging LaStarza with a whirlwind of punches that pounded the challenger unmercifully. Still Rollie did not go down. In his eagerness, Rocky threw a wild right, the force of which caused him to slip clumsily to the canvas.

Timekeeper Al Berle started to count, but Goldstein waved him off, signaling that it had been a slip and there was no knockdown. The timekeeper appeared startled, as if he had missed the action.

Rocky jumped up quickly and the referee wiped his gloves. Embarrassed and wild-eyed, he seemed to have acquired new reservoirs of stamina as he hurried back to chase LaStarza around the ring.

In the eleventh, Rocky threw a right that landed high on the head. LaStarza looked as if he would buckle, then moved away, stumbling across the ring. Marciano trapped him on the ropes, spraying the punches until a particularly hard right sprawled LaStarza out of the ring onto the apron.

LaStarza was on his knees at five. Almost unbelievably, he staggered up at nine—dazed, battered, and defenseless, yet willing to continue, unable to accept defeat.

Marciano punched wildly. LaStarza was almost unconscious, but he remained on his feet. Then, midway through the round, Goldstein wisely stepped between the fighters and stopped it.

In the dressing room, weary and sore, LaStarza said, "I was stopped by the champion of the world, and I don't hesitate to say that anybody who beats him will have to be five thousand times tougher than I was tonight. Rocky's improved a hundred percent since I fought him last."

Later, when LaStarza was examined by Dr. Nardiello, it was discovered that Marciano's punches had broken blood vessels and damaged bones in his arms. LaStarza had been unable to raise his arms for protection against the unrelenting punishment.

AT THIRTY-THREE, EZZARD CHARLES was about three years older than Marciano. Always underrated as a champion, the lean and stylish heavyweight from Cincinnati had been a professional since 1940, eight years longer than Rocky. He had defeated many of the top boxers of his era: Joey Maxim and Archie Moore, each three times, Jimmy Bivins, Joe Baksi, Jersey Joe Walcott, Gus Lesnevich, Freddie Beshore, Nick Barone, Lee Oma, Joe Louis, Rex Layne, and Cesar Brion.

Ezzard had won more than 80 fights, lost 8, and KO'd 50. He was an excellent boxer who could hit with power, but he lacked the charisma to be a crowd pleaser. He was too refined and mechanical, never really savage, a civilized fighter without a killer instinct.

Charles had won the title with a decision over Walcott in June 1949. He had defeated Louis and eight other contenders before losing the championship back to Walcott by a seventh-round KO in July 1951. He then lost the return go with Walcott and dropped a decision to Rex Layne before returning to his winning ways.

BARBARA MARCIANO WAS PREGNANT AGAIN. As usual, Rocky seldom saw her during training. As he prepared to take on Charles, he arranged for Barbara to take a trip with friends.

Rocky's brothers and some of his friends noticed a slight strain in the relationship between Marciano and his wife. Barbara had a glandular problem and had gained much weight. She had bleached her hair blond, and friends recalled that she was almost a chain smoker and sometimes drank too much to relieve her loneliness. She loved Rocky very much, and was one hundred percent behind him, willing to make whatever sacrifices were necessary.

While Barbara was vacationing in Acapulco, she suffered a miscarriage. She never became pregnant again.

High in the Catskills, Marciano was unaware of his wife's miscarriage. The training was going well except for the continual tension between the Marcianos and Al Weill.

One Saturday, Sonny Marciano and his cousin Duna Cappiello left Rocky's camp for a night on the town. They saw a show at the nightclub, had some drinks, and danced with the girls. It was 4 A.M. when they arrived back at Grossinger's. Cappiello slammed the door and they went into the kitchen, laughing and joking as they made some sandwiches.

"You jerks," Weill said at breakfast the next morning. "Are you crazy? What makes you think you can barge in here making all kinds of fucking noise at four inna morning? I should throw you outta this camp. You think this is a picnic? Rocky's gotta train. He don't want to be listenin' to no couple of jerks like you at four inna morning."

When Rocky was embarrassed he would curl his upper lip, drawing the skin tight against the partial plate that bridged his upper front teeth.

Sonny recalled that Rocky had stopped eating. His face was flushed and the lip curled upward, "Okay! Okay, Al!" Rocky shouted. "For Christ sake, lay off, will ya. I didn't wake up, did I? You gonna keep this up all day?"

"So what if you didn't wake up," Weill said. "You could'uv. I've got enough headaches without these jerks. Once more and they're out."

"Weill stomped out of the kitchen then," Sonny said. "He'd be almost insane if he didn't get the final word. I could see Rocky was still embarrassed. 'Fuck him,' Rocky said. 'Don't listen to him. He's not your boss. You want to have some fun, go ahead.' "

SHORTLY BEFORE THE FIGHT, Marciano received an anonymous letter: "If you beat Charles, you'll be killed, because you are a bully and Ezzard is a gentleman."

Rocky shrugged it off. He had been threatened before. It was something he had come to expect as part of being a champion and a celebrity.

"I'm not worrying about something like that," he said. "The guy's a crackpot. Anyway, if it's your time nothing's gonna change it."

The afternoon before the fight, Marciano was a 19 to 5 favorite. There were few takers.

"I couldn't get a bet on a knockout," Rocky's Uncle Mike said. "They'd only bet on a fifteen-round decision. I found one guy so sure that Charles would win if it went the distance, I talked him into giving me four to one."

Rocky was making no predictions. "I'll be in there to win," he told reporters. "That's all I can say."

Some claimed Charles was nervous about facing Marciano, and had dropped from his normal 189 pounds to 185½.

Nevertheless, Charles seemed confident. "I'm well trained and I believe that I have the boxing ability to defeat Marciano," he said.

Charles's critics questioned his courage, implying that when the going got rough Ezzard would quit on Marciano. Some felt that Charles was not the same fighter, never punched as hard as he had in 1948 when he KO'd Sam Baroudi in ten rounds in Chicago. Baroudi later died of injuries. He was certainly a ghost whose presence must always be felt, but one that a champion would not allow to interfere once the bell sounded and the fighting began. Those who felt Baroudi's death had influenced Charles's ability or desire overlooked the fact that Ezzard had gone on to win the heavyweight championship and score numerous knockout victories. Before the night of June 17, 1954, was over, Charles would make believers of the 47,585 fans in Yankee Stadium.

In the first round, Charles took control of the fight. He was very fast with the hooks and jabs and there was heavy power behind his punches.

Rocky forced the fight, throwing plenty of hard punches of his own, but Ezzard was a picture-book boxer, always moving away and scoring effectively with sizzling countershots.

In the fourth, Charles opened a deep cut at the side of Rocky's left eye. It was the kind of a gash that would have been enough to stop a nontitle bout, and it spilled so much gore that a photograph of Rocky's bloody face appeared on the cover of the *Police Gazette* above the caption; "When to Stop a Fight!"

But Charles's fortunes declined from this point. The injury to Rocky's eye, which should have been an advantage to the challenger, was perhaps the source of Charles's downfall. For it converted Rocky's ordinary aggressiveness to immeasurable ferocity.

Commanded by his primordial instincts to survive, Marciano pursued Charles relentlessly. From the fifth round on, the puzzled but game challenger found it increasingly difficult to defend himself against the champion's assault.

But Rocky had serious cause for concern. The cut over his eye blossomed and spurted blood, appearing even more gory than it was. Charles was concentrating on the eye, sending in stinging jabs that spread the gash to fearful proportions.

In the sixth Rocky delivered some very hard blows to the head. Charles was hurt. But he fought back, managing to land some punches of his own.

They were toe to toe in the seventh and eighth, when Charles appeared to be recovering from the initial surprise of Rocky's surge, regaining some of his poise and punching prowess. But Ezzard was still getting pounded. His right eyelid was cut in the eighth, and despite flashes of brilliance, he lost almost every round from then on.

By the tenth, Charles was weary from the battering. His ordeal had been terrible in the ninth, a round he was fortunate to have survived. Several times his knees buckled and it appeared as if he might go down, but he kept going deep into the well of his inner pride, gamely resisting the inevitable, unwilling to concede anything to Rocky's awesome attack. But the men scoring the fight unanimously gave Marciano the ninth, tenth, and eleventh rounds.

"Charles was a game fellow," Referee Goldstein said years later. "He wanted to stay the limit, and he held on in the last five rounds. But when you hold on and don't do any fighting you get credit for being courageous, but you don't get credit for winning the rounds. Marciano won the last five rounds by himself, and there was no question that he won the fight."

Rocky spent punches like a sailor on leave buying drinks. They came from all directions, in all sizes, shapes, and forms, and although he was wild, enough of the punches landed solidly to begin the gradual process of melting the iron in Charles's legs. As a conservationist Rocky was a failure. He seemed unable to pace himself. It was an open question whether he would run out of energy before dispatching Charles.

"Maybe some of Rocky's punches didn't land just where he intended them to," Goldstein said. "But he landed one or two in the right place, and some on the arms and some on the elbows. At the end of the tenth round, I could see that Charles was unable to lift his arms up to punch back."

But the blood of a champion flowed in Ezzard's veins, and in the fourteenth he staged a rally that defied explanation and earned him a split in the scoring. He was punching and moving and hitting Marciano, even though the blows might have been mistaken for friendly pats of affection or respect.

In the fifteenth, Marciano called upon every hidden devil in him to pour on the misery as he went desperately for the knockout, as if the outcome of the fight were in doubt. But Rocky had thrown enough leather to carry the average heavyweight through half a dozen fights, and though his spirit was eager, his arms had begun to grow very heavy. A KO punch no longer existed in his fists, and Charles stood and took it, and remained on his feet, while the crowd roared its approval of Marciano's victory by unanimous decision.

It was the only time Marciano was ever forced to go the fifteen-round distance. He was exhausted and happy in the dressing room, high in his praise of Charles.

"It was my toughest fight," Rocky said. "What can I say? The guy's a terrific boxer, and he can really punch."

"Sure," Marciano said, as he recouped. "It was much harder than my first fight with Walcott. Yes, I'd like to fight him again, but of course that's up to Al."

In the loser's dressing room, Charles was battered, tired, and dejected. His voice had been reduced to a hoarse whisper by a Marciano punch that damaged his Adam's apple.

"I thought I won," Charles said. "I felt I had him beaten. I just don't believe I lost."

There was nothing but praise from the crowd, the judges, and the referee for the performance of both fighters. Already they were anticipating a rematch.

"Ezz was a very good, smart fighter, who

still employed the same tactics he had as a middleweight," said Goldstein. "He gave Marciano trouble for the first ten rounds. He came at him fast with an assortment of punches, and he hit Rocky with a lot of combinations where he'd put together five or six punches in a row. Most fighters would grab on and wait for their head to clear after being hit by a good combination. But this was where Marciano was a discouraging-type fighter. After a fighter hit him with some of his best punches, Rocky would come chasing right after him, back him up against the ropes, and throw seven or eight punches of his own."

Goldstein scored the fight eight rounds for Marciano, five Charles, two even; Judge Art Aidala, nine Marciano, five Charles, one even; and Judge Harold Barnes, eight Marciano, six Charles, one even.

"What I really liked about this fight was that I didn't have to break them once in fifteen rounds," Goldstein said. "You figure at least once they're going to have to fall into a clinch that you're going to have to break up, but they never did. Whenever they came together they always got themselves out of it right away before I had to move in. I'll never forget that."

ANTICIPATING A BIG GATE, Jim Norris and the IBC hurried to schedule a return go for September 15, less than three months away. Rocky soon went back to Grossinger's, although his damaged eye required more mending before he could risk any sparring or contact training.

After the second Walcott fight, Colombo and others had noticed that the miles of daily roadwork and hours of isolated exercise were becoming more and more of a drudgery to Rocky. He had already achieved his major goals—winning the heavyweight championship and earning enough money so he would never have to worry about being broke. But he would always be insecure about his finances, and he wanted to go on to be remembered as one of the greatest of all fighting champions. He kept reminding himself that this required a commitment of total dedication and self-sacrifice.

He had given up sex almost entirely because someone had once mentioned that "it takes something out of a fighter."

Lou Goldstein, an executive at Grossinger's, recalls the time a wealthy businessman trying to impress Marciano sent a gorgeous hooker to a room where he and Rocky were having a conversation. Rocky was training, but there were no fights scheduled in the immediate future.

"You take her, Lou," Rocky said.

The night after the LaStarza title fight, Ernie Clivio had accompanied Rocky and Barbara to Pickering, Ontario. Ernie shared a room with Rocky, who didn't sleep with his wife.

"Most men would have been looking for the booze and broads to celebrate after a big victory," Clivio said. "But not Rocky. He was up at five in the morning to do roadwork."

Clivio had noticed the beautiful girls that came up from the resort to watch Rocky train for the rematch with Charles and how the champion forced himself to ignore them.

One evening, as they were walking around the airport, Ernie said, "Hey, Rock, tell me something. Are they feeding you saltpeter here? You know, like they used to do to guys in the service to keep their minds off sex."

"Hell, no," Rocky said. "What're ya, crazy?"

"The reason I'm asking, Rock," Clivio said. "Well, you know, you never talk about going to bed with Barbara."

"God no," Rocky said. "No saltpeter. That's not it. Sex takes something out of you, Ernie. I can't afford it. There's plenty of time for that after I quit fighting."

Clivio had returned to Stoneham to manage his dairy business when he received a call from Rocky.

"Ernie, when you come up again, bring some jerseys with the name of your dairy on them," Rocky said. "I've got an interview with the editor of the Chicago Tribune coming up. This'll be a great thing for you. We'll have everybody wear the jerseys, and they'll take a bunch of pictures that'll go all over the country."

"I don't know, Rock," Clivio said. "The people at Grossinger's might not like it."

"Listen, Ernie," Rocky said. "Don't argue. I want you to take advantage of me while I'm still the champ. Remember, if I ever quit, nobody's gonna care about me."

Although he was nervous and reluctant, Clivio had the jerseys made up and brought them to the training camp. He realized that Rocky really wanted to do something for him, but he knew also that it wasn't going to please the management at Grossinger's, whose main reason for providing the training facilities was the publicity.

Rocky took off his Grossinger's T-shirt, and put on Ernie's, with its large green letters: SUNNYHURST DAIRY. Then he ordered everyone in his entourage to change into Sunnyhurst shirts. Soon Allie Colombo, Charley Goldman, Lou Ambers, and all of the sparring partners were wandering around with the milkman's advertisement across their chests.

Clivio's worst fears were realized when a Grossinger's public relations man confronted him. "What're you trying to do?" the man said. "This is ridiculous."

"Rocky insisted," Clivio explained.

But the PR man only became angrier, and he went stalking off, convinced that it was Clivio's idea to have them wear the shirts.

A few minutes later, word filtered back to Rocky that Jennie Grossinger, owner of the resort, was on her way up to the airport. There was a scramble to get out of Sunnyhurst Dairy shirts and into the ones provided by Grossinger's. But Rocky pulled on a plain white T-shirt over the Sunnyhurst jersey. Jennie Grossinger was walking toward him when he realized the T-shirt was transparent and the Sunnyhurst Dairy letters were clearly visible through it.

Rocky stood grinning, talking to Jennie with his huge arms folded across his chest to hide the letters. Everything looked fine to Jennie, who always got along marvelously with Rocky and his family.

But Rocky wasn't satisfied. "Next time bring some bottles of milk, Ernie," he said. "We'll get some pictures of me drinking your milk. I've got another good idea too, I want you to put my picture on your milk bottles."

Clivio liked the publicity angle of featuring a photo of the champ on his bottles, so he had some made. But he still had many plain bottles in his plant, which were mixed in with the new ones during deliveries.

Clivio soon received a letter from the superintendent of schools in Melrose, Massachusetts, asking him to please send all bottles with pictures of Rocky on them or all plain ones. The way the kids were fighting to get milk with Rocky's picture was disrupting the entire school.

"The new bottles are working out great, Rock," Clivio said. "But I've been thinking.

You know, I really don't have any right to use your name and picture. Weill's your manager. If he finds out we're doing this without his permission there could be problems."

"Ernie, he'll never give you any trouble," Rocky said. "You're my friend."

But just to ease Ernie's conscience, Rocky wrote a letter giving him permission to use his picture and name for any purpose. It was probably not legal without Weill's concurrence, but Rocky didn't worry.

The drudgery of training was temporarily assuaged by Rocky's strong desire to make a better showing against Charles. Even though the June decision had been unanimous, he was unhappy because the fight had gone the full fifteen rounds. He was convinced he could knock out Charles, and he not only craved the KO, but envisioned one that would impress the entire boxing world.

And so spurred by the spirit of his mission, Rocky went about his work as zealously as ever and never once complained, just as he had done for six long years. It seemed as if he was always in training, never able to enjoy the spicy foods he loved so much, the people, the parties, the glamour and excitement of being a champion.

Sonny Marciano noticed the effect it had on his brother.

"Rocky had about fifteen pairs of shoes, given to him by businessmen who wanted to make an impression," Sonny said. "One night I borrowed a pair to go out on a date. I scuffed them up a little."

"What the hell're ya doin'?" Rocky yelled. "Those are my best shoes. You ruined them."

"I couldn't understand it," Sonny said. "Rocky had dozens of suits, shirts, and shoes. He never cared about clothes. He'd dress up in an old pair of brown slacks and a blue shirt and scuffed-up loafers to go to a fancy restau-

rant. I could always go right in the closet and help myself. Not money. Even two dollars would bother him. But clothes meant nothing."

"For Christ sake, Sonny," Rocky kept saying. "Look at them. You ruined the goddamn things."

"I couldn't believe it," Sonny said. "Except he was training so hard, I figured maybe he'd gotten too much of an edge."

MARCIANO ARRIVED IN NEW YORK CITY on a gray, drizzly Monday afternoon, a trim 184 pounds, the injured eye completely healed. He was convinced that he would KO Charles in the early rounds, stifling once and for all the rumors that had begun to circulate in some boxing circles that Rocky was beginning to lose his knockout punch. But on Wednesday, September 15, the scheduled day of the fight, it rained, postponing the fight. On Thursday it rained again, forcing another delay.

Rocky was edgy. He was not only keyed up for the fight, but more important, he was losing money because of the postponements. In two days, more than $60,000 in ticket money had to be refunded. Marciano was like a caged lion isolated from his prey. He could wait forever for Charles, because he was convinced he would destroy him. He was not so confident about the money.

More than 34,000 people spent $350,000 to occupy the stands of Yankee Stadium that Friday night, September 17, 1954. Theaters, radio, and home television added another $650,000. Few gave Charles a chance, but everyone wanted to see how Marciano would defeat him.

As in the Walcott return match, there was no resemblance between this bout and the first Charles fight.

Marciano took charge almost immediately. Charles came out fast with a two-fisted flurry in the first round but was stopped cold by Rocky, who never yielded a step.

In the second, Charles tried to jab Rocky with his left. Marciano crashed a right over the jab that slammed against the side of Ezzard's head and staggered him. Rocky then threw everything but the cat, the dog, and the vacuum cleaner at the bewildered challenger. Ezzard's knees had already begun to buckle. Rocky kept punching. Charles crumpled to the canvas.

Surprisingly, he bounced to his feet at the count of two. Everyone figured him to take at least an eight-count, for seconds can melt mountains of fog in a fighter's brain. But the challenger appeared to be all right. As Marciano charged forward, Ezzard returned the bombardment with his own heavy guns, ramming home a hard right that shook the champion.

From then on Charles was strictly a defensive fighter. Marciano kept coming straight at him like a freight train crossing Texas, and Ezzard used all his resources to avoid him. For four rounds Charles employed only occasional spurts of counterpunches and, unlike his aggressiveness in the first fight, resorted frequently to clinching.

But in the sixth, with Marciano way ahead on rounds, Charles came out punching, realizing this probably would be his last chance to regain the precious title, determined to mount some kind of an offense to offset the battering he had been taking. No longer content to wrestle, waltz, dodge, and duck his way out of trouble, Ezzard exploded a flurry of lefts and rights that flew like bullets from a high-power rifle and struck their targets with double force as Marciano walked squarely into the onslaught. Blood spurted in great, dark geysers from Marciano's nose. He trembled with fury and charged, so angry he could not land punches cleanly. Charles moved away, clinched, and assessed his position. The fight had taken on an entirely new complexion.

"It's split in half," Goldman groaned in the corner as he inspected Rocky's cut. "How we gonna stop the bleeding?"

"You ain't," Allie Colombo shouted. "There's no way you're gonna stop that. Rock, you gotta get him! You gotta get him, or they could stop the fight!"

Marciano's left nostril had been completely bisected, halved as cleanly as a pear. It was not the kind of a cut that would normally be caused by a punch, perhaps more like the pointed bone of an elbow catching him as he moved toward Charles. It was in no way connected with the injury before the second Walcott fight, which had impaired his breathing. That time only some blood vessels had been damaged by a sparring partner's punch. But now all the blood vessels had been cut in half and there were two pieces of flapping skin; immediate sutures were necessary to stem the flow of blood, which was all over Rocky's face, chest, and lap.

The doctor was examining Rocky, very unhappy with what he saw. Marciano's handlers pleaded with him not to stop the fight. The doctor himself was reluctant to take a man's championship away on what appeared to be a freak accident. But soon he might not have any choice.

Marciano charged out of his corner at the bell for the seventh. A swab that had been left in his nostril fell to the canvas. Blood poured from the wound.

For the first time since they had begun their long trip toward the title, Allie Colombo panicked. He was pale with fear, running along the ring apron, screaming up at Rocky: "You gotta get him, Rock! You gotta get him! Watch out! Watch out! Don't let that son of a bitch hit your nose!"

Charles was trying to hit the nose, like a mongoose going for the head of a cobra, but he was dealing with a wild man. Rocky's punching accelerator was jammed to the floor. As the round ended, Charles was floundering under the assault.

"Go after him now or you'll bleed to death," Goldman moaned in the corner.

Rocky stormed out of his corner and ran into a solid right by Charles. Blood trickled from the corner of the champion's vulnerable left eye. Then he roared after Charles and crashed a right to the head that dropped Ezzard to the canvas.

Confused and dazed, Charles got up at the count of four, only half-recovered from the effect of the punch.

Weill and Colombo were hysterical. "Go after him! Go after him! Finish him, Rocky! You gotta knock him out!"

His dark, thinning hair soaked with sweat and glued to his forehead, the punctured nostril spraying blood as he snorted for air, the champion delivered his final punishment.

It's impossible to tell which of the punches finished Charles. At the end Rocky had just thrown a right-left, right-left combination. Ezzard collapsed to the floor. He had risen to his knees as Referee Al Berl counted him out with 24 seconds remaining in the eighth round.

"It was amazing," said Sam Silverman, who had been sitting ringside in Marciano's corner.

"The fight couldn't possibly have gone another round without the ref stopping it. They just couldn't stop the bleeding. It had to be an elbow. No punch could make a cut like that. There was Rocky in the middle of a tough fight, but when he had to KO Charles, he did. It was unbelievable."

18.

Something Missing

"**I** DON'T KNOW I'm not thinking tough anymore geared just to fight not fun to watch consigned to oblivion cheese champs nocturnal night training . . . "

Rocky wrote those words in his typical unpunctuated style on one of dozens of scratch pads that he used to record his feelings. As he prepared to defend the title against England's Don Cockell his handlers had no knowledge of Marciano's thoughts, but it was obvious that something was missing and Rocky's spirits were low. He was not training with anywhere near the same purpose and dedication of the Rocky Marciano they had grown to know, the man who believed in sacrificing everything to achieve the ultimate in physical condition. It was a dangerous situation, and everyone was worried.

Ernie Clivio had seen the early signs that Rocky wanted to relax more during a vacation to Bermuda that winter. He was thoroughly enjoying himself and didn't seem nearly as anxious to return to training as usual.

Then one afternoon, as Rocky was playfully lifting Mary Anne up from the water, he injured his back. Ernie accompanied him to the cottage. For a while they were alone in the room, talking, as they waited for the pain and stiffness to ease.

"This back can go on me anytime, Ernie," Rocky said. "It's something that's always bothered me."

They talked about fighting and their families; then Ernie summoned the courage to confront his friend on a sensitive matter that had him very upset.

"People would meet me, knowing how friendly I was with Rocky, and say, 'Hey, how's that cheap bastard doing?' I'd get furious and defend Rocky to the hilt. But it was bothering me, and it was on my mind when we went to Bermuda," Ernie recalled.

"Rocky, a lot of people are starting to talk," Clivio said.

"What do you mean?" Rocky said.

"Well, you know," Ernie said. "I'd be the last guy to ever want to see you picking up tabs for all these freeloaders that hang around, but when a guy's taken you out three or four times in a row, it doesn't hurt to reciprocate once in a while."

"I know, Buddy," Rocky said. "I know what they're saying about me being cheap. But don't you worry, Buddy, when I'm all through fighting, when I know I'm financially secure, I'm gonna show you. I'll make you proud of me."

"Rock, I'm so happy to hear you say that," Clivio said. "I'm so relieved."

It had been an embarrassing conversation for both men. About fifteen minutes had passed when Rocky turned to Ernie and grinned. "But remember one thing, pal," he said. "I'm talking about confederate money."

ROCKY'S PAINFUL NOSE INJURY had been slow in healing. It had withstood the test of sparring sessions, but there was no way to be certain that the tender scar tissue would not reopen should a heavy slugger concentrate on the wound in a real fight. Weill and Goldman were apprehensive. And with this in mind, and with an international angle adding to the appeal of the bout, they selected Cockell for an opponent.

Don Cockell was a beefy brawler who owned a farm near Eastbourne, England. At twenty-six, he'd been fighting two years longer than Rocky and had a record of 61 wins, 11 losses, and 1 draw. He had 36 knockouts, including KOs over Nick Barone and Harry "Kid" Matthews, but he had been knocked out five times himself. Even though he was five years younger, Cockell did not come close to matching Marciano's stamina and power. A flat-footed fighter who waded in and exchanged punches, his style was geared perfectly to Marciano's offense.

"I just can't get excited about this fight, Allie," Rocky told Colombo. "Everybody says the guy's nothing. If he's nothing, what am I fighting him for?"

"How could he be nothing?" Colombo said. "A guy who's been British and European champ can't be just nothing."

"That doesn't mean anything," Rocky said. "I don't know, I just can't get up for this fight."

Rocky no longer seemed willing to punish himself. He showed no enthusiasm and lacked concentration in his sparring sessions.

That spring Rocky's training camp was shifted from New York State to Calistoga, California, since the fight was to take place in San Francisco's Kezar Stadium on May 16. But Rocky had been more comfortable in the Catskills with his friends at Grossinger's. Nothing about the approaching fight seemed to interest him.

During a sparring session shortly before the fight, a powerful punch to the chin sent Rocky to the canvas.

"Time!" Colombo shouted. "That's it! No more today."

"Rocky! Rocky! What're ya doin'? What're ya doin'?" Goldman said. "The guy shouldn't even hit you."

"That's all," Weill roared. "That's it. No more distractions. Get everybody out of here. The guy does this against Cockell and we're all dead."

Marciano's handlers knew that without the hunger—the dedication, desire, and total commitment—Rocky might be vulnerable to even an average heavyweight like Cockell. But nothing they tried seemed to lift his spirit.

"I just can't get going for this one, Allie," Rocky told Colombo. "There's no goal to shoot for. Everybody knows I'm gonna beat this guy. So what's there to get excited about?"

"But the guy's a good fighter, Rock," Colombo said. "You've got to get that out of your mind. This is for the title."

The mayor of Calistoga sponsored a dinner in Rocky's honor, and during the evening asked the members of Rocky's entourage to introduce themselves and explain how they were associated with the champion.

"I'm Pete Marchegiano, Rocky's father."

"I'm Charley Goldman, Rocky's trainer."

Then Nicky Sylvester stood up and grinned. "I'm Nicky Sylvester," he said. "And I'm a very good friend of Al Weill's."

Weill bolted from his seat with his fists clenched. "Sit down, you bum!" he stammered.

Rocky went into a fit of giggling that he could not control. He was tittering like a schoolboy, and everyone in the restaurant was staring at him.

"But Al," Sylvester said. "Aren't we pals?"

Weill was very brusque with most of Rocky's friends, including Marciano's brothers and other relatives. He seemed to view everyone closely associated with Rocky as a threat to his own total authority. But Sylvester, with his constant flow of wisecracks and complete disregard for Weill's importance, irritated the Vest more than any of them. He kept glaring across the table at Sylvester. And the harder Weill stared, the more Rocky giggled. He loved to see Nicky get under Weill's skin.

There was a rumor that reached Mary Anne years after her father retired. The story was told by a Mafiosa underling who was friendly with the family.

He claims a top Mafia figure from New York approached Rocky weeks before the fight, while he was training in Calistoga.

"Rocky, you lose this fight, and we'll take care of you," the mobster said. "There's a lot of money to be made. You're the champ, Rocky. You'll beat Cockell easy in the rematch."

"Get away from me," Rocky said. "How could you even suggest it? You disgust me of the Italian race. I'm ashamed you're an Italian."

"I was told that my dad was offered two million dollars to throw the fight," Mary Anne said. "Afterward, when they thought about it, the Mafia guys were very proud of him, being a young Italian fighter, making the decision that he did and standing up to the big guy."

Mary Anne believes the story, although her father never mentioned it to anyone. It seems unlikely and cannot be substantiated, although other champions, including Sugar Ray Robinson and Jake LaMotta, have told of New York mobsters trying to influence them to throw fights.

Although he was a 10 to 1 underdog, Cockell came to fight. He had the attitude of a challenger who realizes he is being given the greatest opportunity in his life. He was naturally chubby but, despite the roll of flab around his midsection, had trained hard and at 205 was lighter than he had been in many bouts.

Marciano appeared trim and solid, but he weighed 189, the heaviest he had been since amateur days.

For three rounds the burly Englishman pushed, pulled, and slugged with Rocky on even terms. But although Cockell had the heart and seemed to rise to the occasion as the fans cheered him on, he lacked the power, skill, and stamina to slug it out with Marciano in a sustained battle. The roar of the crowd encouraging the challenger irritated Rocky. Just before the end of the third round, he ripped a left hook to the jaw that buckled Cockell's knees. Things were not the same for the former European champ after that.

Rocky staggered Cockell in the fifth and sixth rounds, and the challenger's knees sagged both times. At the end of the seventh, Rocky was battering Cockell against the ropes. Even though the Englishman was fighting back doggedly, it was obvious he couldn't hurt

Marciano and only a miracle could save him.

In the eighth, Marciano erupted and smothered his opponent with a volley of punches. Cockell had nothing left but heart. Just before the bell, Rocky crashed a right to Cockell's head that sent him through the ropes out onto the apron.

Early in the ninth, Rocky floored the challenger again with an explosive overhand right. Cockell got up wavering and bleary-eyed. He was bleeding, battered, and thoroughly exhausted. Marciano charged, punching furiously. Cockell crumpled and went down again. He staggered up at five, too dazed to take advantage of a longer count. Cockell was helpless and Marciano wanted to destroy him, but just as Rocky was about to attack, Referee Frankie Brown jumped between the fighters and grabbed the reeling Englishman up in his arms, signaling an end to the slaughter.

"He could take a lot of punishment," Rocky said in the dressing room. "I hit the guy with some of my best shots."

The Marciano camp was happy. The fight had been a crowd-pleasing brawl. Rocky's injured nose had withstood the test of Cockell's best punches. And more than $130,000 had been added to the Marciano-Weill bankroll. But Rocky's suspicions and dislike for Weill continued to increase as the result of an alleged deal that had taken place during negotiations between Weill, Norris, and Jimmy Murray, who promoted the Cockell bout. According to testimony taken in a California investigation of the IBC, Truman Gibson, the IBC attorney, had sent a letter to Murray to confirm an agreement that $10,000 be skimmed from the promotional profits. Rocky was told nothing about it.

Almost a year later, though, a California Boxing Commission investigation uncovered the letter and the information was made pub-lic. The check for $10,000 had been cashed the day after the fight. It was alleged that the money went to Al Weill.

Weill denied any knowledge of the deal. But Marciano was furious.

Publicly, Rocky said, " Al wouldn't do that to me. He's an honest guy." But privately he was saying, "That son of a bitch has screwed me again."

It was the last straw.

19.
The Final Challenge

THERE HAD TO BE A GREAT CHALLENGE, a goal to restore the toughness and overwhelm the apathy that had tarnished Rocky's spirit as he prepared to face Cockell. For it was the enemy within, the monotony of indifference, that sapped the fighting heart and the champion's supremacy. Rocky knew it and so did his handlers. With this in mind and the prospects of a very big purse, Weill chose Marciano's next opponent.

Archie Moore, light-heavyweight champion of the world, had been pressing for a chance at Marciano's crown. One of the truly great boxers of his era, Moore had been fighting top contenders and champions for almost twenty years. At thirty-eight, Archie had a record of 149 wins, 22 losses, and 6 draws. He was a skilled and very tricky boxer and a ruinous puncher who had KO'd 111 opponents. There was not another contender so worthy of facing Marciano.

"This may be your toughest fight," Colombo said. "Moore's won his last twenty-one in a row."

"I'm going all out for this one, Allie," Rocky said. "I really feel good about it." He was training relentlessly at Grossinger's.

In his last three fights, Moore had KO'd

Harold Johnson and Carl "Bobo" Olson and decisioned Nino Valdez. Since winning the light-heavyweight title from Joey Maxim in 1952, he had successfully defended it four times.

Only Ezzard Charles, whom he had fought in the mid-forties, had been able to dominate Moore. Ezzard had faced Archie three times without defeat, decisioning him twice and knocking him out once, a considerable feat since Moore had only been KO'd four times before facing Marciano.

The fight, scheduled for September 20, 1955, was postponed one day because of the threat of a hurricane moving up the Atlantic Coast. The largest crowd ever to see Marciano in the ring, 61,574, showed up at Yankee Stadium while hundreds of thousands crammed closed-circuit-television theaters across the country. (The fight would gross $2,248,117, then second only to the second Dempsey-Tunney bout in earnings.)

AFTER A CAUTIOUS FIRST ROUND, Moore amazed the fans by smashing Rocky with a solid right early in the second round that caught the champion squarely on the chin as he was moving in to attack. For only the second time in his career, Marciano dropped to the canvas.

Rocky was down on his right knee with both gloves braced against the floor. He didn't hear the count, but got up instinctively at two. He seemed to stare out over the crowd as he walked toward the ropes.

The roar of the crowd swelled Moore's breast with the pride of a champion. He wanted to charge Rocky and go for a knockout.

But Referee Harry Kessler, caught up in the excitement of the moment, continued counting. He had reached five before he realized his mistake and stopped, for in a championship bout the count ends once the fighter has regained his feet.

Moore was enraged. In writing his autobiography Archie called the chapter on his fight with Marciano "Fouled." He claimed the referee cost him his big chance at the ring's greatest prize by not allowing him to go after Marciano immediately.

What Archie had on his hands was the boxing jungle's equivalent of a wounded tiger. His pride damaged more than his body, Rocky soon began attacking his quarry with hard, hurting punches. And Archie, in his own rage, fought toe to toe with him.

By the third round Rocky's nose was bleeding and he had a slight cut over his left eye, although he had been battering Moore.

In the sixth, advancing in his relentless crouching style, Rocky caught a left hook, a solid jab, and a right to the jaw. He stormed back with a crunching right to the jaw that floored the challenger. Archie came off the canvas at the count of four, and Rocky rushed after him. They were trading punches on the ropes when Rocky threw a flurry of rights and

lefts that dropped Moore again. Archie came up shaky at the count of eight. Marciano smelled his blood and moved for the kill, but the challenger was punching back at the bell. Both fighters appeared on the verge of exhaustion when they returned to their corners.

In the seventh, Moore continued to slug it out, but Rocky had the best of it. It was obvious the challenger could not keep up the blistering pace much longer.

In the eighth, Marciano crashed a looping right to the head that floored the challenger. Moore's eyes were vacant. He was still down when the bell ended the round at the count of six.

In the corner, Dr. Vincent Nardiello asked the challenger if he wanted to continue.

"I too am a champion," Moore said. "And I'll go down fighting."

Early in the ninth, Marciano drove the battered and weary challenger into the ropes. He threw a wild volley of punches, the cumulative effect of which overwhelmed his exhausted opponent.

Moore sank grudgingly to the canvas. He sat bleary-eyed in his own corner while the referee counted. Clutching the ropes, he attempted to rise. Then he slumped back down and was counted out.

In the dressing room, a tired and happy Rocky was surprised when reporters seemed more intent on questioning him about rumors of retirement than the fight.

"Yeah, I've given it some thought," he said. "My family would like it. My mother and father have been after me to retire. But there's nothing definite."

"I was really disappointed," he told Sonny. "Here I was, coming off a helluva fight, and all they were interested in was whether I was planning to retire. It was a great fight. Why didn't they ask me more about that? Maybe I am thinking about retiring. Who wouldn't with Al Weill around?"

Moore showed the class of a champion and offered no excuses. "Marciano is far and away the strongest man I've ever encountered in almost twenty years of fighting," he told Frank M. Blunk of the *New York Times.* "And believe me, I've met some tough ones."

Archie held the optimistic philosophy that remained through many more victories after his loss to Marciano. "I believe I put up a good fight," he said. "I think the crowd liked it. If they did, I'm satisfied."

That night ageless Archie, his right eye throbbing and swollen completely shut, was seen in a local nightclub playing string bass with a band.

An enormous victory party was held for Rocky at the Concourse Plaza Hotel.

"Forget all this talk about retirement," Weill said, pacing nervously about the room. "Rocky can have lots more fights. I'm the manager. I'll know when it's time for him to retire."

Weill pleaded with Rocky, advising him to squelch the rumors publicly. The Vest explained that even if Rocky never entered the ring again, they could still make plenty of money as long as he was champion and people thought he was going to fight.

"I've got no plans for retiring at the present time," Rocky finally told reporters.

But Weill was losing his grip on Rocky and he knew it. He wanted to schedule an exhibition tour in Italy, but Rocky turned him down in favor of a vacation with Barbara in South America. They had planned to make it a long trip to make up for all the time he had been away during the years of training. But Rocky inexplicably cut the holiday short at ten days and returned home.

That spring, the investigation in California

confirmed Rocky's suspicions that Weill had cheated him on the Cockell fight.

"Weill got that dough, the son of a bitch," Rocky said. "I don't care what it costs me, I'm not fighting for that guy again."

Sam Silverman recalled that Rocky showed up at a boxing show he was promoting in Holyoke a short while later.

"I'm gonna quit fighting," Rocky said. "But I'll take one more fight for you if you can handle it with Weill."

"Weill and I are bad friends," Silverman said. "He'll never go for it."

"Rocky wanted me to give him twenty-five thousand dollars under the table that Weill wouldn't get a cut on, because he figured Weill screwed him on the promotion money for the Cockell fight," Silverman said later.

On Saturday, April 28, 1956, the newspaper headlines read: MARCIANO RETIRES TO SPEND MORE TIME WITH HIS FAMILY.

The day before, flanked by the somber-faced Weill, Goldman, and Norris, Rocky had seemed lonely and sad, almost reluctant to announce he was leaving the ring.

"I'm retiring because of my wife and daughter, Mary Anne," he said softly at a gathering in New York's Hotel Shelton. "Actually, I feel good. My mother never did want me to fight. She never saw any of my fights. My decision puts her very much at ease."

But it really wasn't the family that was pushing Rocky into retirement.

"There were many reasons why Rocky retired," Sonny Marciano said. "But the absolute main one was Al Weill. He just hated the guy and didn't trust him."

"Rocky and I discussed it," Ernie Clivio said. "Several times his back had gone out on him, and he was really crippled up when that happened. He knew the back could go anytime in the ring, and Rock was too proud to use that as an excuse. The Rock was no dummy. I believe you'd have had to kill him to stop him, but he knew he wasn't getting any younger and that a fight can end with one punch. He'd already proved his greatness as a champion. I think it was a combination of Weill, his family, and everything else."

"The family had nothing to do with it," Mike Piccento said. "Rocky was burned up about the ten thousand dollars from the Cockell fight. He and Weill had split up almost half a million from the Moore fight, and Rocky had worked a deal to have the money spread out over three years. Then he heard Weill had scalped thousands of dollars of tickets on the Moore fight. Rocky wanted his cut, but Weill wouldn't give him anything. He was bullshit. He figured with all that dough spread over three years, with the taxes he'd be fighting for nothing."

AT THIRTY-THREE, ROCKY HAD lost the hunger. He had reached his goals of wealth and athletic prowess. It was no longer easy to make the commitments of dedication and self-sacrifice necessary for a champion. He was beginning to think more and more about the good life away from the isolation and punishment of the training camps.

Rocky had plenty of money. The undefeated heavyweight champion's forty-nine fights had earned over four million dollars. Rocky himself had made more than two million dollars including purses, television, radio, films, and personal appearances. He had not squandered it like many champions. He had hidden it, buried it, put it in banks, and invested it. But he had spent very little.

HAD ROCKY BEEN UNIMPRESSIVE in his conquest of Archie Moore, it is quite possible he may have fought again. The image was very important. The last battle of an undefeated champion has to be remembered as a major victory. It would add to the legacy of greatness when in later generations the ghost of Marciano returned to haunt the castles of new and younger kings.

But it had been a great fight. And there were no contenders on the horizon that compared favorably with Moore's fame and skills as a boxer. Another fight would be anticlimactic, proving nothing.

"Actually, after Rocky became champion, I figured he'd reached his goal," Piccento said. "In a few fights he'd made all the dough he'd ever need. I figured it's time for him to think about quitting. I remembered how my sister used to throw me out of the house when I first encouraged Rocky to be a fighter. So I went to see her . . .

" 'All right, Pasqualena,' I said. 'You always gave me hell about Rocky's fighting. Now we can talk to him about retiring.'

" 'Retiring?' Pasqualena said, beaming with pride. 'But he's a champeen now.' "

THAT SPRING OF 1956, James D. Norris and the IBC were in trouble. When Marciano retired, the IBC lost its biggest drawing card. And two days before Rocky quit, the federal government had filed an antitrust suit against Norris, Jacob Wirtz, the IBC, and the Madison Square Garden Corporation for conspiring to monopolize championship bouts in the United States. The suit claimed the IBC had promoted 80 percent of all championship fights from 1949 to 1953. The Norris empire was crumbling. In June 1957, the court finally ordered the IBC dissolved.

One of the IBC's most bitter adversaries was Sam Silverman of Boston. "Because of the way they treated me with Rocky and a few other fighters, I sued Norris for nine million dollars for trying to monopolize not only champions but contenders too," the promoter claimed. "But I was broke at the time. I settled out of court for $125,000. If I could have held out I'd have probably gotten two million dollars. Rocky hated Weill and those guys. He wanted to get out from under."

But before his fall, Norris made several attempts to get Rocky into the ring.

"Come to my place in Miami and talk," Norris said. "Maybe we can work something out."

"Sure, Jim," Rocky said. "I'll be happy to talk with you."

"What're you doing, Rock?" Sonny Marciano asked as they drove to Norris's estate in Coral Gables. "I thought you hated Norris? And didn't you say you were through with boxing? This isn't like you, Rock, giving in to a guy who's screwed you."

"Don't worry," Rocky said. "I'll handle it."

He'll probably offer plenty, Sonny was thinking. This guy's losing a fortune as long as Rocky stays out of the ring.

"Would you believe when I was coming up I only got a grand for those Friday-night TV shows?" Rocky said. "The most was four thousand. They sure made the dough off us boxers."

Rocky had never forgotten how Norris had held his thumb on Weill, forcing him into deals that cost Marciano vast sums of money, such as the second Walcott fight, when the champion received more than a hundred thou-

sand dollars less than the challenger.

Norris lived in pure luxury. The stamp of his enormous wealth and self-indulgence was branded lavishly over everything that occupied the spacious estate. But as Rocky and Sonny entered Norris appeared strangely nervous, as though he already sensed the outcome.

"What will it take to get you back?" Norris said. "Can we talk money?"

"No, Jim," Rocky said, very softly, very friendly. "It's not a question of money."

"How does a million dollars sound to you?" Norris said. "I could get you that much if you're willing to fight again."

"That's a lot of money, Jim," Rocky said. "But my mind is really made up."

"What would it take to change it?"

"Maybe three million would interest me," Rocky said.

"That's ridiculous," Norris said. "No fight would ever draw that kind of money."

"Then I guess there's no sense in talking about it, Jim," Rocky said. "I've made my decision, and I'll stick by it."

As they drove back toward Miami, Rocky was grinning.

"You know something, Rock," Sonny said. "You never intended to take his offer."

"Are you kidding?" Rocky laughed. "Of course I didn't. I just wanted to see him squirm. That dirty mother."

"**D**o me a favor, Rocky," Mike Piccento said. "Stay in shape. Maybe you don't want it now, but someday they're going to offer you a lot of money to fight again. And you're going to want to make a comeback."

"I'll never make a comeback, Mike," Rocky

said. "I've seen what happened to the other fighters who tried to come back. I've got too many good memories for that."

"You will," Piccento said. "Remember I told you so. Because all fighters want to make a comeback."

For three years Rocky kept his promise. He was offered huge sums of money, as much as $2 million, to return to the ring. He always refused.

Then, in June 1959, the big Swede Ingemar Johansson startled the boxing world by flattening heavyweight champion Floyd Patterson in the third round of a title bout at Yankee Stadium.

"He's awkward. He's clumsy," Marciano said. "The guy looks like an amateur." Rocky failed to remember that these same words had often been used in describing him during his rise to the title.

After the fight, Marciano went to Grossinger's with Johansson to celebrate the new champion's victory. For several days he was observed constantly in Ingemar's company.

He basked amid the parties, celebrities, autograph seekers, and others who clamored for the attention of the champion. His mind reveled in memories of past glories, and the dormant hunger came rushing back to his loins.

When he returned to Brockton, Rocky went to his Uncle Mike's sportswear shop. He was sloppily dressed, with a large roll of flab bulging against the buttons of his untucked-in sport shirt.

"I'm going to make a comeback, Mike," Rocky said. "This guy Johansson's nothing. He looks like an amateur. He doesn't even think tough. What the hell did I retire for?"

"Rock, you're too far gone," Piccento said. "Are you crazy? You've been eating all that rich Italian food, partying, chasing the broads, staying up all hours of the night. You can't make a comeback."

"You watch," Rocky said. "I'm gonna get in shape and make a comeback."

Rocky worked out for a month—running every day, sweating in the gym, punching the heavy bag until his arms were leaden.

"You're right, Mike," he said finally. "It's too tough. The hell with it. I could never get in shape. Not the kind of shape I'd want to be in. And I'd never fight under any other conditions. Not for any amount of dough."

It was the last time Rocky ever seriously considered returning to the prize ring.

Maybe Rocky was thinking about the many letters he received from fans urging him never to go into the ring out of condition and risk spoiling his record as the only undefeated heavyweight champion in history.

"Will you please do me a small favor by sending me a full-sized photo of you in boxing kit signed personally," wrote Alfred Leavenley from Stockport, England. "I want your photo to put in my bedroom to give me inspiration to keep fit . . . I'd say you are the fittest man in the world today Rocky . . . Rocky, a man's as old as he feels, but do me a favor pal, and when you do meet a fighter who nearly beats you, and Oh! you'll know it! He will be younger and fitter, and you will have surpassed your peak. Rocky a man only keeps that peak as long as nature permits, and it would be your losing battle Rocky, so don't fight it. When that time comes, turn it in Pal, and be an Undefeated Champ. The 'Supreme Title.' You are a wise man. Keep it that way."

The letter, written in February 1956, shortly before Rocky announced his retirement, was signed: "Just an admirer."

Or perhaps it was something far more personal. For possibly his thoughts returned to that distant night when he fought his first battle in Brockton, and was humiliated before dozens of his paesanos, when his own poorly conditioned body failed him against Ted Lester.

Book Three

The Golden Key

1.

A Cuban Adventure

After he retired from boxing, Rocky seemed more restless than we'd ever known him. When we'd see him, it was only for a day or two, and then he'd be gone again. He wasn't at home with Barbara and Mary Anne much at all. We knew Rocky was moving everywhere, bouncing from city to city, and if you wanted to be with him you had to be prepared to travel. But we didn't know why. It was like he was running or searching for something. Whatever it was, I hope he found it before he died.

—Peter Marciano

THEY HAD BIG PLANS FOR ROCKY MARCIANO in Cuba that spring of 1957. People with gambling interests, business deals, and even a movie producer had offers that could bring large sums of money to the popular former champion.

Rocky flew to Havana in May with Barbara, his brother Sonny, and Dominick Papia, an executive at the Belmont Plaza Hotel in New York who had idolized Rocky and helped him early in his career.

Joe Cambria, a scout for the Washington Senators and sports columnist for a Havana newspaper, had watched Sonny playing minor league baseball in Florida and invited him to Cuba to negotiate a contract to play in the winter league there. The Marcianos were planning a nice vacation as well as a profitable trip.

Rocky had told his wife and brother nothing about the business aspect of the trip other than that he had an offer to make a movie for a television series. Sonny was surprised when a large crowd greeted them at the airport, including "a bunch of photographers taking pictures of Rock, and some very wealthy-looking businessmen."

"Most of these guys were Italian, all well dressed, with three black limousines waiting for them," Sonny recalled. "One guy was obviously the kingpin. Everyone else waited for him to speak. Finally he asked Rocky to come with him."

They went to a conference room on the second floor of an automobile agency building in Havana. About forty people, almost all Italians, gathered around a long table with Rocky and Sonny seated next to the kingpin. Bottles of wine and an elaborate, catered meal were spread before them.

"Rocky, this is beautiful country," the king-pin said. "This is the place to be. The United States doesn't have anything to compare to this. I can make you more money than you'll ever make there. This is the land of opportunity, *paesan*."

"It was all sounding pretty good to me," Sonny recalled. "But I was just a kid. I didn't really understand what was going on."

"I want you to get involved in my automobile dealership and the gambling clubs," the kingpin said. "And besides that, I've got a fantastic offer for you—a soda distributorship here in Cuba."

"Sure," Rocky said. "I'm interested."

"You can deal in big money here," the kingpin said. "And it's money you won't have to report to the United States. It's very important that you stay close by and work with me. You can work strictly with cash, and you won't have to come up with any money of your own. That's what you need, Rocky. You need to be working with cash."

Then the conversation began to change. For a while Sonny did not comprehend much of what the kingpin was implying.

Then the kingpin began criticizing the American system: the FBI, taxes, unscrupulous politicians. He kept emphasizing how much better it was to live in Cuba.

"Rocky, it doesn't hurt to make insinuations," he said. "Be outspoken about your political feelings. You're a champion. People respect you. They listen."

Rocky glanced at Sonny, frowning and looking as if he was about to become very angry. He turned to the kingpin and said, "I'm sorry. I just realized I've got to be at the Sans Souci right away to close the deal on my movie contract."

"Let me make a call," the kingpin said. "I'll take care of it."

"No," Rocky said. "I've really got to go now. I'll get back to you."

Rocky motioned to Sonny, Barbara, and Dominick Papia to follow him, then got up and bolted out of the room.

Sonny ran ahead of the others and caught up with Rocky, who had been charging down the steps two at a time. "Rock, what the hell are you doing?" he said. "You insulted the guy. The man was talking to you and you showed a complete lack of interest by jumping up and leaving."

"For Chrissake, Son," Rocky said. "Didn't you get the picture?"

"What picture?" Sonny said.

"Didn't you understand what was going on?" Rocky said. "These guys are a bunch of Communists."

"Are you kidding?" Sonny said. "They're really Communists, Rock? Why the hell would they want to be Communists?"

"What do you mean?" Rocky said. "Didn't you hear the guy say he was deported? Some of these guys can't even go to the United States. I don't want to have a fucking thing to do with it."

Barbara and Dominick Papia caught up with them, and Rocky quickly changed the subject. "Let's go," he said. "We've got a lot of things to cover today."

Eumile Charde, a Cuban businessman who had managed Kid Gavilan late in his career, was waiting to drive them to the Sans Souci nightclub.

That night they had dinner at the Havana Hilton with the production company of the group that was making the television series *Captain David Grief.*

"The contract looks good," Rocky told a director. "But I want a part for my brother Sonny."

The director argued that it would not be

possible because of union rules. But Rocky was adamant. Finally the director suggested that he might give Sonny a walk-on part without dialogue.

"That's not good enough," Rocky said. "I want Sonny to have a part. I want him to make a few bucks."

The director argued but then reluctantly agreed to Rocky's demands.

The following morning they drove across the Cuban countryside toward a filming location in a desert area by some quarries near the ocean. Peasants moved on ox-driven carts along the dusty dirt road. *"Compione!"* they shouted. *"Compione, Rocky Marciano!"* It sent shivers up Sonny's spine that even there, where few people read the newspapers, they recognized his brother.

Rocky was to be a guest star on the show that featured the tall English actor Maxwell Reed in the role of Captain David Grief. Rocky had the role of an Irishman named Captain Riley.

"How do you like that, Son?" he said. "Imagine me playing the part of an Irishman? Isn't that a joke?"

"Chrissake, Rock," Sonny said. "What're all our paesanos in Brockton going to think? You can't be an Irishman. They'll disown us."

Sonny played the role of a lookout man on Captain Riley's ship. Rocky was holding a bag of gold he had stolen from Captain David Grief. Then Sonny raised his binoculars and shouted, "Captain David Grief is coming into port!"

The scene went perfectly until it came to the part where Sonny was required to run to Rocky and make a report. When Sonny reached his brother he burst out laughing.

"Cut! Cut!" the director shouted.

Rocky was embarrassed. "For Chrissake, Son," he said. "What'd you do that for?"

"I can't help it. Rock," Sonny said. "You look ridiculous in that outfit."

Rocky had on a striped polo shirt and a sailor cap, and he was wearing two guns on his belt. He was taking the situation very seriously, which made Sonny laugh all the more.

"You've got to be able to do these things. Son," Rocky said. "This is important. Do you want these people to think we can't act? Now the next time just look over my shoulder. Don't think of me as your brother. Have a little imagination."

The next time they shot the scene it went perfectly. There was only one other problem.

"The script called for the hero to knock Rocky out in a fight," Sonny recalled. "But Rocky said that would never happen. He'd never been KO'd in the ring, and he didn't intend to have it done to him on the screen."

"There was a discussion about it and then they changed the script so that Rocky got shot instead of knocked out," Sonny said.

"That's fine," Rocky said. "I don't mind getting shot. That's much better than being knocked out."

When they returned to the hotel, Sonny and Rocky heard that there had been some flare-ups and that a showdown between Batista and Castro would soon take place.

"Cuba was tense," Sonny said. "You could almost feel the danger everywhere you went."

Some of Battista's contingent who were looking out for the Marcianos while they were in Cuba advised Sonny not to leave the hotel unescorted. But Sonny was single and anxious to do the town. He'd never seen a wide-open city like Havana before, with its nude shows, sexual exhibitions, and big casinos. The night before he'd been out with a dancer from the Sans Souci, and later with a starlet from the television series. He ignored the advice.

Sonny wandered out of the hotel, looking

for the strip that contained the nightclubs and the showgirls.

"I'd gone only a few hundred yards when I approached some houses that were guarded," Sonny said. "One of the guards called out in Spanish for me to identify myself. I remembered just enough Spanish from prep school to understand the guy."

"Tourista," Sonny said. "Americano tourista."

"Then the guards motioned for me to put my hands up, which I did very quickly. They told me to get out of there as fast as I could, and I wasted no time in complying with their wishes."

On another trip, Rocky and Sonny went to Cuba with their cousin Duna Cappiello. Rocky had been searching for Dominick Papia, who had vanished from sight.

"Rock had given Dominick more than forty thousand dollars in cash to hold for him," Sonny recalled. "It was early in Rocky's career as a businessman, and he still didn't really know where to hide the cash. So he gave the forty thousand to Dominick to lock up in the hotel safe. Rocky trusted Dominick completely, and he forgot all about the cash for a while. Then one day he called the Belmont Plaza, looking for Papia."

"I'm sorry Dominick Papia is no longer here," a stranger answered.

"What?" Rocky said. "Where is he?"

"We don't know," the man said. "He didn't leave a forwarding address."

Rocky called Papia's home, but his mother said she had no idea of his whereabouts and that she had been going to call Rocky to see if he knew.

"Son of a bitch," Rocky said. "How could Dominick do this to me?"

Rocky spent the entire evening calling people all over the country. "He had people in every city looking for Dominick," Sonny said.

"I was really impressed. Rocky must have made three hundred phone calls, and everybody kept assuring him that all the major hotels would be checked. My brother had a better network of connections going for him than the FBI."

Rocky and Sonny discussed the situation. They knew Dominick was a lifelong bachelor who had always lived according to strict Italian tradition. He had never made it big, but he idolized Rocky, and Rocky had told him that someday he was going to build a big hotel and put Dominick in charge of it.

"But Dominick had been very depressed, because he had recently broken up with his girlfriend," Sonny recalled. "He really loved her and he was having a hard time rebounding from it. We knew that Dominick had been an alcoholic, and Rocky thought he might go off the deep end because of the romance breaking up. We tried for weeks to locate him, but it seemed as if he had just vanished from the earth."

Then, months later, as he was walking down a street in Havana, Sonny could not believe his eyes as he watched the man strolling down the opposite side.

"Duna," Sonny said. "For Chrissakes, Duna. Look at that guy. It's Dominick Papia!"

Dominick barely smiled. It was as if he had just seen them yesterday. "Sonny, how're you doing?" he said.

"Dominick! Where the hell have you been?" Sonny said. "Rocky's looking for you."

"Oh, really," Papia said.

"Where are you staying?" Sonny said.

"Never mind," Papia said. "I'm going over to see Rock right now. Just tell me where I can find him."

"I never thought twice about it," Sonny said. "We always trusted Dominick so implicitly. I just told him how to get to the hotel, and

Duna and I kept on walking. That was the last time any of us ever saw Dominick Papia."

"You stupid bastard," Rocky said, when Sonny told him. "Didn't you know what that meant to me? Couldn't you have grabbed him and choked him or something?"

"Rock, I didn't know," Sonny said. "I figured the guy would show up."

"You dumb bastard," Rocky said. "You shitheel. I really ought to kick your ass."

"We heard later that Dominick had been found dead," Sonny said. "But we never did get the details, so I don't really know what happened to him. All I know is we never saw him again, or the forty thousand dollars."

In October 1958, three months before Castro took power, Sam Silverman, Allie Colombo, and Rocky made a trip to Cuba. Silverman was booking Kid Gavilan toward the end of his career, and Gavilan had introduced him to some Cubans who wanted Marciano to work for them in the gambling casinos.

"The deal was for Rocky to run either the Sans Souci or the Montmartre Club, big casinos and night spots in Havana," Silverman said. "A high Cuban official who owned a casino was going to set it up. Rocky would run the joint, and he and Kid Gavilan would be the hosts."

A huge crowd was waiting at the airport, including representatives of a local television station.

"Rock, these guys want you to go on TV," Silverman said.

Rocky frowned, figuring it was going to be a gratis appearance. "Yeah, I guess so, Sam," he said. "It'll be all right."

"I got you a G-note," Silverman said.

Rocky beamed. "Beautiful, Sam. Beautiful."

"Batista was supposed to meet us at the airport," Silverman said, "but he wasn't there. I think he was out of the country. We were greeted instead by Batista's brother-in-law, who was then commissioner of sports and also had a side deal running the slot machines. These Cubans were really enthusiastic. From the minute we arrived they wined and dined us. The guys who owned the casinos were all very close to Batista. They had the action sewed up. And they figured Rocky would be a magnet—he'd attract the American tourists by the droves."

For three weeks they made the rounds of all the nightclubs, eating the best food and drinking the finest wines, all courtesy of the Cubans. But then Silverman began to notice that they were being followed everywhere they went.

"Who the hell are those guys?" Silverman asked.

"Secret service," the Cuban said. "It's nothing to worry about. Some of Castro's people grabbed Juan Fangio a while ago. These men are here to make sure they don't get any ideas about Rocky."

"Fangio was a famous race car driver and a sports hero in Cuba," Silverman said. "It was embarrassing to Battista's forces to have him kidnapped. It wasn't long before I realized that they were really looking to grab Rocky before we ever got this thing off the ground."

"Those assholes," Rocky said. "Are they kidding?"

"Everywhere we went, Rocky and I tried to shake these tails," Silverman recalled. "But we couldn't. It was like they were stuck to us with glue."

"There was another guy around us too," Silverman said. "He used to tell everybody he was a banker, but he was full of shit. He sold a lot of worthless swampland. He sold Rocky some swamps too, and took him for about five thousand dollars."

"Tell him to call me," Rocky always used to say. "Tell him it's important."

"But as far as I know the guy went back to Puerto Rico, and nobody ever got anything back from him.

"We left Cuba on a Thursday and were supposed to return the following Tuesday with our lawyers to finalize the deal for the casino," Silverman recalled. "On Saturday night, the chief of Batista's secret service, some generals, and their wives were machine-gunned down right at the slot machines in the casino Rocky was supposed to run. That was the end of the whole Cuban deal. The entire revolution came to a head right there in what would have been Rocky's casino. Castro screwed it all up, and we never went back."

2.

What Made Rocky Run

EVERY MORNING AT EIGHT-THIRTY, Dale Miltimore, a tall, gregarious former cab driver and short-order cook, pulled his old sedan to a stop in front of Rocky's home in Fort Lauderdale.

"Where to, Rock?" Dale would say.

Invariably Rocky would shrug his shoulders. "I don't know," he'd say. "Just drive. We're bouncing today."

"Bouncing" could mean anything from spending the day with a couple of gorgeous girls, completing a business deal, meeting Jimmy Durante or Jackie Gleason or some other celebrity at the Diplomat or Fontainebleau, or flying to Chicago or Cleveland to be with Frankie Fratto or Pete DiGravio or some of Rocky's other Mafia friends. Miltimore never knew what to expect, and he never questioned him.

Miltimore was just one of many people throughout the country that Marciano could depend upon to deliver when asked to perform a service. There were two kinds of people in the "clan" that Rocky was assembling: friends who could also provide valuable services, and outsiders who bought their way in with money and influence.

"He considered the rich guys strictly from the standpoint of survival," Miltimore said. "Rocky had a scheme for survival. You lived each day on zero expenses, and everything you took in was profit. In order to do this you had to have connections with hotel owners, restaurateurs, lawyers, legitimate businessmen, syndicate people, celebrities, and so on. Rocky had all of these.

"Rocky was the world's greatest schemer," Miltimore went on. "He could leave town with thirty cents in his pocket and tour the country and he'd come back with the same thirty cents. He never had transportation, money, or a system, just the connections to get all of these things. The plane tickets, the hotel rooms, the meals, were always on somebody, but never Rocky."

The way Miltimore joined Marciano's clan was typical of how many people got to know and travel with the former champion.

In 1958, Miltimore became friendly with the manager of Julius LaRosa's Italian restaurant in Hollywood, Florida.

"A lot of celebrities including Marciano hung out there," Miltimore said. "But Rocky didn't go there to be seen. He went there

189

ee. It was strictly a
ere was a heavy wind and
99, and Rocky's house supposed a lot of damage. Mike Richel
manager of LaRosa's restaurant] got a call
rom Rocky to see what he could do. Then
Mike called me and asked me if I'd like to
meet Rocky and try to help him out. I was
dying to meet him and I jumped at the
chance."

But when Miltimore arrived at Marciano's
house, he discovered that "there was really not
much damage done by the storm."

Rocky had gone on a trip and left the windows open. In order to make it appear like
legitimate storm damage, somebody had
thrown boards through the windows.

It was up to Miltimore to work with the
insurance agents toward a settlement. Rocky
was watching to see how Dale could produce.

"I got Rocky ten thousand dollars for no
real storm damage," Miltimore said.

Miltimore recalled that he was "supposed
to have gotten a cut" for helping with the
storm case, but he never saw the money. What
he did see was a lot more of Rocky Marciano.

"For the next ten years, I was Rocky's
valet, chauffeur, secretary, cook, butler, bodyguard—you name it. Whatever the situation
called for, I was it," Miltimore said.

"One thing I wasn't, though, was Rocky's
manager," Miltimore said. "Rocky had more
personal managers than any man in the world.
He had them in Chicago, New York,
Cleveland—every big city in the country. But
nobody was ever really Rocky's manager. They
never really influenced him. Rocky made his
own decisions. The only reason he listened to
some of those guys was to make them feel
important. He always liked to make unimpor-
tant people feel important."

For BARBARA AND MARY ANNE there was
always the loneliness of not being with Rocky.
He would come home for a week and be gone
for three. They loved him very much and cher-
ished the time they could spend with him. And
yet they knew he could never be tied down,
could never live the life of a normal husband
and father.

"Live fast, die hard," Mary Anne found
written among the scribbled notes her father
left. It was the way Rocky ran, and they did not
question it.

"I don't think my dad could have ever been
married to anyone else except Mom," Mary
Anne said. "She gave him the freedom he had
to have. He just couldn't sit still. He couldn't
have been happy. I could never picture my
father as an old man or crippled or sick. He
was constantly on the go."

From her earliest memories, Mary Anne
had been a "Daddy's girl." She was caught up,
as was everyone in the family, in the shadow of
fame and glory that had come to her father
even before she was born. She followed him
around like a puppy, and savored the moments
when they were together.

"All my memories of him are good," she
said. "He always gave me a lot of love."

But it wasn't always easy being the daughter of a heavyweight champion.

There were the times when she was a baby
and her father came home from a fight, his
face battered and swollen, the stitches closing
a gash over his eye. Mary Anne was afraid and
cried and hid behind her mother.

When she was six years old and in the first
grade at Sylvester School on Court Street in
Brockton, Mary Anne discovered what it
meant to be daughter of the champ.

Several boys cornered her on the way home from school. "Let's see if you're as tough as your father," a boy said. "Come on, we're gonna fight."

Mary Anne was knocked to the ground and punched, and when she ran home it was discovered that her nose had been broken.

Rocky was furious. He immediately began teaching Mary Anne how to fight in much the same fashion as his Uncle John had taught him. "Punch. Punch," Rocky told her. "Don't back away. You've got to hit him."

"Because of all the publicity and photographers and everything that was constantly surrounding us, I became very shy and introverted," Mary Anne said.

Although Rocky was often gone, he tried to make it up to Barbara and Mary Anne when he was home. They traveled during summer vacations when Mary Anne was out of school, visiting England, Germany, Hawaii, Austria, and many other places.

Rocky never held back with his money when it involved Mary Anne. "I was always hitting him up," she said. "He'd play tough with me with the money. 'Aw, what do ya need it for?' he'd say. But he loved it. He'd always pull the cash out and give it to me."

When Mary Anne was fourteen she wanted a car. Rocky wanted her to get a Thunderbird.

"Daddy, that's too big," she said. "How about a Firebird?"

A few weeks later Rocky returned home with the car. He had gotten it as a gift and paid nothing, Mary Anne wasn't even old enough to drive.

Mary Anne soon learned of her father's fierce pride and how it sometimes placed him in embarrassing and humorous situations.

Once when Rocky, Barbara, and Mary Anne were vacationing in Hawaii, the manager of a pineapple plantation asked them to visit the groves. The man was very honored to have Rocky there, and did everything he could to make the trip enjoyable.

Rocky wore Bermuda shorts and a short-sleeved shirt. He had on a hat, which he had become accustomed to wearing over his toupee. As they were walking through the groves, Rocky and the manager were talking when a strong gust of wind caught Rocky's hat and blew it off. The toupee was still clinging to it as the hat bounced along behind them.

"Quick! Quick! Get the hat!" Rocky shouted as he ran after it so fast his knees were almost hitting his chest.

The groves were crowded with visitors, and everybody was watching.

"Look! There's the champ chasing his hair," someone shouted.

The people began giggling and pointing as Rocky pounced on his hat. His face was crimson. He was so embarrassed, he bolted out of the pineapple grove, and even though the manager felt badly and pleaded with him to stay, he wanted to be as far away from there as possible.

Another time they were with Ernie Clivio, vacationing at Arrowhead Springs. Rocky and Ernie were relaxing in the cottage when suddenly Barbara screamed: "Rocky, there's a tarantula in our bedroom. Rock, come here quick!"

Rocky dashed into the bedroom, but when he saw the large hairy bug crawling along the floor, he ran for the dresser and jumped up on top of it. "Don't worry, honey," he said. "I'll get him."

Rocky leaned over and eased a drawer out of the bureau. Then he carefully took aim and threw it, crushing the spider. "I got him," he said, grinning.

"It was a big, ugly, hairy bug," Clivio said. "I don't know if it was a tarantula, but it sure looked like one. But the thing that struck me funny was that here was the heavyweight champ of the world up on the dresser, afraid of a bug on the floor. It reminded me of an elephant and a mouse."

"The Rock was a serious guy, but he had that dry humor, sort of like Jack Benny, and he could be very funny sometimes," Clivio said.

Once, before his retirement, they had interrupted a vacation because Barbara had to go to Pratt Diagnostic Clinic in Boston for some tests. Rocky was very worried. When he and Ernie picked Barbara up at the hospital, they learned that the tests had given her a clean bill of health.

"Barbara, honey," Rocky said, "now that I know you're all right, I'm gonna let you buy anything you want."

"Really, Rock," Barbara said. "Honest, hon?"

"Absolutely," Rocky said. "Anything at all."

Ernie was driving slowly through the traffic when Rocky suddenly ordered him to stop the car.

"What for?" Clivio said, pulling up to the curb. They were parked in front of a five-and-ten-cent store.

"All right, Barbara," Rocky grinned, pointing at the store window. "You go right in there and buy anything you want."

Rocky was acquainted with many show business personalities and other celebrities, but he developed close friendships with only a few stars. He always enjoyed being in the company of Jimmy Durante, Vic Damone, Sergio Franchi, George Raft, Bob Hope, Joey Bishop, Jerry Lewis, Dean Martin, and Johnny Weissmuller, and he liked to be with sports heroes such as Ted Williams and Joe DiMaggio. But most of Rocky's really close friends were average people who had no particular claim to fame.

Mario Lanza and Rocky were good friends and shared many of the same interests. Rocky was one of the few persons Mario entertained at his home.

Mario had a tremendous ego, and he wanted to be recognized as a true artist more than anything. A huge, barrel-chested, rugged man, he enjoyed physical challenge; he really was a frustrated fighter, and had once built a boxing ring in his backyard.

Rocky and Mario both loved to eat, and when they got together they sometimes gorged themselves on the rich Italian food. Afterward they relaxed, drinking wine, talking about boxing, sports, and their own careers.

"Mario," Rocky would say, toasting his paseano. "You were the greatest, even greater than Caruso."

"Rocky," Mario said. "You would have murdered Dempsey. You would have beaten them all."

Clivio recalled the singer's shyness. It was almost eerie. Rocky and Ernie had gone to visit Mario at his home. Mario had grown a beard. He grinned when he saw Rocky. But when Clivio, a stranger, entered, he cringed and backed away. And yet there were times when Lanza was very outgoing and boisterous.

In public Mario and Rocky always defended each other and tried to enhance each other's reputation. When Lanza appeared on Ed Sullivan's television show and said, "I want to say hello to my good friend Rocky Marciano," Rocky was so proud that he mentioned it to all of his relatives and friends. The same comment by another celebrity might have gone completely unacknowledged by the champ.

In *The Mario Lanza Story*, a biography by Constantine Callinicos with Ray Robinson, there is an anecdote that describes Mario's loyalty to Rocky.

Former heavyweight champ Max Baer came to visit Mario one evening.

"Any friend of Rocky's is a friend of mine," Mario said.

But as they talked, Baer began belittling Rocky's ability and claimed he could have beaten Marciano.

"I'll use Rocky's style," Mario said, "and you show me how you would have licked him."

They were both notoriously high livers and a long way from being in condition, but Max and Mario began boxing in the living room. Baer threw a right; Lanza blocked it and ripped a left hook that sent Max sprawling onto the sofa. Mario was elated.

But Mario was an alcoholic given to wild sprees of excessive drinking and self-abuse that left him drained and depressed. He was "desperate, lonely and afraid" when he died in October 1959.

It was a sad day for Rocky, and caused a brief interlude of respite from his running pace, a time for reflection and self-analysis.

As much as Rocky enjoyed being with men who were strong-minded, aggressive, and masculine, he sympathized with those who were not and seldom criticized them.

Sonny Marciano recalled the time some wealthy businessmen took him and Rocky to a nightclub in Greenwich Village. Rocky had not wanted to go but the men persisted. It was a gay bar, frequented almost exclusively by lesbians and male homosexuals.

"It was dark and smoky with dim blue lights, and there were guys sitting at the bar with their arms around weaker, shy guys," Sonny said. "They were buying drinks and fawning all over each other, and you could smell the marijuana in the room. Some hard-looking broads in slacks and shirts, with hair cut shorter than men's, sat at tables kissing young, petite, very feminine girls. Some of them were beautiful, and they looked confused and lonely, almost as if they didn't know what was happening to them."

The men who had taken Rocky and Sonny to the gay bar began joking and making wisecracks about the homosexuals.

"They thought they were impressing Rocky," Sonny said, "but I could tell that it was working in reverse. Rocky didn't find it funny at all."

One of the men with Rocky called a homosexual to the table. The stranger was anxious to meet Rocky. He came walking over with a wide grin on his face.

"Then this rich guy began insulting him," Sonny said. "He was really ridiculing the gay guy."

Rocky shook hands with the homosexual and signed his autograph on a napkin. The rich man kept up his banter. Rocky was becoming infuriated. Then the gay man got very uptight and excused himself.

Rocky was seeing black. He stared at the businessman and said, "What the hell's the matter with you? How could you do something like that to the guy? Those people can't help themselves. For Chrissake, leave them alone."

For a while they watched the girls dancing together, kissing and caressing on the floor, making no pretenses. Rocky was fascinated, but he respected the entire scene.

"What the hell are we doing here?" Rocky said suddenly. "Who the hell are you to be criticizing these people? Come on, let's go. We're the ones who don't belong in this place."

Once Rocky had written in a note pad: "When women kiss it always reminds one of fighters shaking hands before the fight . . ."

It is possible Rocky was thinking of scenes like the night in Greenwich Village when he wrote of women kissing, but some of his close friends feel he may have been referring to the many times he had watched women embrace and kiss as they greeted each other at social gatherings. Rocky knew that often these women not only had no affection between them but in fact disliked one another.

Rocky himself always felt shaking hands before a fight was hypocritical.

"What the hell's the sense of shaking hands when you're out to ruin the guy," Rocky said. "You can't be friendly with a guy you've got to destroy."

ROCKY ALWAYS CAREFULLY GUARDED his personal life from public scrutiny and maintained the image he thought was important for a champion to present to the public. What we know of the real Marciano after his retirement is nowhere to be found in the public record, but is gleaned mostly from Rocky's own notes, which he constantly jotted down on scraps of paper and in notebooks, and from the anecdotes and observations of the people who were closest to him from 1956 on.

"Rocky was a mysterious guy. I don't think anybody ever really knew him completely, because unless you were directly involved he didn't tell you anything," Dale Miltimore said. "He had his key people all over the country, and these were the guys he'd be with. He even rated them on the basis of one to ten, depending upon how much he liked them and their ability to produce. I always felt it was patterned after the Mafia, based upon unquestionable service. One was the best, and you never got a call if you fell below a five. You could shift ratings in an instant, depending upon what you did that either pleased or annoyed him. You never went to the

Fontainebleau with Rocky unless you were a number one, and there were people who waited for months for Rocky to call, and never really knew what had gone wrong."

Wherever Rocky went there were these people who wanted to be with him and who would willingly supply transportation, hotel rooms, credit cards, and women to impress him. These newly acquired friends would introduce Rocky to the dignitaries of their city and arrange lucrative personal appearances. Sometimes they'd cancel business appointments in order to drive to Brockton and pick up Marciano's parents and take them to Florida because Rocky thought it would be nice if they got a little sun for a week or two. Or often they would help Rocky's brothers Peter and Sonny with social and business contacts.

Whatever these people, who were almost always of Italian descent, did for Marciano was performed as a service out of loyalty and respect for Rocky. He not only never gave them a penny, but if he even suspected they were involved strictly for the money, he immediately cut them off.

"This is a merry-go-round," Rocky used to tell his friends. "Anytime you want to get off, just jump."

But the ones who did not jump usually found themselves in far better shape both financially and socially than they had been before they met Marciano. Some of his Italian friends went from modest-paying jobs to positions of considerable wealth because of the favors Rocky did to reward their unquestioned loyalty and service. Marciano would never give them a nickel of cash. But he went out of his way to help them through personal appearances, business contacts, and any other ways that did not involve his own money. An Italian acquaintance, who had just entertained

Marciano and some friends for a week and had spent hundreds of dollars, once casually asked Rocky to leave the tip after he had paid the bill in an expensive restaurant Rocky trembled with rage, which he concealed as he almost always did.

"Oh, all right," Rocky said. "You go ahead. I'll take care of it."

When the men had gone, Rocky followed them, having left the tip for the waitress. But it was the last time the wealthy Italian was ever with Marciano.

"You never took from Rocky," Dale Miltimore said. "You never asked him for things, because if you did you embarrassed him. But Rocky would do things for you because he wanted to. He was the kind of a guy who showed his appreciation in strange ways, and anybody who was ever loyal to him never regretted it.

"Rocky never left a dime with a doorman or a waitress in his life," Miltimore recalled. "If you were with him, you paid. He never let a rich guy get out of a joint without taking care of the poor working people."

Among Rocky's new friends, his number one contact on the West Coast was Lindy Ciardelli, a short, flamboyant, self-made, wealthy businessman from San Jose.

Ciardelli came from a large family of poor, immigrant Italians. He had worked and saved until finally he owned his business, Linco Engineering Company.

By the time Marciano met him in the late 1950s, Ciardelli had plenty of money, a private plane, two cars, a luxurious bachelor apartment, and carte blanche at the finest hotels in Las Vegas. Lindy was a mover who craved elegance and extravagance and did not mind paying to go first class. He wanted excitement and lived in a whirlwind of lavish parties, high-priced hookers, expensive suites, and posh gambling casinos. Like Marciano, Ciardelli could not sit still. He was among the handful of men chosen by Rocky to join him in his race against time. Wherever they went, Lindy picked up the tab—unless Rocky met another rich acquaintance, who would pay for them both.

Ciardelli was expected to get the girls, take care of the hotel rooms, find the transportation, and make the business contacts. And he did. He always delivered for Rocky, whether it meant giving an ex-champion like Willie Pep a job, hiring Rocky's brother Sonny, getting a beautiful hooker up to the apartment, or taking care of Rocky's mother and father. But Ciardelli was another of Marciano's newly acquired paesanos who never regretted doing things to please the former champion.

"There was a name that some people used in referring to Rocky," Ciardelli recalled. "They spoke of him as 'The Golden Key.' This was because Rocky had a knack, a special talent, for being able to make things happen. He could put two people together and turn two bad deals into one great big money-making proposition. He could move into any city and penetrate almost any situation. It didn't matter if it was Chicago, New York, Cleveland, Des Moines—Rocky knew all the key people. He was always with guys who would get things done, and who knew how to move and protect his interests on the money. Rocky had the Golden Key to open all the doors.

"And every place we went, they wanted Rocky to do something for them, like appear at a benefit, or show up at somebody's business and shake hands with the customers, and maybe play golf with some guy they were looking to close a deal with. They usually paid him good money for doing these things, but if they were really his close friends he'd do it for nothing. Rocky would never refuse. He couldn't say no to anything. But he was notorious for going back on his word. He'd break any kind of a commitment on a whim."

But although Rocky never worried about the wealthy people who used him as a showcase, he hated to let a little guy down. He was always ready to help out former boxers who had fallen upon hard times. Again, Rocky wouldn't spend his own cash, but he'd go out of his way to do other things that benefited them. And nobody could criticize fighters without getting Rocky angry.

Rocky loved Willie Pep more than any other fighter. For William Papaleo was an Italian *spaccone* who had proven to be one of the greatest champions in boxing history. Willie became featherweight champ at twenty, and held the title from 1942 to 1951. He had an amazing overall record of 238 wins and only 11 losses, most of which came near the end of his twenty-year career, when Willie was an old man in the short-lived world of the boxer. He had won his first 62 fights in a row, lost 1, then won 73 more with just 1 draw.

Willie was just one year older than Rocky. When the flashy little boxer won the title he became an idol. He was an Italian, a sharp dresser, a fast mover, and a champion. At twenty, Willie had everything going for him, and Rocky was an obscure private in the army. And so Rocky admired Willie, and hungered for the champion's way of life.

Not long after Rocky retired from boxing, Willie Pep got a call.

"I'm involved in this electronics company around Brockton," Rocky said. "I think I can get you in as a public relations guy for about two hundred a week."

"Sure, Rock," Willie said. "I'll take it."

One afternoon, Rocky came to the Soundex Company building where Willie was working. Rocky was in a happy mood.

"I just made a big score, Willie," he said, removing a thick roll of hundred-dollar bills from his hip pocket. "You need some cash?"

"I'll tell you what, Rock," Pep said. "Loan me a hundred, and I'll give it back when I get paid Friday."

But on Friday Willie was out of town. The following Monday he went to the office to pick up his pay. He was handed an envelope that contained just $100 instead of the usual $200.

"Where's the other hundred?" Willie said.

"Rocky took it," the company paymaster said.

"Rocky?"

"Rocky came in and said you owed it to him," the paymaster said. "Then he took it out of the envelope."

"Yeah, that's right," Willie said.

"Rocky would always loan me anything I wanted," Pep said. "He'd hold out the cash and tell me to take as much as I needed. If you were a man of your word, The Rock was always right there anytime you needed him."

From 1956 on, Willie was with Rocky often, and Rocky always tried to help him. There was such demand for Rocky to make personal appearances that frequently he booked two on the same night. Rocky would go to one, Willie to the other.

Once they were together for the opening of a municipal auditorium in Baltimore. Willie had received $1,500, but he didn't know what Rocky was paid. After the program, Rocky and Willie were invited to join a group of wealthy men in a Baltimore nightclub. The men had bought several rounds of drinks when Willie reached into his pocket and pulled out a hundred-dollar bill.

"I figured I'd take care of the next round," Willie said. "But then I saw Rocky was squirming in his seat. The next thing I knew he kicked me under the bar."

"Willie, come over here, I want to talk to you," Rocky said, moving away from the bar.

"Sure, Rock," Willie said, excusing himself from the group.

"Listen, Willie, I'm not gonna spend any money, and I don't want you to spend any. Don't make me look bad, Willie. These guys have got plenty of dough and they want to buy you drinks. So don't spend anything."

"That's okay with me," Pep said. Then he went back and took his cash off the bar.

"Rocky was a tough guy with a buck," Willie said. "He earned it all the hard way, and he was determined to keep it."

Sometimes Willie would marvel over the way Rocky went to extremes to avoid spending his money. Pep himself was high-living and never worried about how much he spent.

"How do you do it, Rock?" Willie said.

"Willie," Rocky joked. "Money flows out of my pockets like glue."

But in a more serious mood, he said, "It was rough for me when I was a kid, Willie. It's never gonna be like that again. I'm never gonna be broke now, Willie. Never."

"But don't ever kid yourself," Pep said. "When I was with Rocky alone, he picked up all the tabs. Rocky never let me go for anything. I always understood why he didn't want to spend his money. But that just wasn't my style."

Willie Pep was number one, but any fighter Rocky respected received his loyalty and support.

Miltimore recalls that Rocky always became very upset when he discovered that a former fighter down on his luck was being mistreated.

He recalled an incident in the late 1950s or early 1960s, when Rocky got very upset over the way a boss treated a former outstanding fighter.

Dale was operating a taxicab company then and was on his way to pick up a fare in Miami when he noticed a man hitchhiking.

"The guy had the battered head, the fighter's head," Dale said, "so I picked him up."

"Where're you goin'?" Dale said.

"The Fontainebleau Hotel."

"Good. I'm going right by there. I'll drop you off."

"Thanks," the man said.

"You're a fighter, ain't you?" Dale said.

"Yeah, I'm Georgie Abrams."

Georgie Abrams, Dale thought. He was a helluva fighter. I wonder what the guy's doing now.

"Where ya workin', Georgie?" Dale asked.

"At the Fontainebleau," the ex-fighter said. "I'm parking cars."

Jesus, Georgie Abrams parking cars, Dale thought. That's a damn shame.

Abrams had been an outstanding fighter who had lost a fifteen-round decision to Tony Zale for the middleweight title in 1941.

"The first chance I got, I told Rocky that Georgie was parking cars at the Fontainebleau," Dale recalled.

A short while later, Dale and Rocky went to the hotel with two of his millionaire friends to see Frank Sinatra. The first thing Rocky did was go downstairs to where Beau Jack, former lightweight champion and top welterweight fighter in the 1940s, was shining shoes.

"Give Beau Jack twenty dollars," Rocky told one of the men.

Whenever he went to the Fontainebleau, Rocky always saw Beau Jack, and he always insisted that the wealthy men with him leave a heavy tip.

Once Beau Jack had glanced down at Rocky's scuffed-up brown shoes and grinned. "How 'bout it, Champ?" he said. "Let me shine 'em up for you."

"Rocky almost got mad at Beau Jack then," Sonny Marciano recalled.

"You'll never shine my shoes, Beau," Rocky said. "You were too great a champion."

When they were coming out of the Fontainebleau after the show, Rocky nudged one of his friends and said, "That's Georgie Abrams. Remember him? Helluva fighter. The poor guy is parking cars now."

"Have Georgie get our car," Rocky said to the doorman.

"I can't do that, Rocky," the doorman said. "They're working on an up system."

"Tell him to have Georgie get the car," Rocky told Dale.

After some conversation with the doorman, Dale convinced him that Rocky would really appreciate it if Georgie got the car.

"Up comes the Cadillac," Dale said. "And then Georgie Abrams steps out."

"Hey, Rocky," Georgie said, delighted to see the ex-champ.

"Hey, Georgie," Rocky said, grinning.

They had been talking only a few minutes. Dale recalled, when the doorman shouted, "Hey, Punchy George, get this car."

"I'll be with Rocky just a minute," Georgie said.

"Get this car," the doorman repeated.

Rocky walked over to Dale. His face was flushed and his arms were trembling. "Hit that mother before I do," he said.

"But, Rock, we're standing outside a multimillion-dollar hotel," Dale said. "How'm I gonna hit the doorman? What am I gonna do—hit him with my hands? I won't get out of jail for five years."

Rocky was ripping mad. He took Georgie

by the arm and says, "Leave the car there. Come on, Georgie, let's sit down here. How are ya, anyway?"

They were sitting on the steps at the entrance to the Fontainebleau, Dale said. The people were walking around them, all dressed up in their fancy clothes, and Rocky couldn't have cared less. He just sat there with his arm draped around Georgie's shoulders and talked.

"Tell these guys to each give him a hundred," Rocky whispered to Dale, glancing toward his millionaire friends, when they were ready to leave.

Dale remembered them going over to the ex-fighter and saying, "Here, Georgie, this is for bringing up the car."

When they were in the car driving away from the Fontainebleau, Rocky turned to Dale and said, "I never liked that fucking doorman. If you ever get a chance, hit him with the car. Run that mother over."

He was constantly moving, but fighters and ethnically informed Italians could often stop Rocky's rush.

There was an old Italian around Fort Lauderdale named A. Victor Rennie, and whenever Rocky saw him he would spend hours talking to the man. Rennie had once taught history in Italy, and Rocky was fascinated by his knowledge and appreciation of the Italian people and their culture.

"They'd talk for hours," Dale said. "They'd discuss all the ethnic things that I didn't even understand. You couldn't tear Rocky away when he was with that guy. It wasn't like Rocky, who was usually restless and wanted to be bouncin' all the time.

"Haven't we got an appointment to be at the Diplomat at three o'clock, I'd say to Rocky. 'Naw,' Rocky would say. 'Sit down, Dale, you gotta hear this.'

"A. Victor Rennie was the only man that I

can ever remember where when they went to lunch together Rocky would always pick up the check," Dale said.

During the late 1950s, Rocky lived in jets and small private planes and motels and fancy hotel suites. A week in Chicago, two days in Des Moines, back to Chicago, then on to New York, Brockton, and Fort Lauderdale. It was disorganized and hectic, but that's the way Rocky seemed to like it. And whenever his path crossed Willie Pep's, The Rock made a point of getting in touch with him.

In 1959 and 1960, Rocky saw a lot of Willie in New York. Willie owned a little bar and grill on Fifty-seventh Street called Willie Pep's Melody Lane.

"Rocky used to bring all his friends in to eat," Pep recalled. "He'd have all these big shots and celebrities with him. Rock was always surrounded by the money men. They paid everything. I'd have gladly fed Rocky and his friends for nothing. But Rocky always made them pay. The place was like a headquarters for Rocky. He'd get all his phone calls there. He didn't drink much, only a little Lancer's rosé, but the guy could eat for hours. Rocky was an unbelievable eater."

Rocky had starved himself to stay in shape for fighting, but in retirement he certainly made up for it. His weight sometimes soared to more than 240 pounds, and he was constantly promising himself to go on strict programs of diet and exercise to shed the blubber. Sometimes he did follow through and would lose many pounds. But he'd always gain it back again on the Italian food that he loved. Without the challenge and goals of his fighting career, it was very difficult for Rocky to make sacrifices.

Toward the end of 1960, Rocky went to his friend Lindy Ciardelli to see what he could do for Willie, who was out of the bar and grill business and unemployed.

"Lindy, I've got a terrific deal for you," Rocky said. "I just saw Willie Pep in New York, and he isn't doing anything. He could be a helluva PR guy for you. He was one of the greatest champs in history. How about it, Lindy? Can you give Willie a job?"

Lindy didn't really have a spot on his staff for Willie, but he could tell it was very important to Rocky. And he knew that Rocky didn't plead with his friends for anything. He told them what he wanted and then waited to see if they produced.

"Sure, Rock," Ciardelli said. "Don't worry. If you want it, I'll find a place for Willie. Get me together with him."

Rocky was elated. The next time he was in New York, he drove to Hartford to tell Pep.

"Willie, I've got a guy who loves fighters," Rocky said. "He'd love to be with you. He's a class guy and a real high flier. This'll be great for you, Willie. He'd love to have you travel with him and be his companion."

"That sounds great, Rock," said Willie, who wasn't married at the time and was living in Hartford with his mother. "Yeah, I think I'd really like it."

The next time Ciardelli came to New York, Rocky called Willie to come to the city and meet him.

"I'd love to have you come to California and be with me, Willie," Lindy said.

"Lindy was a real mover," Pep recalled. "He had his own private plane and pilot, a big limousine, and a chauffeur. The guy paid all my expenses, got me the best clothes, a little Chevy to run around in, a charge account at Angelo's Steak House, an apartment, and everything else I needed. He even sent some money home to my mother."

Every morning Willie picked Lindy up and they had breakfast together before going to Lindy's plant. Then, while Ciardelli spent four or five hours in the office, Willie waited in the lounge.

"Every week we flew to different places—San Diego, Sacramento, LA, Vegas," Willie said. "Once a week we hit the Thunderbird Motel in Vegas. I had my own room there. I liked to gamble. With Lindy the sky's the limit. We had some good times."

Rocky often traveled with Lindy and Willie, and he spent a lot of time with them in Las Vegas.

Since they were both *spaccones,* it was almost inevitable that friction would develop between Lindy and Willie.

"Lindy was pretty demanding," Willie said. "He wanted me around all the time. I was beginning to think he wanted me to be a stooge, and I could never let that happen. He was a nice guy, but he always had to be on the move. He'd worked hard all his life and finally made it big. And now he wanted to make up for lost time. He wanted to be everywhere and do everything. We had some great times. Rocky would come in once a month for a few days, and Lindy loved to show him off. We really moved when Rocky was around . . . But at the end of three months, Lindy and I were both beginning to get on each other's nerves. Finally we just couldn't make it. I gave him back his car, and he gave me a ticket."

"What bugged me was that Willie had no respect for money," Lindy said. "The Rock would never allow himself to be in Willie's position."

Ciardelli would okay Willie to buy clothes, to gamble at the Thunderbird, where he had carte blanche with Joe Wells, and in other Vegas casinos.

"Rock, I can't hack Willie anymore," Ciardelli said.

"Aw, you've gotta be patient with Willie," Rocky said. "He's a great guy, Lindy."

Not only could they not stand each other's company anymore, but Willie's father was very ill in Hartford. Willie was now the patriarch of the family and wanted to be home.

"What should I do, Rock?" Lindy said,

Rocky shrugged his shoulders, knowing that Willie wasn't happy with Lindy either, and had been considering leaving. Proud champions like Rocky and Willie were not accustomed to taking orders, nor did they remain for long in the company of persons with whom they were uncomfortable.

"Make sure Willie gets home all right," Rocky said. "That's all."

Willie and Lindy agreed on five hundred dollars and a plane ticket.

ON SEPTEMBER 5, 1961, Rocky wrote a letter to his brother Sonny from the Dunes Hotel in Las Vegas.

Sonny—Finished my TV series and what a relief Spent four days with Lindy + wife in Vegas He promised to help you out now take all the help he wants to give you I have reasons for this I bought you a ticket to Florida plus $50 cash so try and protect me on this at least with his equipment or car both if you can I'm going to be in Vegas again on the 18th of Sept to referee a fight so I'll either be up to see you or talk to you then.

I wish you'd learn all you can about Lindy's business I may buy in before the year is up I'll want lots of good business information out of that particular type of business. Plus Lindy's behavior it all adds up.

I'll send you 24 Klub Karts to your home

try to get at least $60 per Kart look for bigger distribution so we can get a better price on them in quantity. Bill Blackburn at San Francisco SK 19496 is there dealer now try to work with him. I may have to come out for a promotion with him so meet him at least.

Pete should be leaving for school in a week wish he'd give football a try I guess we'll let Mary Anne go to school again in Brockton I need at least 3 months to square thing away in the east

Keep punching I believe things are going to work out for you out there with Lindy

Rocky

The letter shows another contradiction in Rocky's character. Often he would trust someone he barely knew with large sums of money. Yet sometimes he was privately very critical and suspicious of his brothers and closest friends. It was as if he expected more of them.

"Rocky let me down a couple of times very badly. I was really hurt, and I was damn well pissed off," Ciardelli said. "I mean, The Rock and I had a lot more going than just an ordinary business relationship like these other guys that he stood up. After a couple of times, we had a long, serious talk about it.

" 'You tell me what I have to do.' Rocky said. 'You tell me when I've really got to be there, and I'll come.'

"From then on we had an understanding," Lindy said. "If something was important enough, I told him, and he'd make sure he was there."

But nobody really told Rocky what to do. If he wanted to please Ciardelli he might go somewhere for him. But if Rocky really didn't want to make an appearance, no force on earth could move him.

"Sometimes it wasn't his fault that he missed these things. He always figured he'd make it when he first agreed to take a date. But everyone close to The Rock knew he was totally disorganized," Ciardelli said. "He was a great thinker, and he had a mind that could really retain a lot. But as far as notes, records, appointments were concerned, the guy was all screwed up. He'd jot everything down on the nearest scrap of paper. Then he'd lose the papers. He had so many scraps of paper, he didn't know where to look for them."

Lindy sometimes went to Brockton with Rocky, and Pasqualena was always after her son to be neat.

"Rocky, look at Lindy," she'd say. "See, why don't you wear a ring, put on your good suit. You're a champeen. You gotta lose weight. You gotta look nice. Get a wig. Please, Rocky, promise me you're gonna get a hairpiece."

His mother haunted him so much about the hairpiece, that Rocky finally started asking his friends about it.

"What do you think, Lindy?" he'd say. "You think I should get one? Aw, what the hell, who cares if ya got a little hair missing in the front."

"Somehow I got the feeling that he was uncomfortable about the piece because he figured it might get in the way of his manliness," Lindy said. "He never cared what he looked like. But wearing a toupee might make people think he was vain. We grew up in a time when the really rugged guys never bothered to cover up their bald spots. When we were kids it seemed like any guy wearing a rug was some kind of a fairy, a guy you'd snicker at. Now almost anybody who's bald has a toupee. It's the natural thing to do, just like hair styling for men. Imagine some guy trying that back in the forties and early fifties."

"THE BIG THING THAT REALLY MADE US JELL was that we both wanted to move, we both craved excitement," Ciardelli said. "He couldn't sit still and neither could I. I don't think Rocky would have been held down if he was seventy. He couldn't have stayed still if he was sitting on a gold mine. He had to be on the move, always running. He was on an excitement kick, just like me. I've had to tone it down a lot. Doing exciting things is like taking dope. The more you get the more you want. The difference between me and Rock was that he used to always try to combine his business deals with the excitement.

"But Rocky went past the point of being sensible about his own indestructibility," Lindy said. "He went to extremes, almost as if he was testing himself. I consider myself a tough individual who can take care of myself in most situations. But not like Rocky. He seemed to want to flirt with danger. Half a dozen times we came close to being smashed up in car wrecks. I'd get concerned and nerved up over it. If it was some guy's fault who was driving us, I'd be bullshit. I could never see taking unnecessary risks. But not Rocky. He was like ice water. 'What are you worried about,' he'd say. 'Nothing happened, did it?' "

At various times, Ciardelli had five planes. Rocky never cared who the pilot was, and he never worried about the weather. "Let's move," he'd say. "Come on, Lindy, let's move."

Once Rocky and Lindy went to the airport on a gray, drizzly morning with the fog so thick they couldn't see the tops of the trees.

"Forget it, Rock," Lindy said. "We can't fly today."

"Aw, it'll be all right," Rocky said. "We gotta go to Vegas don't we?"

"Let's wait until tomorrow," Lindy said. "Maybe we'll have better weather by then."

"Aw, fuck the weather," Rocky said. "I wanta go now. C'mon, Lindy, have a few balls."

"I got the balls. Rock," Lindy said. "I just don't think it's too smart. We don't even know if the pilot can handle this kind of a situation."

"Well, let's see what he says," Rocky said. "If he's willing, it'll be all right. Figure it this way, Lindy, we got at least as much going for us as the pilot does."

"Fortunately for all of us, the people at the airport wouldn't clear us for a takeoff that day anyway," Lindy recalled. "Our guy wasn't checked out for that kind of flying."

3.

The World's Worst Businessman

ON CHRISTMAS EVE, 1959, Frank Saccone was at home with his family in Brockton around the Christmas tree. He was about to pour himself a glass of warm brandy when the telephone rang.

"Is this Frank Saccone?" a soft, vaguely familiar voice asked.

"Yes, it is," Saccone said.

"Listen, Frank, I got a deal here and I understand you're the accountant for this outfit I want to buy," the man said.

"Well, who is this?" Saccone demanded, suddenly annoyed that a stranger had the nerve to call him about business at ten o'clock on Christmas Eve.

"This is Rocky."

"Rocky who?"

"Rocky Marciano."

Saccone removed the receiver from his ear, covered the mouthpiece with his palm, and grinned sheepishly at his family.

"You won't believe this," Saccone said. "It's Rocky Marciano."

Frank Saccone was a struggling accountant who had just been certified to practice in Massachusetts. He had never met or spoken with Rocky Marciano.

"Look, Frank, I want to buy this restaurant in Taunton out on Route One thirty-eight," Rocky said. "I was wondering if you could get me a good deal . . . I'd appreciate it if you could give me some figures. You know. What's the place worth? What's it taking in?"

"Sure, Rocky," Saccone said. "I can put the whole package together for you. When do you need it?"

"How about tonight?" Marciano said. "I'm here at my mother's house on Dover Street. Can you make it over? That's only a couple of miles for you, isn't it?"

"But, Rocky," Saccone said. "It's Christmas Eve. I'm here with my family."

"Aw, so what, Frank," Rocky said. "This will only take a little while."

"All right," Saccone said. "Just give me time to get my papers together."

When Saccone arrived at the Marchegiano home, Rocky led him up the back staircase. They stood alone in the hallway outside Rocky's sister Alice's second-floor bedroom. There, beneath a dim, uncovered light bulb, Saccone described in detail the financial operation of his client's restaurant.

"Get me the best deal you can, Frank,"

Rocky said. "I'd like to buy that place, but I'm looking for a deal."

"Well, I think you can get the price down," Saccone said.

"You handle it for me, will you, Frank?"

"Sure, Rocky," Saccone said. "But you'll have to meet with the owner."

"All right, Frank," Rocky said. "You set it up."

FRANK SACCONE HAD NO IDEA how much that Christmas Eve meeting with Marciano would change his life.

"I figured I'd be with Rocky for this one deal and that would be it," Saccone recalled. "I had no way of knowing then that when Rocky liked you, you were with him for as long as you wanted to be, and it was almost as if you were a member of the family."

Saccone became Rocky's personal accountant and traveling companion, and was involved in all of Marciano's future business transactions.

"The deal on the restaurant fell through finally," Saccone said. "It wasn't because we didn't get a good price. The guy really wanted to do business with Rocky. He came way down from the original price. But Rocky kept missing meetings and putting it aside. Finally, the owner got disgusted and called the whole thing off. That didn't seem to bother Rocky a bit, even though we'd put all that effort into it and gotten a good thing set up. I didn't really know Rocky then, and it was hard as hell to figure out."

It was in 1961 that Rocky met George DiMatteo in the elevator of a New York City hotel. DiMatteo, a handsome, dapper, smooth talker was a partner in a Massachusetts firm. He talked Rocky's language—big deals, multi-million-dollar ventures. By the time the elevator reached the ground floor, Marciano was convinced he should meet with DiMatteo at his office in Natick.

"Frank, this guy DiMatteo has really got something going," Rocky told Saccone. "I like the way he moves. I think I'm going to buy in."

"But, Rock, you don't know a thing about him," Saccone said. "At least let me check the guy out before you do anything."

Saccone soon learned that that wasn't Marciano's way of doing business. It was a source of continued frustration to the meticulous accountant, who was trained to keep exhaustive records and move very cautiously.

"George is all right," Rocky said. "What the hell's there to know? I like the guy. He's got a few balls. Besides, I hate the telephone company. I gotta get back at those mothers."

DiMatteo had an invention that his company had sold to Bell Telephone. At the time he met Rocky, the company was collecting royalties on it.

"This is beautiful," Rocky said. "If I could only get in a position to demand things."

Rocky's relationship with George DiMatteo is a clear example of the great lengths he'd go to to help a friend.

"In 1966, George DiMatteo was in a bind again," Saccone said. "He had another big real estate deal going, and he needed some quick cash to swing it."

"Rock, I really need the dough," DiMatteo said. "This deal is gonna be worth a fortune."

"I'll see what I can do," Rocky said. "I can't spare the cash right now, but maybe we could hit someone for it."

"How about Jimmy Hoffa, Rock?" DiMatteo said. "He'll give it to you."

Hoffa often spent time with Rocky, and

enjoyed being seen in his company very much.

"Hoffa actually idolized Rocky," Saccone said. "We went to see Jimmy in Washington once and spent the entire day with him. Hoffa was a little guy, but tough and in beautiful physical condition."

By this time Rocky had lost so much in deals with DiMatteo that he refused to put up his own cash anymore. But he was still willing to go to great lengths to try to get the money for his friend.

"Yeah, that's a good idea," Rocky said. "We'll go see Jimmy."

Hoffa, the head of the powerful Teamsters Union, could loan millions from the union's pension fund.

"We arrived at the Teamsters Union building early in the morning," Saccone recalled. "Hoffa was sitting at a huge desk in a fantastically elaborate office. He was really happy to see Rocky, and as soon as we got there we went right out for breakfast. They had a beautiful restaurant right in the same building— French chefs, fancy gourmet dishes, the whole works. I think we had something like pheasant under glass for breakfast. Rocky didn't go for it. He'd rather have had some nice common food."

Hoffa was a fanatic on physical fitness and worked out every day in the gym. After breakfast, he took Rocky, Frank, and George to his gym, where there were saunas, weights, exercise machines, and everything a professional gym would provide.

"Hoffa insisted that all of the people in his organization keep in condition," Saccone said. "If anybody in his outfit ever got out of shape, he ordered them right into the gym for a three-day workout."

The union boss did about sixty push-ups, a routine of other exercises, and weight-lifting while Rocky watched.

"Rocky didn't work out, but he took a sauna, a rubdown, and a shower," Saccone said. "He loved rubdowns. He'd take two or three a day if he could get them."

After lunch, they went back to Hoffa's office and talked about the money. DiMatteo wanted about $300,000, but he had no collateral to put up.

"Rocky had been burned so many times in DiMatteo's big deals that he had had it with George as far as risking any of his own cash. He'd help the guy, just like he would any of his friends. If it meant taking a trip and spending some time, he'd go. He'd do anything but take a chance of losing money.

"Hoffa wanted to let George have the dough, but he couldn't loan out the teamsters' funds without collateral. Hoffa was shrewd, and probably sensed the risk involved.

" 'Can you put up something?' Hoffa asked.

" 'I haven't got it,' DiMatteo said.

"That was the end of the deal."

Sonny Marciano recalls Hoffa as "a cocky little guy" who had once told Rocky, "I've got a son who can handle himself pretty good, maybe he could fight you."

Rocky grinned. "No kidding, Jim," he said, "A real fighter, huh?"

"That's good, Jim," Sonny said. "But he'll have to get by me first. And he'll never do that."

Frankie Carbo came to Clivio once and said, "Jimmy Hoffa needs a favor. There's a big charity affair coming up in St. Louis and Jimmy wants Rocky to be there. I understand you've got a big milk business in Boston. You do Jimmy this favor and you'll never have to worry about any union problems. Just make sure Rocky's there."

"I didn't have anywhere near the huge business they thought I had, and there's never been a union in my place," Clivio recalled, "But Rocky always wanted to make his friends look good and important to everyone."

"Rock, I'm really proud of you," Clivio had said once after a championship fight. "You really made it the hard way."

"I'm proud of you too, Ernie," he said, "You're not so different than me. You had to fight your way up against the big milk companies just like I fought to get where I am."

ROCKY'S WAR WITH THE TELEPHONE COMPANY went back as far as most of his friends could recall, and placed him in many comical and sometimes embarrassing situations. It was almost as if he felt the phone company had a personal grudge against him and he had to show them he couldn't be pushed around. He was constantly thinking of ways to avoid paying for calls, and to beat the telephone company out of even a dime was a personal victory that gave him great satisfaction.

He went to great pains to use such devices as wires that would trip the change return lever inside the phone and small pieces of string, which he had telephone servicemen attach to pay phones. The strings would release all the money Rocky deposited the instant he pulled it.

Saccone and other friends recalled dozens of times where Rocky's obsession with beating the phone company caused him to do foolish things that could have put him in serious trouble.

"Rocky was always using somebody else's credit card or reversing the charges," Saccone said. "But the operators were always fouling him up."

Once Saccone and Marciano flew into La Guardia Airport before dawn. Rocky only had one dime; Saccone had none. Rocky had to make a few calls to get things going—transportation, hotel rooms, and so on. He dialed the first number, and the line was busy. The dime didn't come back.

"Operator! Operator!" Rocky yelled. "Give me back that fucking dime!"

"He was furious," Saccone said. "I thought he'd break the phone in half. He was squeezing it so hard he was shaking with rage. 'Mother,' he screamed. Then he went all the way down the line and ripped the phones off all the booths."

Another incident that Rocky's friends love to recall happened at the Waldorf-Astoria in New York.

Marciano had been at a meeting, and when it broke up he went to the lobby to make some calls. He had with him a piece of wire that was exactly the right size and shape so that when he pushed it down the change slot it would trip the mechanism and his money would be returned.

Saccone and DiMatteo waited while Rocky went into a booth and began dialing numbers. Rocky was struggling, trying to get the wire to work. The lobby was crowded, and people passing the booth recognized Marciano and waved to him. "Oh, hi. How' re ya doin'?" Rocky would say. Then he'd go back to wrestling with the wire, getting angrier all the time.

Finally he came out of the booth and handed the wire to DiMatteo. "Hold this for me, George," he said.

"Rocky had never explained to DiMatteo what the wire was for, because he figured George was such a classy mover he wouldn't appreciate it," Saccone said. "So George just kind of frowned and put the wire in his back pocket."

Rocky talked to some reporters and other people in the lobby for about an hour. Then he decided he had to make another phone call. "George, you got that wire?" he said.

"What wire?" DiMatteo said.

"The wire," Rocky said. "You know, the one I gave you to hold for me."

"Well, no. Rock," DiMatteo said. "It was cutting a hole in my pocket, so I threw it away."

"You threw that fucking wire away?" Rocky said. "You threw it away?"

"Well, I didn't think it was that important, Rock," DiMatteo said. "What the hell's a little piece of wire? I'll get you another one."

Rocky grabbed George by the shirt.

"You threw that wire away," Rocky shouted. "I don't believe it. How the hell could you do something like that, George?"

"Everyone in the lobby was staring at them," Saccone said. "Rocky kept shouting about the wire. The people seemed really concerned. They must have figured George had thrown away a valuable telegram or something."

All the while, Rocky was making large sums of money through personal appearances and deals that friends and admirers set up for him. He always insisted on being paid in cash, and if he got a check he was nervous until he got it to the bank. He didn't trust banks, lawyers, or consultants, and instead hid money like a squirrel. And to this day people are still searching for it.

Once Rocky showed up at the University of Miami and handed his brother Peter several paper bags full of money.

"Hold this for me, Pete," he said. "I'll be back to get it."

There were thousands of dollars in the bags and Peter was nervous about it. Rocky was gone for about three weeks, and one day Peter, finding himself short of cash, took fifty dollars from one of the bags.

Rocky returned and got the bags from Peter. That night he called his brother long distance. "Peter, what the hell's going on here?" Rocky said. "There's fifty dollars missing from those bags I gave you to hold for me."

"Well, Rock, I needed a few bucks one day, so I figured you wouldn't mind," Peter Marciano said.

"Don't ever do that again," Rocky said. "If you want money, ask me. But don't you ever take any again without asking."

Another time, Rocky handed Sonny an attaché case containing $25,000 and the key to a safety deposit box in Cuba.

"Take this over there and lock it up," Rocky said. "Then bring the key back to me."

"He had all kinds of keys like that," Sonny Marciano said. "Something happens to him, and who'd ever know where to look. He never put it on paper. It was just a bunch of keys."

"It used to amaze me the amount of cash Rocky carried around in his pocket," Lindy Ciardelli said. "Once we were at the Fairmont Hotel in San Francisco with George DiMatteo. Rocky had a zipper bag with $14,000 in hundred-dollar bills in it. He hid the bag under the mattress in our room. But we had a big, swinging party that night, and when it was over Rocky had forgotten where he put the cash. He looked under the mattress two or three times, but he didn't look far enough.

"Finally, Rocky found the money. He was grinning like a little kid. 'Christ sake, Lindy,' he said. 'Imagine that? It was right there all the time.'"

Ciardelli recalled the time he needed $45,000 in a hurry.

"I was running a big business, and I had to make a quick investment," he said. "Rocky went to New York and got the money. When he got back, we laid it out on twin beds and counted it: hundreds, fifties and twenties."

Ciardelli put the cash in an attaché case and slept with it in his lap as he flew west to take care of the business.

"The next morning I got a phone call from Rocky," Ciardelli said.

"Lindy, I had a bad dream," Rocky said. "I dreamed the plane crashed and the money was blowing in the wind."

"When I counted the dough that day in San Jose, I was three hundred dollars short," Ciardelli said. "Rocky had loaned me the cash for six months with no interest. He didn't care. 'Don't worry Lindy,' he told me. 'There's no interest on this. Just make sure I get it all back.'"

WHILE SOME OF MARCIANO'S FRIENDS and associates claim he was a very shrewd businessman, Frank Saccone, the dapper little accountant who was closer to Rocky's business dealings than any of them, didn't agree.

"Rocky was the world's worst businessman," Saccone said. "He never wanted to be bothered with small details. He never wanted contracts, never trusted lawyers, never consulted banks. If you stiffed him on a little two-dollar deal, he'd kill you for it. But a guy like DiMatteo could beat him out of thousands and he wouldn't get mad at all."

Saccone remembers DiMatteo as the first person who took Rocky for a lot of money.

At first they wanted $50,000 from Rocky for the telephone company deal, Saccone said. But then Rocky and George talked DiMatteo's partner into taking $25,000.

"DiMatteo said he was going to make Rocky a vice-president, but he had a way of avoiding all talk about stock," Saccone said. "I advised Rocky not to give him ten cents until the thing was worked out in black and white. There were no lawyers, no contract, nothing. But you just couldn't talk Rocky into doing the right thing."

"I trust this guy, Frank," Rocky said. "If I trust him, what do I need a lawyer for? Why do I need a piece of paper? What the hell, I'll kill the bastard if he ever goes in on me. You know that don't you, Frank?"

Rocky trusted and liked DiMatteo so much that he first brought him to his friend Ernie Clivio for a loan.

"Ernie, this is the most live-wire hustling guy I've ever met," Rocky said. "He's downstairs now. He wants me to lend him twenty thousand for two months and he'll pay me back twenty-two thousand and ten percent of his business."

"Rocky, please don't get involved with this guy," Ernie said. "Nobody in the world gives you something for nothing. If this guy was legit, he wouldn't come to you, he'd go to a bank. And he certainly isn't going to give you ten percent of his business."

"We've got to make the deal, Ernie," Rocky said. "This guy's the greatest. I'll tell you what I want you to do for me. I want you to make it look like you're giving him the twenty thousand, like it's your money. You draw up a note as though he owes it to you."

"Rocky," Ernie chuckled. "I'll only give him twenty thousand when I get your check to cover it."

"Don't worry, pal," Rocky said, and he made out a twenty-thousand-dollar check for Clivio.

"It's your money, Rock," Ernie said. "I can't fight with you. But I really think you're making a big mistake."

DiMatteo came upstairs to Ernie's office and immediately began giving him a sales pitch.

"I don't want to hear it," Clivio interrupted. "I'm only giving you this money because Rocky's asked me to. Quite frankly, between you and I, he's guaranteed it to me. But I don't want to see Rocky lose this dough. Sixty days is going to go by awfully fast. You make goddamn sure you've got the money in my office in sixty days."

"It was just before Christmas, and when I didn't get a card or even a phone call from a guy I'd just loaned twenty thousand to, I was convinced the deal was bad," Clivio recalled. "I telephoned him two weeks before the note was due and told him to make certain he showed up with the money."

"Don't worry," DiMatteo said. "I'll be there."

On February 15, DiMatteo showed up with Rocky but no money.

Rocky took Ernie into the office alone again. "Ernie, this is a good deal," he said. "But he needs another twenty thousand."

"No way," Clivio said. "This man's a phony. He hasn't even made an attempt to pay you back. If he did that'd be one thing. But this man's a con artist. I wouldn't give him a nickel."

"I argued with DiMatteo in my office, and then he finally left," Clivio recalled. "Allie Colombo had a fighter, Mike Pusiteri, that he wanted Rocky to see, so we went over to the Friend Street Gym. We were talking to Allie and Sam Silverman when I realized that DiMatteo had followed us."

After they watched Colombo's fighter, Rocky and Ernie went to the Lucerne Restaurant for dinner. DiMatteo followed and sat at another table.

"Give him a chance, he's really a good guy," Rocky said.

"Please, Rocky," Clivio said. "Please don't have anything more to do with him."

"DiMatteo was a smooth talker with a big Cadillac equipped with a bar and telephone in the back seat," Saccone said. "He moved fast, and he spent money like it was going out of style. He had the broads, the connections, everything, and he lived like a king. But if George made it big, he lived like two kings. If the guy made two hundred thousand dollars, he spent four hundred thousand dollars.

"I couldn't talk any sense to Rocky," Saccone went on. "He'd hand this guy thousands like it was nothing. But it was in the New York World's Fair deal where DiMatteo really got to him."

Marciano signed a note for DiMatteo that committed him to a speculative business involving hundreds of thousands of dollars.

DiMatteo and others had invested in a pavilion at the fair.

"Rocky lost about a hundred and twenty-five thousand dollars," Saccone said. "It was just like another of DiMatteo's businesses. But that was one that started off small. Rocky would give him five and ten thousand at a time. He never got a dime back."

Prior to the World's Fair, Marciano had lost large amounts of money cosigning notes for DiMatteo for an environmental testing company on Long Island.

"The company was going out of business, but DiMatteo convinced Rocky he could save it," Saccone said. "But after a couple of years the deal went sour. It was partly Rocky's own fault. Rock was supposed to go around and meet people and make the necessary connections to bring up sales. But Rocky was always moving, and even though he had that big dough invested, he never found time to work for the business."

The bank foreclosed and brought suit

against Rocky for about $75,000, Saccone said. The day Rocky was informed of the action, they were supposed to go to a party in New York.

"Jesus, Rock," Saccone said. "How can you think about a party at a time like this? You've got big trouble here."

"Christ sake, Frank. We did everything we could," Rocky said. "Whatever's going to happen will happen anyway. Forget it. We're out for a good time tonight. I don't want to hear about it anymore."

Rocky went out that night and acted as if he didn't have a care in the world. Nobody at the party could have ever known he was about to lose $75,000. The next morning, he and Saccone went to the bank.

Rocky took one of the Italian bank officers aside. "Look, I'm hooked," he said. "Don't embarrass me. I've got a reputation to protect."

"They had a long conversation, and the bank official became very compassionate," Saccone said. "Rocky kept telling him the bank had all his money, which was far from the truth."

"I had nothing to do with this deal," Rocky said. "I just signed a piece of paper. You're Italian. Haven't you embarrassed me enough?"

Largely due to the Italian bank official, the case was settled for about $35,000, less than half of what the bank had originally sought, Saccone said.

But no matter how much he lost through these investments. Rocky never got angry with DiMatteo. In fact, he kept trying to help him.

"Rocky took DiMatteo along for the ride on a lot of deals," Saccone said, "He set the guy up time and time again. He made a lot of money for DiMatteo, but George blew it. Because George was a compulsive spender."

Although Rocky never bothered DiMatteo about the money he was losing, he still expected complete loyalty from him, just as he did of everyone who was allowed to enter his entourage.

Rocky would call DiMatteo in the middle of the night and say, "George, I'm out at Logan Airport. Can you come and get me?"

"But Rock, it's two in the morning," DiMatteo would say.

"Well, you're a pal, aren't you?" Rocky would say.

Half an hour later, DiMatteo would be shivering behind the wheel as his Cadillac warmed up for the long drive to Logan Airport.

For several years Rocky kept handing cash to DiMatteo for deals that never seemed to materialize. Then DiMatteo disappeared. Saccone and others searched for him; Rocky thought he was dead.

"Some guys were saying George had gotten into trouble with the Mafia," Saccone said. "Six months before he went out of sight, he borrowed a lot of money from Rocky. But all Rocky seemed to worry about was that he was gone. DiMatteo beat Rocky out of a hundred and ten thousand in cash, easy."

"By the way, Rock, did you ever get your money back on that deal with DiMatteo?" Clivio asked years later.

"That son of a bitch," Rocky said. "He grabbed me for nincty thousand."

Clivio turned pale. "Jesus, Rocky," be said. "How could you let a guy like that do it to you?"

Rocky went home and told Barbara, "The next time you see Ernie, tell him not to bring this DiMatteo thing up. It really bothers me."

Barbara telephoned Ernie.

"I never mentioned it again," Clivio said. "I would never for the world have wanted to make Rocky feel uncomfortable."

But almost as soon as he had resolved some of the problems with DiMatteo's deals, Rocky was taken in by another high-flying Italian *spaccone.*

"He was a real con man, a majority stockholder in a big company, which he was bleeding dry," Saccone said. "This was in nineteen sixty-five, right after the World's Fair, and I kept advising Rocky to stay away from the guy. But Rocky didn't listen. This heavy roller was his type of guy. He'd make a ring out of fifty-dollar bills and put it on a girl's finger. He'd spend a thousand on four or five of us in a club in a night and think nothing of it. Sometimes there'd be twenty-five or thirty people in his party, and he'd take them to the finest shows, the best restaurants. The sky was the limit.

"But he used Rocky for personal gain," Saccone said. "I could always see it. I tried to talk Rocky out of it a hundred times. But he wouldn't listen. In the end, Rocky went for about fifty thousand with him."

There were many other deals where Marciano's unorthodox business practices resulted in his losing large sums of money or not making as much as he should have had there been negotiated contracts involved.

In 1957, Jimmy Serniglia, known by Rocky's group as the Tomato King, involved Rocky in a potato- and tomato-growing business in Florida that went bad only because a rare frost that year wiped out the crops.

"Rocky lost about ninety thousand on that deal," Saccone said. "I have records of at least that much."

Ernie Tomanio, one of Rocky's Italian paesanos, wanted to buy a restaurant near the Naval Academy in Annapolis, Maryland. Marciano put up the entire down payment of about $40,000 to get it for him, according to Saccone.

Tomanio was a nice guy; he always gave Rocky and his friends rooms, fed them the best meals, and treated them like kings. But he wasn't giving Rocky any money.

"Rock," Saccone said. "Ernie's not paying you anything. That's a thriving business. We should be keeping some books on it."

"Ernie doesn't say much," Rocky said. "But if he was doing that well, he'd give me something, I suppose."

"What do you mean, 'suppose'?" Saccone said. "Ask him who the auditors and accountants for that business are. He may be making plenty of money, and if he is it's yours. Or he may be mortgaging you to the hilt."

Tomanio was proceeding on the assumption that the restaurant was his and that Marciano was just loaning him the money.

"That wasn't the case," Saccone said. "Rocky owned the restaurant, and the money was his. I kept telling him to get an accounting. We talked about it for six months, but Rocky never did anything. He didn't want to hurt Ernie's feelings."

Peter Marciano recalled going to the restaurant with his brother. "Jesus, Ernie," Rocky said. "You never give me anything. Give me something at least, even fifty dollars."

"I've got a lot of bills, Rock," Tomanio said. But then he gave Marciano the fifty dollars.

"See, Frank," Rocky said when he saw Saccone. "He gives it to me once in a while. Cash."

"Are you kidding, Rocky?" Saccone said. "That restaurant is making a bundle, and you're paying for it. Let me go down there and inspect the books."

Finally, after months of stalling, Rocky said, "All right, Frank, go down and see what he's making."

When Saccone arrived, Tomanio called Rocky and told him it was impossible to pro-

212 EVERETT M. SKEHAN

vide records since he was just like Marciano and he never kept any.

"All right, Ernie," Marciano said. "Forget the past records. We'll start now."

"For Christ sake," Saccone said. "After four or five years of running the place, the guy doesn't want to come up with anything?"

Then, according to Saccone, Tomanio called Rocky again and said, "Rock, if you don't trust me and I have to start keeping books, I don't want it. You come and take over the restaurant."

"Of course I trust you, Ernie," Rocky said. "But Frank says we need books. That's the way it's done."

"That's it, then," Tomanio said. "I'm leaving."

"Jesus, Frank," Rocky told Saccone. "See what you did. You've got him all nerved up. He's leaving. I don't want this to happen."

"Listen, Rock. I told him if he wants to quit because you want records, then to go ahead and leave," Saccone said. "You're responsible to the government for taxes down there, Rocky, and you don't even know what the hell is going on. This could be very serious."

"Talk to him," Rocky said. "Try to explain it."

Saccone claims he spent a long time explaining, but Tomanio refused to listen, said he didn't want any books, and quit.

Saccone finally helped Rocky hire another manager, then he took time off from his practice in Brockton and spent every weekend for three months trying to resolve the situation at the restaurant.

"Finally the place was showing a nice profit," Saccone said. "Then Tomanio called Rocky and said, 'I put five years into that restaurant and you kicked me out.' Rocky put Ernie right back in charge. And in no time things were right back to where we started."

"Don't ever ask me to go there again, Rock," Saccone said. "Everything we put into that place is going right down the drain."

"Ernie's my friend," Rocky said. "I've got to help him, don't I?"

"Tomanio stayed there until the day he died," Saccone said. "Ernie died the night of the first Clay-Frazier championship fight."

Saccone had called in Lee Lovitt, a Washington lawyer, to handle legal matters concerning the restaurant

"When it was done, Lovitt wanted to he paid immediately," Saccone said. "Rocky was out of town, so I paid him. Then Lee asked me if I was getting paid, and I told him I never took any money from Rocky. Lee got very angry, and insisted I couldn't work for nothing, that I should put in a bill. Against my better judgment, I gave Rocky a bill for five hundred dollars and told him Lovitt had insisted on getting his money so I had given it to him."

"Rocky was furious," Saccone said. "He wanted to kill both me and Lovitt."

"Are you crazy?" Rocky said. "Never do that again. I don't care what it is, don't ever pay anybody or turn in a bill to me."

"I thought about it a lot," Saccone said. "I'd never taken a penny from Rocky, but he always did all right by me. He always introduced me to people, and set me up with the right connections for big accounts. Wherever we went, he made certain I was really taken care of, wined and dined, the whole bit. Rocky never let me pick up a check or spend a dime, and he told me I was never to do so as long as I was with him. I figured the money thing was Rocky's way of testing your loyalty. If somebody wanted to get paid, he wasn't a true friend. Rocky expected to take care of people in his own fashion. If I wanted to get paid, then I wasn't a friend, I was just another accountant, and I should leave him alone, because he didn't want people like that around him. That was the only time I ever did it. I've gone all around the world with Rocky, been in on every deal, but I've never charged him a cent."

If Rocky was overtolerant to a flaw with the people he admired, he was just the opposite with people he had no respect or warm feelings for. And his business practices with them bore no resemblance to the carefree manner in which he dealt with a hustler like DiMatteo.

Rocky was taking care of the Marchegiano family in his own fashion. As patriarch, he paid the bills, but usually he didn't use his own money. He schemed for ways to get them paid by others who owed him either favors or cash.

Once, while Rocky was out of town, his mother broke her leg. She went to the Brockton Hospital, where she was admitted and treated. Months later the hospital pressed for payment of the bill, which came to a little more than $1,000. Rocky was still out of town, and Pasqualena, being thrifty and afraid of being in debt, was very nervous. Saccone, who technically was authorized to take care of Marciano's finances, decided to pay the bill.

"When Rocky found out, he was enraged again," Saccone said. "He almost tore my office apart."

"What the hell is this?" Rocky said. "You paid the whole goddamn bill?"

"Well, yes, Rock," Saccone said. "It was overdue."

"Christ sake," Rocky said. "Couldn't you have made a deal? This is ridiculous. Did you have to pay the whole thing?"

"He was so pissed off, I just couldn't talk to him," Saccone said. "What kind of a deal could you make with the Brockton Hospital?"

But to Rocky Marciano deals were the name of the game. He had deals going with the oil man, the grocery clerk, the man who ran the clothing store.

He was the patriarch, and nobody questioned his methods when it came to the family's financial matters, even though he had made no will and there was nothing on paper to give the slightest hint to where much of his cash could be found in the event that anything ever happened to him.

When Peter Marciano got $4,000 as a bonus for signing with the Milwaukee Braves, Rocky took it away from him. For months, Rocky doled the money out to Peter, $50 and $100 at a time.

Rocky's insecurity and anxiety about money were largely responsible for some embarrassing and tense situations that concerned people he had been friendly with since his boyhood.

Nicky Sylvester, who was with Rocky from their sandlot days at James Edgar Playground through his rise to the heavyweight championship, has never fully understood the emotional turmoil that placed Rocky in conflict with him.

In 1960, Sylvester went to the Commodore Hotel in New York to see Rocky and to get some tickets for the return match between Floyd Patterson and Ingemar Johansson.

"How many tickets do you want?" Rocky asked.

"Two," Sylvester said.

"Who's the other one for?" Rocky said.

"It's for Joe [Barbara Marciano's cousin]," Sylvester said.

"Oh, that asshole," Rocky said.

Rocky had been told that Barbara's cousin

had bet against him on a fight, and he had never forgiven him.

"Oh, shut up and give me the tickets," Sylvester said.

Rocky gave him two hundred-dollar tickets, which he had received as part of a complimentary block, and mentioned that there was a twenty-dollar tax on each of them.

Sylvester thought nothing more of it until the night he and Rocky were sitting together ringside for a fight between Carmen Basilio and Paul Pender at Boston Garden.

"Nitch, do you owe me some money?" Rocky said.

"What money?" Sylvester said.

"You know. For the Johansson-Patterson tickets," Rocky said.

"Stop it," Sylvester said. "You got those tickets for nothing."

"No," Rocky said. "I had to pay the tax. You owe me forty bucks."

"Please," Sylvester said. "Don't be ridiculous."

"All right," Rocky said. "If that's the way you want to be."

Months later Sylvester, who was out of work with a broken arm, was driving along Ames Street in Brockton and saw Rocky in a Cadillac headed up Montello Street toward Boston.

"I flagged him down and Rocky got out of the car," Sylvester said. "I had a roll of bills in my pocket, and I flashed them at him. I always flashed my money at Rocky, just to bug him."

"Give me the forty dollars," Rocky said.

"What forty?" Sylvester said.

"For the Johansson-Patterson tickets," Rocky said.

"Oh, why don't you stop it," Sylvester said. "You know you got them for nothing."

"I'll get you," Rocky said. "You've been liv-

ing the life of comedy with me for thirty years, and it's all over."

Sylvester floored the accelerator and sped off down the street. How could he say that when he was the champ? he kept thinking. How could he say it?

"I kept agonizing over it," Sylvester said. "How could Rocky say something like that to me, his best buddy, when he knew I was drinking the hootch like crazy? How could he, when he was the champ?" Sylvester wondered if it were possible that their friendship could end over a forty-dollar misunderstanding.

For months after the incident there was no communication between the two men. It was as if Rocky had disappeared and Sylvester had fallen completely out of the inner circle of his friends.

Sylvester recalls that he saw Peter Marciano once in Brockton and said, "Hi, Peter, buddy."

"Fuck you," Peter said.

It was not that Peter Marciano ever really disliked Nicky Sylvester, but he was and always did remain completely loyal to his brother. If Rocky felt Nicky had cheated him, then Peter would have nothing further to do with him.

The dispute lasted for months, and Sylvester and Rocky never saw each other. Then, one time while Rocky was visiting his parents, he asked Peter, "How's Nicky Sylvester? What's he doing now?"

"What're you asking me that for?" Peter said. "I thought you were mad at him."

"No, Pete," Rocky said. "That's ridiculous. Nicky was my real pal."

"Then why don't you tell him that?" Peter Marciano said.

Rocky seemed embarrassed. "No, Peter," he said. "You tell him. All right? Will you do that for me?"

A few days later, when Peter saw Sylvester

coming out of a package store near the Brockton Fairgrounds, he went over to him.

"Nicky, Rocky thinks you're the greatest," Peter said.

"Oh, come on, come on," Sylvester said.

"No, Nicky. Really. He thinks you're the greatest," Peter said.

Sylvester thought about it many times. He never did get together with Rocky again.

"I really wanted to believe it, but I still think Rocky went to his grave figuring I owed him forty dollars," Sylvester said. "Sometimes I wonder if he's looking down at me saying, 'Come on, Nitch. Where's my forty dollars?'"

MOST OF THE TIME ROCKY had dozens of loans out all over the country. They always involved cash of varying amounts, from a few hundred dollars to many thousands. Rocky handled these deals personally, without contracts, and charged a small interest. These were the kind of deals he liked to make—with no taxes or legal fees involved. But occasionally Rocky had difficulty collecting, for some of the people he did business with were often unreliable and had proven many times to be poor risks.

The case of Brockton Eddie exemplifies the way Rocky handled people who were reluctant to pay back loans.

There was a club on Center Street in Brockton called the Liberty Club, where the local gamblers went to play cards.

"We used to call it steam, clean, and press," Izzy Gold said. "Because the minute you walked through the door they cleaned you out."

Eddie "Brockton Eddie" Massod ran the games at the Liberty Club and handled part of a thriving bookie business in the city. He was a slender man about five-eight, in his mid-forties; he always needed a shave and walked hunched over as if he had a permanently injured back. Eddie had a reputation as a sharp card player and a hustler interested in anything that would turn a buck.

A couple of years after Marciano retired, Brockton Eddie contacted Izzy Gold about the possibility of getting a loan.

"Izzy, we need some money," Brockton Eddie said. "Can you get Rocky to lend it to me?"

"How much?" Gold asked.

"We need five thousand," Eddie said.

"If I tell Rocky you're okay, he'll lend you the dough," Gold said.

When Marciano came to visit his parents, Gold approached him about Brockton Eddie's proposition.

"Sure, I'll let Eddie have the dough," Rocky said. "And for only a small percentage."

"But what if this guy doesn't pay it back?" Sonny Marciano said when he heard about the deal. "You've got nothing to prove you gave him the cash."

"What do you mean?" Rocky said. "If he doesn't pay it back, I'll ruin him. He wouldn't dare not give me back that dough."

But when the time came for Brockton Eddie to return Marciano's money, he was nowhere to be found.

"Where is this fucking guy with my dough, Izzy," Rocky said, whenever he came to Brockton.

"I don't know, Rock," Gold said. "I can't pin him down. But don't worry, we'll get it."

When several months had passed, Marciano went to see Willie Pep at his home near Hartford, Connecticut. He had done many favors for Willie, and now he was calling upon him for a service.

"This guy in Brockton owes me five thousand dollars," Rocky said. "How can I get it, Willie? Is John still in Providence?"

"Yeah," Pep said. "He's around."

"Good," Rocky said. "This guy can get my money."

"Okay," Pep said. "We'll go see him."

Rocky and Willie drove to Providence and found the man.

"Rocky and I knew this guy John had ways of doing things," Pep said. "We didn't know too much about him, but he was an ex-boxer, and he had some very good connections."

"This Brockton Eddie owes me five grand," Rocky told the man.

"We'll pay him a visit," John said. "Don't worry, we'll get your money."

While they were driving home, Rocky said to Pep, "Willie, if these guys get my money, it'd really be nice. I'd give them a hundred bucks apiece."

"Rocky if they get five grand for you, you've got to give them five hundred apiece," Pep said.

"What?" Rocky said. "But it's my money."

A short while later, Pep and Marciano drove to Brockton with John and "some other guy he'd brought along."

Rocky and Willie went into a restaurant and ordered coffee while John and his friend went after Brockton Eddie at the Liberty Club.

John was grinning when he returned to the restaurant less than an hour later.

"Rocky," he said. "This guy hasn't got the money now, but he wants to pay. He'll give you so much a week."

"Beautiful, John," Rocky said. "I knew you could do it for me."

Later John told Pep that they had taken Brockton Eddie into the men's room and kicked him in the legs and roughed him up.

"I didn't know Brockton Eddie," Pep said.

"But he must've been a helluva guy, because Rocky didn't go for no stories. If Rocky loaned the guy money, there must have been a deal."

John was eventually found murdered in a car in Boston, Pep said. "He'd been shot. He was a former fighter, and that's how Rocky and I met him. Beyond that, we knew nothing."

Even after the visit from John, months went by and Brockton Eddie never paid up.

"I'm going after this guy," Rocky said. "Where can I find him?"

"He's always at the Liberty Club," Izzy Gold said.

The way Gold recalls the story, just as he and Rocky were arriving at the Liberty Club they saw Brockton Eddie going out the back entrance.

Rocky grabbed Eddie by the shirt, spun him around, and said, "This is it, Eddie. Where's my money?"

"I haven't got it right now," Brockton Eddie said.

"Rocky whacked the guy with a left, and Eddie went down like a dead mackerel," Gold said. "Then Rocky went through his pockets and took every cent he had."

"When I tell you you've gotta pay, Eddie, that means you'd better pay," Rocky said.

"I don't think Rocky ever had any trouble with Eddie after that," Gold said. "He got his money, and everything turned out all right."

Eddie was the type of hustler who knew the risks and held no grudges against the kind of tactics Marciano had used to collect. When he saw Peter Marciano on Main Street in Brockton, he smiled and shook his hand.

"Gee, I'm awful sorry about that, Eddie," Peter said.

Eddie's jaw had been cracked and he could barely speak, but he was still grinning. "That's all right. Peter," he said. "I'm lucky he used the left. With the right he might have killed me."

"**T**HAT'S THE WAY IT WAS," Frank Saccone recalled. "It wasn't unusual for Rocky to get into these situations. We just kept traveling and traveling, making deals wherever we went. There were usually no contracts involved, and when Rocky got a check, he'd be nervous until he got it cashed."

"Despite those guys who took him for a lot of dough, Rocky was making plenty," Saccone said. "Bernie Castro really liked to be with Rocky. He showed Rocky a lot of business tricks and how to spread his money around, and he made a bundle for Rocky on land deals around Ocala, Florida. Castro made big money for Rocky on investments. Others like Pete DiGravio in Cleveland, who idolized Rocky, got him into deals that made plenty of money. There were more guys helping Rocky than there were guys who were trying to take the money away from him.

"Toward the end of his life, I know Rocky was hiding money," Saccone said. "He was burying a lot of it somewhere. I kept all of his books, and they just didn't jive with what he was taking in. Rocky wasn't accounting for a lot of the cash, most of which has never been found."

Marciano's family and friends have spent years searching and speculating as to where Rocky might have hidden his money. Some of his friends said he kept making secretive trips to a small town in Pennsylvania. Others, including Saccone and Mike Piccento, feel Marciano may have hid a lot of his cash in a bomb shelter that a wealthy friend had built on his estate. But nobody knows for certain what Rocky did with it, or how much he actually had.

"They haven't found much," Saccone said.

"Not anywhere near the amount I'm sure Rocky had. I believe the biggest chunk of Rocky's money is still out there someplace. Maybe we'll never find it."

4.

A Favorite Son

ON THE EVENING OF JUNE 21, 1968, Rocky Marciano hastily left Cleveland, where he had just gone to settle some business with local racketeer Pierino "Pete" DiGravio. Before they could get together, DiGravio was a dead man—a 30-caliber rifle slug ripped through his back as he prepared to tee off on the sixteenth hole of the Orchard Hills Golf and Country Club in Chesterland, Ohio. Had the murder occurred a day later, Marciano quite possibly could have been on the golf course with DiGravio.

In any case, while the unknown gunman was making his escape from a makeshift blind he had built in order to ambush DiGravio, Rocky and Frank Saccone were on their way to Cleveland to resolve an Internal Revenue case that involved some investments Marciano had made with DiGravio.

"We had left New York with Ben Danzi and Frank DaLucca to go to Cleveland and straighten things out," Saccone recalled. "But then Danzi and DaLucca had an argument over something, and Ben got off. So we drove to Cleveland without him."

DiGravio's assassin had to be an expert marksman, sending three rapid shots from long range that struck the victim in the back, at the base of the skull, and in the back of the head. DiGravio was killed instantly, as his three golfing companions ran from the scene, screaming. They had nothing to fear, since the professional hit man was interested only in DiGravio.

"We finished up the business quickly, and then got right out of Cleveland," Saccone said. "Pete had been a good friend, but there was nothing Rocky could do for him then, since he was already dead, and it was senseless to hang around. Rocky had nothing to hide. All of his dealings with DiGravio had been legitimate. But people were sure to ask questions, and there was Rocky's reputation to think about."

Stories about the still-unsolved murder in the *Cleveland Plain Dealer* told of speculation at the time of DiGravio's death that he was the number three man, or *consigliere*, of the Cleveland Mafia. There had been a rumor that DiGravio had been offered the Mafia leadership in that city and had refused. But nothing could be substantiated, and DiGravio was never officially linked to the fraternal Italian crime organization.

"We're dealing with a cold-blooded professional, who cased his contract to kill for at least a week before shooting DiGravio in the back," said County Sheriff Louis A. Robusky.

DiGravio was one of many Mafia- and rackets-connected persons who sought the friendship of Rocky Marciano after the fighter had become the heavyweight champion. Although he was never involved in any of their illegal dealings, Rocky knew and was friendly with underworld figures throughout the country.

ROCKY HAD ALWAYS BEEN FASCINATED by the elements of suspense and danger that engulfed the Mafia style of life. In some respects, he was still the child who had always listened faithfully to his favorite radio program, "Gangbusters." He viewed these shady characters through rose-colored glasses, thinking of them mostly in terms of adventure without considering the misery and hardship their activities often caused innocent people.

Almost every heavyweight champion has been entertained by some segment of the underworld. For hoods gravitate to champions in much the same way that they go for flashy clothes and big black Cadillacs and bleached blondes in tight dresses. And when the champion happens to be Italian, he has particular appeal to members of the Mafia, who take great pride in Italian paesanos who rise to glory through their own hard work and legitimate achievements. To such people, the heavyweight champion stands on top of Mount Everest.

DiGravio and Marciano had enjoyed a long friendship. They had once shared an apartment; Rocky had invested in a machinery business that DiGravio owned; and he had also helped Rocky in other legitimate and profitable ventures.

"Pete DiGravio idolized Rocky," said Lindy Ciardelli. "I think Rocky used Pete like he used a lot of people. Even though Rocky liked the Mafia style, that element was secondary as far as DiGravio was concerned. Pete used to put Rocky into a lot of good deals. Rocky spent time with Pete only for his own purposes and at his own convenience."

As he rode out of Cleveland on the night of DiGravio's murder, Rocky wrote in a manila note pad: "Italian good killed by lightning." Below that Rocky had printed in traced-over capital letters the single word "insecure."

DiGravio and other underworld figures shared something that drew Marciano's respect. For DiGravio could be brash, arrogant, completely unafraid, and impossible to intimidate. And yet he could also be compassionate, even protective, toward less fortunate paesanos who posed no threat to him.

"Slain loan shark Pierino 'Pete' DiGravio may have been a rackets figure to area police departments," a *Plain Dealer* story said. "But to residents of Little Italy, DiGravio was a man who cared for other people."

The story went on to explain how DiGravio "aided the helpless in Little Italy" and made sizable contributions to churches and charities.

"The government and police may think Pete DiGravio was a loan shark, but that's not what people around here think," the newspaper quoted Mrs. Patricia LeForce as saying. "He was the kind of man who helped poor people without question. I borrowed three hundred dollars from him in May 1967 and took eight months to repay it. He charged me no interest at all. I told him I had heard he charged interest, and it was only fair that I pay the usual rate."

"Lady," DiGravio said, "you heard wrong."

"When we got out of Cleveland that night, Rocky made us drive way out of our way to an Italian restaurant owned by one of his friends," Saccone said. "The guy put out a fantastic spread. We sat there all night, and Rocky just ate and ate for hours. It reminded me of a Roman orgy. It was like he was obsessed. I never saw a guy eat so much."

WHEN FORMER MAFIA DON VITO GENOVESE was dying in a federal prison hospital early in 1969, Marciano visited him.

"Do you think it's wise?" Rocky's friend Ben Danzi asked. "Everybody'll know. Think of what it'll do to your reputation."

"It'll be all right, Ben," Marciano reportedly said. "The guy's really sick. Besides, Benny Trotta wants me to go with him."

The key was Trotta. Rocky could not refuse a friend. Trotta, a fight promoter around Baltimore, had been a close friend of Marciano's and always took good care of him.

"A lot of us have done some bad things in our lives," seventy-year-old Genovese, once head of New York's most powerful Mafia family, told Marciano. "But you've made us proud."

A short time after the visit, in February 1969, Genovese died of a heart condition in a prison hospital in Springfield, Missouri.

There is little doubt among those who knew him that Marciano was looking for something to replace the danger and excitement he had known in the ring. Rocky could never adjust to a routine nine-to-five type of life, nor would he ever be content with a life devoid of risk.

Perhaps Rocky's own writings in a small black address book inscribed HOTEL AMERICANA DI ROMA—ROCKY MARCIANO best describe the way he was: "If you want to live a full life then live dangerously." Opposite that was printed in capital letters and underlined the single word "insecure."

Lindy Ciardelli recalled a night in Chicago when "Rocky took me into a big room where the Mafia held meetings. There was a long table surrounded by chairs, and on the wall there was an American flag and an Italian flag. Rocky was fascinated by that room."

"This is where they make the contracts, Lindy," Rocky said. "This is where it's all decided. Right here in this room."

Another time Rocky pointed out a Mafiosa acquaintance and told his friend, "The guy's got seventeen credits [alleged murders]. Imagine that."

ONE EVENING ROCKY AND FRANKIE "ONE-EAR" FRATTO stood outside of P. J. Clarke's in New York. A long line of people waited to get in. As they walked along the side of the line, the manager of the club spotted Rocky and beckoned to him. "C'mon in, Rock," he said. "Follow me."

Frankie Fratto grinned and began to stride past the line of waiting customers. "C'mon, Rock. Let's go," he said. "This guy's gonna get us in."

Then a tall, bald man in the line glared at them and said, "I guess you have to be a fuckin' dago to get in here."

Inside the nightclub, Fratto fumed over the comment. He knew that Rocky had not heard it.

Frankie Fratto was a Mafiosa who is described in *Captive City*, a book about the Chicago underworld, as a syndicate henchman on the North Side who "muscled his way into the aluminum siding and storm window business. His brother Rudolph is known as the 'garbage king' of the Rush Street saloon strip." His criminal record dated back to 1941, with more than ten arrests for theft, and assault with intent to murder. He was a suspect in the 1957 murder of Willard Bates and the 1963 murder of Alderman Benjamin Lewis. Frank Fratto, also known as Frank Frappo, One-Ear Frankie, and Half-Ear, did not enjoy being called a "fucking dago," nor would he tolerate anybody who called Rocky Marciano a "fucking dago."

Frankie saw the big, bald guy and four others take seats at a table directly opposite him and Rocky.

"Hey, Rocky," he said, "You see those five guys at that table. Well, when we were walkin' in I heard that guy call us 'fuckin' dagos!'"

"Aw, Frankie," Rocky said. "Don't pay any attention to those guys. They're probably a bunch of drunks."

"I'd like to punch that bald guy right in the ear," Frankie said.

"Naw, Frank," Rocky said. "Forget it. Enjoy the show."

Then, Fratto recalled, the big guy came over to the table and said, "Hey, Rocky, you see those four guys I'm with. Well, they said I should come over here and give you a fat lip."

When he said that, Rocky bolted upright and grabbed him by the suit coat and pulled him down over the table. "Listen, you jerk," Rocky said. "If you don't get out of here, I'll take you and those four other guys and put you right through that wall."

"Oh no you won't," the bald guy said.

Fratto jumped out of his seat and grabbed the big guy by the neck and slammed him up against the wall.

"I was just about to punch the guy," Frankie said, "when Rocky jumped up and grabbed me. Then the manager and some other guys joined in and they pulled me off him. In the meantime, my cousin Louie, who can handle himself very well, walked in and helped the people get the five guys out of the place."

"Do you know who that was?" one of the men asked.

"No," Frankie said. "Who was it?"

The man explained.

"Hey, Rock," Frankie said. "Good thing you didn't hit that guy. He was a Yankee pitcher. He would have liked the publicity of saying he fought the Rock."

When Rocky Marciano came into Des Moines, Frankie Fratto and his brother Lou would be waiting at the airport "to give him the town." The same thing would be repeated in Omaha and even more so in Chicago.

Rocky could pick up the phone from anywhere in the country and say, "Frankie, I'll be coming in Monday, could you meet me at the airport?"

Frankie would not only be at the airport, but he would have made all the arrangements for whatever Rocky wanted to do.

Among the syndicate people that Rocky knew, Frankie Fratto was one of his best pals. He always made it a point to see Frankie whenever he was in Chicago. They traveled, partied, and spent time with each other's families.

When Peter and Linda Marciano got married in Brockton, on September 4, 1965, Fratto flew out from Chicago to attend the wedding.

When Rocky had an appointment to meet with President John F. Kennedy in Washington, he stayed overnight at Frankie's house in Chicago. "Why don't you come with me to meet the President, Frank," he said the next morning.

"No, Rocky," Frankie said. "I think it would be best if you went down alone. The President didn't invite anyone else."

When Rocky returned from Washington, the first thing he did was give Frankie a framed picture of himself with President Kennedy.

Frankie arranged for Rocky and Jimmy Durante to appear at the grand opening of the Tiara, a high-rise apartment building on Sheridan Road in Chicago.

"Jimmy Durante loved The Rock very much," Frankie said. "He would kiss his hands when he saw him."

Fratto said he sometimes had Vic Damone and Rocky to his home for Sunday dinner. "Vic loved The Rock too," Frankie said. "They were the best of pals."

Frankie often traveled to Florida to visit with Rocky. Once he spent three weeks there with Rocky's mother and father.

"Rocky told me to take care of Ma and Pa while he was busy," Frankie said. "I took them all over town, and they had a wonderful time. One night they had a big dinner at the Doral and Rocky was the honored guest. He told me to take Ma and Pa there and I did. They treated Ma and Pa with the greatest respect."

"Once we went to the Diplomat Hotel in Hollywood," Pasqualena said. "Alla the biga stars were there—Buddy Hackett, Frank Sinatra, Eddie Fisher, Sammy Davis, Jerry Vale . . . 'Everybody get up,' Frankie Fratto said. 'I want the best seat for Pop and Mom Marchegiano.'"

Ernie Clivio was also fascinated by the lifestyle of the Mafia. He enjoyed their company as much as Rocky did.

"Whenever we met these people, they always greeted us warmly and gave Rocky the greatest respect," he said. "From our vantage point, they were sincere and friendly and exciting to be with. They would do everything they could to make us comfortable and show us a good time. Anything else that went on was not our business. Rocky would no more be involved with the shady stuff than I would. But it was an adventure just being around those guys."

Once he and Rocky had gone to a suite in the Hampshire House in New York where some of the biggest syndicate bookmakers in the country were having one of their periodic meetings. After the business was finished, they began to leave the hotel to visit the kingpin in the Bronx.

"As we were going down the elevator, the guy who was the oddsmaker for the entire country handed me a wad of hundred-dollar bills," Clivio said. "I figured it had to be about a hundred thousand dollars."

"Ernie, here, you carry this, because if they pick me up they'll keep it, but they won't bother you," the syndicate man said.

Clivio was shaken, but didn't know what to say. It wouldn't be good to refuse. He put the clump of hundreds in his coat pocket. The syndicate man grinned and handed him three more wads of hundred-dollar bills.

"By the time we got to the bottom of the elevator, I must have had about four hundred thousand dollars in my pockets," Clivio said.

When they entered the Bronx gangster's house, Clivio was stopped by two men.

"Can we have your coat?" one of them said.

"No, thanks," Clivio said. "I'm fine."

The men followed Ernie into a large room where everyone was seated at a long table. They stood directly behind him. It didn't occur to Clivio why they were there until two Italian women came into the room and began chatting about a recent trip they had made to Italy.

"You know, I was in Italy just a few weeks ago," Clivio said.

"Are you Italian?" one of the Mafia men standing behind him asked.

"Of course I'm Italian," Clivio said.

The man laughed, and soon the two standing behind Ernie moved away from the table.

"With my glasses on I looked like a Jew," Clivio said. "They must have figured the bulges in my pockets were guns."

Mary Anne and Ernie recalled the time when a low-ranking Mafia soldier had insulted Rocky.

Barbara and a girlfriend had gone to the Poodle Lounge in the Fontainebleau Hotel in Miami.

There was a man at the bar who was cocky and swaggering, trying to impress Barbara with his importance.

"Rocky's no goddamn good," the Mafiosa said. "He's a cheap son of a bitch. You just take care of yourself, and get all the money you can out of him."

Barbara was becoming very upset when the man took a business card out of his wallet and pushed it down her dress into her breasts.

As soon as she saw Rocky, Barbara told him of the incident. He was furious and immediately made some phone calls.

Mary Anne recalled that her mother and father were picked up at their home in Fort Lauderdale "by some men in a bulletproof limousine, who drove them to a small hotel."

The man who had made the insults was sitting by the pool. Barbara was asked to identify him. When she did, they took the man into a private room in the hotel and sat around a long table with Rocky and Barbara at opposite ends. There they had a lengthy session, eating dinner and drinking wine, while the entire story was reviewed.

"Apologize to Rocky and Barbara," the Mafia leader said. "Then I want you to leave Miami. Get out in twenty-four hours, and don't come back."

When the bill came, the Mafia soldier paid it. Then he got up from the table and very respectfully excused himself. It was the last the Marcianos ever saw of him.

5.

A Farewell to Allie

THAT SPRING OF 1956, when Marciano retired from boxing, there was a huge celebration in Brockton in his honor.

Allie Colombo stood on the open-air stage and faced the crowded bleachers with tears glistening in his eyes. "It was never easy," Colombo said. "But in the end, it was all well worth it. All I can say now is I'm grateful and happy to have been a part of the Golden Years . . ."

THE THUNDEROUS APPLAUSE for the sons of two immigrant Italians that echoed from the stands that cool evening was Colombo's final, dying glimpse of fame. From then on Allie's fortunes declined. There were no more Golden Years, although he would forever dream of them. Instead, Colombo labored at an obscure job as a fork lift operator in a supermarket warehouse.

Rocky and Allie had drifted apart. They seldom saw each other anymore, and then only briefly, when Marciano, the wanderer, made an occasional visit to Brockton.

Colombo had spent whatever money he had managed to save from the Golden Years. He had a family to support and could not afford to be out of work. But he never gave up his private fantasies.

On Saturday mornings Colombo would meet Art Thayer, the former middleweight, at Sullivan's Donut Shop. He was still dreaming. Still figuring that he, Allie Colombo, would discover another heavyweight champion of the world.

"I don't know, Art," Colombo would say. "This guy's got bad knees. Kids from Boston don't want to train. What can you do? Half of them haven't got any guts. They don't want to be fighters. Nobody's hungry anymore."

Sam Silverman chuckles when he talks of the fantasies that Weill and Colombo had after Marciano retired.

"You can't replace a Rocky Marciano," Silverman said. "Marcianos come along once in a lifetime, if you're lucky. Weill had nothing but bums after Rocky. Colombo had a couple of fair kids. What the hell, they weren't even in the same ball park with Rocky Marciano."

Whenever Rocky came to Brockton, he

would express concern about Colombo's situation to his friends.

"What can I do for him?" he asked Izzy Gold. "I put him with people. I give him all the right connections. But Allie doesn't know how to move. He's not like you, Izzy. If I set something up for you, then you're going to take advantage of it."

Rocky always told his brothers that Colombo could have been with him as long as he wanted to. But Allie had a wife and two young daughters. He was settled. He could not afford to be a compulsive runner like Rocky.

AND SO THAT COLD, RAW WINTER NIGHT of January 6, 1969, there was some disappointment, perhaps even sadness, and certainly longing in the life of Allie Colombo as he made the trip from Brockton to the warehouse in Readville. He was forty-nine years old, and there were no more Golden Years on the horizon.

Colombo was reading the sports section of a Boston newspaper as he and a friend walked along the row of trucks that were backed up to the loading platform.

"They never saw the truck backing in until it was too late," Colombo's brother Eddie said. "They were walking along the platform. The other guy bounced off, but Allie got caught between the truck and the platform. He was shouting, but the driver couldn't hear him over the roar of the engine. The truck backed up and crushed his chest. You know, the guy that was driving the truck was one of Allie's best buddies."

The accident happened about 11:20 P.M.

Colombo was rushed to Boston City Hospital, where he died in surgery at 2:05 A.M.

"ROCK, I'VE GOT SOME BAD NEWS," Peter Marciano said when he telephoned his brother in Las Vegas. "Allie's dead. He got crushed by a truck."

There was a long silence. Then Rocky's voice came over the line very softly: "Wow. Wow."

It was the word that Marciano always used to express great shock or disbelief. And now it was all that he could say.

"When are you coming out, Rock?" Peter said finally. "Do you want me to pick you up at the airport?"

Another long silence.

"Gee, Pete, I don't think I can make it," Rocky said.

Peter Marciano was stunned.

"What do you mean, you can't make it?" Peter said. "You've got to make it, Rock. He was your best friend."

Rocky got angry.

"I can't make it, Pete," he said. "That's all. I'm tied up. I just can't make it."

"Why, Rock?" Peter said. "What in hell could tie you up so you'd miss Allie's funeral?"

"You wouldn't understand," Rocky said.

"Well, at least give me a shot," Peter said, suddenly becoming angry himself. "Try me."

More silence.

"Pete, I remember Allie one way," Rocky whispered. "I remember him running beside me. And I don't want to remember him any other way. Because I remember Allie very much alive."

When the conversation ended, there was

no doubt in Peter's mind that Rocky did not intend to return home for the funeral. There was great concern and dismay in the Marchegiano family. Finally Rocky's mother called him.

"What's everybody gonna say if you don't come?" Pasqualena said. "How they gonna feel? You and Allie, the best friends. You gotta come, Rocky. You just gotta come."

Rocky could never stand to hear his mother pleading and be sad that way. "All right, Mom," he said. "I'll be there. Don't you worry. I'll be there."

Peter Marciano went to Logan Airport in Boston to meet Rocky's plane. It was the final day of the wake; the funeral was scheduled for the following morning.

"Gee, Rock, we'll have to hurry," Peter said as they pulled onto the expressway. "I don't think we're going to get to the funeral home in time."

"That's all right, Pete," Rocky said. "Take your time. Do me a favor. Don't hurry."

Marciano never did see his friend Colombo laid out in the casket at Pica Funeral Home. They arrived after the wake was over and went directly to Colombo's home.

Rocky embraced Colombo's wife, Lilly, and tried to console her. Then he went to Allie's father, Michelange "Mike" Colombo.

"He was my real friend," Marciano .said, embracing the old man.

On the morning of January 10, they drove in the funeral procession from Our Lady of Lourdes Church toward Melrose Cemetery. Rocky, who had been a pallbearer along with several other boxers, was dejected. They were riding the same streets where thousands had lined the sidewalks to cheer them in the championship days. Only now the streets were empty. And there was only the long gray line of cars, filled with somber, gloomy people.

A Lincoln Continental pulled in front of the car in which Marciano was riding.

"Do you know who that is?" Peter said.

"No."

"It's Art Thayer."

"No kidding," Rocky said. "Is that his car?"

"Yeah," Peter said.

"Wow," Rocky said. "Well, what does he do? What kind of business is he in?"

"Rubbish disposal, Rock. He's got a fleet of trucks. Doing real well."

"Wow," Rocky said. "That's great. You know, I always knew he'd make it someday, Pete. Arthur was a bright guy, and he knew how to hold onto a buck. I always knew if he didn't stick to boxing he could make it in something else."

"Do you really believe that, Rock?" Peter Marciano said. "I mean, look at you."

"What do you mean, look at me?"

"What would you have done if you hadn't made it big in boxing?" Peter said. "You didn't make it as far as Sonny or me in baseball. What makes you think you could have been successful at something else?"

Rocky was enraged. "Don't you ever compare yourself to me," he said. "I could have done anything I wanted to. I could have been successful at anything I decided to do."

Peter was very upset. They barely spoke during the rest of the drive.

After the burial, Colombo's close friends and relatives were returning to Allie's house, as is the Italian custom.

"I'm not going back there again, Pete," Rocky said. "Do me a favor, and take me to the airport."

"Sure, Rock," Peter said. "Only, don't you think you should pay your last respects?"

"Peter, don't ask me any more questions. Just get me to the airport."

It was cold and windy at the airport and

snow swirled around their shoulders. Peter Marciano could sense the loneliness that overwhelmed his brother. A big part of Rocky's life, the most important and irreplaceable part, had died with Allie Colombo.

He was getting on the plane now, a lonely runner, faced perhaps, if only briefly, with the stark realization of his own mortality.

And Peter Marciano recalled the way his brother's voice had sounded when he said, "Pete, I remember Allie one way. I remember him running beside me. And I don't want to remember him any other way. Because I remember Allie very much alive."

6.

Never Play Safe

In 1968, Frank Saccone, along with a group of ten professionals and businessmen, bought a Cessna 172 single-engine plane and formed the Flying Club of Brockton.

"Rock, maybe I'll be a pilot myself," Saccone said. "I think I'll take lessons."

"Wow, that'd be beautiful, Frank," Rocky said. "Then we could fly everywhere."

Rocky was so excited that he insisted that Frank go with him that very afternoon to sign up for instructions at Norwood Airport.

"This is my friend, and I'm getting him to fly these things," Rocky told the flight instructor. "Teach him all you can. Maybe you could spend all next week with him."

Rocky convinced the pilot to take him and Frank up in a plane.

"Why don't you let Frank take over," Rocky said, almost as soon as they had left the airport.

"But, Rock, I can't fly yet," Saccone said.

"You've got to learn, don't you?" Rocky said. "Just take the controls, Frank. Go ahead."

"It ended up with me flying all the way to Providence," Saccone recalled.

As soon as the Cessna arrived, Rocky insisted that they hurry over to the airport to see it.

"Beautiful," Rocky said. "Beautiful, Frank. We've got a plane now. We can fly anywhere. Let's go."

"But, Rock, I'm not qualified yet," Saccone said. "I've only had a few lessons. I don't have that type of license."

"Come on, Frank," Rocky said. "Who's gonna know? We can take a little flight. Just fly me down to Providence."

"But my license doesn't allow me to take up passengers, Rock," Saccone said.

"So what?" Rocky said. "Let's go. What's the matter with you? Nobody's gonna catch us."

"He kept insisting, so we went up," Saccone recalled, "but all we did was circle the airport. I wasn't about to try for Providence. We just kept circling and circling, and Rocky thought it was the greatest."

Ernie Clivio was also very concerned about his friend's callous disregard for safety in aircrafts.

"Once, I think it was in 1955, we were visiting Frank Sinatra on the set while they were filming *Guys and Dolls* in Hollywood," Clivio recalled. "Rocky mentioned that he had to get to Palm Springs in the morning, and Sinatra said to take his plane.

"We were supposed to be at Lockheed

Airport at ten in the morning, but when Sinatra's pilot showed up it was about eleven-thirty. The pilot hadn't shaved and his eyes were bloodshot. The guy looked to me like he was really hung over. I wasn't that brave, I didn't feel like going, but Rocky climbed in front and said, 'Get in back.'

"We hadn't been flying five minutes when Rocky was sound asleep. Then a little while later I noticed the pilot's head was nodding. I shook Rocky and said, 'For chrissake, wake up. This guy's sleeping.' Rocky mumbled and closed his eyes again. I thought, if this guy's falling asleep in the daylight, what's it going to be like tonight when we have to fly to Vegas after dark. I had a premonition we were going to get killed, and there's Rocky taking a nap."

Another time they were flying toward Brockton when the single-engine plane lost power and the pilot had to land in a farmer's field. For Rocky it was almost fun, sort of like a game, while Ernie was shuddering in his seat.

Mary Anne recalled that a tree had once saved her father's life by cushioning the crash of a plane in which he was a passenger.

"Gee, Dominick, it's been nice knowing you," Rocky had said to a friend who accompanied him on the flight. "Better put your head between your knees."

Once Rocky had written on his note pad: "Champs are not (never) supposed to play safe playing against the clock jab and move" Another time he had scrawled in an address book: "If you want to live a full life then live dangerously." Opposite that, in printed capital letters, was "insecure."

In blacker moods, he had taken a dim view of himself. "Are you really needed?" he wrote. And on the same note pad: "Am I worth all of this honor sneaky lie cheat *bad thought* cold unconcerned"

"Rocky wasn't a lonely man," Lindy Ciardelli said, "but he was unhappy. He was always too busy living to be lonely, but he hated the word 'content.' "

"What is content, Lindy?" Rocky said. "Break it down into little pieces for me. How can anyone say they're content? There's too much to life to ever be content."

But Rocky often felt sad for people who were lonely.

"Once we were going to see Marilyn Monroe at her apartment in New York," Ciardelli recalled. "Rocky had talked to Marilyn on the phone about seven in the evening and told her we were coming, but then he had gone in to take a nap. When he woke up it was one A.M. but he still wanted to see her.

"Why don't we forget it for tonight, Rock," Lindy said. "We can get in touch with her again later."

"No, I want to settle it now," Rocky said.

From where Rocky and Lindy were staying it was a very short cab ride to Marilyn's apartment. The fare was only $1.60.

Lindy had nothing smaller than a twenty-dollar bill, so Rocky handed the driver two dollars.

"Give the driver the forty-cent tip," Lindy said.

"Oh, sure," Rocky said.

But when they got out of the cab he was enraged at Lindy. "You've got a helluva nerve," he said.

Marilyn was still awake, and she invited them into the apartment.

Lindy mixed some drinks, and they had a long chat. Rocky was trying to convince Marilyn to come on his television show, *The Main Event,* and the conversation was very pleasant. But Rocky was impressed by the strange loneliness that seemed to be a part of Marilyn.

When they went back outside, Rocky challenged Lindy again about the cab fare.

"It was one of the few times I was ever really miffed at Rocky," Lindy said. "I'd been going for all kinds of money at parties and dinners and things. I just couldn't understand how something so insignificant could be so important to him."

The point was not the forty cents. Rocky was not about to take orders from anybody. It could have been forty cents or two million dollars, a guy like Ciardelli didn't tell Marciano what he should or shouldn't do.

Afterward, in the room, Rocky and Lindy were discussing what a beautiful girl Marilyn was.

"Gee, it's really too bad," Rocky said. "Marilyn's got everything going for her. It's too bad she's so lonely."

"Rocky had eyes for her, I think," Lindy said. "But he never made his move. The bigger a girl's name was, the less aggressive Rocky was toward her."

In the mid-1960s, Rocky was still running—running from the only thing he ever feared, the specter of going broke. "Money was his greatest obsession. He lusted for it. And he'd go to great lengths to get it. He didn't care at all about material things; a home, a car, fancy clothes—they meant nothing. Cold, hard cash was what he wanted.

"I used to act as his manager," Ciardelli asserted. " 'We've got to hit those mothers,' Rocky'd tell me. I'd go out and get him twenty-five hundred dollars for the appearance, seven hundred dollars for expenses, five hundred dollars for the plane tickets. Then he'd come up with a free plane ride and pocket the ticket money. He never offered to take care of my expenses, but that was the price I paid to be with the guy, and it was well worth it. Just being with him did things for you, opened up doors that would otherwise have been closed tight."

To a guy like Willie Pep, Rocky was loyal to the end.

"Willie, Willie, what're ya doin'?" Rocky said every time he saw him.

"Yeahh, yeahh, Willie, yeahh," Rocky said, whenever he liked something they were doing. "Yeahh, Willie."

"In 1966, I had a television program in Hartford called *Pep Talk*," Willie recalled. "They wanted guest celebrities. I asked Rocky, and he came on the show for fifteen minutes. Any other former heavyweight champ, you couldn't bring in for less than a thousand dollars. Rocky did it for nothing.

"Well, almost for nothing," Willie said. "All we did was feed him. We took Rocky and Ben Danzi to Frank's Italian Restaurant, the finest place in town. I joked about it later, that I'd rather pay Rocky than feed him. The guy ate all day, I think he ate forty dollars' worth of food all alone.

"For as long as I knew him, Rocky was always trying to do things to help me," Pep said. "He was really excited about introducing me to Bernie Castro, his millionaire friend from Fort Lauderdale."

"This is the guy you oughta meet, Willie," Rocky said. "He can do a lot for you. He'll put you to work around New York. This is the spot for you."

"But it never came to be," Willie said, "because of this terrible thing that happened to Rocky."

"Friend? There was never one like Rocky," Dale Miltimore said. "Rocky really cared about his friends. If someone did something to hurt me, he would hit them. He would attack them physically and in every other way possible. I never really had much of a family life. Rocky was the best friend I ever had."

There were dozens like Dale Miltimore

throughout the country, every one of them believing that Rocky was his best friend.

✴

ALTHOUGH FRIENDS SAY THAT FRANK DaLUCCA and Ben Danzi were closer to Rocky than anybody toward the end of his life, both men hold their relationships with Rocky as personal and private and are unwilling to discuss them publicly.

"DaLucca had a lot of influence over Rocky toward the end," Frank Saccone said. "He's a weird guy. He pretends to be a real bug on religion. He never fools around with girls. He's a vegetarian, a fanatic on not eating meat. He's into yoga and a lot of deep philosophy stuff. He claims to believe in reincarnation. He's a real strange guy.

"Frank used to be an altogether different type at one time," Saccone said. "He owned a nightclub in New Jersey, he drank, smoked a pack of cigarettes a day, and did just about everything else most guys associated with that life would do. Then he got disgusted and went to Florida, and changed his whole way of living. He went into the scaffolding business, and became very successful.

"DaLucca used to travel around with Rocky and spend weeks with him," Saccone said. "Rocky had loaned him money. They were the best of buddies. Frank was sloppy just like Rocky, always had his shirt hanging out, wouldn't shave. He had a strong influence on the way Rocky was thinking toward the end."

Sometimes Rocky came to Brockton to see his relatives, but he remained there only briefly.

"Whatsa matter, can't you leave that phone alone for a minute and visit with us?"

Pasqualena had snapped angrily. "Your father and your sisters and brothers want to see you. We don't ever see you no more, Rocky."

"Aw, Ma, you know I got these commitments," Rocky answered, going over to her and putting his arms around her shoulders and whispering to her in Italian. "I gotta make a living," he said.

"I know, Rocky," his mother had sighed, "I know, *figlio mio*. But if only you could be with us more often. It would be so much better then."

In the evening Rocky would become even more restless. He would be talking with his father, and then suddenly, for no apparent reason, he would get up and leave the room. He always did this very quietly, never informing anybody of his intention to leave, and sometimes his father, resting his eyes as he sat in the soft-cushioned chair in the living room, would go on speaking for several minutes before he realized that his son was gone.

Rocky would go into the bathroom and splash cold water on his face. Or he would go outside in the cool night air and walk alone around the edge of the ball field. Then he would come back into the house and pick up the telephone, and they would hear him say, "Operator, I want to talk person to person to Ben Danzi in New York at area code 212-. Charge this call to credit card . . ."

Frank Saccone had picked Rocky up at the airport one day, and they were on their way down the expressway toward an appointment in a town near Boston, when Rocky suddenly got the urge to drive. "Pull over will ya, Frank," Rocky said. "I'd like to drive for a while if you don't mind."

Not being able to think of any ready excuse, Frank replied, "Sure, Rock. I'd be glad to let you try the car."

Rocky wasn't doing too badly, Frank

remembered, although he did have trouble staying in the lanes and would go from the driving lane across to the passing lane back over to the breakdown lane. "Then, as we were talking away, we suddenly realized that he had passed the exit we needed to go to our business appointment."

"Hey, that was the exit," Rocky said, twisting around so that he was almost facing the back seat looking out the rear window. "Jesus Christ."

"That's all right. Rock," Frank had said. "There's another exit a few miles down."

"No! No!" Rocky had shouted, taking both hands off the wheel and throwing his arms up in disgust. "That's the exit we want."

Then, before Frank realized what was happening. Rocky let a few cars go by, then suddenly spun the wheel around and turned the car directly into the path of the high-speed, one-way traffic. "Get out of the way, you mothers!" he shouted, driving straight up the highway in the wrong direction between the onrushing cars. "Out of the way, you mothers," he kept hollering, waving his arms at the horrified drivers as they swerved to miss Saccone's shiny new Pontiac.

"My legs were like jelly and I could barely speak," Saccone said. "But somehow Rocky had managed to drive several hundred yards through traffic to get to the exit he was determined to take."

"Gee, Frank, I hope I didn't scare you," Rocky said, when they were safely driving toward their appointment. "But we had to make the right exit. We could've really gotten ourselves screwed up there if we took the wrong turn."

And Rocky was as calm as if nothing had even happened.

7.

The Final Glory

HE WAS AN OLD MAN FOR A FIGHTER, with a bad back and sixty pounds of flab to lose as he prepared for what would be his final moment of glory in the ring. He had not fought, nor had he done any serious training, in almost fourteen years. And the pain that Rocky experienced—going to the gym every day, working on the heavy bag, sweating and running in the cool morning breeze—was as intense as any he had ever known.

It was billed as the heavyweight championship fight of the century—a battle of the supreme undefeated heavyweight kings: Muhammad Ali, also known as Cassius Clay, dancing across the giant screen in living color to test his boxing skill against the sheer power and animal savagery of Rocky Marciano.

The computerized film version of a fight between Marciano and Ali was born in the mind of Murry Woroner, a short, chunky, Miami promoter with thinning black hair, horn-rimmed glasses, and a penchant for making the big bucks. Woroner had everything going for him when he hired Ali and Marciano to make a film that summer of 1969.

Ali, who had been stripped of his title and banned from boxing because of his refusal to

be drafted into the army in 1967, needed the money.

Marciano had plenty of money, but could always use more, and he truly missed the excitement and charisma of the ring wars. It was something that would enhance his image across the world. It would not be a real fight. But it was an excuse to be a fighter again, and he accepted it eagerly.

And so Rocky sweated and ran and went back into the gym to sharpen his boxing skills, skills he had not used for almost a decade and a half. They remained as imperishable as the instincts of a killer shark. It was pride, more than anything, that forced him to sweat and grunt and give up the rich Italian foods. For he trained as hard as any champion making a serious comeback, and by July 1969, he had shed almost fifty pounds, and his muscles were hard and strong. Five weeks before the crash that claimed Rocky's life, he was eager again and happy in something that just ever so slightly resembled his old stamina and physical condition.

When Rocky went to the dingy gym on the North Side of Miami Beach he was thinking tough, expecting things to go smoothly but prepared for anything. He had been briefed, knew that the punches were to be pulled, and that it would not be a real fight. But Rocky wouldn't go into the ring that way. Even at forty-six, he had to feel that if something went wrong, if suddenly the punches became real, he would be ready to win.

Ali seemed indifferent. He had not trained and the roll of fat around his midsection appeared larger than Rocky's bulge as they stood face to face in the makeshift ring.

The fights were filmed in secrecy, with only twenty people allowed inside the hot, dirty gym. There was more security than you'd expect to find at the White House. If word of the outcome reached the public before the film's release, Woroner's brainstorm could become a financial disaster for him.

Against a black backdrop, Ali and Rocky sweat for eight hours a day fighting one-minute rounds under the bright lights while cameras grind away miles of film. They pull the punches thrown to the head, and the body blows are like you would expect in a normal sparring session. Nobody is in there to hurt or be hurt.

The ring action is filmed like a Hollywood scenario. There are trainers and a referee. The fighters grunt and groan and twist, and the sounds of leather slamming into flesh and bone are dubbed in through a special effects system. Ketchup is substituted for blood and gore, most of it poured on the scar tissue over Rocky's eye and beneath his nose, which must be bloodied by Ali's fast jabs.

Two men work the corners.

Angelo Dundee is a familiar and true figure as Ali's trainer.

Marciano's trainer is a stranger. Mel Ziegler plays the role of Charley Goldman, trainer of The Rock. Little Charley, the man with the derby hat who resembled an older

Mickey Rooney, had passed away the previous November at the age of eighty. Gone too was Allie Colombo, the loyal pal who had been at Rocky's side for all of his important fights. Al Weill was sick in a Miami nursing home, and died less than two months after Rocky's fatal plane crash.

Every possible situation is filmed, including seven endings, some of which show Rocky winning and others that give Ali the victory. All of this information is supposedly fed into the computer, which makes the ultimate decision.

Ali later claims he chose the ending that was finally used, in which Rocky knocks him out in the thirteenth round. It is an unimaginative carbon copy of the night Rocky, far behind in rounds, KO'd Jersey Joe Walcott in the thirteenth round to win the title.

But while the film is being made, while they punch and tug and dance for the cameras, neither fighter knows the outcome.

Rocky was a good friend of Angelo Dundee, but he had never met Ali. Angelo had often told Rocky that he'd like Ali, but Rocky didn't think so. Before they finally got together in Miami, Rocky had disliked Ali because of his public image.

"This guy likes to shoot his mouth off too much," Rocky said. "I know he's just trying to build up the gates, but it's not good for boxing. People don't like that kind of thing. He should do all his talking in the ring with his fists."

But in Miami they became friends. They spent hours discussing the things that great fighters have in common. Rocky had always had much respect for Ali as a fighter, but now he discovered a different person than he had imagined, a man he could relate to completely and understand as a friend. And Ali wrote that during this filming session he became closer to Rocky than to any other white fighter.

"Muhammad acquired a lot of respect for Rocky," Angelo Dundee recalled. "He said Rocky was a lot harder to hit with a jab than he looked. They never really lost their tempers. A few heavy punches got thrown, but it was nothing unusual, and these guys remained friendly. There was no grudge stuff or anything like that involved. They were just trying to do the job, the best they could."

There was a funny incident that Angelo recalled. Rocky had been fitted with a new toupee for the film. It blended perfectly with his dark hair and made him look years younger. In keeping with the new image of being well groomed and trim he was trying to project, Rocky was very fussy about the wig.

They were exchanging punches when Ali threw a jab that grazed the back of Rocky's head and picked up the toupee.

"Cut! Cut! Cut the camera!" Rocky shouted, his high-pitched voice almost in a panic. "Watch the piece!"

Some of Rocky's friends who had been allowed to view a few of the sessions remembered Rocky's concern about his hair. "Guy better stop messing with the piece," Rocky said. "You don't think he's doing it on purpose?"

"No, Rock," his friends assured him. "It's just an accident."

"Well, he'd better start aiming those punches better," Rocky said.

"Rock was really uptight about the toupee," Dundee said. "He had this guy in New York that made his toupees. I remember when he got the first one. *Mingia!* It was terrible. It looked like a dead cat. I said, 'Rocky, watch out. That thing might get up and run away.' "

"Rocky was always after me to get a toupee," Dundee said. "Every time I saw him he'd say, 'Ange, why don't you get yourself a piece?' "

"Excuse me," Peter Marciano said, interrupting the interview. "But isn't that a piece you've got there now, Ange?"

"No, this is my God-given," Angelo said, patting the clump of shiny black hair that covers his crown. "It's a little thin on top, but I go to the hair stylist once a week, and he combs it down in front for me."

"No kidding," Peter said, grinning.

But Rocky seemed very happy during the filming, and even though he pretended to be concerned about the outcome in conversations with Ali, he projected the old confidence of a consistent winner when around his friends.

In his autobiography, Ali suggests the entire fight is a fake, including the computer, and claims that Rocky said he felt the fight would be rigged for the benefit of the promoter and that "the computer is bullshit."

One thing is certain, Rocky never thought he would lose. He had refused millions to make a comeback in the ring. There was no way he would risk losing a fight to a computer for a few thousand dollars.

Angelo Dundee figured everything was done fairly. "The intriguing thing is that nobody knew who the winner was going to be," Dundee said. "Muhammad wasn't told, I wasn't told, the referee wasn't told. The only guy who knew was Murry Woroner, and he wasn't telling anybody. It was done strictly by the computer. Nobody set the thing up,"

"To err is a machine," Dundee said later, when the films showed Marciano to be the winner.

"The guy from Mississippi must have been running that machine," Ali said jokingly, but he was boiling mad.

Rocky had already won the all-time heavy-weight championship in a Woroner-sponsored radio computer tournament. Rocky had KO'd Jack Dempsey in the fifteenth round of the final bout. But Clay had been eliminated in the preliminaries by Jim Jeffries. Ali, then called Cassius Clay, ridiculed the outcome, and criticized both the computer and Jeffries, calling him the slowest, clumsiest heavyweight champ in history.

It is surprising that Ali would have even agreed to the computer fight with Marciano, having so little faith in the computer and the promoter. But he claimed he needed the money. It amounted to $999.99, according to Ali.

Rocky claimed his cut was about $10,000, and he didn't know what Ali was paid.

The fight grossed at least $2.5 million when it was shown the following January at a thousand sites in the United States and five hundred in Europe and other areas, according to the *New York Times*.

A few days after the filming was completed, Rocky came into his hotel room and flopped in a chair. He was in obvious pain.

"What's the matter, Rock?" Peter Marciano said.

"My back stiffened up," Rocky said. "Guess I hurt it getting ready for Clay. It'll be all right, Pete."

"How do you think you'll do in that fight?" Peter asked.

"I'm a winner in thirteen," Rocky said, grinning.

"You know you won?" Peter said.

"I told you," Rocky said. "I take him out in the thirteenth round."

Peter knew better than to pursue the matter beyond that point. Rocky told people only as much as he wanted them to know.

"Gee, that's great. Rock," Peter said.

"Clay's a great fighter, but I knew you'd beat him."

It was August now, and Rocky had tasted the last glory. He was anxious to move again. He planned trips to several cities before going to New York and then on to Brockton to visit his parents.

Following the rigorous training for the Ali fight, he was in the best physical condition he had been in for years, and he was happy.

8.
Destroyed but Not Defeated

Iᴛ ᴡᴀs 5:30 ᴘ.ᴍ. when Glenn Belz readied his plane at Midway Airport, Chicago, for the flight to Des Moines. He had just received a weather briefing, warning of stormy skies including fog, clouds, and low ceiling in the vicinity of the Iowa airport where he planned to land. He was not cleared for instrument flying. He should not have taken his Cessna off the ground. But there were important things waiting in Des Moines. Rocky Marciano and his friend Frank Farrell were depending upon him. The warning was ignored. It was Sunday, August 31, 1969, the evening before Rocky's forty-sixth birthday. His wife, Barbara, had observed her own birthday just a day earlier. Rocky was planning to return home to Fort Lauderdale for a party in the morning. But first he had a favor to do for a friend.

Frank Farrell was Louis Fratto's son, a Des Moines businessman who had done many favors for Rocky and who is also a brother of Frankie Fratto.

"From what I heard, they were taking off on a combined business and pleasure trip," Peter Marciano said. "Rocky was going to help Frank take care of some things in Des Moines, and then they were planning a little celebration."

Baltimore boxing promoter Ben Trotta had been in Chicago that day with Rocky to discuss signing a young amateur to a professional contract.

"Rocky wanted to go back to Fort Lauderdale on Monday to celebrate his birthday with his wife and two children," Trotta told reporters. "But Farrell asked Rocky to go to Des Moines with him. He didn't want to do it, but he decided he would. He was only going to stay a few hours and then come back to Chicago and fly from there to Fort Lauderdale. He offered to take me to Des Moines with him, but I refused. Rocky hugged me and kissed me the way old Italian friends do and then left."

At 6 ᴘ.ᴍ. the Cessna lifted off from the Chicago airport. Rocky was seated in front beside the pilot; Farrell, the twenty-two year-old insurance salesman who had flown in from Des Moines to pick Rocky up, was alone in the back seat. That was the last anybody knew of them until almost 9 ᴘ.ᴍ.

At 8:50 ᴘ.ᴍ. Belz contacted Des Moines Radar Approach Control by radio. The pilot said he was above a layer of clouds and could not see the airport. Belz was apparently confused, and in need of help. His total flying time was 231 hours, with only 35 hours at night.

Belz requested radar assistance, but a minute later radioed that he had broken out of the clouds over Newton (Iowa) Airport and was landing to refuel. There was no further communication with the flight.

At nine o'clock, a man saw the plane come skimming in less than a hundred feet off the ground about two miles south of the airport. The Cessna disappeared into a maze of clouds, then came back into view and began to climb before falling off to vanish near a hill where the wreckage was later found.

The plane crashed into an oak in the middle of a cornfield. It was located in the only stand of trees in the entire field. The plane was totally demolished by the impact, which killed all three passengers. A wing was sheared off and landed 15 feet from the tree; the battered hull skidded on and came to rest in a drainage ditch 236 feet away.

Rocky's shattered body was found braced firmly in the seat of the wrecked Cessna, but Belz and Farrell had been thrown clear of the plane.

Inspection of the wreckage produced no evidence of mechanical failure or malfunction. The fuel system was working properly and there was gas in both tanks.

"The true tragedy of this accident, in addition to the loss of a nationally known and respected sports champion, is the tragedy of hundreds of other similar accidents; it could have been prevented," said the report of the National Transportation Safety Board. "The pilot attempted operation exceeding his experience and ability level, continued visual flight rules under adverse weather conditions, and experienced spatial disorientation in the last moments of the flight."

The news of Rocky's death echoed in a wave that brought sadness to the world.

Mary Anne had returned home and was in her room when Jack Sherlock, of the Fort Lauderdale police, entered and said, "Barbara, Rocky's dead."

Mary Anne heard her mother scream, and knew instantly that something terrible had happened to her father. There was no way to avoid the vibrations of a fate she had dreaded all along.

It was late at night when Pasqualena Marchegiano received the news. She had answered the phone eagerly, expecting Rocky to call as he always did on his birthday if he was unable to visit her. Only then Pasqualena heard the soft, apologetic voice of a stranger. The words were measured, strained, and emotional, but they exploded in her brain like cannons.

"Rocky! My Rocky!" she screamed, refusing to believe the stranger's message. And even under the family physician's heavy medication she could not control the agony and loneliness that overwhelmed her.

Pierino absorbed the shock with great strength. Although he was torn apart inside, pale and weak with grief, his old man's face, lined and tired as it was, never lost its firm and steady stare.

Strange that such tragic words had reached them from a complete stranger, a member of the Fort Lauderdale Police Force, and not through Barbara Marciano or some other relative. But a separation had developed between the Marchegiano and Cousins families that even Rocky's death could not immediately penetrate. They had seen each other less and less until finally there were no words left to be said between them.

The estrangement between the families resulted largely from minor differences between the elders that had developed over a long period of time and were magnified and made more difficult by the many miles that separated them.

But despite the strained relationship between the grandparents, it never filtered down to the children. There was much love between Rocky's brothers Peter and Louis and Barbara and Mary Anne. Although their own hearts were heavy with sorrow, the men gave their strength to Rocky's wife and daughter as they escorted the women into the funeral home and the church and helped them through the final moments at the cemetery.

The ring of the telephone startled Peter Marciano from a sound sleep.

"Figlio mio, cuore di mama" (My son, heart of my life), Pasqualena kept shouting, hysterically.

"Ma! Ma! What is it?" Peter pleaded. But there was no calming his mother, and even as he dashed from his house to go and be with her, instinctively Peter sensed the tragedy.

"I've got some very bad news," Kitty Vingo told Carmine the next morning. "Rocky's dead. He was killed in a plane crash."

"No," Vingo said. "No, that's wrong. Are you sure? Maybe you misunderstood. Maybe it was somebody else. Rocky can't be dead."

In Fort Lauderdale, Barbara Marciano packed away the presents and prepared for the trip to Brockton. She and sixteen-year-old Mary Anne would follow Rocky's body home, while the Marcianos' seventeen-month-old adopted son, Rocky Kevin, remained in Florida with relatives. The youngster had just learned to walk, and was going to surprise his father at his birthday party.

Pete and Sonny Marciano sat on the porch of their parents' house looking out over the ball park, each trying to be strong to comfort the other through his deepest moments of despair.

"They had helped each other through many things before, but it didn't work this time," Peter's wife, Linda, said. "They both broke down. They had a good cry out there. They stayed together all night until the sun came up just trying to console each other and figure out why Rocky did it, how it could have happened. And in the morning it was better. It was very much better."

A light rain was falling Tuesday night as the long line of mourners formed outside the Hickey Funeral Home along Main Street in Brockton.

Willie Pep stood with his head bowed waiting in the solemn line that stretched for several hundred yards along the dismal, wet sidewalk. He appeared oddly conservative in the dark suit and tie, preoccupied with his own thoughts as he spoke softly with former champion Tony Zale.

Former middleweight champion Paul Pender was there along with many other boxers both famous and obscure, all suddenly very equal in the shadow of lonely tribute they had come to pay to the man who was one of their truest friends and greatest champions.

It was a procession that in a happier time would have been ablaze with the glitter of famous politicians and celebrities, and yet it was the great tribute of the forlorn multitudes of unknown faces in the crowd that most clearly expressed the sharp sense of loss that had befallen all of them. For they had been Rocky's true friends: the struggling athletes, the Italian paesanos from the shoe factories, the average working people whom he had always found time to know and into whose lives he had brought immeasurable pride and pleasure.

"I've been in the funeral business almost thirty years, and this was one of the largest funerals I've ever seen," said Joseph Pica, owner of a funeral home located adjacent to Mickey's. "I decided to open my parking lot to the public. I did it out of respect for Rocky and his family. That was the only reason. I went to all of Rocky's fights, every single one of them. I felt very sad about Rocky, and I wanted to do everything I could."

About ninety percent of the Italians who live and die in Brockton are taken to the Pica Funeral Home. It's almost a foregone conclusion. So when Barbara Marciano decided to bring Rocky's body to Pica's Irish competitor, located directly next door, the Marchegianos were concerned that Pica's feelings might be hurt.

"The family came to me to explain," Pica said. "It hurt them more than it hurt me. I told them I understood."

When Pica opened his parking lot to the public he did not inform Hickey, but mentioned it only to the Marchegiano family.

"I've spoken very little to Hickey, and he very little to me," Pica said. "But I knew that Rocky's wife and mother-in-law had taken charge of all the arrangements. The Marchegianos didn't even get a list of the people who came to the funeral. But I remember a lot about Rocky, and all of it was good. I remember the night he won the title. Nicky Sylvester got me the ticket, and I was sitting right at ringside beside Sugar Ray Robinson and Dr. Vincent Nardiello. I remember the feeling when Rocky knocked Walcott out. You never forget a night like that or the way it makes you proud."

And so Joseph Pica, a proud Italian, walked across the lot and joined his paesanos in paying a final tribute to their hero. It was the only time Pica ever went inside Hickey's funeral parlor. A few days later, Hickey's son-in-law Joseph Connolly thanked Pica for the use of the parking lot.

Izzy Gold, the tough little Jewish kid who had grown up with Rocky, broke down and cried like a baby at the news of his death. And Nicky Sylvester was ashen and grim, his eyes locked in an immovable stare as he passed his paesano's bier.

People who had barely known him were also shaken.

"Johnny Lorenzo, an average working guy from Connecticut who happened to meet Rocky once in his life, took the time off and came all the way to Brockton," Peter Marciano recalled. "He was a big rugged-looking man who loved boxing and used to send Rocky cards after every fight. But when he passed the casket, Johnny fell to his knees and began sobbing and praying. Sonny and I had to help him out. I could feel shivers running all through me. For a while I thought I was going to break down too."

On Thursday, Saint Coleman's Church, where Rocky and Barbara were married almost twenty years earlier, was filled to its two thousand-person capacity, and about a thousand other mourners stood outside while eleven priests participated in the solemn requiem high mass. That night hundreds of Rocky's friends followed when his body was flown to Fort Lauderdale for services and burial there.

The Marchegiano family was inconsolable in its grief as the long trip south began. Ernie Clivio accompanied Rocky's sisters, Alice, Betty, and Connie, who had become so dejected they did not want to go and summoned the courage only when their mother insisted and said, "This is the last thing you can do for your brother."

Pierino and Pasqualena remained at home, keeping their silent vigil.

"This is the saddest news I've ever heard," said Joe Louis. "When he defeated me, I think it hurt him more than it did me. He was always talking about it. After the fight, he sent a message to my dressing room saying how sorry he was the fight turned out the way it did. He just had a good heart. Everything I remember about him is good."

Pete Farley, sports editor of the *Brockton Enterprise-Times*, captured the sincere emotion of the great Brown Bomber in his story that Saturday, September 6:

No minister of God—no man of the cloth—could have said it any better, though, than Joe Louis said it here yesterday afternoon.

"Something's gone out of my life," the man who felt the thunder of Rocky's fists on an October night in 1951 said reverently, "I'm not alone, something's gone out of everyone's life."

Then in an emotion-packed moment the balding former heavyweight champion leaned over and kissed Rocky's casket.

SHORTLY AFTERWARD, PETER MARCIANO asked Louis to "tell me something about my brother."

"He was the greatest, Peter," Louis answered in a barely audible whisper. "He was the greatest."

"The world of boxing that was so much a part of Rocky when he was alive saw to it that he wasn't forgotten in death," wrote Farley continuing:

They saw to it by coming by plane, by train, and by auto to kneel reverently in front of his casket or to bow their heads in meditation.

There was heavyweight champion Joe

Frazier saying, "He was a great fighter and a great man." There was former light heavyweight champion Joey Maxim saying, "There was no pretense about Rocky. He was the genuine thing." There was Beau Jack saying, "When I was down on my luck Rocky made it a point to look me up."

EVEN THE USUALLY TOUGH, unbreakable stare of Sonny Liston appeared to soften and assume a faraway look as he prepared to enter the funeral home. "This man was one of the greatest champions ever," Liston said. "He refused to accept defeat. And nobody beat him."

The fighters showed the fiber of which champions are made as they solemnly paid their respects to Rocky. There was no showboating among the boxers, although some celebrities did take advantage of the situation by using the time to sign autographs for the gawking tourists who had been attracted to the scene.

In his autobiography, *The Greatest—My Own Story*, with writer Richard Durham, Muhammad Ali told of how he had driven to Fort Lauderdale in a rush, breaking speed limits and ignoring red lights to get to Rocky's funeral on time.

Ali had been disturbed by the "big names" giving out their autographs and steadfastly refused to sign his own. "I looked on and hoped Rocky was somewhere taking down their names, so that whenever they joined him, he could whip them for upstaging him at his own funeral."

Rocky's casket was closed, but Ali imagined he could see through the bronze lid to a face that looked "the way they fix dead faces, heavy and stiff and waxy. Not like Rocky and I had fixed it only a few weeks before, with all kinds of life and action, the face of a member of our trade after a terrible battle. I believe he would have liked it better to go out looking that way."

Peter Marciano had stood in the reception hall of the funeral parlor beside Joe Frazier. Some reporters, anxious for a new twist to the story, had cornered Frazier.

"How do you think you'd have made out against Marciano?" a reporter asked.

Frazier stared at him coldly. " 'Scuse me, mister," he said. "I'm here to pay my respects to one of the greatest champions ever. If you want to ask them questions, you come down to Philly next week. Then I'll answer all the questions you want."

"I never forgot that," Peter Marciano said. "Frazier really showed his class. He could have taken advantage and used that situation. But Joe just blew them all off. He didn't want to hear it. I didn't really know Frazier, and it gave me a great lift that he showed so much class and respect for my brother."

The crowd was so enormous and there was so much confusion in the procession that followed Rocky's body to the Queen of Heaven Cemetery for entombment at Lauderdale Memorial Gardens Mausoleum, that some of Rocky's best friends, including Ben Danzi and Frank Saccone, missed it entirely.

"We kept telling the cop we were supposed to be with the family, but he just kept motioning us back across the street," Saccone said. "There was just no way we could get into that line of cars."

"They should have done something," Dale Miltimore said. "That was part of the code. That was the way Rocky always operated. You had to improvise. If you couldn't do it one way,

you found some other way of getting the job done."

A WEEK BEFORE HIS DEATH, Rocky had visited his relatives and friends in Brockton. He was trim and in good spirits at the home of his mother and father on Dover Street. He had stood on the screened-in porch and watched the boys playing baseball at James Edgar Playground.

"We're really gonna have a good deal out there in San Jose," he had told Peter and Sonny, enthusiastically describing how he planned to involve them all in managing Papa Luigi's Italian Restaurant.

But Rocky was still restless. He had not been in Brockton long when he asked Ben Danzi to drive him back to an apartment they shared in New York. He wanted to jog in the morning and to be amid the excitement of the city. But in a few days he became uneasy in New York and flew to Fort Lauderdale to be with Barbara and their son Rocky Kevin. Mary Anne had gone to Brockton, and did not see her father. But again he found a reason to keep moving, and he flew out of Florida to join his friends in Chicago.

"He asked me to go with him," Dale Miltimore recalled. "He said it would only be for a few days. But I knew what Rocky's few days could turn into, and I didn't want to be away too long, so I refused. Otherwise, I might have been with him on that plane."

Not long after Rocky's funeral, Peter Marciano moved his family to San Jose and joined Sonny in the management of Papa Luigi's Italian Restaurant.

"We tried it for six or eight months, but it

wasn't working," Peter said. "Our hearts just weren't in it."

When he returned to Brockton, Peter was still grieving deeply over his brother's loss. It seemed a strange and shallow life without Rocky, who had been both a friend and an idol to his youngest brother. But even though he grieved, flashes of his old optimism had begun to return to Peter that summer, for two months after Rocky's death, Linda had given birth to one of their sons—his name is Rocco Francis Marciano.

9.

Promises to Keep

THE SUDDENNESS OF ROCKY MARCIANO'S DEATH was a tragedy for which the former champion and his family were completely unprepared.

The flaws that Rocky had failed to recognize in himself led to a situation he would never have chosen for the loved ones who survived him.

For Rocky truly believed he was indestructible, governed by a fate that somehow set him apart and spared him the burden of mortality. He never thought about dying, never feared it, and never planned for it.

Rocky's only fear was that of going broke, and because of this he was as miserly and as secretive as a squirrel hoarding acorns. Rocky had guarded, hidden, and invested his treasure in ways so unorthodox and mysterious that it was extremely difficult and often impossible for the money to be found and rightfully used for the benefit of his family.

Rocky left no will, no provisions for his mother and father, no security for his brothers and sisters, and only a small fraction of his fortune in assets to be claimed by his widow and children.

"What they haven't found is his cash," said Frank Saccone. "I'd guess The Rock had a mil-lion dollars stashed away for a rainy day, not even counting real estate and loans. Rocky had at least two hundred and fifty thousand dollars out in loans with no contracts, nothing on paper at all."

"Rocky must have had from a million and a half to two million dollars hidden when he died," a close friend from New York said. "The Rock was earning about fifteen hundred dollars a week for personal appearances for fourteen years after he retired, not to mention all the side deals he had going, and the cash he had stashed away during his boxing career. He made all this money, and he never spent a dime because all the expenses, the phones, the transportation, the hotels, the meals were always taken care of by somebody else."

And so the search continues. The Marcianos know many of the people whom Rocky loaned money to at various times. But no one has come forth to return any cash. Did they pay it back before Rocky's death? And regardless, where is the proof?

Speculation is all that remains. Safety deposit boxes, code-written notes, unexplained trips that Rocky made with bags full of cash to Cuba and other places.

"Rocky made a lot of trips to Altoona,

Pennsylvania," a close friend from New York recalled. "He'd go out there heavy with cash and come back empty."

A millionaire friend of Rocky's had built a bomb shelter on his estate in Florida. Barbara, Mary Anne, and some of their relatives in Brockton suspected that Rocky might have hidden cash in the bomb shelter.

"Dad always talked about it," Mary Anne said. "He always said the bomb shelter serves another purpose, but he never really explained it." More speculation.

"Most of the money Dad earned was circulating on the street," Mary Anne said. "We knew he had loaned it out all over the world, and planned on getting it back when he needed it."

Barbara and Mary Anne were convinced that some of Rocky's trusted friends had large amounts of his cash but made no effort to repay it. They knew that true paesanos, like Ernie Clivio, who had always given but never taken from Rocky, would have come forward instantly. But they knew also that there were others who were not beyond taking advantage of the situation.

"At the funeral, they all said, 'Oh boy, I'm sure glad I paid Rocky back last week,'" Mary Anne recalled. "Every one of them. Even some of his best friends. I don't hold it against them. If a man's dead, I wouldn't expect them to pay back everything right away. But if they'd even just say something."

But Barbara and Mary Anne never received any money voluntarily.

"The only one we got some money from was a couple of thousand dollars from Pete Rigani, because my mother found a note, and from the vice president of a bank, who had given Dad a receipt for ten thousand dollars," Mary Anne said.

Hustlers came like sharks after Barbara and Mary Anne, two women who had never had the responsibilities of taking care of finances.

"We were at their mercy, and they took advantage of it," Mary Anne said. "They took advantage both financially and in terms of publicity. They indicated to us their services wouldn't cost much, but then they submitted enormous fees. Everyone thought the estate was going to be gigantic, but they weren't aware of how my dad did things. It's still not known how much was in the estate. It's been closed out and it's going to be reopened."

Mary Anne knew well her father's habit of hiding money, and suspected that much of his cash was buried in almost untraceable places.

"He was great for hiding money in rooms," Mary Anne said. "He'd take the light fixture off the ceiling, and usually there was a big hole and he'd stuff money in it. He'd tape it into toilet bowls and roll it up and use a coat hanger to push it up inside of curtain rods."

"I always thought he might have hidden money right in our old beach house in Fort Lauderdale," Mary Anne said. "He loved that beach house. He'd go out and jog along the ocean every morning when he was home. It was a logical place for him to keep some cash."

Once, about five years after his retirement, when Rocky was staying at a home he owned in Hanson not far from Brockton, his sister Alice noticed that he was sluggish and seemed to be ill. He appeared to have difficulty breathing and lacked his usual enthusiasm and vigor, Alice knew that as a baby Rocky had almost died from pneumonia. She feared that he might have contracted it again, and so she sent a doctor to the house.

"Who called you?" Rocky said when the doctor arrived.

"Your sister Alice," the doctor said.

"Well, for crying out loud," Rocky said.

"There's nothing wrong with me."

But the doctor persisted and finally Rocky consented to an examination. The diagnosis was pneumonia. Rocky had a temperature of 103, and for the first time in years he was ordered to stay in bed, although he did not like it at all and kept insisting it was not necessary.

Alice had seen other instances that showed that Rocky never considered the possibility that anything might happen to him. She knew he never kept records or prepared for emergencies. And so, shortly before his death, she had approached her brother on the subject.

"Rocky, what if something ever happened to you?" Alice said. "What would become of Mom and Pop?"

Rocky shrugged it off. Nothing was going to happen to him. He was perfectly capable of taking care of his family in his own fashion. It was annoying to think otherwise.

But Rocky did not want Alice or the family to be concerned, so he scribbled a name on a scrap of paper.

"This guy's a lawyer around Providence," Rocky said. "If anything ever happens to me, he'll take care of it. Get in touch with him."

The scribbled name was DiSpirito. But later when Alice tried to contact him, she could not locate any lawyer named DiSpirito. Peter Marciano checked further and his friend Ben Cerelli, a Providence attorney who had done work for Rocky, said he knew of only one lawyer around Providence by that name and felt Angelo DiSpirito was the man Rocky had designated. But by the time Peter got this information, Angelo DiSpirito was dead.

According to the files of the *Providence Journal*, DiSpirito, forty-four, a Woonsocket lawyer who had lived in North Smithfield, Rhode Island, was found dead aboard his yacht adrift off Long Island on May 15, 1970. His brain had been blown out by a shotgun

blast through the roof of the mouth, and the death was ruled "an apparent suicide." The newspaper account identified DiSpirito as a local "political figure," who had once been named in an alleged scheme to obtain a $25 million loan from a Teamsters Union Pension Fund in 1968. Among the six named in the alleged conspiracy were three suspected members of the Mafia.

Possibly this was not the lawyer they were supposed to find. Maybe there was another DiSpirito somewhere who was in a position to take care of Rocky's mother and father. But if there was, Peter could not locate him. It was just another of the many dead ends in the search for Rocky's money.

For months after Rocky's death, Pasqualena refused to accept that he was gone. She waited by the telephone, half expecting Rocky to call as he always did.

Rocky's death had undermined his decision to retire his father from the shoe factory. Because there was no will, the Marchegianos had been left with no income from Rocky's estate. And Pierino's early retirement from the factory sharply reduced his Social Security benefits.

Barbara and Mary Anne visited Brockton several times after Rocky's death, but never talked to the Marchegiano family. Pasqualena grieved to see her granddaughter and did not understand.

"Whenever they were here we tried to keep it from Mom," Peter Marciano said. "It was better that she didn't know."

A week after her forty-sixth birthday, in September 1974, Barbara died of cancer. She went into the mausoleum five years to the day after Rocky.

"Mom always dreaded her forty-sixth birthday," Mary Anne recalled. "She always said she'd never make it."

"Rocky, I'm not ready," she pleaded, delirious from her illness shortly before her death.

"Mom, Dad's not here," Mary Anne said. "He can't hear you."

Rocky never intended things to end the way they did. He was determined to resolve the family problems. He wanted his wife and children and mother and father to be secure and happy. He wanted to settle down and restore old friendships with pals like Nicky Sylvester.

And some of his friends claimed he was changing. That the compulsive Rocky had finally begun to slow down. He was growing mellow, even sentimental, and for once in his life he had begun acting secure about his money.

Saccone recalled going to a fancy restaurant with Rocky and Ben Danzi. When the check came, Rocky picked it up.

"I'll take care of this," Rocky said.

"Come on. Rock, who are you kidding?" Danzi said.

"I've got it," Rocky said.

"Ben and I ribbed him about it, but Rocky took it all good-naturedly," Saccone recalled. "He even joked about it himself. Five years before, you'd have had to kill Rocky to get him to pay a check. The Rock was really beginning to relax about money. His whole style was changing. In the last six months of his life, he was becoming more and more conscious of his looks and the way he dressed. He had taken off a lot of weight. He jogged every morning. Rocky really wanted to improve his image."

But even though he was slowing down, Rocky was still on the run. There were promises to keep. Important promises. Overdue promises. Secret desires shared by very few. But Rocky was like the compulsive mountain climber, always searching for the next peak to conquer. And the promises would have to wait.

Family unity was the most important promise. Rocky held the key to this delicate lock and he knew it. He wanted to bring the family together, but it would take time. He had begun the first steps.

Rocky had promised himself that someday he would help boxers less fortunate than himself who were exploited by the system. He had always felt strongly that so many fighters gave their all to the sport and, when they were finished, they were given a ticket to oblivion. Rocky thought that boxers should have a union and a pension fund, benefits to fall back on and keep them off the docks, the welfare rolls, and the factories when they could no longer fight.

It was often the subject of his talks when he tried to influence VIPs to improve conditions for boxers. Once, before a speaking engagement, he jotted his thoughts on a sheet of stationery from the Town House Motel in Altoona, Pennsylvania. He called it "Boxing Hour."

"Today mostly paper tigers," Rocky wrote, using only spaces for punctuation.

Game run by men of greed little interest in long range plans for the good of all federal government partly responsible I remember they've heard our problems [Senate investigations of boxing in 1950s] classic image of the gallant gladiators in battle giving their all more $ less effort effect of soft living on our times fear boxing is in trouble things are not good every sport is better all should join as one and be proud to excel I've become a computer (no human element) nature of the man be better never quit toy people in a make-believe world

FROM NOTES LIKE THESE, Rocky made many speeches he hoped would improve the condition and image of boxing. But boxing continued to decline in Rocky's final years. He would have been encouraged by the great battles between Frazier and Ali, and later George Foreman, that kindled a new spark in the heavyweight division. But he would have been appalled by the showboat tactics that pitted Ali against a Japanese wrestler, making a mockery of the heavyweight title in the pursuit of millions.

Another promise Rocky had made to himself was to help underprivileged boys who were interested in sports but could not afford to get the proper training.

"Rocky knew what it was like to go without a glove or a bat when he was a boy," Sonny Marciano said. "He always found time to visit kids in hospitals and in ghetto areas where they had nothing, and he was always moved by what he saw."

Since Rocky's death, Sonny and Peter Marciano have established the Marciano Foundation, a nonprofit organization dedicated to helping underprivileged youths develop their potential in sports.

"We hope to build a gymnasium either near Brockton or somewhere on the West Coast where these kids can learn boxing under expert guidance," Sonny said.

IN THE SPRING OF 1973, Pierino Marchegiano had died of a respiratory ailment at the age of seventy-nine. Many of Rocky's old friends had attended the funeral services at Pica Funeral Home and Saint Patrick's Church.

Pasqualena managed to hold her composure and mask her grief through the wake and church services, but at the cemetery, when they began to lower Pierino's casket into the ground, it was more than she could bear. Pasqualena threw herself across the coffin and began sobbing loudly. "God, give me back my husband," she cried. "Rocky! Rocky! I want my Rocky!"

Sonny and Peter Marciano raised their mother gently by the arms and led her away from the burial ground into a waiting automobile.

After the funeral, relatives and friends gathered at the Marchegiano home on Dover Street. They sat at the kitchen table sipping warm glasses of brandy and Strega and eating the pasta, antipasto, and freshly baked Italian pastries. There were people from Las Vegas and New York and other cities throughout the country, but mostly they were the friends and relatives of the family who had spent their lives living in the little Ward 2 neighborhood. The conversation was not of Rocky Marciano, the fighter, although he was largely responsible for some of the people being present. It was mostly the small talk that transpires between Italian mothers and friends in times of stress, talk of children and weddings and babies and how the work was going.

"Isn't it something?" a nightclub owner from Las Vegas said, standing out on the screened-in porch sipping a drink of whiskey and soda. "They're all gone—Allie, Rocky, Goldman, Weill, and now Rocky's dad."

It was amazing, almost like the fate that Rocky was convinced controlled their destinies. Norris, Goldman, Colombo, Weill, Wergeles, Trotta, Charles, Savold, Rocky, Pierino, and Barbara—key persons in Marciano's rise to the title, all dead in such a relatively short span of time.

But the spirit of Marciano lives on in

Brockton. Young athletes, not even born when Rocky won the title twenty-five years ago, strive and strain within the shadow of his legend. For in a city long devoted to athletic excellence, The Rock stands at the pinnacle, a perpetual example of courage, determination, and glory.

ON JANUARY 20, 1970, almost five months after his death, Rocky was resurrected on screens in theaters throughout the world as millions of loyal fans viewed the champion's final glory.

For those who had idolized him it was an emotional experience not soon forgotten. To his paesanos, who savored the good memories, it was as if The Rock had been miraculously reincarnated. Suddenly it was 1952 again, and there he was, going for the title.

But for Sonny and Peter Marciano, as they entered the theater at Pebble Beach, it was also a time of great anxiety. Rocky had told them he defeated Muhammad Ali in thirteen rounds, but now that he was dead, they feared the fight might end differently.

"After Rocky was killed, I was worried they might change it," Sonny said. "I knew if Rocky was alive it would never happen, because he wouldn't allow it. But with Rocky gone, it seemed like they had nothing to lose and everything to gain by making Ali the winner. Ali was still undefeated. He had the potential for earning them a lot of money in the future. I called Murry Woroner on the phone and told him he'd better not change it. He assured me he wouldn't, but I was still worried."

Chills rushed through Peter Marciano's spine as he watched his brother charging across the ring after Ali. For it was not just a fight that Peter saw, but a whole panorama of life swirling before him.

To the fans it was as if Rocky's ghost had returned to stalk the heavyweights of any generation who dared lay claim to his title. Raging out of his corner, smeared with make-believe blood, the old fury burning in his eyes, he was to them much more than the forty-six-year-old former champ acting out the scenes of a play with the twenty-six-year-old champion of another era. For to many Rocky was a symbol. He was a pillar of indestructibility. He was the unwavering proof that man is undefeated and can prevail to overcome any challenge through sheer determination and sacrifice. And to the believers in the power of The Rock, it was not a film they were watching—the fight and the man were real.

In most theaters, Rocky was the sentimental favorite. The fans remembered him as a great and humble champion who had met a tragic end. Their views of Ali were mixed. He had been a great champion, but many who valued unquestioned patriotism above all else resented him deeply.

They were good actors. Rocky punching Ali was much more convincing than Bogart against Cagney or Garfield could have ever been. They had the moves and instincts of real fighters, something even the greatest Hollywood actors have never been able to master.

If only the scriptwriter had used a little more imagination. Other than giving Rocky a couple of extra knockdowns—he had had three and Ali one—it was almost a rerun of Marciano's first championship fight against Walcott.

There's Rocky smeared with blood, fighting desperately, but being held at bay by the faster, more stylish champ. The time of judg-

ment is drawing near, and Rocky senses he is behind in rounds. He charges his opponent, batters him in the corner, and knocks him out in the thirteenth round, in a sensational Cecil B. De Mille ending.

But the fans were well satisfied. In Boston the cheers were deafening. Someone had finally gotten a pound of Cassius Clay's flesh. And to some it was no film they had seen; it was as real as they wanted it to be.

"I just couldn't believe it," Peter Marciano said. "I saw Clay going down for the count, but it seemed impossible. I never thought they'd let it end that way. They had nothing to gain and everything to lose."

Peter felt the sweat under his collar as he began to leave the theater. He had been as nervous as he was at any of Rocky's championship fights. The fans recognized him—the image of his brother—and shook his hand and congratulated him.

"The Rock was the greatest," they said. "There'll never be another like him."

Even to many sportswriters in the audiences, the film was a clear indication that Rocky would have beaten Ali in a real fight.

"My impressions of the film are that Rocky might have licked Clay any day he ever lived, including when the 46-year-old man and the 26-year-old kid tangled on celluloid," wrote John F. Buckley, sports editor of the *Evening Gazette* (Worcester, Massachusetts).

"We've got to call Ma and tell her Rocky won," Peter said proudly, as he and Sonny walked down the aisle toward the exit.

The last thing Peter remembered, before the night air snapped him back to reality, was Rocky in the center of the ring. Ali had taken the final count, and the fans were cheering loudly. Rocky acted the scene very well, as if he felt it was real. He looked out sternly over the crowd, and there was fierce pride in his

battered face. He was immortal as Referee Chris Dundee raised Rocky's hand in victory to haunt the heavyweights for all time.

Book Four

Echoes of a Legend

Introduction to Book Four

UNDEFEATED IS THE STORY of a great athlete, Rocky Marciano, the "fighter who refused to lose."

Rocky did not have your classic fighter's background—whatever that might be—as Everett Skehan made clear in his 1977 book *Rocky Marciano: Biography of a First Son*. What he did have, and maintained, were profound ties to his hometown—the eastern Massachusetts city of Brockton. Therein lies an interesting story. . . .

When we first began Rounder Books, Richard Johnson of the Sports Museum approached us within weeks of our first publication to tell us of Everett's manuscript. Long out of print, Johnson was hoping to help *Rocky Marciano: Biography of a First Son* again see the light of day in time for the fiftieth anniversary of Rocky's retirement as the world's only undefeated heavyweight champion.

Richard was also aware of the wonderful collection of photographs taken by a man from Brockton, Stanley Bauman. Stanley knew Rocky since Rocky's elementary school days. He began photographing Rocky well before he became heavyweight champ and continued to cover him, documenting championship fights, tender exchanges with his family and friends, and the champ's more private, pensive moments. And Stanley was there at the funeral services where Brockton mourned the premature loss of Rocky.

Looking through the Stanley Bauman photographs—there are almost 1,000 images in his Marciano collection alone—we were very taken with what they offered. Here was a unique opportunity to present the life of a champion in the context of the community from which he came, and to which he was deeply loyal to throughout his boxing career. Most of Rocky's family still live in the Brockton area today. Some of the Bauman photographs bear witness to those roots—Rocky strolling the streets of Brockton with his wife, pushing a baby carriage, Rocky meeting with local business and civic leaders at an awards luncheon of one sort or another. There are images, too, of young boys from Brockton gathered outside a local grocery store cheering on the champ.

It is that sense of Rocky rooted in community that we hope to convey with a selection of

the Stanley Bauman photographs and a brief
essay which Everett Skehan wrote for the
newly-compiled Book Four of *Undefeated*.
Everett also interviewed Stanley Bauman, asking him about his photography of Rocky
Marciano. Even though the demands of being
champion took Rocky many different places,
he always remained a son of Brockton and he
remains to this day a source of great pride for
the people of this humble city.

> BILL NOWLIN
> Rounder Books
> *Cambridge, Massachusetts*
> May, 2005

Rocky's Brockton Legacy

Rocky Marciano's influence as an unbeatable fighter who overcame tremendous odds to rise to the top of his sport has continued into the twenty-first century with no sign of declining. He has inspired many athletes and others to battle seemingly impossible challenges and emerge victorious.

But nowhere is Rocky's example more evident than in his hometown of Brockton, Massachusetts. From the achievements of his brothers and sisters and the winning athletic accomplishments of their children, to the unmatched record of the coach and players of Brockton's championship high school football team, the continued progress made by the city's mayor, and many other sports stars, businessmen and friends that credit Rocky as a strong motivator, the champion's image and influence has never faded.

The legend and legacy of Rocky is carved clearly and permanently on a large rock at James Edgar Playground that faces the old two-story house on Dover Street where the champion grew up. It bears his likeness along with an inscribed bronze plaque that reads:

ROCKY MARCIANO
1923–1969
THE BROCKTON BLOCKBUSTER
UNDEFEATED HEAVYWEIGHT CHAMPION
OF THE WORLD
49–0
SEPTEMBER 23, 1952–APRIL 28, 1956
HE BEAT THEM ALL
BECAUSE HE REFUSED TO LOSE
THE MOST OUTSTANDING ATHLETE EVER
TO COME FROM BROCKTON–WHO IN HIS
YOUTH PLAYED ALL SPORTS AND SPENT
COUNTLESS HOURS AS A YOUNGSTER
HERE AT JAMES EDGAR PLAYGROUND.
DEDICATED 1979

The "Rock" that honors Brockton's most famous son has become a symbol of glory and hope. On every Labor Day weekend, to mark the anniversary of Rocky's death and celebrate his unequaled achievements, admirers arrive at James Edgar Playground: the Marciano family, dozens of baseball players and other athletes, politicians including the mayor and fans from throughout the region.

They come there to honor Rocky at the "Brockton Invitational Tourney," which is a

255

showcase for baseball talent that attracts scouts from professional and college teams to watch 120 outstanding baseball players compete in Saturday and Sunday games. The competition is played at the same James Edgar ball field where Rocky spent hundreds of hours pursuing his dream of becoming a major league catcher. Two of the tourney's many accomplished alumni include Tom Glavine, famed pitcher of the Atlanta Braves and New York Mets, and Rich Gedman, Red Sox catcher.

The year 2004 was the first time that tournament play was temporarily suspended. This was done to honor the memory of Connie Spillane, a Brockton athlete and lifelong promoter of amateur baseball in Massachusetts.

Spillane, who admired Rocky and was the founder of the Invitational, died at age 92 just a week before the competition was scheduled to begin. The tourney was set to resume in 2005.

Tommy Frizzell, head baseball coach and professor of business at Massasoit Community College in Brockton, has been a major contributor to the tribute's success. He addressed the participants at the inaugural tournament and has been speaking there for more than twenty years.

"To be a player selected to participate in the tournament is quite an honor, and many of the players have gone on to professional careers," Frizzell said. "I remember that first tourney and the excellent response we received. I had memorized my speech, but when I turned around and saw the crowd I blanked out for the only time in my life. I had to wing it all the way but it came out fine."

Frizzell said that he was just five years old when Rocky was winning his big fights, but he and all of the other kids knew of Rocky and how he was a big hero from Brockton that had won the heavyweight championship of the

world. And today there are still many reminders throughout the city to keep Rocky's image before youngsters that were born almost half a century after his final fight.

"We wait until the first game is finished at the tourney and then, just before the second game, we hold a ten minute ceremony," Frizzell said. "I talk to all of the players about Rocky. It gives them something to remember and reflect upon."

🥊

BROCKTON MAYOR JOHN T. UNITS, JR., is another high achiever from a family of Italian immigrants, who values the lessons of Rocky Marciano and the impact the champion has had on the city.

"Rocky has been a very important role model in Brockton," he said. "Rocky was the one who put Brockton on the map; there's no question about it. He was genuine. Brockton was always his home. He started it all and much progress has taken place after Rocky's glory years."

Units said with Rocky's magnificent accomplishments as the primary influence along with the greatness of Brockton's Middleweight Champion Marvelous Marvin Hagler in the 1980s, and the award-winning Brockton High School Band that has dominated competitions for many years and the unmatched winning record of Brockton's high school football team it was time to make some important changes.

"We wanted to change our image," Units said. "In 1969, we could see Rocky's fiftieth anniversary coming up soon. We changed the city's name from the "Shoe City" to the "City of Champions." It was a very appropriate move. Brockton is a city of immigrants and there is no finer example of what they can accomplish than that provided by Rocky Marciano. The spirit of Rocky became the basis of the logo "City of Champions." And Marvin's, too. His spirit is very inspiring. Although Rocky's unmatched accomplishments are the greatest ever, they were both magnificent champions. We give them a lot of credit for the uplifted spirit of Brockton and its neighborhoods."

The changes are quite apparent to anyone who grew up in Brockton but has been away from the city for a long time. For many years Brockton was a city of mostly immigrant families with blue collar workers from mostly Irish, Italian, Lithuanian and Jewish neighborhoods, who made their livings by working in shoe factories, textile mills, machine shops and foundries.

"The city has come a long way since Rocky's time," Units said. "The shoe factories and textile mills are almost all gone. Footjoy is one of the few shoe factories left." Most of the other factories moved away in the late 1940s and 1950s to southern states and overseas locations to take advantage of cheaper labor.

"We have mostly service industries now," Units said. "And we've been making lots of other improvements."

The racial and ethnic mixes of the city have also changed greatly in the years since Rocky's fighting days. Back then there were few black and Hispanic families in Brockton. But today the city is a smorgasbord of white, black, Hispanic and others. For many of the kids going to school there today English is still a second language.

Units said the city still has an outstanding sports tradition with winning high school teams, and a professional baseball team called the "Brockton Rox" that is also doing well. And

Brockton also has a competitive boxing program run by Rocky's cousins, the Cappiellos. They sponsor some large fight cards that attract the best boxers available.

"I was just a young kid when Rocky was fighting, but I was always kept aware of his greatness," Units said. "Later on I went to a lot of Marvin Hagler's fights. Marvin is a really nice guy and he still comes to visit me."

Units said that the younger generation doesn't fully understand or appreciate Rocky's historic record and the tradition he established, "so we try to constantly repeat and remind them that Rocky was the only undefeated heavyweight champion in the history of the sport.

"I bring it up all the time when I'm speaking to the kids. I tell them they can be whatever they want to be in this country. I tell them to look at Rocky Marciano; he was awkward, he was much smaller than some of the fighters he fought, and yet none of them could beat him."

As the grandson of an Italian immigrant, who knew and respected the challenges of coming to America and working hard to gain success, Units relates strongly to the journey of Rocky's rise to glory.

"My grandfather, Poppa Units, came with his family from Italy to Everett, Massachusetts. He was on the Everett High School football team from 1914 to 1917. That team never lost a game and it was never scored upon.

"When Rocky died my father had tears in his eyes. That was how much Rocky meant to the Italians. I can still remember the arguments in the kitchen, when my father kept insisting that Rocky was the greatest heavyweight champion of all time. Nobody could ever convince him of anything different. And he was right."

"Anyhow, the only similarity between me and Rocky is that I'm in my fifth term as mayor now and I haven't lost a precinct yet in a final election. Rocky and I are both short, both Italian, and we both hate losing."

ARMOND COLOMBO, THE HERO THAT learned from Rocky.

It may seem strange to some that the winningest high school football coach in the history of Massachusetts, and possibly all of New England, is Armond Colombo, brother-in-law of Rocky Marciano. But that is no coincidence to Colombo who credits Rocky with providing the inspiration that has afforded him much of his success.

"I grew up in Rocky's neighborhood and knew him all my life," Colombo said. "I was seven years younger but I played baseball on teams with and against Rocky as a kid."

Colombo not only was close to Rocky and his family from the beginning, but Rocky's sister, Elizabeth "Betty" Marchegiano, was his childhood sweetheart. He and Betty were married in 1955, the year that Rocky had his last fight, which was a ninth round knockout of Archie Moore.

Colombo said he saw the dedication and courage that Rocky displayed from those earliest days right through the immense challenges and obstacles he overcame during his fighting career. The lessons he learned have stayed with him forever, and he has passed them along to dozens of athletes.

"Rocky influenced me and my teams very much," Colombo said. "I always went to his fights and I talked with him often. The advice and insights he gave me helped me greatly in my coaching career.

"I'd ask him how he felt before a fight and what he thought about when he was in the ring and after a fight. Then we mentioned this all the time to our players. We told them how hard he trained and the sacrifices he made to become such a great champion. Before the big games we'd bring Rocky into our talks by telling the players about his life and my personal experiences with him. It would always fire them up and they'd go out and play their hardest. We won a lot of games."

Colombo's record totals include 316 victories, 100 losses, and four ties. His teams have played in 15 Massachusetts Class "A" Super Bowls, and have won eight of them, which is the all-time record for Super Bowl victories.

Colombo said he views Rocky as a role model that set an example of excellence for him to aspire to as well as for many other athletes and people that were not even involved in sports.

"Not only what Rocky did in the ring but what he did before and after a fight was very important to me," Colombo said. "He was always humble, always appreciative of his opponent; he had great respect for an opponent before, during and after a fight.

"In many of the big games we've had at Brockton High we bring Rocky into play by telling the players about his life and my personal experiences with him. I tell them about all of the reasons Rocky was such a great champion and why he was never beaten as a pro. Every team hears the same stories over and over again. In fact, if you asked any of the players if I ever told them about Rocky they'd laugh at you. I probably overdid it sometimes, but it worked.

"It inspired them and very often they won those big games. The reason we won those eight Super Bowls is because we carried the name and example of Rocky Marciano in the back of our minds."

Colombo said he considers Rocky to be "the greatest athlete that ever lived" and that he had great loyalty and provided immense inspiration to his family and the athletes and other people of Brockton.

Rocky always supported the teams and went to as many games as possible, especially when his brothers Louis and Peter were playing. When Lou was playing in the 1950s, Frank Saba was the BHS coach. Colombo began coaching at Archbishop Williams High School in the 1960s and Peter Marciano transferred to Archbishop Williams from BHS and played center for the team.

There are two large posters of Rocky in the BHS locker room, one with Rocky's arms raised high and the other wearing his fighter's robe with the team's black and red colors and the name "BROCKTON" on the back.

"Rocky played center on the BHS team," Colombo said. "He was a Brocktonian all the way. Whenever he was asked, he'd tell everybody he came from Brockton, not Boston or Fort Lauderdale."

Although Rocky was proud of Brockton sports teams he missed many of the city's days of glory. He died just a few weeks after Colombo departed from Archbishop Williams and took over the Brockton team.

"I'm very sad that Rocky didn't live to see our greatest heyday, when we won the big championships," Colombo recalled. "He would have been right there cheering us on.

"The year I took over in Brockton was 1969. I was in my first season of double sessions when Rocky had his tragic accident. Brockton football had gone through some rough years, but the very next season, in 1970, we went undefeated.

"That same year of 1970, when we never

lost a game, we went into a new High School and a brand new stadium, which was named Rocky Marciano Stadium. That was very symbolic and I mentioned many times to my players that the first year our team ever played in the stadium dedicated to Rocky Marciano, the undefeated heavyweight champion of the world, we also went undefeated."

The team's name was also changed in 1970 from "Shoe City and Red and Black" to the "Brockton Boxers" in honor of Rocky.

The first high school Super Bowl ever played in Massachusetts was held in 1971, and the Brockton Boxers also won that. Colombo's son, Peter, was the quarterback on that championship team. He went on to star as the quarterback at Holy Cross College, in Worcester, and piloted the team to two straight wins over Boston College (1978-79), spearheading the effort and winning the coveted O'Meara Award in 1979 as the game's most valuable player. Those were the last victories that Holy Cross football teams ever had over BC.

Armond's youngest son, Tommy, also played quarterback for the Brockton Boxers and set the Massachusetts record for touchdown passes with eighty-five. Tommy threw more touchdown passes than Doug Flutie and many other stars. The closest to him had touchdown throws that totaled in the low seventies.

Some of the so-called boxing experts claimed that Rocky was too small to ever become a heavyweight champion. But lack of size has never been a factor that discouraged or impeded the success of members of the Marciano clan.

Peter Colombo was only five-foot-eight when he enjoyed his many high school and college victories. And Tommy was a diminutive five-foot-six when he set those records at BHS and went on to star for Villanova at the college level. He was a walk-on at Villanova and few thought he would be successful, but Tommy proved them all wrong. He became captain of the Villanova team and took them to the collegiate playoffs two years in a row.

Armond Colombo himself was the quarterback for Brockton High School in 1948, when the team won a national title in the Orange Bowl by defeating Edison High School of Miami. The Brockton team had a record of twelve wins and one defeat that year, which is the highest number of victories in BHS history. That was the same year that Rocky Marciano started fighting as a professional.

Armond retired as the BHS head coach in 2003, and his son, Peter, is now the team's coach. But Armond still works with Peter every day and assists as much as possible.

In 2004 the football field inside of Marciano Stadium was named Armond Colombo Field. The memory of Rocky is never far from the hearts of the Colombos or those of the members of the team.

August 28, 1940 – St. Patrick's Baseball Team. FRONT ROW: Mascots, William F. McCann and James R. Finnegan
SECOND ROW: Edward M. Smith, Vincent J. Hayes, Edward F. Mason, Capt. Michael F. Brugliera, Herbert M. O'Connor,
Tully Colombo, and John F. Kilroy, Jr. THIRD ROW: Rev. Jeremiah J. Minnihan, Rocco Marchegiano (Rocky), Eugene Slyvester,
Joseph J. Mahoney, William A. Roland, Vincent G. Colombo, and Jack Kilroy

1941 – Rocky with Thomas and Ben Giaquinta, trying out for the Brockton High football team.

Rocky in training at the Brockton YMCA early in 1947.

Rocky Marciano and Allie Colombo run along the streets of Brockton when the title was still a distant dream.

Rocky training at the Brockton YMCA November 1948 for a fight in Providence.

January 10, 1950 – Rocky trains at the Brockton YMCA for his March fight with Roland LaStarza.

Rocky receives a robe from Allie Colombo, Charlie Goldman, and Samuel Kovner.

Rocky with his mother Pasqualena and his father Pierino Marchegiano.

Rocky praying for boxer Carmine Vingo, who remained in critical condition after his fight with Marciano.

October 24, 1951 - As she always did before every fight, Rocky's mother praying at church before the fight with Joe Louis. In every case, after her prayers, Rocky won.

Rocky Marciano and Barbara Cousins being married at St. Coleman's Church, Brockton MA by Msgr. Leroy Cooney.

1950 – Rocky with a crowd in front of Marconni's Market.

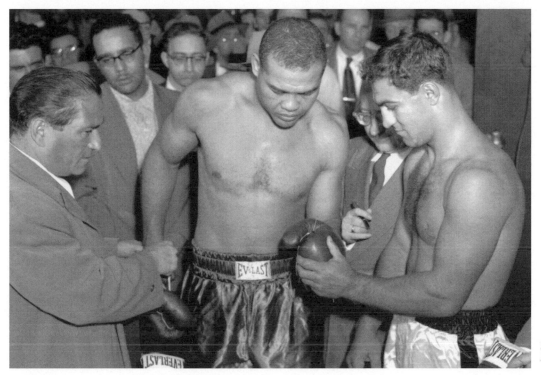
October 26, 1951 – Joe Louis and Rocky weigh in.

Following the fight with Joe Louis.

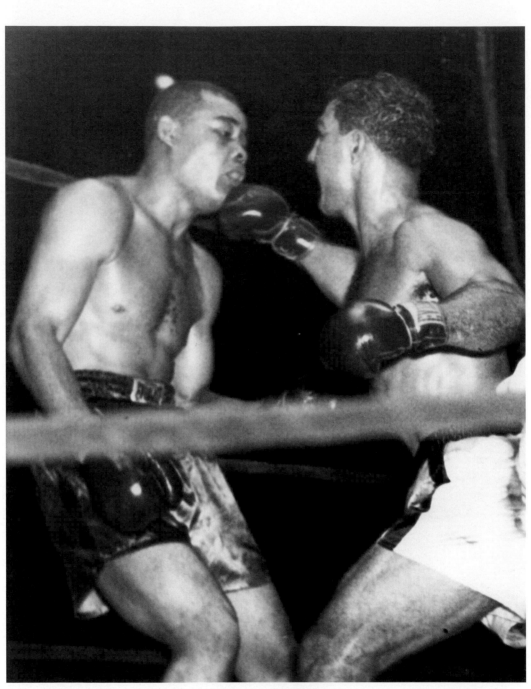

October 26, 1951 – Rocky versus Joe Louis at Madison Square Garden. This shot was taken in the eighth round, when Louis seemed exhausted, and was the knockout blow.

February 13, 1952 – Rocky waving to a crowd from his hotel room before his fight with Leo Savold.

Newsmen with Rocky in his locker room after his fight with Savold in Philadelphia.

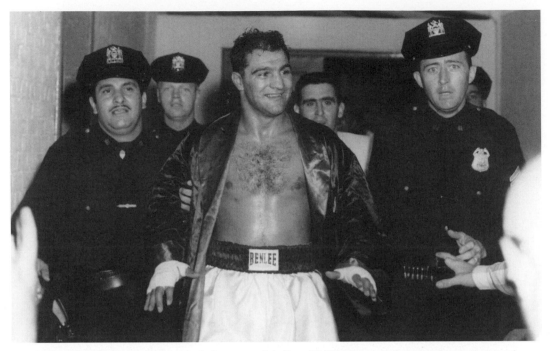
July 28, 1952 – Rocky in New York, leaving the locker room to fight Harry "Kid" Matthews, who he knocked out in the second round.

July 28, 1952 – Rocky in the locker room following his fight with Harry "Kid" Matthews.

July 28, 1952 – Rocky after the fight with Matthews.

February 13, 1952 – Rocky celebrating a victory with Allie Colombo and Charlie Goldman.

1952 – Rocky showing his father Pierino around Philadelphia prior to his fight with Walcott.

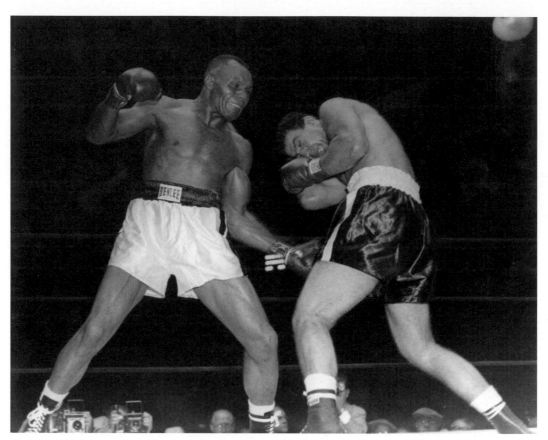

September 23, 1952 – Rocky versus Jersey Joe Walcott in Philadelphia for the title. Marciano won by knockout in the 13th round.

July 28, 1952 – Rocky's mother, Pasqualena Marchegiano, surrounded by a crowd at the Ward 2 Club after Rocky's defeat of Harry "Kid" Matthews.

July 16, 1951 – Rocky's welcome home parade.

October 2, 1952 – Rocky with a "welcome home" poster celebrating his feats as a fighter.

October 2, 1952 – Rocky is presented with the key to the city of Brockton following his fight with Walcott.

October 2, 1952 – Brockton's celebration of Rocky following the Walcott fight.

October 2, 1952 – Rocky speaking on radio station WBET.

Pasqualena Marchegiano dishes out the spaghetti to Rocky after her son won the title.

Rocky receiving kisses from his wife Barbara and his mother Pasquelena.

Rocky with Stanley A. Bauman.

Rocky mowing the lawn of Stanley Bauman.

November 12, 1952 – Rocky with his Cadillac.

April 11, 1953 – Rocky and Barbara Marciano with their infant daughter Mary Anne, on the streets of his hometown of Brockton, MA.

April 2, 1953 – Rocky's wife Barbara Marciano reads to their daughter Mary Anne – then four months old – at a family gathering on the eve of the postponement of the April 10 battle between Rocky and Joe Walcott.

April 11, 1953 – Followed by a crowd and accompanied by wife Barbara, Rocky pushes a baby carriage containing their infant daughter Mary Anne through the streets of Brockton.

November 11, 1952 – Rocky posing with the Ring Magazine diamond and gold belt.

September 24, 1953 – Rocky versus Roland LaStarza.

September 24, 1953 – Rocky posing after his fight with LaStarza.

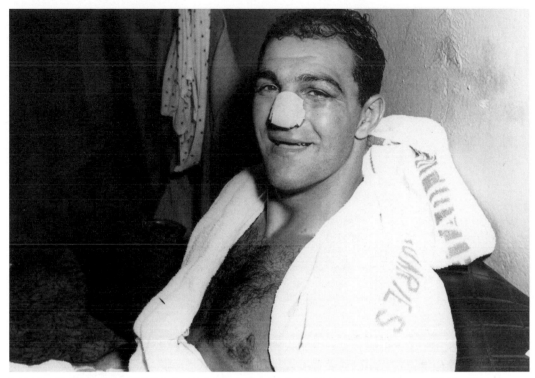

September 17, 1954 – Rocky at Madison Square Garden, smiling despite his damaged nose after his second fight with Ezzard Charles. Marciano won by a knockout in the 8th round.

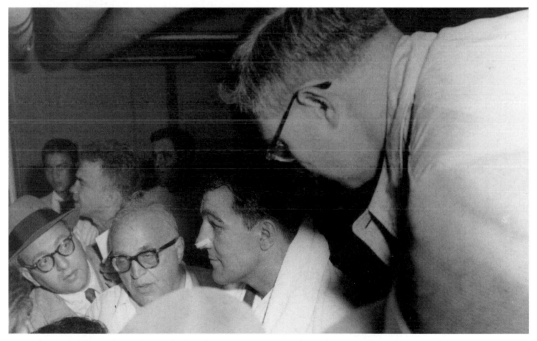

September 17, 1954 – Rocky explaining his knockout to reporters at Madison Square Garden.

July 4, 1954 – Rocky surrounded by children upon his arrival in the old neighborhood.

1954 – V. Robert Pereira sits on Rocky's lap as Santa at the Ward 2 Club.

June 12, 1953 - Sonny Marciano (at bat) takes his cuts at James Edgar Playground, while Rocky (catching) takes a brief fling at his first love, baseball, shortly after defeating Walcott for the second time.

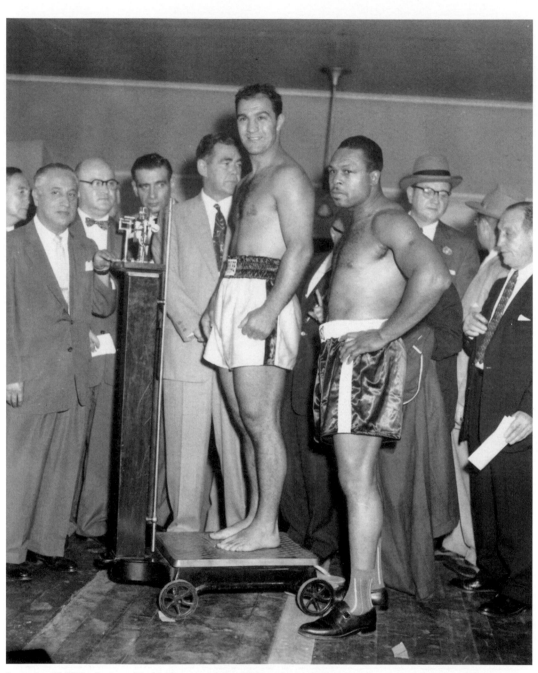

September 20, 1955 – Rocky and Archie Moore weigh-in at Madison Square Garden.

September 21, 1955 – Rocky, in his last fight, delivers a blow to Archie Moore.

September 21, 1955 – Rocky standing over Archie Moore.

Rocky's mother and brother Pete, among others, celebrating at the Ward 2 Club.

Henry L. Tartaglia, Peter Marchegiano (Rocky's brother), Louis E. Tartaglia, John A Picciuto, and William Rodenbush read the newspaper to learn the outcome of Rocky's fight the previous night.

Rocky's wife and daughter looking at a painting of him in the ring.

May 16, 1955 – Attentively listening to Rocky's fight against Don Cockell at the Ward 2 Club.

June 27, 1955 – Rocky holding daughter Mary Anne after returning home from training in California.

Rocky waves to fans from a plane after announcing his retirement.

May 17, 1960 – Dorothy Dale, sports reporter for WBET, interviews Rocky.

May 3, 1956 – Rocky, after his retirement, with longtime friend Allie Colombo.

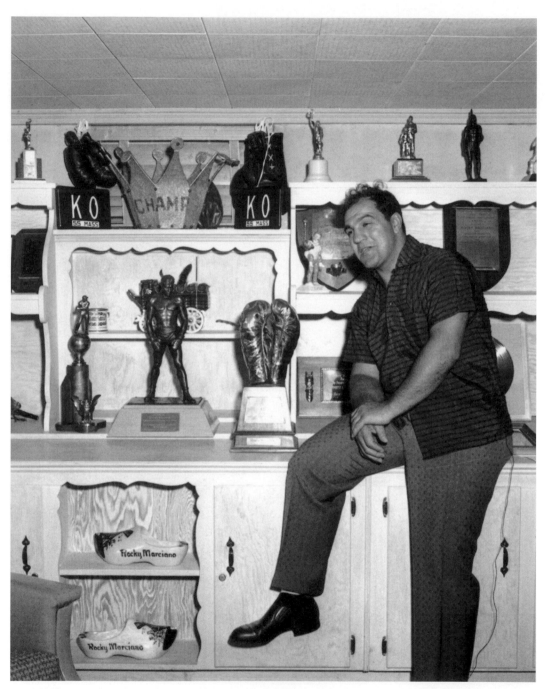

June 1, 1956 – Rocky during his coast-to-coast telecast from his basement.

September 3, 1969 – A huge crowd lined up for Rocky's funeral at the Hickey Funeral Home in Brockton, MA.

September 17, 1962 – Rocky makes a prediction on the outcome of the Liston-Patterson fight.

Stanley Bauman on Rocky and Brockton

I'VE KNOWN ROCKY MARCIANO since he was nine years old. Back then his name was Rocco Marchegiano; he played baseball all the time and never gave a thought to boxing.

When he finally did get involved in professional fighting, in the late 1940s, a lot of people laughed at him at first and only a few thought he'd be successful. But then when he started winning all the time he created great excitement around Brockton and everybody jumped on his bandwagon. Before long the whole city was proud of Rocky and bragging about him.

I had many thrilling experiences as a photographer: I covered five presidents; several disasters, such as the Strand Theater fire in 1941, and the great hurricane of 1938; and countless other historic functions and events around Brockton and all over the state. But being ringside at Rocky's big fights and covering all aspects of his life and the impact he had on our city and everywhere else rate as some of the most interesting and exciting of all of my adventures in news photography.

I had been on the *Enterprise* staff for seven years when the hurricane hit on September 21, 1938. It was a monstrous storm, the worst hurricane in the New England region's history. Many people died. There were torrential rains, floods, high winds, and everything went down: power lines, trees, telephones, drinking water, railroads and trolley cars. The entire region was crippled.

And on top of that we'd never had a hurricane before in Brockton, at least not in my lifetime. Nobody knew what to think or do. The city and the entire region was in turmoil and experiencing the kind of danger and challenges that stressed everybody to their limits.

I took scores of pictures of that storm. Everywhere I went there were flooded streets, buildings and telephone poles and electrical wires down, people injured and in grave danger. I got stranded on one avenue and had to drive through a field to get out.

The Strand Theater fire and collapse, which took place on March 10, 1941, was another tragedy in Brockton that made nationwide history. I was on the scene and took fifty pictures of that sad occasion.

The fire at the movie theater in downtown Brockton was reported after midnight (12:38 A.M.), so fortunately the building wasn't full of people watching the movies. But it turned out to be a tragic night for the firemen. There were thirteen firefighters killed, which was the most firefighters that ever died in a single building fire in this country's history. It was a record that stood for more than sixty years, until the tragedy that took place on September 11, 2001 in New York. *(There were 343 firemen killed and hundreds more injured during the terrorist attack at the World Trade Center in New York.)*

For years afterward people always talked about what a raging fire it was at the Strand and how the theater was completely destroyed, but it really was nothing like that. It wasn't a huge fire; I'd covered much worse as far as flames were concerned.

What happened was that there was fire in the eaves of both sides of the building. The firefighters were up there hosing it down and when they put the water on it the roof collapsed. It came down with a bang right on top of the firemen.

The thirteen firemen that died were not killed by the flames; they were buried under the rubble. It was a very sad day and nobody that was around back then ever forgot it.

(The city is planning a memorial tribute to those firemen that will include a bronze statue and a plaque. It's long overdue and greatly deserved. But, as tragic as the Strand fire was, the deadliest blaze that ever took place in a public building in the United States happened on November 28, 1942 at the Cocoanut Grove nightclub in Boston. That was a raging inferno in which 487 people died, most of them succumbing to suffocation and trampling as they tried to escape through the crowded exits. A number of people from Brockton also perished or were injured in that inferno. However, Stanley Bauman wasn't on hand to photograph that fire, for he had already departed to serve his country in the Army.)

I covered hundreds of weddings and anniversaries, babies, school kids, mayors, all kinds of other politicians and plenty of political meetings, crime scenes, picnics and outings, sporting events, parades, opening days of the fishing season, trains, ski slopes, and you name it, everything and anything that captures the flavor and pulse of the city. It all goes with the territory of being a news photographer.

I can remember a lot of them quite well, but the really important and exciting ones remain as sharp as if I took the photos yesterday. Rocky was one of the most special of them all. He had a profound and lasting impact on the city of Brockton.

The paper didn't send me to Rocky's early fights in Providence, because I had lots of territory to cover and loads of work to do and the craze over Rocky, when everybody went wild and couldn't get enough of him, didn't start until he went to New York and started winning big fights.

Then I began going to all of the fights. I watched Rocky train and saw first-hand the great determination and confidence that he possessed. I witnessed how hard he constantly worked on his conditioning and how no sacrifice was too great if it would help him achieve his goal.

I'd already seen some of Rocky's punishing workouts in Brockton and the way he and Allie Colombo constantly ran through the streets in order to improve his already amazing stamina and power. It was amazing. I never saw anybody else who trained nearly that hard: he was at it all the time.

I always felt the success of Rocky was due to his absolute addiction to a strict and punishing regime of training. And that dedication wasn't just limited to boxing or when he got older. He was that way when I first started taking pictures of him as a kid playing baseball. He never wanted to quit. He never wanted to stop hitting baseballs or trying to improve his skills as a catcher. He was absolutely committed to making himself the very best that he possibly could be.

Then I saw him in the ring during those important, tough fights in New York and Philadelphia and how hard he went after those opponents. I didn't know a great deal about boxing, but it didn't take much to realize that Rocky was a winner. He wasn't the kind of guy that was ever going to let himself lose if there was anything at all that he could do to prevent it. He had the heart of a true champion. He was determined to win at all costs.

I was ringside for all of Rocky's big fights; when he beat Joe Louis and Roland LaStarza on the way up and at all of the title fights from the knockout of Jersey Joe Walcott to his final KO over Archie Moore. I saw some terrific action and Rocky was the biggest part of it.

We had our cameras up so close that they were resting on the ring apron. It provided great opportunities when I was on the side of the ring where the action took place, but when I was on the opposite side it wasn't good. Then I couldn't always get the picture I wanted.

The best picture from my standpoint was when I captured Rocky nailing Roland LaStarza *(for an 11th round KO on September 24, 1953 in New York)*. LaStarza was the best looking of the fighters: he wasn't a pug like a lot of them; he looked more like a movie star. But this picture I got of him shows his face all distorted by the tremendous blow that Rocky threw.

Rocky had such powerful legs and he went into the punch with his whole body when he hit LaStarza. That picture is one of the most famous ones that I have. It shows clearly just how powerful and devastating Rocky's punches were and the toll they took on his opponents.

I also have pictures of Rocky knocking out Joe Louis, Jersey Joe Walcott, Ezzard Charles and clobbering Archie Moore in Rocky's last fight. They were all great champions and Rocky took them all out. But it wasn't always easy, far from it, and I've got the pictures to prove it.

Those were all thrilling fights, but the most exciting of them all were when Rocky knocked out Jersey Joe Walcott in the 13th round in 1952 to win the title, and when he came roaring back to knock out Ezzard Charles in the 8th round of a title fight in September of 1954.

The referee was going to stop that fight with Charles because Rocky's nose had been split wide open and the blood was pouring out of it and the doctor couldn't stop it and didn't want the bout to continue. But before he could take action the bell rang and Rocky raced out of his corner and pounded Charles into submission.

I've got the pictures of the doctor trying to repair that injured nose and it wasn't a pretty sight. It looked like Rocky's nose had been cut in half with a pair of scissors. Afterwards Rocky had to go to a plastic surgeon and have an operation to repair it, but nothing was going to stop him during the heat of that battle.

There were lots of parades in Brockton over the years, but Rocky had more than anybody and they were always exciting. I took pictures of five presidents; Franklin D. Roosevelt, Harry Truman, John F. Kennedy, Richard Nixon and Ronald Reagan.

I remember how big the crowd was when Harry Truman came down Legion Parkway in the center of Brockton. I took his picture flanked by the mayor and the chief of police.

But Rocky had great parades after every big fight with thousands of fans cheering as he proceeded up Legion Parkway with motorcades and bands and everything else to celebrate one great victory after another. He was the biggest hero the city had ever known.

I'll never forget Rocky or all those sensational fights that put a little industrial city such as Brockton on the map of fame and glory all over the world.

Stanley Bauman is the legendary photographer, who covered all of Rocky Marciano's championship fights for the Brockton Enterprise Times. *A lifelong bachelor, who devoted his life to capturing the news and profiling the region on film, Bauman was the area's premier news photographer for half a century and at the age of 92 is still pursuing his craft on a part-time basis. His work is well known and admired by newspaper readers in Brockton and many other New England communities.*

Bauman was born in Brockton in 1913 and began working as a reporter-photographer for the Enterprise *in 1931 soon after graduating from High School. He enlisted in the Army in 1942 and eventually became a regimental sergeant major in charge of training units of combat photographers at a camp in Louisiana. He later served in China and India.*

After he was discharged from the Army in 1945, Bauman returned to the Brockton Enterprise *and continued his lengthy career as a photographer. He covered all of the major stories for the paper until 1970, then became semi-retired, but still did work for the Brockton newspaper as well as freelancing for the* Boston Globe *and others. Throughout most of his career, he compiled a file of more than 3,500 photographs a year. The Bauman collection includes 920 photos of Rocky Marciano and some of those pictures of Rocky, his family and friends and champion opponents are featured prominently in this book.*

Stanley Bauman at home, 2005. (Photo by Bill Nowlin)

Brotherly Reflections

Louis and Peter Marciano, younger brothers of the champion, were closer to Rocky than most and were greatly influenced by his accomplishments and presence. The lessons Rocky taught and the pride and determination he instilled have carried the brothers forward and pushed them to being their best. What follows are some of their observations of Rocky's career and the impact of life with the Champ.

PETER MARCIANO—Rocky was seventeen years older than me and when I was growing up he was always a father figure to me. I speak at Marciano Scholarship functions and a lot of other events and I always close by saying that if every kid had an older brother like I did the world would be a lot better place. I believe that strongly because Rocky always told me to try my hardest and do my best at all times no matter what, and I've always made sure I followed that advice.

Many people have told me how much they were influenced by Rocky's example. That is evident everywhere you look and it grows stronger all the time. It gives me a very good feeling.

For me the experience of learning from my brother has been very personal. Rocky's example has followed me all through my life and I've passed it down to my entire family.

Rocky came to my games and always supported and encouraged me. I was a good athlete in my own right, but with Rocky's great achievements a lot of people got the impression that there was a jealousy factor involved. Not at all: nothing could be further from the truth. Because Rocky always made it very clear that what I did I did on my own.

(Peter played football and baseball in high school and was inducted into his high school's hall of fame in those sports. He received a baseball scholarship to the University of Miami in Florida as a catcher.)

After college I signed with the Braves as a catcher and played for two years in the minor leagues. But I didn't make it to the top. When I was released by the Braves it was very depressing. The first person I called was Rocky.

We met in New York City. It was an extremely difficult time for me. It was like the end of my world because I thought I was going to be a major league baseball player. That was my life's goal and I couldn't imagine not being able to achieve it, or what I would do next.

265

(As described in the biography's text, almost five years before he became a champion and world-renowned celebrity, Rocky had seen his own dreams shattered as he failed in his attempt to advance beyond the minor leagues and reach major league stardom as a catcher. He knew all too well the feelings that Peter was experiencing. He knew also that he had risen above the pain and humiliation of that defeat to a place of far greater accomplishment and glory.)

Rocky softened the blow by talking to me and comforting me. He said, "Peter, if in your own mind you feel that you gave it your best shot then you have no regrets and you went a lot further than ninety-nine percent of the guys that play baseball."

I felt a lot better after that. I was able to put it behind me and go on to enjoy a happy productive life. I'll never forget my brother or all that happened back when he was with us, but it's not like I think of Rocky all the time. I've got a wonderful family, a business, and a very active life.

(Peter and his wife Linda have three sons, Peter, Rocco "Rocky," and Stephen, and a daughter named Elise. All three of the boys were outstanding athletes in both high school and college.

Their first son, Peter, played football and baseball for Brockton High School and went on to be a star football player at the University of Iowa.

Peter's stardom is described in the written tribute that accompanies his 1985 induction into the Brockton Athletic Hall of Fame, which begins by proclaiming that "Peter, a four-year starter, has to be considered one of the finest wide receivers, punt and kick returners in the history of Brockton High School football."

It goes on to state that Peter scored thirty-three touchdowns, and that his greatest per-

formance took place when he scored 18 of Brockton's 20 points during the team's 20-6 victory over Lexington in the 1984 Class A Eastern Massachusetts High School Super Bowl. Peter returned the opening kickoff 76 yards for the game's first TD, then went on to score two more on receptions of 43 and 46 yards.

Peter also played three years of varsity baseball for Brockton High School. His batting average was .326 and his 51 stolen bases led the team. He spearheaded the baseball squad to three Suburban League Championships, two South Sectional Championships and a state tourney final game.

Although at five-foot-eight, 175 pounds, Peter was undersized for Big Ten competition, he went on to star and set records at the University of Iowa. He was a freshman on the Iowa team that lost 45 to 28 to UCLA in the 1986 Rose Bowl. He was a letterman for Iowa four years in a row and held the school's record for punt returns at 124 and return yards totaling 759. As his father, Peter, said, "He was undersized and over-achieved."

Peter and Linda's middle son, Rocco "Rocky" Marciano, and their youngest son, Stephen, were also schoolboy stars. Rocky went on to star and was captain of the football team at Plymouth State College in New Hampshire. Stephen went to Boston College on a football scholarship and also was captain of the BC baseball team.)

My brother Rocky had an important influence on all of my sons. They got pumped up by listening to tapes and learning about Rocky's accomplishments. It was very inspirational.

But Rocky was gone when they were growing up. He never got to see them play in the high school and college games where they were stars. I always worked with them and encouraged them to give their all and be the best that they possibly could. Although he inspired them, I don't think Rocky had the influence on the boys that I did. I was with them all the way.

As far as Rocky as a person, I feel that, although he was undefeated as a fighter, like all human beings he wasn't perfect, and if he had it to do over there are certain things he would change. But even though I say that, my feeling is that overall he was a great man, a dedicated family man, and a wonderful brother.

LOUIS "SONNY" MARCIANO—In my travels throughout the country, I've met hundreds of people that admire Rocky and think he was the greatest ever. Almost all of them are very curious about Rocky's life, especially how he overcame what appeared to be overwhelming odds to become such a great, undefeated champion.

If they knew Rocky the way I did, if they slept in the same bedroom with him and grew-up watching him play ball and seeing how hard he always worked out and tried to become better, and if they could only have listened in on some of our conversations then the reasons would become obvious. They would see what drove Rocky and made him run farther and higher than his competition.

Actually Rocky loved all sports, and when he was young he was especially obsessed with baseball and to a lesser degree football. He was the type of guy who would never be satisfied until he made himself the best that he could possibly be and he wanted that to be the best of all. But if he gave his all at one thing,

such as baseball, and fell short of his goal, such as happened when he tried out in the minor leagues and failed, he'd never quit. He'd never be discouraged for long. He'd go right on to something else and go after it with that same determination and hard work, always with that goal of becoming the greatest.

Fortunately for Rocky, and the boxing world in general, after baseball he turned to fighting and went at it with such pride and passion that he rose to the very top. My older brother, a kid who never even thought about becoming an amateur boxer until he went into the Army in the 1940s, and didn't turn pro until he was twenty-five: my brother, who was considered by most experts to be too light, too short, too clumsy to become even a good journeyman heavyweight, became the greatest champion of them all.

I know the reasons why, because I was right there with him all the way. I was ten years younger than Rocky and he was my idol and greatest inspiration. I tell them how Rocky trained like no one else they've ever seen pushing himself on and on to the point where most guys would collapse. I know because I watched him in the gym and the ring and often I had to run with him while we kept throwing footballs and he tried to convince me it was to my benefit because he was getting me ready for high school sports. Rocky had more stamina and power than much younger opponents but it was no accident. He sacrificed more than any of them to get it.

People ask why it was that Rocky rarely clinched during a fight. I tell them it's like the newspaperman Arthur Daley wrote in one of his columns praising Rocky; a clinch is for fighters who are either tired or hurt. The fighter that has the stamina to go the distance and hasn't been staggered has no need for clinches.

I was at every fight and I saw Rocky just keep on charging forward throwing punches, because the truth is he was never tired and never hurt enough to slow him down for more than a few seconds. In all of his fights Rocky was only knocked down twice, once by Walcott and the other time by Moore, and even then he was never badly hurt and was on the canvas for only a total of seven seconds.

But two of the biggest reasons that Rocky could never be beaten were his tremendous confidence and utter lack of fear.

Early in Rocky's career, before all the money and fame came along, Rocky and I slept in the same big bed in our family's house. We used to talk about lots of things but mostly about sports and Rocky's boxing.

I remember asking him, "How does it feel when you see a guy across the ring from you that wants to come out and beat the hell out of you?"

"You know something, Sonny," Rocky said. "I don't even think about it. I've never feared anybody. It's not in me to be afraid. Besides what do I care what the guy wants to do? He won't be able to hurt me. I'll get him."

Rocky said he felt that he'd been blessed with great genes, big fists, plenty of power and the ability to take a punch. "I just think that if I'm in great shape then nobody can beat me," he said. "And you know I'll always be in great shape."

He said that to me way back then but he also repeated it to me in almost the same words as we walked along the streets of New York the day after one of his big fights at Madison Square Garden.

Even then I asked him, "Rocky, you're gonna be fighting Jersey Joe for the title one of these days; does that scare you at all?"

Rocky got a little miffed. "What's the matter with you?" he said. "What's all this crap about being scared? Why're you asking me that again? How many times do I have to tell you, I don't fear anybody. I'm in great shape and as far as I'm concerned nobody can beat me."

I remember that one of the biggest criticisms I heard of Rocky was that he fought a lot of old fighters. Even some of the so-called fight game experts used that excuse to knock my brother and claim he wasn't the greatest of the heavyweights. But that's ridiculous. If they want to fault Rocky for that then they'd better fault all the other great champs, too. You always see younger boxers fighting older fighters on the way up, but then, if they stay too long, they fight the younger guys on the way down.

I did a lot of research on this and it certainly should make those critics see Rocky in a different light. For example, Rocky was nine years younger than Jersey Joe Walcott from whom he won the title, but Jack Dempsey was thirteen years younger than Jess Willard when he KO'd Willard for the title: James Jeffries was twelve years younger than Bob Fitzsimmons, Joe Louis was twelve years younger than James Braddock, and Cassius Clay (later known as Muhammad Ali) was ten years younger than Sonny Liston when he took the title. Rocky was nine years younger than Joe Louis and ten years younger than Archie Moore, both of whom he knocked out. But Ali was nineteen years younger than Moore and Floyd Patterson was 21 years younger than Moore when they fought. And Joe Louis was nine years younger than Max Schmeling when Schmeling KO'd him.

In my opinion, Ezzard Charles was one of the greatest and most underrated fighters of all time. But Charles was only two years older than Rocky; he was thirty-two and Rocky was thirty when Rocky beat him twice in 1954 to retain his title.

There are dozens of examples of the young meeting the old on the way up and the old former champs and contenders on the way down meeting the young hopefuls that are climbing the ladder; because that's the way it is in the boxing game.

The important thing that I always remember is that Rocky fought them all, never ducked a single fighter the way a lot of guys do these days, and he never lost to any of them. He beat every one of them, whether they were older or younger than him. He retired with a record of forty-nine and zero with forty-three knockouts and only six fights that went the distance. That gave Rocky a knockout percentage of eighty-eight, which was twelve points better than the runner-up, Joe Louis, who ended his career with a percentage of seventy-six.

And Rocky didn't retire because he had any doubts about being able to win more fights. He was still in great shape and he knew he could keep winning, because there were no challengers that could even come close to beating him. Rocky quit because he didn't like his management and felt he was being cheated. If he could have gotten out of his contract he'd have stayed longer and won more fights.

SOME OF THE COUNTRY'S TOP SPORTS WRITERS, Jimmy Cannon, Red Smith, and A. J. Liebling to mention just a few, have described in their columns how tenacious and physically fit Rocky was and how he could absorb all kinds of punishment and keep coming on to win the fight. Some described cuts and hard punches that would have stopped most fighters but barely seemed to even faze Rocky.

Another misnomer that people had was that Rocky was too small to fight all those huge heavyweights. The truth was that Rocky loved fighting big guys; he found them easier to beat and knock out than those faster little guys that ran all over the ring and tried to escape. Larry Merchant used to always praise the big guys but then the big guys all started getting KO'd and he changed his view.

Many of the top champions and trainers, legendary winners like Joe Louis, Joe Frazier, Joe Walcott, Ezzard Charles, Angelo Dundee, Lou Duva, Goody Petronelli, Al Certo and numerous others, have expressed great praise and admiration for Rocky.

I always recall the day I got a call from my good friend Al Scoma, owner of the finest seafood restaurant in San Francisco, which is located on Fishermen's Wharf. Al said Gene Tunney was there and wanted to meet me.

I went to Scoma's and met with Tunney, one of the great legendary heavyweight champs, and we had a conversation about Rocky and boxing in general. Tunney told me that in his opinion Rocky was the greatest heavyweight champion of them all.

Rocky had a tremendous influence on me. He taught me many valuable lessons and supported me all the way. I played third base in baseball and linebacker in football and did very well in both sports. My sons, Lou Jr., Terry, and Tony, were also inspired greatly by Rocky. They were all good athletes, who played football and baseball in high school.

I remember when Rocky was winning all those fights Charley Goldman came to our house and wanted me to become a fighter. I was very interested at the time, but my mother put an end to that. She insisted that one fighter was enough in the family. She had almost stopped Rocky from fighting in the beginning, but nothing could discourage him.

I THINK I WOULD HAVE BEEN a better boxer
than I was a baseball player. Rocky used to put
me in to spar with some very good fighters at
the training camp and I always did well. I was
in high school then and concentrating on
baseball, but Rocky kept telling me I could
become a top notch middleweight boxer. I
knew he'd never encourage me to pursue that
unless he really thought I could make it.

But by the time I considered going for it
even despite the family's objections it was
already too late. I'd always figured on baseball
and by the time I changed my mind I was too
old and inexperienced to start out in the fight
game. I wouldn't have wanted to get involved
if I couldn't go all the way to the top.

One of the best examples I can recall of
how much Rocky inspired me took place the
day after Rocky knocked out Joe Louis at
Madison Square Garden.

After the fight, Allie Colombo and I drove
back to Brockton. It was a Friday night in late
October of 1951 and I was scheduled to play
for Brockton High in a football game against
Malden High the next day. But I was so excited and proud that there was no way I could
sleep. Allie and I stayed up all night talking
about Rocky and the fight.

By the time the game started I hadn't slept
at all in about two days. But I was still so
pumped up that the adrenalin was flowing like
crazy and I didn't feel the least bit tired.

In fact, I was so inspired by Rocky that I
played my best game ever. I made all kinds of
tackles and was so energized that I felt unbeatable as if nobody at all could ever stop me.

That was the effect Rocky had on me. That
was the way I'll remember my brother for all
time.

Trainers of Champions Assess Rocky

At 82 years old when this interview was conducted in 2004, Angelo Dundee was one of the most accomplished and highly recognized trainers of champion boxers in the world. Dundee, who was inaugurated into the International Boxing Hall of Fame in 1992, has been training and managing fighters for almost seven decades and has helped shape the careers of fifteen world champions.

Dundee, who was born in Philadelphia in 1923 as Angelo Mirena Jr., learned his trade as a young apprentice by studying some of the sport's greatest trainers, cut men and others as they handled top fighters at the Stillman's and CYO gyms in New York. He absorbed the best that those master craftsmen had to offer and then added innovative touches of his own.

One of the best from which Dundee learned a great deal was the crafty little ring-wise wizard called Charley Goldman, whose brightest rising star in the late 1940s was a promising but unpolished heavyweight named Rocky Marciano.

Dundee applied much of the knowledge garnered from Goldman's imaginative techniques that brought out the greatness in Marciano, as well as the skills he learned from trainers such as Whitey Bimstein, Ray Arcel, and several others, in shaping the careers of many of his own impressive champions.

Among those who benefited from Dundee's artistry were Angelo's first world champion, Carmine Basilio, who won the welterweight title with a 12th round TKO of Tony DeMarco in 1955 and went on to numerous championsip victories both as a welterweight and middleweight. Other accomplished champions handled by Dundee included Sugar Ray Leonard, Willie Pastrano, Ralph Dupas, Sugar Ramos, Aleson Rodriguez, George Scott, Jose Napoles, Pinklon Thomas, Michael Nunn, Slobodan Kacar and Jimmy Ellis. Angelo also worked George Foreman's corner when the then 46-year-old former champ came back in 1994 to win the title from Michael Moorer.

The greatest of them all was Muhammad Ali, who Dundee developed and nurtured during a span of twenty years (1960-1980) starting with the professional debut of a gifted 18-year-old from Louisville, Kentucky called Cassius Clay and ending with a record of 56 wins and five losses by the highly skilled boxer, who changed his name to Muhammad Ali after becoming Heavyweight Champion in 1966 *with a 7th Round TKO of Sonny Liston.*

As this book went to press Angelo had just finished working on the movie Cinderella Man, *which is based on the life of heavyweight champion James J. Braddock and stars Russell Crowe in the title role. Angelo was a consultant that polished Crowe as a boxer and he also played the role of a cut man. He had also worked with actor Will Smith in developing his techniques in portraying Muhammad Ali in the movie of Ali's career that was released a year earlier.*

Here's what Dundee had to say about Rocky.

ANGELO DUNDEE—Rocky was a friend, number one. After he retired Rocky moved to Florida and we got to know him real well. He was always a nice guy and a pleasure to be around. He had a great personality and was very down to earth.

As a fighter Rocky was the best of his time. I mean there was nobody that could beat him. He retired undefeated and that says it all.

The first time I saw Rocky was when he came to New York for training. He was an unknown, a raw kid from Brockton, Massachusetts that had done most of his fighting out of Providence and hadn't been seen around New York.

My dear friend Charley Goldman asked me to come to the CYO Gym and watch him work. "He's got bad balance, got those stooped shoulders and short arms, but, oh, how he can punch," Charley said.

I went over to the CYO and watched Rocky work out with the heavyweight Keene Simmons, who was a tough guy and a good fighter. It was a great workout and Rocky was absolutely sensational.

(About three years later, in January 1951,

Rocky and Simmons fought for real in a scheduled ten-rounder in Providence. It was a brutal battle with vicious exchanges when in the seventh round Simmons opened a large gash over Rocky's eye. The doctor was in Rocky's corner and about to call it off because the cut man could not stop the bleeding; but before he could declare the fight over the bell rang and Rocky went running out into the ring.

Marciano stormed all over Simmons battering him with what seemed like hundreds of rapid fire punches and then, with Simmons out on his feet and defenseless, the referee stepped in and waved Rocky off, declaring him the winner by a technical knockout. It was one

Angelo Dundee and Muhammad Ali. (Photo courtesy of Angelo Dundee)

of the many examples of Rocky's determination, undaunted heart, seemingly endless stamina and relentless pursuit of opponents; he simply refused to accept defeat.)

Rocky overcame a lot of things and came out keeping the fans happy because he always made great fights. He never gave up and he never backed down or allowed himself to lose.

The best thing about Rocky was his leverage. He'd be in a crouch and then come up banging. He stopped a lot of fighters that way.

He was really a good defensive fighter, too, which is something a lot of people didn't realize. Rocky gave the impression that he was a tough guy but he really wasn't just tough, he was slick. I found that out when we did the computer fight between Muhammad and Rocky. Muhammad had a hard time reaching Rocky with a jab. Rocky has his own technique with his leg. It looked like he was standing still, but he was actually sliding away from the punch.

The two champions learned a great deal about each other during that computer fight. A lot of fans and fighters had the wrong impression of my kid.

(They called Ali the "Louisville Lip" because despite his immense skill he was viewed by many as a braggart, who constantly blew his own horn and predicted the downfall of opponents.)

The truth is though that Muhammad changed the whole approach to the promotion of boxing and fighters because he talked the super-star talk. Before him all the fighters said "I do my fighting in the ring." Well, that's not enough today; you want to hear from the star himself. You want to get his insights concerning the opponent and how he thinks he'll beat him.

I taught Muhammad the importance of publicity and projecting a positive and confident personality. He learned that the press was not his enemy but could be his best friend and was a necessary part of any athlete's success. He always liked being around people anyhow and it was natural and easy for him to interact and communicate. He'd always give interviews to reporters and he'd sign dozens of autographs and spend a lot of time talking to his fans.

But during the computer fight Rocky got to know the real Muhammad, who is a very kind and humble man. One day during that computer fight Rocky became very warm toward Muhammad. He came to me and said, "You're right, Ange. He's really a good guy."

People ask where to rate Rocky or Muhammad or Joe Louis, and others. But that's not the way to look at it; for all of the different eras and different times there are different challenges. Nobody can say who the greatest fighter of all-time was.

It falls short because each era had its greatest fighter. Rocky was the greatest fighter of his era, Muhammad was the greatest of his, Joe Louis the greatest of his, and so forth. There was nobody of their eras that could compare to them; they were far above the rest of the heavyweights.

The fight game is in limbo right now; there is no superstar, and there are too many divisions and not enough talent. It's an ever changing thing and it's been in a downward swing, but the game is still there. You can always grab negative stuff, but I think if we get another superstar, if a fighter like Rocky or Muhammad shows up, it'll come back.

But don't get me wrong; it won't be the same. The new guy won't be a Rocky or a Muhammad, because they were one of a kind. The thing is, though, we have to get somebody to hang our hat on so the fight fans will recognize him.

When Rocky was killed in that plane crash,

Muhammad and I were both very upset. We took Jimmy Ellis with us and headed for Brockton. Muhammad was driving and it was a scary ride because we were a little late and Muhammad had us flying.

But Muhammad was an excellent driver. We arrived without any trouble and well in time for the service. There were many past champions and hundreds of others there and all were sad and respectful. It was a fitting tribute to a great champion.

As far as Rocky's place in boxing history goes; Rocky beat everybody out there and never got licked. What more can you say besides that? To me Rocky was very, very special.

Lou Duva received his introduction to boxing as a fifteen-year-old fighter in a 1937 bout during the Great Depression for which he was paid five dollars. He went on from there to become a premier trainer, manager, promoter and matchmaker, who developed and showcased the talents of eighteen world champions in fights before thousands of fans with proceeds that totaled many millions. He was elected to the International Boxing Hall of Fame in 1998, and at eighty-two years old he was still at the top of the sport and going strong when this book went to press.

Duva polished his training skills in the 1950s by watching the great handlers and their champions at Stillman's Gym in New York. He was a dedicated student, a tough guy himself always ready to do battle, who knew well the immense challenges that faced aspiring fighters.

Duva was one of those loyal trainers from the old school, who wanted to help his fighters in every way possible both in and out of the ring and became a strong advocate for their success. He knew all of the tricks and crooked deals that were pulled by some promoters, managers and ring officials and he would fight tenaciously to protect his fighters. It was a trait that sometimes placed him in the midst of headline-making controversy and scraps.

After years of hard work, when his talents were divided between boxing, working in his family's restaurant, running a large trucking company that he owned and managed and being a bail bondsman pursuing fugitives charged with criminal offenses who had failed to appear in court, Duva began to enjoy large measures of success in the fight game and quit his other interests to devote full-time to the sport.

His first and favorite champion was Joey Giardello, who in 1963 banged out a fifteen round decision over then middleweight title holder Dick Tiger. Giardello was elected to the International Boxing Hall of Fame in 1993.

But it was after Duva and his late son Dan joined forces in 1978 to form the promotional company called Main Events that many of the champions and great measures of fame and financial success came along. Lou served as the trainer and manager and Dan ran the business aspect of the company that soon provided strong competition for the two promoters, Don King and Bob Arum, who until then had largely controlled the boxing matchmaking scene.

Duva's champions include; Giardello, the outstanding heavyweight champion Evander Holyfield, Leon Spinks, Rocky Lockridge, Bobby Czyz, Livingston Bramble, Johnny Bumphus, Tony Tucker, Mike Callum, Mark Breland, Pernell Whitaker, Meldrick Taylor, Vinny Pazienza, Darrin Van Horn, John-John Molina, Eddie Hopson, Vernon Forrest, and Fernando Vargas. He also worked with several other champions who were not signed to Main Events, two of whom were Michael Moorer and Arturo Gatti.

LOU DUVA—I say Rocky Marciano was the greatest heavyweight of them all. I can only go by one thing; no one ever beat him. Rocky had the perfect style. He made this style to beat any fighter at all, and he had the tools.

I worked with Rocky and had a chance to watch him train. He was my partner for a while with some fighters.

I met Rocky at Stlllman's Gym when he first came to New York, and later I went to Brockton to watch him train there. Rocky would hit a tire with a baseball bat. He'd climb a hill with a bag of sand on his shoulders. He'd jump in a pool or a lake and start punching and running doing aerobics under water.

I relayed that over to my fighters. I've got a kid right now that idolizes Rocky because I gave him your book and he read that and I told him so much about Rocky.

His name is Mike Marrone, from Vero Beach, Florida. He's won everything down there. He thrives on Rocky's inspiration. He absolutely idolizes him.

Rocky had Charley Goldman, a very great trainer, and Rocky was a great pupil. It was a combination that would be very hard to beat, and it never was beaten.

I'm one of the old timers; I never watched a fighter as much as I watched the trainer. You've got to show a fighter and tell him why. And that's the main reason that Goldman was such a great trainer. He explained everything to Rocky and told him why he should do it.

Rocky was relentless. He'd bang your body, arms, head and all over. He'd charge an opponent and keep going after him throwing punches. He never backed off, always went forward. He was the best; not because of the style but the tenaciousness and his heart. In fact, I adopted Rocky's motto myself, which was don't ever hold back, just go right in there and "keep punching." How could a guy put together an offense of his own if he had to keep blocking Rocky's punches?

I'll never forget when his nose was split wide open by Ezzard Charles and several other times when his eyes were busted up and cut so bad he could barely see. Rocky just kept on going forward and punching relentlessly until he knocked them all out. He was one of a kind.

Jersey Joe Walcott was another dear friend of mine. I remember at Rocky's funeral Jersey Joe almost collapsed. And I recall talking to him about when Rocky knocked him out to win the title. He said he was planning to take Rocky out with a left hook and suddenly realized he couldn't even feel his left side. Rocky

Lou Duva and Rocky. (Photo courtesy of Lou Duva)

had hit him with so many punches to the ribs, arms and body that Jersey Joe's left side was just about paralyzed.

I went to dinner with Muhammad Ali during the computer fight. We started kidding around and Ali told me some things about Rocky. He said when he started moving Rocky around in the ring Rocky would keep hitting him in the ribs. Muhammad's ribs were sore from all of the punches. And that was what Rocky did with every fighter. He'd just keep banging away until they couldn't take any more.

Was Rocky finished after he knocked out Archie Moore for his forty-ninth victory, or could he have fought some more? Only foolish people would ask that question. Rocky was thirty-six years old and still in great shape. Of course he could have kept winning. There wasn't anybody on the horizon that could have come close to beating him. He retired because he was having too many problems with his manager, Al Weill, who treated him lousy and had cheated him.

The fact is that in 1959, after Ingemar Johansson knocked out Floyd Patterson in the third round at Yankee Stadium to take the heavyweight championship, Rocky almost made a comeback. He was offered a million and a quarter to fight Johansson, which was a fortune for fighters in those days. It would have been a big draw that the fans would have loved and Rocky would have taken him easily.

I know; I was right there with Rocky when the deal was proposed. We were in the Victoria Hotel in New York and Andy Robustelli was with us. (*Robustelli was a famed defensive lineman with the Los Angeles Rams and New York Giants in the 1950s and 1960s. He was a six-time Pro Bowler and was inducted into the Professional Football Hall of Fame in 1971.*)

I remember Andy Robustelli smiled at Rocky. "Are you kidding?" he said. "Just looking at that Swede, I'll fight him myself. I've got a lot tougher people to deal with in football."

Ed Kelly, a lawyer for Rocky, who also knew Johansson's people, was there with us, too. It would have been a firm deal except that Patterson's manager, Cus D'Amato, came up with a hidden contract for a return bout between Patterson and Johansson and that was the end of it.

(*Patterson went on to knock out Johansson in the fifth round in June of 1960 at the Polo Grounds in New York.*)

In 1964 Rocky and Joe Louis were doing a radio show. I took them both to see Cassius Clay fight Sonny Liston for the title at Miami Beach. After Clay beat Liston with a seventh round TKO, Rocky said, "Can you imagine he's gonna get a million dollars a fight?"

Joe Louis looked at Rocky and said, "What're we waiting for? Let me start running with you."

Then another time Rocky was interviewing Liston for his radio show. Liston started to get wise with him. He said, "What do you think I'd have done to you, Rocky?"

Rocky tried to be diplomatic and said, "Well, you're a pretty big guy Sonny . . . "

But Liston cut him off and said, "I'd have destroyed you."

Rocky said, "You think so? Well then let's get our gear and go into the ring right now and we'll find out."

The "Boys" that were taking care of Liston rushed Sonny out of the place in a hurry.

They don't make fighters like Rocky these days. Today's boxing is entertainment; there's a lot of promotion, a lot of glitz. The big shows are put on before the fights, but once they get inside the ring too many of the performances are mediocre.

The promotion is one of the big things. It's all about building the fight up, creating a lot of drama, doing a lot of hype on television and getting the public's interest to a peak.

As far as Don King goes, I can take him or leave him. I think he's a good promoter. He certainly knows how to attract attention and interest and bring in the bucks. He's flamboyant, but don't get me wrong, he does things for his own interest; he takes advantage of fighters and the sport of boxing. He controls everything; the fighters, the opponents, the money, where they have to train, the return matches; everything involved with a fight that King puts on is under his strict supervision. The guy who makes out better than anybody is always Don himself.

Bob Arum is different. He does his promotions in a dignified way. He's a lawyer. He's smooth and knows how to put together good, entertaining shows. But he doesn't exactly love all the fighters either. It's strictly a business.

The trainers and handlers of today could use some lessons. There's more to boxing than just sending fighters into the ring. A lot of these handlers and trainers that are around nowadays just don't know; they haven't got the experience. They put on a suit and hold press conferences and act important like they know it all. But in reality too many of them are ignorant. They haven't served their time.

How would Rocky have done against these modern heavyweights? That's easy; he'd have beaten them all.

If he was still around and in his prime today Rocky would put all of those fighters away. The size means nothing. He'd just wear them all down. Pretty soon you'd hear someone holler "timber." There are about eight so-called champs up there right now. Rocky could have lined them all up, one right after another, and taken them all out a day apart.

Rocky would have knocked out Lennox Lewis without any question. He'd have bobbed and weaved and got under Lewis and destroyed him with a thousand punches. Then he'd have nailed him with that right hand.

For a while they tried to put Mike Tyson on the same level as Rocky Marciano; but it could never happen. When Rocky was in there he didn't just have the punch; he had the heart and the will to win that not Tyson or any of the others could ever come close to matching.

They say as the heavyweight division goes so goes the sport of boxing. It's at its lowest now; there's no real star; but it seems like another great always emerges, somebody comes along for every era; a Marciano, a Joe Louis, a Joe Frazier.

But it doesn't look like anybody's coming for this one; I hope so, but I don't see it. There are no fighters of Marciano, Louis or Frazier's caliber at the top and none coming up the ladder.

Those guys that call themselves heavyweight champs today wouldn't have a chance against the great champions of the past. When you see guys like Roy Jones Jr. and Johnny Ruiz fight for the heavyweight title, come on, that's ridiculous. They're not even anywhere near in the same league with a guy like Rocky.

What do you think Roy Jones would do right now if he had to fight guys like Ezzard Charles, Archie Moore, Billy Conn, and Joey Maxim? Roy's a friend of mine, but there's no chance he'd win.

(Two weeks after this interview was completed, on September 25, 2004, Roy Jones Jr. fought International Boxing Federation Light Heavyweight Champion Glen Johnson, a journeyman with a record of 41-9-2, who was making his first defense of the title. Jones, the heavy favorite, was knocked out in the ninth round by the thirty-five-year-old Johnson, and had to be taken to a hospital after the bout.

It was the second fight in succession in which Jones had been KO'd, having been stopped in the second round on May 15, 2004 by Antonio Tarver to lose his WBA and WBO light heavyweight titles.

Jones had a record of forty-nine victories and three losses with thirty-eight knockouts and had held world titles as a middleweight, super-middleweight and for eight years as light heavyweight champion. He had exceptional speed and was considered by many to be the greatest fighter of modern times.

However, Jones ducked a number of the best fighters of an era that had few stars to begin with and rarely was tested against high class opponents. His only fight as a heavyweight was in March 2003 when he won a twelve round decision over the unimpressive WBA champion, Johnny Ruiz. What this fight really showed was that Jones would not have fared well against outstanding heavyweights.

Lou Duva most likely accurately concludes that light heavyweight champions from boxing's golden era such as Moore, Maxim and Conn, and contenders such as Charles, who moved up to become heavyweight champ, would have defeated Jones.)

I respect the old time fighters much more than the boxers that are in there today. None of these modern guys could beat those old time fighters.

When they ask me, I tell everyone my favorite fighter of all-time was Rocky Marciano: he was clearly the best of the heavyweights. But my opinion of the greatest all-around fighter of all-time was Sugar Ray Robinson. Sugar Ray could do it all; he could box, punch, and had superior defense and other amazing skills. He could knock you out going backwards, like he did with Gene Fullmer.

I doubt if we'll ever get fighters like Sugar Ray and Rocky again. And the heavyweight division is the worst of all. These guys that call themselves heavyweight champs today wouldn't even get to be contenders against the great champions of yesterday.

(Duva was then asked whether he thought Evander Holyfield, who was one of the most talented, dedicated and courageous of the modern heavyweight champions, might have taken Rocky?

"Nobody would have taken Rocky," Duva said. "Nobody.")

Goody Petronelli, trainer of the outstanding Middleweight Champion Marvelous Marvin Hagler, is a lifelong resident of Brockton, Massachusetts and was a devoted friend and admirer of Rocky Marciano. Goody, who was the trainer and co-managed Hagler with his partner and brother, Pat Petronelli, shaped and handled Marvelous Marvin from the time he was a green sixteen-year-old kid off the streets of Brockton that had never had a fight in a boxing ring through his rise and reign as middleweight champion of the world.

Hagler held the undisputed world championship belt throughout thirteen fights from 1980 to 1987 before losing his title in a controversial split 12-round decision to Sugar Ray Leonard. Marvin and Goody thought they'd won and Petronelli said he tried hard for a rematch but his attempts were rejected.

Hagler retired and never fought again. He had compiled a record of 62 wins, three losses and two draws. He was inducted into the International Boxing Hall of Fame in 1993 and is considered by many to be one of the very best of the great middleweight champions.

After Hagler and Leonard, in 1987-88, most boxers who won titles were no longer recognized as undisputed champions of the world. The division that had already begun to be watered down was then clearly defined and splintered into three fragments, the International Boxing Federation, World Boxing Association, and World Boxing Council. The majority of the fighters since then have been beneath the class and talent of Hagler, Leonard and a number of the great champions that preceded them.

Goody, a member of the National Italian American Sports Hall of Fame, trained and developed numerous other good fighters, including champions such as Hagler's brother, Robbie Sims, Pat Petronelli's son, Tony Petronelli, Steve Collins and Drake Thazdi, but none were undisputed world champions and none approached the greatness of Hagler.

The connection and passion toward Rocky Marciano was evident at the old Petronelli Gym in Brockton, where each night, after he had finished training the fighters, as he departed from the gym Goody would look up at a large poster of Marciano on the wall and, as if the ghost of Rocky were present, would nod his head and say, "Goodnight, Rocky.")

GOODY PETRONELLI—Rocky and I were both from Brockton and about the same age, but we came from different neighborhoods and didn't chum together as kids. We really got to know each other well and became friends in later years because of our involvement in boxing.

Shortly after I graduated from Brockton High School, I joined the Navy and stayed in the service becoming a master chief petty officer toward the end of a long career that lasted until the late 1960s. I served as a hospital corpsman, did some fighting in the service,

and coached Navy and Marine boxing teams.

I also did some fighting around Brockton. A short time before he died, Rocky's childhood buddy, Izzy Gold, told me that I was one of the inspirations for Rocky getting started in boxing. The Rock came to some of my fights near Brockton.

It was 1963 or 1964 and I was a chief petty officer training the Navy-Marine Boxing Team at the Grosse Isle Naval Air Station in Michigan, when I decided to ask Rocky if he'd come up there to referee some fights.

I flew down to the Naval Air Station in South Weymouth, Massachusetts and my brother, Pat, and I had breakfast with Rocky at a little restaurant there.

I said, "Rocky, it'd be nice if you came up and refereed our matches. It'd be a good plug

Goody Petronelli and Rocky. (Photo courtesy of Goody Petronelli)

for the station and for me in particular."

Rocky never hesitated. He said, "Sure, Goody. I'd love to do it."

Rocky flew in that day. I gave him my boxing shoes and he refereed all of the matches. It was a full house and they all loved seeing Rocky in the ring. After it was over, Rocky never asked me for a penny: he did it all for nothing, never even wanted expenses. That was the way Rocky was if he really liked a guy.

When I took him to the airport, Rocky asked me when I would be retiring from the service. I told him in a few years. Then he asked what I was going to do when I got out of the Navy. I told him I planned to open a gym in Brockton and train fighters.

"That's great," Rocky said. Then he stunned me by adding, "How about if I go in with you?"

"Fantastic," I said. "With your reputation we can't go wrong."

It almost happened but we never did become partners. I'd been stationed on the West Coast and had just been discharged in 1969. I was driving back to Brockton, when I heard over the car radio that Rocky's plane had crashed and Rocky and the pilot were killed.

I pulled over to the nearest restaurant and went in for coffee. I couldn't move for quite a while, the news was so devastating. I was in total shock.

There will never be another Rocky. He had the greatest heart and will to win of them all. He had a chin of iron and he could hit you with either hand. He was always in the best of condition and could go at full speed for as long as it took to nail an opponent. He had that confidence, unmatched determination, and

(L-R) Pat Petronelli, Champion Marvelous Marvin Hagler, and Goody Petronelli, following a championship victory. (Photo courtesy of Goody Petronelli)

complete belief in his ability to win. It doesn't matter how good you are as a trainer; you can't give a fighter those things.

I got Marvin Hagler when he was sixteen years old. He came into my gym right off the streets of Brockton. I started working with him right away and he won the (amateur) Nationals. He had outstanding natural physical talent to work with, but it was his attitude and determination that impressed me most.

All I kept telling Marvin was great things about Rocky Marciano. I said here was a guy that nobody thought would ever make it except Rocky himself. I told him how Rocky was considered by the so-called boxing experts to be too old, too small, too inexperienced, too clumsy, but that nothing discouraged him.

I was constantly telling Marvin about the greatness of Rocky Marciano and how he made it to the top from Brockton, Massachusetts against the toughest of odds. The poster of Rocky on the wall of our old gym on the second floor above a hardware store on Center Street off Main Street in downtown Brockton was always there as another reminder as Marvin went through his grueling training routines. And then there were the slogans mounted on the wall; *Train until it hurts, and then train some more, When the going gets tough, the tough get going, The more you sweat in the gym the less you bleed in the ring* and half a dozen other motivators.

Pretty soon Marvin told me he was going to be a world champion just like Rocky. He was going straight to the top and nothing would stop him. That was the kind of talk I liked to hear.

Marvin had that determination that I saw in Rocky. He was very focused. Of course, being a military man, I went by the numbers: you get in there and there's no talking, you do what you have to do.

(In fact, that was Rocky Marciano's motto throughout his life; "Do it: don't talk about it." He gave that advice many times to his brothers, friends and acquaintances in the boxing world.)

Just as it had always been with Rocky, it was all business with Marvin, too. He knew that to climb that mountain wasn't going to be easy. There was no time to relax or give it anything less than all he had. We'd get up at the crack of dawn and do our road work and then we'd go right through the entire schedule. He knew he was going to become a champion right from the beginning.

Later, after Marvin became a celebrated world middleweight champion, we got a new more modern and spacious gym across the street on Ward Street, and then they changed the name to Petronelli Way. So it's been quite an experience.

What I saw in Rocky was the heart of a lion. Nobody could stop him. He bobbed and weaved, always punching, never giving an inch of ground until he either wore-out or most often knocked-out his man. He was a guy that had that extra something that makes a really great champion.

For my money Rocky was the greatest fighter in the world of his time. Nobody can ever question that. Jack Dempsey was the greatest of his time; Joe Louis the greatest of his time, and so forth.

But who knows who the greatest heavyweight champion of all-time was? That's open to opinion. But if I had to make a pick overall, I'd put Rocky on top. I say he was the best. He had the greatest record of all-time. He was the only one who never lost; forty-nine fights, forty-three knockouts, six decisions. You couldn't ask for a better record than that.

And there weren't twelve or so different

champions and all kinds of divisions in Rocky's time. He was the undisputed heavyweight champion of the world, as were the greats that preceded him. The fighters that followed were not in their class.

The heavyweight division of this era is in an awful mess. There's no big star up there, nobody even close to Rocky's talent or crowd appeal. It's wide open.

I've got an excellent heavyweight prospect myself in Kevin McBride. He's thirty years old, six-foot-six, 260 pounds, and he's a good puncher and boxer. [On June 11, 2005, as this book was going to press, McBride scored a seventh-round TKO over Mike Tyson, after the former heavyweight champion refused to leave his corner and failed to answer the bell.] I've also got a good middleweight named Ian Gardner, who is twenty-three and has a record of sixteen and one.

I'm looking for another champion. You don't quit. You never give up.

But finding another Rocky would be like catching lightning in a bottle, just about impossible. And getting another Marvin would be like beating the odds of the biggest lottery out there.

The slogan adopted here and widely known and respected throughout the boxing world is, "BROCKTON: City of Champions."

There are plans to have bronze statues made of both Rocky and Marvin and place them side-by-side in a prominent location in Brockton. It would be a fitting tribute to the two greatest champions in the history of this city and two of the greatest in the world.

Appendix*

ROCKY MARCIANO (September 1, 1923—August 31, 1969). Manager Al Weill. Trainers Charley Goldman and Allie Colombo.

Marciano won the heavyweight championship from Jersey Joe Walcott by a knockout in the thirteenth round in Philadelphia's Municipal Stadium on September 23, 1952. He defended the title six times, winning five by KO and one by decision, before retiring undefeated in April 1956.

The only heavyweight champion ever to complete a professional career without a loss, Rocky's record was 49-0, with 43 KOs. He was the greatest slugger in boxing history and knocked out 88 percent of his opponents compared to 76 percent by runner-up Joe Louis.

Marciano's Professional Record

Year	Date	Opponent	City	Result
1947	March 17	Lee Epperson	Holyoke, Mass.	KO 3
1948	July 12	Harry Bilazarian	Providence, R.I.	KO 1
	July 19	John Edwards	Providence, R.I.	KO 1
	Aug. 9	Bobby Quinn	Providence, R.I.	KO 3
	Aug. 23	Eddie Ross	Providence, R.I.	KO 1
	Aug. 30	Jimmy Weeks	Providence, R.I.	KO 1
	Sept. 13	Jerry Jackson	Providence, R.I.	KO 1
	Sept. 20	Bill Hardeman	Providence, R.I.	KO 1
	Sept. 30	Gil Cardione	Washington, D.C.	KO 1
	Oct. 4	Bob Jefferson	Providence, R.I.	KO 2
	Nov. 29	James Patrick Connolly	Providence, R.I.	KO 1
	Dec. 14	Gilley Perron	Philadelphia, Pa.	KO 2
1949	March 21	Johnny Pretzie	Providence, R.I.	KO 5
	March 28	Artie Donato	Providence, R.I.	KO 1

*Statistics as compiled by *Nat Fleischer's Ring Record Book*

	April 11	James Walls	Providence, R.I.	KO 3
	May 2	Jimmy Evans	Providence, R.I.	KO 3
	May 23	Don Mogard	Providence, R.I.	W 10
	July 18	Harry Haft	Providence, R.I.	KO 3
	Aug. 16	Pete Louthis	New Bedford, Mass.	KO 3
	Sept. 26	Tommy DiGiorgio	Providence, R.I.	KO 4
	Oct. 10	Tiger Ted Lowry	Providence, R.I.	W 10
	Nov. 7	Joe Dominic	Providence, R.I.	KO 2
	Dec. 2	Pat Richards	New York, N.Y.	KO 2
	Dec. 19	Phil Muscato	Providence, R.I.	KO 5
	Dec. 30	Carmine Vingo	New York, N.Y.	KO 6
1950	March 24	Roland LaStarza	New York, N.Y.	W 10
	June 5	Eldridge Eatman	Providence, R.I.	KO 3
	July 10	Gino Buonvino	Boston, Mass.	KO 10
	Sept. 18	Johnny Shkor	Providence, R.I.	KO 6
	Nov. 13	Tiger Ted Lowry	Providence, R.I.	W 10
	Dec. 18	Bill Wilson	Providence, R.I.	KO 1
1951	Jan. 29	Keene Simmons	Providence, R.I.	KO 8
	March 20	Harold Mitchell	Hartford, Conn.	KO 2
	March 26	Art Henri	Providence, R.I.	KO 9
	April 30	Red Applegate	Providence, R.I.	W 10
	July 12	Rex Layne	New York, N.Y.	KO 6
	Aug. 27	Freddie Beshore	Boston, Mass.	KO 4
	Oct. 26	Joe Louis	New York, N.Y.	KO 8
1952	Feb. 13	Lee Savold	Philadelphia, Pa.	KO 6
	April 21	Gino Buonvino	Providence, R.I.	KO 2
	May 12	Bernie Reynolds	Providence, R.I.	KO 3
	July 28	Harry "Kid" Matthews	New York, N.Y.	KO 2
	*Sept. 23	**Jersey Joe Walcott**	**Philadelphia, Pa.**	**KO 13**
1953	**May 15	Jersey Joe Walcott	Chicago, Ill.	KO 1
	**Sept. 24	Roland LaStarza	New York, N.Y.	KO 11
1954	**June 17	Ezzard Charles	New York, N.Y.	W 15
	**Sept. 17	Ezzard Charles	New York, N.Y.	KO 8
1955	**May 16	Don Cockell	San Francisco, Cal.	KO 9
	**Sept. 21	Archie Moore	New York, N.Y.	KO 9
1956	April, retired undefeated			

*Won the heavyweight championship of the world.
**Title bout.

Marciano's Ring Earnings
Overall totals of championship fights

Date	Opponent	City	Attendance	Receipts
Sept. 23, 1952	Jersey Joe Walcott	Philadelphia, Pa.	40,379	$504,645
May 15, 1953	Jersey Joe Walcott	Chicago, Ill.	16,034	331,795
Sept. 24, 1953	Roland LaStarza	New York, N.Y.	44,562	435,817
June 17, 1954	Ezzard Charles	New York, N.Y.	47,505	543,092
Sept. 17, 1954	Ezzard Charles	New York, N.Y.	34,330	352,654
May 16, 1955	Don Cockell	San Francisco, Cal.	15,235	196,720
Sept. 21, 1955	Archie Moore	New York, N.Y.	61,574	948,117
totals:			259,619	$3,312,840

Marciano's Purses and Television Earnings from Title Fights

Opponent	Gate	Television
Jersey Joe Walcott	$69,085	$25,000
Jersey Joe Walcott	76,038	90,000
Roland LaStarza	141,624	53,125
Ezzard Charles	200,586	47,452
Ezzard Charles	120,608	54,000
Don Cockell	64,496	50,000
Archie Moore	328,374	140,000
totals:	$1,000,811	$459,577
combined total:	$1,460,388	

Index

Abrams, Georgie 197, 198
Addie, Jack 100
Aidala, Art 166
Ali, Muhammad 1, 2, 55, 80, 137, 140, 145, 154, 155, 156, 233–236, 241, 248–250, 268, 271–274, 276
Almcida, Manny 59, 61–65, 71, 77
Ambers, Lou 56, 57, 95, 167
Angelo, Joe 121
Araujo, George 54, 62, 63
Arccl, Ray 271
Archibald, Joey 57
Arguello, Alexis 2
Armstrong, Henry 2
Armstrong, Jack 38
Arum, Bob 274, 277
Atwood, Ben 160
Baer, Buddy 119
Baer, Max 192
Baksi, Joe 138, 163
Balzerian (see Bilazarian)
Barnes, Harold 121, 166
Barone, Nick 93, 95, 102, 163, 172
Baroudi, Sam 164
Basilio, Carmen 2, 116, 214, 271
Bassett, Percy 81, 104
Bates, Willard 221
Batista, Fulgencio 185, 187, 188
Bauman, Stanley 253, 254, 261–264
Belz, Glenn 237, 238
Berl, Al 162, 170
Bernstein, Harry 84

Beshore, Freddie 52, 102, 104, 113, 163
Bilazarian, Haroutunc "Harry" 61–63
Bimstein, Whitey 92, 271
Bishop, Joey 192
Bivins, Jimmy 113, 138, 141, 163
Blackburn, Bill 201
Blunk, Frank M. 177
Bocchicchio, Felix 115, 139, 142, 146
Bogart, Humphrey 86, 148
Boland, Eddie 56
Boldt, George H. 115
Bonomi, John 115
Braddock, James J. 39, 141, 268, 272
Bramble, Livingston 274
Berland, Mark 274
Brewster, Lamon 2
Brion, Cesar 74, 75, 90, 91, 100, 106, 110, 158, 163
Brown, Billy 116, 117
Brown, Ethel 70
Brown, Frankie 174
Brown, Freddy 145
Bucceroni, Dan 158
Buckley, Johnny 102,103, 250
Bumphus, Johnny 274
Buonnano, Sharkey 107
Buonvino, Gino 102, 134
Butera, Frank 158
Byrd, Chris 2
Caggiano, Generoso "Gene" 36, 37, 52–54, 56, 65, 66, 103, 104
Callinicos, Constantine 192

287